Nathan Strong

The Doctrine of Eternal Misery Reconcilable with the Infinite

Benevolence of God

And a Truth Plainly Asserted in the Christian Scriptures

Nathan Strong

The Doctrine of Eternal Misery Reconcilable with the Infinite Benevolence of God
And a Truth Plainly Asserted in the Christian Scriptures

ISBN/EAN: 9783337778569

Printed in Europe, USA, Canada, Australia, Japan

Cover: Foto ©Lupo / pixelio.de

More available books at **www.hansebooks.com**

THE
DOCTRINE
OF
ETERNAL MISERY,

RECONCILEABLE WITH THE

INFINITE BENEVOLENCE OF GOD,

AND A TRUTH PLAINLY ASSERTED IN THE

CHRISTIAN SCRIPTURES.

By NATHAN STRONG,

Paſtor of the North Preſbyterian Church in HARTFORD.

HARTFORD:

PRINTED BY HUDSON AND GOODWIN.

1796.

INTRODUCTION.

─────────────

THE friends of truth are often alarmed by the prevalency of error. Meafuring prefent appearances on the fcale of human wifdom, it feems to them as though the caufe of CHRIST is on the verge of ruin, and the truths of divine revelation near being loft, amidft the corruption of human nature. If there were not a GOD to govern, and a Mediator at the head of his own kingdom, who hath all power both in heaven and in earth, this would indeed be the cafe, for there is a conftant warfare between truth and error. Truth is uniformly the fame, and appears in the fame plain and artlefs drefs from generation to generation ; but error appears in every fhape, and is continually changing its drefs. When beaten from the field of enquiry in one fhape, it foon affumes another, and attempts to do that infidioufly, which never will be done by open and candid argument. At one time one error is prevalent ; at another time, fome other error becomes the fashionable way of going to destruction. But though great numbers are ensnared, the promise remains in full force, that the gates of hell shall not prevail against the kingdom of CHRIST, and the very things which most threaten the church and truth of GOD, are through his overruling wisdom, made eventually to promote its interests. By enquiry, the truth is brought out into view, with more incontestible evidence than it ever was before. GOD worketh not as man works, neither is his wisdom like the wisdom of creatures.

By attending to the history of the church, we shall find, that when infinite wisdom designed to collect and bring the evidence of truth into most pointed view, he hath generally suffered some opposing error to arise, and make a most formidable appearance; whereby many have been deceived, and many others who did not relinquish the truth trembled for its safety. In consequence of this, Inquiry hath taken place, and the very errors which seemed to be triumphing, have been totally refuted, and truth prevailed with a new clearness. This method of conducting things is admirably calculated, not only to confute and give a more complete overthrow to error, and establish GOD's own doctrines on a most firm basis; but also to bring the human heart out into plain view. Men of corrupt minds hide much of their corruption from the sight of the world. They do not choose to have the wishes of their hearts known, until they think themselves sure of prevailing. When things are so ordered by an infinitely wise providence, that they

think the wifhes of their hearts are like to prevail ; then they will manifeft them, and fhow
a corruption that otherwife would never have
been fufpected. The human heart is thus
brought out—its pretended obedience to GOD's
fovereignty detected—its oppofition to his law
and its penalties difcovered—and its joy in the
fuppofed fafety of an unholy life, fhows a bad
heart, where the contrary was profeffed.

THIS fact is moft ftrongly illuftrated in the
prefent. day. Individuals will rarely ftep forth,
and endeavor to make a party either in church
or ftate, fo long as they think the public opinion is wholly againft them ; but will fecrete the
defires of their hearts, left they fhould thereby
be expofed to odium. It is neceffary there
fhould be a confiderable prevalence of infidelity,
or denial of the fcriptures ; and fuch an order-
ing of things by divine providence as will manifeft this prevalence ; before men will hazard
their reputation. But when they find that they
have companions in plenty, they will boldly
appear, and fhew that they never loved a holy
bible, and the pure morality of the heart which
it requires ; and that nothing was wanting long
before to have made them reject it, but a want
of company to render them reputable in fociety.

WITH refpect to the doctrine of the falvation
of all men, it is not new in the world. There
have been fome folitary individuals, perhaps in
every age of the chriftian church, who have
efpoufed fuch an opinion ; but there hath been
no period, in which fo many have declared
themfelves converts to it, as in the prefent.—
Such an event is mightily calculated to difcover
the human heart. It fhows how unwilling men

are to acknowledge the righteoufnefs of GOD's law, and its penalties—that they never felt the juftice of GOD, in condemning finners—never faw his glory in punifhing fin—and that they do not choofe to have him for their GOD, if fin is to come to fo awful an end, as the doctrine of eternal mifery predicts. They are willing to have him for their GOD, if men may be made happy at all events, whether they live finful or holy ; but on the oppofite conditions do not choofe him for their fovereign. It is prefumed in the prefent, as it hath happened in former cafes, that the prevalence of this error and the ftrong defire men fhow to make themfelves quiet in fin, and reject the fpirituality of religion on this ground ; will terminate in a more general conviction, that eternal punifhment is threatened in the chriftian fcriptures.

ONE great defign of infinite wifdom, in managing the ftate of this world, is to fhow the nature of fin by fuffering it to be acted out in many fhapes—in many crimes—in many errors of opinion—in many felfifh wifhes of the finful mind—in many ways of refifting the divine fovereignty—and, in many feigned excufes for an unholy life. By all thefe things, at the confummation of time, it will appear that fin is exceeding finful—that it makes the minds of rational creatures mad—and that the GOD of the earth acts a moft excellent part, in forbidding, condemning and punifhing it.

THE friends of truth have no reafon to defpond, becaufe error hath prevailed, or that it now prevails. There is reafon to believe from our moft holy prophecies, that the abounding of error hath not yet come to its heighth. Thefe prophecies fpeak of a day, which is yet future, in which, the earth fhall be filled with righteouf-nefs and peace ; when the glory of CHRIST's religion fhall appear by reigning in men's hearts and purifying their lives. 'It is alfo pro-phefied, that directly before this glorious day there will be a greater falling away from the pure truths of divine revelation, than had been common before.

THERE are alfo many prophetic figns, fhew-ing that we are now in the period of great er-ror and irreligion. Infidelity hath overfpread a great part of the old chriftian world, and is now making a rapid progrefs in the new. The foul-humbling doctrines of chriftianity are defpifed—the divine honors of JESUS are deni-ed—that kind of chriftian life which the fcrip-tures teach, confifting in much prayer, holinefs and felf-denial is rejected—and the work and influences of the holy fpirit in men's hearts is ridiculed. Very great progrefs in this period of infidelity and irreligion is already made, and to how much greater length it is to proceed, no man can fay. Such a ftate of things, be-fore the church fhall put on her glory, is mat-ter of prophecy ; and we have figns enough to know that it hath already commenced; but how far GOD will fuffer it to proceed muft be refolved by the event.

How far old errors will be revived and be-come general, or what new ones may arife, or to what lengths practical ungodlinefs and the defpifing of vital piety may go, it is not wife in us to foretel. GOD hath not revealed the times and the feafons, any further, than is neceſſary, to ſupport the hope and patience of his ſaints. Chriſtians, deſpair not when you ſee this to be the caſe. Your God and Redeemer hath foretold ſuch an event. He reigns in his holy hill of zion—all men and all hearts are in his hand—the reſidue of the ſpirit is with him— and he will ſuffer deluſion and impiety to prevail no further, than he can overrule them for his own glory, and the final advancement of truth.

LET not infidels, and thoſe who depart from the ancient underſtanding of the chriſtian ſcriptures exult. The church hath expected this day—Her children and witneſſes expect to dreſs themſelves in ſackcloth, and in the eyes of the world to be ſlain ſtill longer before ſhe putteth on her joyful robes ; but ſhe looſeth not her hope in the God who died for her. Though ſhe cannot tell certainly, on the principles of human wiſdom, why it is beſt that this falling away ſhould take place ; ſhe doth not wiſh another king, nor doubt his wiſdom, nor fail in her expectations that a day much brighter will ſucceed, than could have been without ſuch a night going before it. Mankind ſeem to be in general ſenſible, that the world has been full of a deplorable wretchedneſs, ariſing from human crimes. All are looking forward to a better day. Some who do not ſeem to have much ſenſe, of the power of religion in the heart ; or the need of God's ſpirit to ſanctify the heart ; ſtill predicate ſuch expectations on the word of prophecy. Others expect ſuch a day, only becauſe it is natural for men to hope better things than they have ſeen or experienced. The rational believers in revelation, expect a more glorious state on earth, because they find promises of a general pouring out of the spirit of God, and of such effects as will always follow, when the spirit is shed abroad in his sanctifying influences. But before such a general outpouring of the spirit of God takes place, much evil is to be expected in the earth —much sin—much error—and great misery. The righteous Lord will punish men by their own hands. He hath already risen from his place, and is dashing the nations one against another. The kings of the earth are gathering together to the great battle of the Lord's vengeance. The clusters of the vine of the earth are ripe, and the blood of them is beginning to run from the wine press of divine wrath. The angel standing in the sun, is beginning to proclaim to the fowls of heaven, to come and eat the flesh of captains and of mighty men. The natural and political state of the world is prepared for such an event; and while the wisdom of men will attribute the scenes which are now opening, to political causes; the faithful believer in God's word traces them up to a higher, a divine agency, punishing the sin of the earth. The same prophecy that leads us to expect these things, also assures us that while they are taking place, men will not in general repent, nor see the hand of God in what is doing. That the eyes of many will be more fast closed than ever—the truth will have many enemies—the friends of the truth be despised—and a flood of error cover mankind in thick darkness.

Much hath been expected from what is called Civilization, to make a happy state on

B

them refpectability in forgetting GOD, and living without him in the world.

To all perfons of every defcription, who either difbelieve or forget that GOD hath prepared a punifhment for the wicked in another
world, the following fheets are dedicated; and
the writer prays GOD, that all our minds may
be fo enlightened on this fubject by his own
Holy Spirit, as to know that our fins not only
difhonor his great name, and injure others;
but expofe our own fouls to a juft and everlafting mifery.

THE

Doctrine of Eternal Misery, &c.

PART FIRST.

IN confidering this fubject, the following order will be obferved :

I. To prove from the fcriptures the doctrine of eternal punifhment, or a ftate of mifery from which fome men fhall never be delivered.

II. To anfwer fome popular objections to this doctrine.

III. STRICTURES on a late publication entitled Calvinifm improved, &c.

IV. A SERIOUS and folemn addrefs to thofe, who place their dependence of future fafety, on a belief that all men fhall be faved.

1. To prove from the fcriptures, the doctrine of eternal punifhment or a ftate of mifery from which fome men fhall never be delivered.

SECTION 1. THERE is no reafon to fuppofe that the Creator of the univerfe delights in mifery for its own fake. The contrary to this ; and that he delights in happinefs, and that his whole fcheme of government is defigned to produce and eternally preferve the greateft quantity of happinefs, may be proved from revelation; and alfo by reafoning from thofe perfections, which an infinite and eternal being muft poffefs.

I SHALL not fpend the time to prove, that an infinite being muft neceffarily delight in happinefs, and have no pleafure in mifery for its own fake. Thofe who oppofe the doctrine of eternal mifery, will doubtlefs agree with me in this point. One of their principal arguments againft eternal mifery, has been drawn from the goodnefs of GOD, of which we are as firm believers as they can pretend to be; and we readily allow, that infinite power and wifdom will forever prevent any event happening in the univerfe, which will leffen the quantity of holinefs and happinefs. Holinefs and happinefs will forever go together. As rational creatures are made, the greateft quantity of holinefs will always imply the greateft quantity of happinefs. One of the principal arguments againft eternal mifery, has been drawn from the goodnefs and benevolence of GOD. Much has been faid againft the doctrine, as neceffarily implying that GOD was not a good being. It is conceived that all this hath arifen from conceiving GOD fuch a being as creatures are—unable as they be to bring good out of evil, and to make eternal mifery the means of a greater happinefs, than could ever take place without it. When men fay that the infinite benevolence of GOD forbids eternal mifery, and build their arguments on this maxim, they not only take that as granted which we deny, but make it the very foundation of their fuperftructure. Finite wifdom, is totally incapable of meafuring, the wifdom which is infinite. Human incapacity to bring the greateft poffible good out of much evil—much fin—and much mifery, is no argument that an infinite God cannot do it; for his ways of working are as much above ours, as his nature is more capacious, and as the endlefs duration of eternity exceeds the momentary limits of time. We therefore wholly deny the maxim of the Univerfalifts, that the goodnefs of God forbids eternal punifhment confifting in mifery. When we view the ftructure of nature, (and that any other ftructure is poffible doth not appear,) from this very confideration, we fuppofe the fcriptural reprefentation to be a true one; and that there will be more happinefs in the univerfe, than if mifery had never entered it. Should this be the cafe, the divine benevolence will be fo far from militating againft the eternal punifhment of finners, that it will furnifh a ftrong argument to prove, that what hath been the common underftanding of the Bible is the true one.

Sec. 2. In a matter of this extent, human reafon can never be a fufficient guide. To make the government of the univerfe the moft right and perfect, it muft have regard to the whole. It muft have a reference to the ftate and condition of the vaft collective body—to the different orders and nature of beings, and to the whole extent of their duration. A government adapted to the private benefit of a fmall part, could not be called a good one for the whole. This would be a partial, but not an impartial government; and if fome praifed, others, with more caufe might difpraife it. As human reafon cannot comprehend, the immenfe fyftem of creation—the variety of created natures which it embraces, nor the connexions and influences which thofe parts have one on another; it muft be impoffible for reafon, without a revelation, to determine in all points what is a good moral government of the whole; and what the infinite parent may and will do, in the treatment of individuals, confiftent with righteoufnefs. For this reafon a revelation is neceffary. There are many points which we never could determine, except by a revelation, or by waiting for the event; and where a previous knowledge of the event is defirable, a revelation from GOD becomes abfolutely neceffary. Of this nature are the following queftions. What is a proper penalty of the moral law, which is the rule both of right and happinefs through the univerfe? Whether it be confiftent with the glory of GOD and the good of the univerfe, that any finning creatures fhould be forgiven? What the beft manner and means of forgivenefs are? Whether it be beft, that all finful creatures fhould be forgiven or only a part of them? How long the probationary period of forgivenefs fhall continue? What the condition of forgivenefs and falvation on the part of the creature fhall be? The wife refolution of thefe queftions, depends on a knowledge of the infinite nature of GOD the creator, lawgiver and governor of the whole; and alfo on a moft perfect knowledge of the nature of the connected univerfe. Without fuch a knowledge, thefe and fundry other queftions, cannot be safely resolved; and it is a knowledge, which none but JEHOVAH himself either doth or ever can possess. The frail man, who supposes himself adequate to the solution of such enquiries, forgets his place in the system of being, and takes on him to determine what is much above his share of wisdom.

To teach us in these things, that revelation was necessary, which GOD hath graciously given.

THIS revelation teaches us that eternal misery, consisting in a separation from all good, and the suffering of all evil, was the fit penalty of the moral law. That all mankind are under the condemnation of the law, and that if GOD should leave them to everlasting sufferings, they would have no reason to complain of him as an unjust GOD. A way of salvation is revealed through JESUS CHRIST, and all men are commanded to repent and turn to GOD through him. There are also abundant promises, that all who do repent and come to GOD, shall be forgiven and delivered from the wrath that is to come upon the impenitent.

HERE the question arises, will all men be saved from future and eternal misery, by the mediator JESUS CHRIST; or will only a part of men be brought to final salvation through him, and the other part remain in final impenitence, and actually suffer the eternal punishment which the law originally threatened?

THE universalists suppose that all men will come to final happiness.—It hath been the common opinion in the christian world, that a very great number will remain in their sins, and be forever miferable. To determine this point, we muft now have recourfe to divine revelation. And let every man endeavour to feel himfelf in the prefence of God—judging on a moft folemn queftion ; and that his own prejudices, and the wifhes which come from his own perfonal ftate, will make no change in the truth.

The Testimony of Jesus Christ,

Sec. 3. It is natural to fuppofe that Jesus Christ would be very explicit on this point. He is the great prophet, by whom all knowledge comes from God. The fpirit of prophecy is his. He is the creator and the judge by whom the ftate of every creature will be appointed. He is the redeemer, through whom falvation comes to all thofe who are faved from among men, and it muft be fuppofed that he knew his own fcheme of grace, and the extent of its efficacious application in the falvation of finners. As it feems fit that Jesus Christ fhould be explicit on this point, more than any other of the infpired teachers ; it appears that he actually was fo. The xvii chapter of John is a prayer, which Christ made to his father, a fhort feafon before his fufferings commenced, commending his church to the divine keeping. This prayer was made in a moft folemn fituation, and he continually refers back to the covenant of redemption between him and the father. It is predicated upon that covenant, and the bleffings requefted are coextenfive with it. The whole prayer is worthy of being read as an argument on this point, but I will only felect feveral paffages from it.

Verse 2. *THOU haſt given him power over all fleſh, that he ſhould give eternal life to as many as thou haſt given him.*

Verse 6. *I HAVE manifeſted thy name to the men thou gaveſt me out of the world : thine they were, and thou gaveſt them me.*

Verse 9. *I PRAY for them : I pray not for the world, but for them which thou haſt given me ; for they are thine.*

Verse 12. *THEM that thou gaveſt me I have kept, and none of them is loſt but the ſon of perdition ; that the ſcriptures might be fulfilled.*

Verse 14. *AND the world hath hated them, becauſe they are not of the world, even as I am not of the world.*

Verses 20, 21. *NEITHER pray I for theſe alone ; but for them alſo which ſhall believe on me through their word. That they all may be one ; as thou father art in me, and I in thee, that they alſo may be one in us : that the world may believe that thou haſt ſent me.*

Verses 25, 26. *O RIGHTEOUS father, the world hath not known thee ; but I have known thee, and theſe have known that thou haſt ſent me. And I have declared unto them thy name, and will declare it : that the love wherewith thou haſt loved me may be in them, and I in them.*

THE whole prayer ſpeaks the ſame ſentiments, as theſe verſes which are ſelected ; and had CHRIST ſtudied the moſt expreſs way of contradicting the univerſaliſts, he could not have done it more effectually. He ſpeaks directly to the father, and in prayer, the moſt ſolemn manner of addreſs. He brings into view the covenant of redemption between the father and the ſon ; and the origin of redeeming and faving grace in the counfels of the deity. He evidently fpeaks of men as divided into two claffes ; thofe whom the father had given him ; and the world. The world here cannot mean the inanimate creation, for he faith that the world hateth thofe whom the father had given him. He prays for all thofe whom the father had given him ; but exprefsly fays, that he doth not pray or intercede for the world. He was praying in the prefence of his difciples, and confidered them as reprefenting his earthly church ; and faith, that of thofe whom the father had given him, he had loft none, but the fon of perdition his betrayer. He was loft, becaufe the father had never given him to CHRIST. This fentiment correfponds with what CHRIST fays of him in another place, that it would have been better for that man, if he had never been born.

FROM this reprefentation of our bleffed Saviour, it appears, that in the covenant of redemption which determined the number of thofe to be faved ; fome were given to CHRIST as his fpiritual feed, and none of them fhall be loft ; and fome were not given to him in this fenfe, and are called the world. He does not even intercede for the world, for they hate him and his people. They are never to be one in a fpiritual fenfe with his father and him ; nor to be in the fame place with CHRIST, nor fee the glory which the father hath given him ; and of courfe they muft be left to fuffer the wages of fin, and be feparated from the holy prefence of GOD.

IF there be any, who are not given to CHRIST as the great head of the redeemed

church, and whom he doth not confider as belonging to him, and for whom he doth not pray;
they muſt certainly be miſerable, for their fins
muſt make them ſo, and there is no ſanctification encouraged.　Common ſenſe doth not ſee
how the ſon of GOD could expreſs himſelf as
he hath done in this chapter, if he ſuppoſed
that all men were to be ſaved by his mediation
and atonement.　The ſaviour always made uſe
of the moſt dignified plainneſs and ſolemnity
in all his words, and ſuch a mode of expreſſion, in ſolemn prayer to GOD, could not be
deſigned to terrify man; but was an affection-
ate ſupplication, grounded on the covenant
between him and his father, praying that GOD
would keep by his mighty power thoſe who
were appointed unto ſalvation.　GOD had already given him power over all fleſh, and put
the government of the world into his hands;
that he might be able to ſave his choſen people; and he here ſupplicates the divine co-op-
eration, in bringing them to glory.

SEC. 4. THE queſtion whether all men
ſhall be ſaved, is expreſsly reſolved by JESUS
CHRIST, in ſo plain a manner, that it ſeems
ſtrange any who profeſs to believe the holy
ſcriptures ſhould doubt the event.　It is in the
xiii chapter of Luke from the 23d to the 30th
verſe.

THEN ſaid one unto him, LORD, *are there few
that be ſaved? And he ſaid unto them, ſtrive to
enter in at the ſtrait gate : for many, I ſay unto
you, ſhall ſeek to enter in, and ſhall not be able.
When once the maſter of the houſe is riſen up, and
hath ſhut to the door, and ye begin to ſtand without, and to knock at the door, ſaying,* LORD,

LORD, *open to us : and he shall answer and say unto you, I know you not whence you are : Then shall ye begin to say, we have eaten and drunk in thy presence, and thou hast taught in our streets. But he shall say, I tell you, I know you not whence ye are; depart from me, all ye workers of iniquity. There shall be weeping and gnashing of teeth, when ye shall see Abraham, and Isaac, and Jacob, and all the prophets in the kingdom of* GOD, *and you yourselves thrust out.*

IT doth not appear that the enquirer had any idea of the falvation of all men. His queftion was, *Are there few that be faved?* It might be mere curiofity which propofed the queftion ; but it is more probable that his motive was the fame, as now moves many enquirers, whether all men will be faved? and that if he had found very many fhould be faved, he would have improved it as an excufe for delaying repentance. CHRIST did not inform him, whether few or many fhould be faved; but affured him that fome fhould not be faved. He evaded the queftion propofed; and anfwered that which is the matter of prefent difcuffion. *Strive to enter in at the strait gate, for many shall seek to enter in and shall not be able.* It is a matter of no concern to thee, whether many or few be faved. A knowledge of this will not help any one in working out his own falvation, and it is referved as one of the fecrets of the divine counfel; but it highly concerns you to know, that many fhall never enter into the kingdom of GOD. Many fhall never be faved, and fome of them fhall be perfons who entertain no confiderable doubt of their fafe ftate. They had eaten and drank in CHRIST's prefence, and he had taught in their ftreets. They had made ufe of CHRIST's ordinances. They fuppofed themfelves not only well inftruct-ed but very fafe, and on thefe grounds, they had a much fairer pretence of hoping, than the very uncertain one that all men fhall be faved. Still CHRIST will tell them, *I know you not whence you are, depart from me ye workers of iniquity.* The ftate into which his mighty pow-er will caufe them to depart, he defcribes by weeping and gnafhing of teeth, and being caft out of the kingdom of GOD where Abraham and the prophets and good people are. A moft lively defcription of extreme mifery. A very fimilar defcription to the above is found in Matt. vii. 21—23.

SEC. 5. SEVERAL of CHRIST's parables feem to be fpoken on purpofe to place this fubject beyond all doubt. Particularly the parables of the *tares* and of the *net*, which CHRIST him-felf explained. Thefe with a number of oth-er parables, are in the xiii. chapter of Matthew. The kingdom of Heaven, and the kingdom of GOD, appear to be phrafes of fimilar import in many of CHRIST's difcourfes. They fome-times mean the future kingdom of glory; and at other times the kingdom of his vifible church in this world. In this chapter it appears that by the kingdom of Heaven is meant, the vifible church ftate on earth.

THE parable of the tares is as follows—*The kingdom of Heaven is like unto a man which fow-ed good feed in his field : but while men flept the enemy came and fowed tares among the wheat, and went his way. But when the blade was fprung up, and brought forth fruit, then appeared*

*the tares also. So the servants of the householder
came, and said unto him, sir, did not thou sow
good seed in thy field ; from whence then hath it
tares ? He said unto them, an enemy hath done
this. The servants said unto him, wilt thou then
that we go and gather them up ? But he said, nay,
lest, while ye gather up the tares, ye root up also
the wheat with them. Let both grow together
until the harvest ; and in the time of harvest
I will say to the reapers, gather ye together
first the tares, and bind them in bundles to burn
them ; but gather the wheat into my barn.*

To prevent all possibility that the parable
should be explained away, or misunderstood,
our Saviour explained it in the following words,
*He that soweth the good seed, is the son of man ;
the field is the world ; the good seed are the
children of the kingdom, but the tares are the
children of the wicked one ; the enemy that sowed
them, is the devil ; the harvest is the end of the
world ; and the reapers are the angels. As
therefore, the tares are gathered and burnt in the
fire ; so shall it be in the end of the world. The
son of man shall send forth his angels, and they
shall gather out of his kingdom all things that offend, and them which do iniquity ; and shall cast
them into a furnace of fire ; there shall be wailing and gnashing of teeth. Then shall the righteous
shine forth as the sun in the kingdom of their father. Who hath ears to hear, let him hear.* That
by the children of the wicked one are meant,
wicked and sinful men ; we learn from what
CHRIST told the Jews, John viii. 44. *Ye are
of your father the devil, and the lusts of your father ye will do.* Also from 1 John iii. 8. *He
that committeth sin is of the devil ; for the devil
sinneth from the beginning.*

· THE parable of the net is in the fame chapter. *Again, the kingdom of Heaven is like unto a net, that was caft into the fea, and gathered of every kind : which, when it was full, they drew to fhore, and fat down, and gathered the good into veffels, but caft the bad away.* Which CHRIST thus explained. *So fhall it be at the end of the world ; the angels fhall come forth, and fever the wicked from among the juft, and fhall caft them into the furnace of fire : there fhall be wailing and gnafhing of teeth.* A man the beft acquainted with the powers of language, could not exprefs in a more definite and clear manner the following truths. That when the prefent earthly ftate of things ceafes, there will be a day of judgment. That men will then be divided into two claffes, the good and the bad ; and that the bad will go into a ftate of mifery, which he defcribes by weeping, by wailing, by gnafhing of the teeth, by being fhut out of the kingdom of GOD, and feparated from Abraham and the prophets, and other good people, who fhall fhine forth as the fun in the kingdom of their father. Language cannot exprefs any thing, if thefe truths are not expreffed. If all the univerfalifts in the world, with the moft critical knowledge of the powers of language, fhould attempt to exprefs the propofition, that all men will be faved ; they could not do it in more definite and pointed language, than JESUS CHRIST hath expreffed the contrary propofition, that at the day of judgment men fhall be feparated, and part of them go into a ftate of the moft extreme mifery. A mifery which is pictured to us by the ftrongeft expreffions, which the nature of our prefent ftate will admit us to underftand ; and all this is faid by JESUS

D

Christ in explaining his own parables, in order to accommodate them to the understanding of every man.

Sec. 6. It is ordered by the wisdom of God, that we should have an explanation of the foregoing parables of the tares and the net, by Jesus Christ himself, in such language as cannot be misunderstood by any unprejudiced mind. As a great number of Christ's parables convey the same truth on this subject, it was wisely ordered that two of them should be explained by his own mouth, and this serves as a most certain key for understanding the others. The parable of the marriage of the king's son is to the same purpose. It is in Matt. xxii. from the beginning to the 14th verse. The six first verses represent the gospel offer made to the Jews, and their rejection of it. The 7th verse represents the destruction of their nation and city. From the 8th to the 10th verse is described the calling of the Gentiles.——At the eleventh verse begins a most solemn representation. All before this had been done by the ministration of servants, but here the king himself appears to sit in solemn judgment.

And when the king came in to see the guests, he saw there a man which had not on a wedding garment: and he saith unto him, friend, how camest thou in hither, not having a wedding garment? and he was speechless. Then said the king to the servants, bind him hand and foot, and take him away, and cast him into outer darkness: there shall be weeping and gnashing of teeth. For many are called: but few are chosen.

The following truths are represented by this parable. That some are called who are not chosen. That at the end of the probationary ftate, when the good and bad are gathered by the miniſtration of ſervants; the king himſelf, God himſelf will come. All ſhall paſs under his in- ſpection and judgment. Some ſhall be found without a wedding garment, or deſtitute of the qualifications for entering into the marriage ſup- per of the lamb. The marriage ſupper of the lamb is a well known ſcriptural emblem of the bleſſedneſs of Heaven. Theſe guilty perſons will be ſpeechleſs. They will have no excuſe to make before their judge. The king will order them to be bound, taken away from him, and caſt into outer darkneſs, where is weeping and gnaſhing of teeth. Here this parable leaves them, as do all the other repreſentations of Christ on the ſame ſubject, in outer darkneſs and extreme ſorrow. Who can bring them from the place and ſtate in which the judge hath left them? They are unworthy, and are caſt out from the marriage feaſt; and if that feaſt is to be an eternal one, as none will probably deny, their miſery muſt be eternal.

Sec. 7. The xxv. chapter of Matthew is wholly on this ſubject, containing the parables of the ten virgins; of the talents; and a deſcrip- tion of the day of judgment.

In the firſt of theſe parables all are called vir- gins, for it is a deſcription of the profeſſors of religion. But it is ſaid, five of them were fooliſh. It is well known that in the holy ſcriptures, fools, folly and fooliſhneſs; mean ſinners, ſin and un- holineſs; and that wiſdom when aſcribed to men, means true grace or holineſs. Part of theſe vir- gins were fooliſh, or unholy profeſſors. They all had the lamp of profeſſion. The wiſe had oil in their lamps; that is, the anointing or ſanc- tification of the ſpirit. The unholy profeſſors had no oil—no anointing from the spirit of God. While the bridegroom tarried they all slumbered and slept. The sincere and hypocritical professors lived too much alike, though there was an essential difference in the state of their hearts. If the wise virgins had lived in the manner they ought to have done, it would probably have given conviction to the foolish, that they were in a very unsafe state; and if christians now conducted in all respects as they ought to do, it would go further to convince Universalists, than all that can be written for their warning. At an unexpected time the bridegroom came. Whether we understand this to be God's coming in death or to the final judgment, is immaterial to the present point. When he came the difference between holy and unholy persons appeared. The unholy could not bear the meeting. They were not prepared, for they had no grace. Their former hopes and expectations were of no avail. Their consciences being now awakened would not suffer them to plead that all the virgins are to be saved; and while in their own sinful way, they were preparing, the wise entered. Mark the event! The doors were shut, and to their pleading for entrance, God answered, I know you not. Can any representation more solemnly describe, the unhappy end of some men? They are shut out from God, and he doth not know them as his. There are no earthly events to which such descriptions as these can possibly apply, and the wise Saviour of the world either spake without any meaning, or they must be applied to the closing of men's probationary state on earth, and the eternal consequences that ensue.

Next follows the parable of the talents, from the 14th to the 30th verse. In this parable the dif-

ferent abilities of men to ferve God, and their
different opportunities and advantages for falvation, are compared to the different number of
talents which a Lord gave to his fervants, before he travelled into a far country. Thefe fervants made a different improvement. The firft
and fecond doubled their number of talents.
When the Lord, after a long time, returned and
called them all to an account, the faithful fervants received his approbation. *Well done, thou
good and faithful fervant, thou haft been faithful
over a few things, I will make thee ruler over many things, enter thou into the joy of thy* Lord. But
the flothful fervant is defcribed as hiding his tal-
ent in the earth; he made no gain for Heaven
with it, but buried himfelf up in a worldly and
fenfual life. He called God unreafonable in
the requirements of a religious life, and his lord
condemned him on this very principle; that he
had knowledge of his duty and what would be
required of him. So that his flothfulnefs could
not be imputed to ignorance, but to a finful dif-
affection of heart. And his fentence was, *Caft
ye the unprofitable fervant into outer darknefs: there
fhall be weeping and gnafhing of teeth.*

These parables of the virgins, and of the talents are in themfelves plain; but left they fhould
be perverted and mifapplied by men who do not
love the truth, Christ proceeded to give a moft
folemn defcription of the procefs and iffue of the
final day of judgment; and this defcription may
be confidered as an explanation of thefe parables,
in the plaineft language; and fhewing that they
applied to the confummation of men's ftate of
probation.

*When the fon of man fhall come in his glory, and
all the holy angels with him, then fhall he fit upon*

the throne of his glory. And before him shall be gathered all nations, and he shall separate them one from another, as a shepherd divideth his sheep, from the goats : And he shall set the sheep on his right hand, but the goats on the left. Then shall the king say unto them on his right hand, come ye blessed of my father, inherit the kingdom prepared for you from the foundation of the world. For I was an hungered, and ye gave me meat : I was thirsty, and ye gave me drink : I was a stranger, and ye took me in : naked, and ye cloathed me : I was sick, and ye visited me : I was in prison, and ye came unto me. Then shall the righteous answer him, saying, Lord, when saw we thee an hungered, and fed thee ? or thirsty, and gave thee drink ? When saw we thee a stranger, and took thee in ? or naked, and cloathed thee ? or when saw we thee sick, or in prison, and came unto thee ? And the king shall answer, and say unto them, Verily, I say unto you, in as much as ye have done it unto one of the least of these my brethren, ye have done it unto me. Then shall he say also unto them on the left hand, depart from me, ye cursed, into everlasting fire, prepared for the devil and his angels. For I was an hungered, and ye gave me no meat : I was thirsty, and ye gave me no drink : I was a stranger and ye took me not in : naked, and ye cloathed me not : sick, and in prison, and ye visited me not. Then shall they also answer him, saying, Lord when saw we thee an hungered, or a thirst, or a stranger, or naked, or sick, or in prison, and did not minister unto thee ? Then shall he answer them, saying, Verily, I say unto you, in as much as ye did it not to one of the least of these, ye did it not to me. And these shall go away into everlasting punishment : but the righteous into life eternal.

THE words tranflated everlafting and eternal in the laft verfe, are expreffed by the fame Greek word in the original, and whatever duration of bleffednefs, the righteous have ; the fame duration of mifery is declared concerning the wicked.

TAKING this chapter in connection, the following things appear to be expreffed by JESUS CHRIST. That there is a day of judgment, when all nations fhall come before him. Among them he will find two kinds of perfons. Firft, his fheep ; the wife virgins, and thofe who have faithfully improved their abilities and advantages for the glory of GOD and good of mankind, in all the works of humanity and righteoufnefs. Thefe fhall enter into the wedding before the door is fhut. The judge will call them good and faithful fervants ; invite them into the joy of their LORD ; make them rulers over many things ; and give them a kingdom prepared for them before the foundation of the world, where they fhall enjoy life eternal.——The fecond kind of perfons he calls foolifh virgins. They are finful and unholy profeffors, who have none of the oil of grace that is given by the fpirit of GOD ——unprofitable fervants——perfons who do not improve their talents for GOD and another world, but hide them in the fenfuality, wickednefs and vices of earth ; denying the righteoufnefs of GOD and the reafonablenefs of religion, and defying the juftice of that punifhment which the LORD threatens to execute on his return. Their character is expreffed by that of goats, compared with fheep ; and as perfons deftitute of humanity and righteoufnefs in their treatment of mankind ; and their end is that they are fhut out from the bridegroom, and the door is clofed that they cannot enter. To their

call, God will answer I know you not. That
which they seemed to have through the restraints
of divine power is taken from them, so that their
sinful hearts appear in all their enormity. They
are bound hand and foot, and cast into outer
darkness, where is gnashing of teeth. They
go into everlasting punishment, in everlasting fire
prepared for the devil and his angels. All this
is said by Christ himself who is to be the judge,
and could he have told in plainer terms the
awful end of the wicked?

Sec. 8. The greatest part of our modern
Universalists, suppose that the happiness of all
men commences at death. But how is this consistent with Christ's representation of the rich
man and Lazarus, in the xvi chapter of Luke.
The rich man fared sumptuously, and lived and
died a sinner, and in hell he lift up his eyes being in torment. Lazarus also died and was
carried by angels to Abraham's bosom. Abraham's bosom was a name used by the Jews, for
the place and state of blessedness after death.
The tormented sinner requested that Lazarus
might be sent to dip the tip of his finger in water and cool his tongue. Abraham's answer
was, *remember that thou in thy life time receivedst
thy good things ; and likewise Lazarus evil things ;
but now he is comforted, and thou art tormented ;
and besides all this, between us and you there is a
great gulf fixed : so that they which would pass from
hence to you, cannot ; neither can they pass to us, that
would come from thence.* Here Christ represents some men as going into torment at death,
and being denied all favor—as having received
their share of good things—and that there could
be no passing between Heaven and them—and
if that gulf could not be passed their misery

muſt be without end. Sundry other parables of CHRIST teach the ſame truth as theſe which we have conſidered. The method of inſtructing by ſuch parables as CHRIST uſed, is ſufficiently plain to give the fulleſt conviction, to thoſe minds which candidly wiſh for truth. It perſuaſively gains the attention to ſubjects, on which men do not like to meditate; and unites the advantages, of drawing on the reader or hearer, by the charms of a ſtory, and of a ſolemn addreſs to the conſcience on ſubjects of infinite importance.

SEC. 9. HAVING noticed the parables of CHRIST, we will now attend to various other teſtimonies of his on this point. In a converſation with the Jews, recorded John viii. 21 to 24 he ſays: *I go my way, and ye ſhall ſeek me, and ſhall die in your ſins: whether I go, ye cannot come. Then ſaid the Jews, will he kill himſelf? becauſe he ſaith, whether I go, ye cannot come. And he ſaid unto them, ye are from beneath; I am from above: ye are of this world; I am not of this world. I ſaid therefore unto you, that ye ſhall die in your ſins: for if ye believe not that I am he, ye ſhall die in your ſins.* The natural meaning of theſe words is this; that death would have no purifying effect upon them, and that they ſhould go out of the world and remain in a ſinful ſtate. He ſays expreſsly, *ye ſhall die in your ſins,* that is with your ſins upon you; unpurified and unſanctified, and *where I go ye cannot come.* CHRIST went to heaven; but they could not come there, and were excluded from the place, where all the redeemed ſhall ſee the glory which the father hath given him. He prays the father that all thoſe who were given to him might be with him, where he is; and he here ſays, there are ſome who never can be with him; the conſequence is plain.

JESUS CHRIST caſt out devils by the ſpirit of God. On a certain occaſion, the Jews charged him with caſting them out, by Beelzebub the prince of devils. Upon which CHRIST ſaid, Matt. xii. 31, 32. *All manner of ſin and blaſphemy ſhall be forgiven unto men: but the blaſphemy againſt the Holy Ghoſt ſhall not be forgiven unto men. And whoſoever ſpeaketh a word againſt the ſon of man, it ſhall be forgiven him: but whoſoever ſpeaketh againſt the Holy Ghoſt, it ſhall not be forgiven him, neither in this world; neither in the world to come.* Mark iii. 29. *He that ſhall blaſpheme againſt the Holy Ghoſt, hath never forgiveneſs, but is in danger of eternal damnation.* Luke xii. 10. *Unto him that blaſphemeth againſt the Holy Ghoſt, it ſhall not be forgiven.* Here is CHRIST's moſt expreſs teſtimony, that there are ſins which ſhall never be forgiven. They cannot be forgiven in this world, and he adds, *neither in the world to come*, to give emphaſis to the awful truth.

THAT theſe words of our Saviour meant a puniſhment and miſery, which ſhall never come to an end, may be argued from the nature of the goſpel ſcheme of recovery. Thoſe who think that it is a reflection on the ſufficiency of CHRIST's atonement, to ſuppoſe any ſins unpardonable, ought to conſider from whence their unpardonableneſs doth ariſe. It is not from the greatneſs of thoſe ſins compared with other ſins; nor from any want of ſufficiency in the atonement of CHRIST. The Holy Spirit hath his own part in the work of ſalvation, and without his awakening, convincing and ſanctifying operation, men will never be ſaved. They will reſiſt truth and duty and continue in unholineſs. The ſin of the Jews, was their denying the work of the Holy Spirit by whom CHRIST caſt out devils; and aſcribing the effect to the ſpirit of devils. Denying the work of the Holy Ghost, and resisting his influences in such a manner as grieves him to depart, and to say he will never act upon the mind again, is an unpardonable sin. The unpardonableness of the sin does not, in strictness, arise from its greatness compared with other sins ; neither from the atonement of Christ being insufficient to pardon sins of such magnitude ; but from a cause entirely different. No sinners can be pardoned without sanctification, and the action of the divine spirit leading them to believe in Christ, and preparing them for heaven. If any sinners have so treated the spirit of God, that in infinite wisdom and righteousness he hath determined to leave them to themselves ; they are as certainly and as eternally in an unpardonable condition, as they would be, if no saviour had been provided.

The words of our Saviour under consideration, are therefore, not only a testimony for the eternal punishment of some sinners ; but also a solemn warning, that they bring not themselves into that state, by resisting the influences, and denying the work of the Holy Ghost. Many, doubtless, have committed unpardonable sin ; and we must expect to find such persons, among those, who, after having been often warned and had many convictions, are now sunk down into deep security, and think nothing of another world. Those who against sufficient evidence, deny the christian scriptures, that were given by the inspiration of the spirit ; or divide them, receiving part and rejecting part, in accommodation to their own wishes ; or pervert them to establish opinions which are contrary to the general scheme of God's truth, are sinning directly against the Holy Ghost. The spirit of God hath left them—they are given up to their own sin—*to strong delusion, to believe a lie, that they might be damned, becauſe they had pleaſure in unrighteouſneſs.*

Sec. 10. Matt. v. 22. *But whoſoever ſhall ſay, thou fool, ſhall be in danger of hell fire.* Could Christ ſay this with truth, if he knew that there is no hell fire, and that all men ſhall be ſaved? Matt. x. 28. *Fear not them which kill the body, but are not able to kill the ſoul; but rather fear him which is able to deſtroy both ſoul and body in hell.* 33d. Verſe. *Whoſoever ſhall deny me before men, him will I alſo deny before my father which is in Heaven.*—Matt. xvi. 25, 26. *For whoſoever will ſave his life, ſhall loſe it; and whoſoever will loſe his life for my ſake, ſhall find it. For what is a man profited, if he ſhall gain the whole world, and loſe himſelf?*

In the 18th chapter of Matthew he deſcribes the fearful end of the unmerciful ſervant, who had been forgiven by his lord, and then ſays, *ſo ſhall my heavenly father do unto you, if ye from your hearts forgive not every one his brother their treſpaſſes.* Would the ſon of God have given this deſcription, unleſs there be ſuch an end to which ſome men ſhall come?—Matt. xxiii. 13—15. *Woe unto you, ſcribes, Phariſees, hypocrites; for ye ſhut up the kingdom of heaven againſt men; for ye neither go in yourſelves, neither ſuffer ye them that are entering, to go in. For ye devour widows houſes, and for a pretenſe make long prayers; therefore ye ſhall receive the greater damnation, for ye compaſs ſea and land to make one proſelyte, and when he is made, ye make him twofold*

*cometh in the glory of his father, with the holy an-
gels.*—Mark ix. 43—48. *If thy hand offend thee,
cut it off; it is better for thee to enter into life maimed,
than having two hands to go into hell, into the fire
that never shall be quenched : where their worm
dieth not, and the fire is not quenched.* Could
CHRIST have faid in more plain words that there
is a future punifhment prepared for them, who
will not part with their favorite fins and lufts?—
Mark xvi. 15, 16. *Go ye into all the world, and
preach the gofpel to every creature, he that believeth and is baptized, fhall be faved ; but he that
believeth not fhall be damned.*—Luke vi. 24. *Wo
unto you that are rich : for ye have received your
confolation.* With what propriety could a Wo
be pronounced on thofe who abound in the
bleffings of this world, or could it be faid that
they have received their confolation, if there be
not a ftate of future mifery where thofe who
have ufed their riches in a wrong manner, fhall
be punifhed?—Luke xiii. 3. *Except ye repent,
ye fhall all likewife perifh.* Doth not this imply
that fome fhall not repent, and actually perifh?—
Luke xiv. 27. *Whofoever doth not bear his crofs,
and come after me, cannot be my difciple.* Can
thofe who are not CHRIST's difciples be faved?
—John v. 28, 29. *For the hour is coming, in
which all that are in the graves fhall hear his
voice, and come forth ; they that have done good
to the refurrection of life ; and they that have done
evil, to the refurrection of damnation.*—John xv. 6.
If a man abide not in me, he is caft forth as a

erable state of sinners in another world. He
speaks of those who have once reformed and
backsliden, as in a desperate condition ; for they
take to themselves seven other spirits more wicked
than themselves, and their last state is worse than
their first. He draws a comparison, between the
condemnation of different sinners at the day of
judgment ; as Tyre, Sidon, Sodom, Gomorrha,
and the cities wherein his mighty works were
done ; telling us it should be more tolerable for
some than others, plainly intimating a state of
misery to all of them.—He speaks of those who
build on a sandy foundation, and of a time of
tempest when they shall be overwhelmed in destruction.—He says with what judgment ye judge,
ye shall be judged ; and with what measure ye
mete, it shall be meted to you again. Many of
an evil character appear to go out of the world
without repentance, must they not suffer hereafter for the fulfilment of such threatnings? He
speaks of the devil as taking the word out of
men's hearts, lest they should be saved ; does not
this imply that some shall not be saved ? Those
who put their hand to the plough and look back are
not fit for the kingdom of God.—He tells us that
those who are not born again cannot see the kingdom
of God.—That he that believeth not the son shall
not see life.—He speaks of those who are in darkness, and hate the light, and this is their condemnation ; of those who hate both him and his father ; of those who do not and will not receive
him ; of many sins in which men appear to continue, which are inconsistent with salvation.—He
describes two characters ; men of different tem-
pers and in different interests, who have different
pleasures and are coming to different ends.

THE doctrine of a future punishment is either
expresly asserted, or most strongly implied in

almoſt every diſcourſe of our Saviour which is on
record, and it ſeemed to be a main deſign with
him to inculcate it. The deſcription of this miſery is expreſſed by a vaſt variety of words, and
expreſſions, denoting perpetuity without end, as
much as language can do it.—Eternal—everlaſting—the worm which dieth not—the fire which
is not quenched—ſhall not ſee life—cannot be
ſaved—ſhall not be forgiven—with innumerable
other modes of expreſſion, denoting interminable
wretchedneſs.

THROUGH all his diſcourſes he repreſents this
life as the time of trial, and the only ſeaſon in
which there is an offer of grace; and ſpeaks of
death as ending this ſeaſon; and of the final judgment as fixing men in a ſtate of retribution. In
all that he ſays concerning future events, and the
nature of that world from which he came, and
to which he was going; there is not a ſingle hint
of any change in men's condition, after it is
once fixed.—Many have been charged with
dwelling too much on the terrors of future miſery; but on faithfully examining the four evangel-
iſts, who have written a hiſtory of CHRIST's life
and doctrines; it will appear, that he did it more
abundantly than any who have miniſtered in his
name. It was fit he ſhould do it; for he came
from the inviſible world, and could have no un-
juſt ideas concerning it. It was all in his view.
All men are in his hands. The grace which ſaves
was purchaſed and is applied by his ſpirit. He is the
judge, and will appoint to every ſoul its eternal
condition. So that the witneſs of JESUS CHRIST
on this point, may be eſteemed concluſive; and
it muſt be ſtrong evidence indeed to overturn
what he hath ſo fully eſtabliſhed. But to ſhow
that there is an agreement of ſentiment on this
point, we will conſider what is ſaid by the other
inſpired teachers.

SEC. 12. THE TESTIMONY OF JOHN THE BAP-
TIST, recorded by Matthew and Luke, in Mat. iii.
and Luke iii. *O generation of vipers who hath
warned you to flee from the wrath to come.——
And now alfo the ax is laid to the root of the
trees ; therefore every tree that bringeth not forth
good fruit, is hewn down and caft into the fire.
——Whofe fan is in his hand, and he will thoroughly purge his floor, and gather his wheat into
the garner ; but he will burn up the chaff with
unquenchable fire.* If there be no wrath to come ;
if there be no trees to be hewn down and caft
into the fire ; if there is to be no feparation between the wheat and the chaff ; how can fuch
addreffes as thefe be either proper or honeft ?

IF, as fome Univerfalifts have attempted to
evade fuch paffages as thefe, it fhould be faid ;
the chaff means fins, feparated from the finner,
and thefe fins are eternally tormented ; it is requefted they would give a defcription of a fin,
that is feparated from the finner, and placed in a
ftate of mifery. A lie is a fin. Stealing is a
fin. Who ever conceived of a lie put into the
ftocks, or of a theft tied to the whipping poft ;
and the liar and thief themfelves efcaping. The
very idea is almoft too abfurd to remark upon.
That men will always be found, abfurd enough
to teach whatever the world will patiently and
ferioufly hear, is to be expected ; but that a
congregation of rational beings, fhould calmly
hear fuch abfurdities in nature, and not feel de-
graded by their fituation, is ftrange indeed ! ! !

SEC. 13. TESTIMONY OF PETER THE APOS-
TLE. 1 PETER iii. 19, 20. *By which he went
alfo and preached to the fpirits in prifon ; which fome-
time were difobedient, when once the long fuffering
of God waited in the days of Noah.* The Apoftle
is here fpeaking of the means of grace, which

were ufed with thofe ancient finners in the days of Noah; when God bare long and warned them, the whole time the ark was building, and they repented not. Why are they now called fpirits in prifon, unlefs they are confined for a public trial and punifhment?—1 Peter iv. 17, 18. *For the time is come that judgment muft begin at the houfe of God; and if it firft begin at us, what fhall the end be of them that obey not the gofpel of God? And if the righteous fcarcely be faved, where fhall the ungodly and finner appear?* Can there be a more clear implication than this is, that the ungodly and finner will not be faved?

The whole of the fecond chapter of Peter's fecond epiftle, might pertinently be quoted, to prove future and eternal punifhment. I will only recite a few verfes. Verfe 1ft. *Who privily fhall bring in damnable herefies, even denying the Lord that bought them, and bring upon themfelves fwift deftruction.* Verfes 3, 4, 5. *And through covetoufnefs fhall they, with feigned words, make merchandife of you: whofe judgment now of a long time lingereth not, and their damnation flumbereth not. For if God fpared not the angels that finned, but caft them down to hell, and delivered them into chains of darknefs, to be referved unto judgment. And fpared not the old world, but faved Noah the eighth perfon.*

These laft words, explain what is meant by the fpirits in prifon, mentioned in the firft epiftle. They are the impenitent finners of the antediluvian world, delivered unto darknefs, and referved in chains with the fining angels, to the fame punifhment. Verfe 9. *The Lord knoweth how to deliver the godly out of temptation, and to referve the unjuft to the day of judgment to be punifhed.* Verfe 12. *But thefe, as natural brute beafts, made to be taken and deftroyed, fpeak evil of the things which*

F

they *underftand not, and fhall utterly perifh in their own corruption.* Verfe 17. *Thefe are wells without water, clouds that are carried with a tempeft ; to whom the mift of darknefs is referved forever.* The whole chapter when read in connection, will appear more forcibly to affert the doctrine of eternal punifhment, than thefe verfes can when detached by themfelves.

THE third chapter is remarkable in many refpects. *This fecond epiftle, beloved, I now write unto you ; in both which I ftir up your pure minds by way of remembrance : that ye may be mindful of the words which were fpoken before by the holy prophets, and of the commandment of us the apoftles of the* LORD *and Saviour : knowing this firft, that there fhall come in the laft days fcoffers, walking after their own lufts, and faying, where is the promife of his coming ? for fince the fathers fell afleep, all things continue as they were from the beginning of the creation. For this they willingly are ignorant of, that by the word of* GOD *the heavens were of old, and the earth ftanding out of the water, and in the water : whereby the world that then was, being overflowed with water, perifhed : but the heavens and the earth which are now, by the fame word are kept in ftore, referved unto fire againft the day of judgment, and perdition of ungodly men. But, beloved, be not ignorant of this one thing, that one day is with the* LORD *as a thoufand years, and a thoufand years as one day. The* LORD *is not flack concerning his promife, as fome men count flacknefs ; but is long-fuffering to us-ward, not willing that any fhould perifh, but that all fhould come to repentance. But the day of the* LORD *will come as a thief in the night ; in the which the heavens fhall pafs away with a great noife, and the elements fhall melt with fervent heat, the earth alfo, and the works that are therein, fhall be burnt up. Seeing then that all these things shall be diffolved, what manner of persons ought ye to be in all holy converfation and godlinefs ; looking for and hasting unto the coming of the day of* God, *wherein the heavens, being on fire, shall be diffolved, and the elements shall melt with fervent heat? Neverthelefs, we, according to his promife, look for new heavens, and a new earth, wherein dwelleth righteoufnefs. Wherefore, beloved, feeing that ye look for fuch things, be diligent that ye may be found of him in peace, without fpot, and blamelefs : and account that the long-fuffering of our* Lord *is falvation ; even as our beloved brother Paul alfo, according to the wifdom given unto him, hath written unto you ; as alfo in all his epiftles, fpeaking in them of thefe things : in which are fome things hard to be underftood, which they that are unlearned and unftable wreft, as they do alfo the other fcriptures, unto their own deftruction. Ye, therefore, beloved, feeing ye know thefe things before, beware lest ye alfo, being led away with the error of the wicked, fall from your own fteadfaftnefs.* In this chapter, he exhorts the brethren to attend to the things written by the holy prophets, and not forget what God hath denounced. He warns the church, that in the laft days fhall come fcoffers, walking in their own lufts, and in the pride of human reafon, who fhall call in queftion the truth of what God hath threatened. They fhall fay, where is the promife of his coming, for fince the fathers fell afleep all things remain as they were? Where is this punifhment of fin, that hath been fo long threatened? We do not feel it ; we will not believe it. And he fays they willingly are ignorant, both of the ancient and future punifhment of the ungodly. They call the fcripture hiftory of ancient punifhments, and the threatening of wrath to come, incredible. He afferts, that as it is a fact, the earth and its inhabitants were once destroyed by water; so the visible heavens and earth that now are, are reserved for a second destruction by fire.—That this shall be at the day of judgment, which is the day of the perdition, the perishing or destruction of ungodly men. He then tells them, that this delay of God in punishing, is not through slackness and irresolution; and that it affords no room for sinners to hope they shall escape with impunity; but is to show his lenity, and give them an opportunity for repentance; that they may appear exceedingly sinful and justly condemned. They are not impenitent for want of time to repent, nor for want of warning; but having time enough, continue in sin, because they love it; and spend the season allotted for repentance, in endeavouring to dispute God out of his threatened judgments. He also says that notwithstanding this infidelity concerning future punishment, *the day of the LORD will come as a thief in the night, in which the Heavens shall pass away with a great noise, and the Elements shall melt with fervent heat, and the earth also and the things that are therein shall be burnt up.* This is the time of the perdition of ungodly men; when their compleat punishment in body and soul shall take place.—After this the apostle, from the 11th to the 15th verse, gives an exhortation of warning and consolation to christians. That in expectation of these things, they should watch *in all holy conversation and godliness*, looking for and holding themselves in readiness, for the coming of the day of God; and lest they should be terrified by the awful truths he had been stating, tells them, that christians may look for new heavens and a new earth wherein dwelleth righteousness, in the place of the old heavens and earth, which are reserved unto fire for the destruction of ungodly men. The 15th

and 16th verfes of this chapter are very remarkable, and have not been underftood by many
chriftians. The words are thefe, *even as our beloved brother Paul alfo, according to the wifdom
given unto him, hath written unto you; as alfo in
all his epiftles, fpeaking in them of thefe things: in
which are fome things hard to be underftood, which
they that are unlearned and unftable wreft, as they
do alfo the other fcriptures, unto their own deftruction.* On thefe fingular words of Peter many
remarks have been made. Infidels have pleafed
themfelves that Peter was at variance with Paul,
or did not underftand his writings; and many
chriftians, hardly knew how to reconcile the reprefentation with pure friendfhip. The beauty
and propriety of Peter's defcription, could not
be feen, until the events to which it related took
place. He is defcribing the herefies of the laft
days; which are the days in which we now live.
He afferts the doctrine of future and eternal
punifhment; he defcribes the character of fome
who fhould fall into the error of denying that
punifhment; and goes fo far as to fay, that they
would appeal much to the writings of Paul as a
proof of their errors. It is a well known fact,
that many Univerfalifts, in fupport of their fcheme,
fo far as they depend on holy fcripture for proof,
appeal much to the writings of Paul. Take away
his writings, and it is prefumed many of them
will allow, that in all the remainder there is little
evidence for their opinion.* Peter under the infpiration of the bleffed fpirit, forefaw that this

---

* Doctor Chauncey, a Univerfalift writer, takes almoft the
whole of his fcripture proof from the writings of Paul. This
work of Dr. Chauncey hath been learnedly refuted, by Dr. Jonathan Edwards, both on the principles of reafon, and by the
teftimony of revelation. Dr. Edward's reply to Dr. Chauncey,
is recommended to the perufal of thofe who wifh to be thoroughly acquainted with this fubject.

would be the cafe, and predicted the event. He did not mean to reflect on his beloved brother Paul; but to vindicate his character, and leave a public warning that his writings would be perverted, to fupport the very error we are now confidering. He fays that there are fome things in Paul's writings hard to be underftood, being written in the deepnefs of that wifdom given unto him, and that unlearned and unftable men would wreft them to their own deftruction. Could there be a more exact prophetic defcription of the prefent day? and doth not this warning given by Peter, furnifh great occafion to fufpect, that thofe paffages in the writings of Paul, which have been adduced to prove the doctrine of Univerfal Salvation, are totally mifapplied, and mifunderftood by thofe who make this ufe of them. And ought not fuch perfons, before they determine pofitively, to paufe and enquire, whether they are not either unftable, or unlearned in the true fcripture fcheme. How admirable is the wifdom and plenitude of divine infpiration, and what a full proof of the omnifcience of that holy fpirit, who guided all the facred writers, thus to give a warning by one of them, of the mifufe that would be made of the writings of another.

SEC. 12. TESTIMONY OF PAUL THE APOSTLE.——EPISTLE TO THE ROMANS. This epiftle hath generally been efteemed an intricate part of the facred writings. It contains much truth brought into a fhort compafs, and connected by a train of reafoning, that cannot be underftood without the clofe attention and ftudy of the reader. And few readers have either patience, or a difpofition for this. Great ufe of the Epiftle, hath therefore been made by errorifts of various denominations. They have detached certain paſſages, and applied them to their own purpoſe ; but we know, that particular paſſages detached from a connected train of reaſoning, and viewed by themſelves, give very little light on any ſubject, and they may be improved directly oppoſite to the intention of the writer.

ALL the writings of Paul abound with this kind of reaſoning, which makes them difficult to be underſtood, and expoſes them to be miſapplied, by the unlearned and unſtable, as Peter hath forewarned. In the Epiſtle to the Romans, the final rejection and puniſhment of ſome men, is both plainly expreſſed, and neceſſarily implied in other truths, which are fundamental pillars in his ſcheme of doctrine. One principal deſign of the apoſtle, was to explain the nature, manner, and effects of the chriſtian juſtification by faith in CHRIST ; and alſo to deſcribe the character, of thoſe who are juſtified. The general plan of the Epiſtle, is this. He, in the firſt place, deſcribes the utterly ſinful, guilty and condemned ſtate of mankind by the law. He gives a view of the ſin and guilt of the Gentile nations ; and recites proofs from the Old Teſtament, which were the Jewiſh ſcriptures ; that the Jews alſo were all guilty. It ſeems to be his deſign in the ſecond chapter, to convince thoſe who had the Jewiſh ſcriptures, and who were as much under a diſpenſation of grace, as members of the chriſtian church now are, that without a holy obedience through faith in CHRIST, they are expoſed to damnation. In this chapter we find the following words. *And thinkeſt thou this, O man, that judgeſt them which do ſuch things, and doeſt the ſame, that thou ſhalt eſcape the judgment of* GOD ? *Or deſpiſeſt thou the riches of his goodneſs, and for-bearance, and long-ſuffering ; not knowing that the*

goodness of God *leadeth thee to repentance? But,
after thy hardness and impenitent heart, treasurest
up unto thyself wrath against the day of wrath, and
revelation of the righteous judgment of* God *; who
will render to every man according to his deeds : to
them, who by patient continuance in well-doing, seek
for glory, and honor, and immortality,* he will render *eternal life ; but unto them that are contentious,
and do not obey the truth, but obey unrighteousness,*
he will render *indignation and wrath, tribulation
and anguish, upon every soul of man that doeth evil,
of the jew first, and also the* Gentile.

He afterwards speaks of those, who having sinned without a written law, shall perish without a
written law ; and of those, who having sinned
with a written law, shall be judged by the written
law. Also he says, that the Gentiles who have not
a written law, are a law unto themselves.   Their
consciences shall accuse or excuse, in the day when
God shall judge the secrets of men by Jesus
Christ.   Is not all this explicit enough, that
there is a day of wrath, and revelation and of the
righteous judgment of God? that to some tribulation and anguish will be rendered? that the
light or law of nature, is sufficient to justify God
in doing this? and that it will be in the day when
the secrets of men are judged by Jesus Christ.

In the latter part of the third, and through the
whole of the fourth chapter, he describes the
righteousness of faith in Jesus Christ, by which
sinners are pardoned and justified.   He goes back
to Abraham, who is called the father of the faithful, whether they be Jews or Gentiles, and describes how faith was efficacious in him, and in
all his spiritual seed.   In the 5th chapter, he describes the benefits that come to the believer
through faith, and shows that he gains more by his

connexion with CHRIST the fecond Adam, than he loft by the apoftacy of the firft Adam.*

THE Apoftle having fpoken in ftrong terms of the abounding benefits of grace, and knowing how apt men are to deceive themfelves into fecurity, becaufe GOD is merciful; in the 6th and 7th chapters, fhows the neceffity of holinefs or fanctification, as evidence that we have any benefit from the abounding grace of the gofpel, either for time or eternity. Verfe 1ft. *What fhall we fay then, fhall we continue in fin that grace may abound?* that is, fhall we remain eafy in unholinefs, or think that we ourfelves, or that all men fhall be faved, becaufe GOD's grace abounds in JESUS? To the queftion he gives a long anfwer. It begins in thefe words. Verfe 2d. *How fhall we that are dead to fin live any longer therein?* The meaning of which is; the perfons who have any right to this abounding grace, are mortified to fin, and do not wifh to live in it, and if they appear to love fin, it fhows that whatever the abounding of grace be, it doth not belong to them. *They have been baptized into* CHRIST'S *death*, as an emblem of their being dead to fin, and if fincere in this, fo as to entitle them to the promife of grace, *will walk in newnefs of life, and henceforth not ferve fin.* Verfe 13. *Yield yourfelves unto* GOD, *as thofe that are alive from the dead.* Verfe 16. *Know ye not that to whom ye yield yourfelves fervants to obey, his fervants ye are whom ye obey; whether of fin unto death, or of obedience unto righteoufnefs.* Verfe 18. *Being then made free from fin ye become the fervants of righteoufnefs.* Verfe 21, 23. *What fruit had ye then in thofe things, whereof ye are now afhamed,*

---

* From this Chapter is taken one of the moft notable arguments of the Univerfalifts, a confideration of it is referred to part 3d.

C

*for the end of those things is death. But now be-
ing made free from sin, and become servants to* God,
*ye have your fruit unto holiness, and the end ever-
lasting life. For the wages of sin is death; but the
gift of* God *is eternal life through* Jesus Christ.——
The whole of the 6th and 7th Chapters, are not
only descriptive of the common exercises of holiness, in those who have it; but also contain, a
limitation to that abounding of grace, which had
been mentioned in the 5th chapter; and that it
is only to those who are dead to sin, and alive to
holiness. Also that if men are the servants of sin,
sin must be unto death; because eternal death is
as much the wages of sin as it ever was. If the
Apostle had supposed that all men would become
holy, and share in the abounding grace of God,
quite another method of writing on this subject
would have been proper.

In the 8th Chapter, the Apostle goes on further to describe the character of those who share
in the abounding grace of God, and to mention
the benefits, which they receive in this life. *They
walk not after the flesh but after the spirit. They
do not mind the things of the flesh, but the things of
the spirit. They are spiritually minded. Being
the Sons of* God *they are led by the spirit; and the
spirit of* God *assists them in a prayerful and religious life.*——Certainly there are many of mankind,
who do not manifest any thing of this character;
and of those who are disobedient, in this same
chapter, the Apostle saith, *They that are in the
flesh cannot please* God. *For if ye live after the
flesh ye shall die.* All this, was manifestly designed to limit that abounding of grace, which he
had before mentioned; and was meant, both to
instruct christians, and to guard against Universalism. When we see Universalists living such
lives, as the Apostle describes in those to whom

the grace of GOD abounds; when we fee them meek, humble, and eminent in all holy converfation and godlinefs ; when we fee them imitators of the blefled JESUS, prayerful, weaned from fenfual pleafure, and feeking the comforts of godlinefs, we will then allow them to be in a ftate of fafety ; but thinking that all men fhall be faved, will not on apoftolic principles give any fecurity unlefs gofpel holinefs is joined with their hope.

HITHERTO, a connected view of this Epiftle, appears to be much againft the opinion of Univerfal Salvation, and if the apoftle had faid nothing further, an attentive reader, would gather from his writing, his belief of eternal punifhment. The weight of evidence from this Epiftle remains ftill to be confidered, and is found in the 9th, 10th, and 11th chapters ; where the point is decided with as great plainnefs as language can do it.

HE takes up the fubject, of the blindnefs of his own nation, the Jews ; and their rejection by the fovereignty of GOD, from the benefits of the gofpel. His defign was to juftify the righteoufnefs of GOD in doing it, and reconcile all the former promifes made to that people, with fuch an event. If part of the Jews are eternally rejected by GOD, the opinion of Univerfal Salvation is unfounded ; and part of every other nation may alfo be forever loft. To fhew that this was actually the cafe with the Jews, he enumerates in chapter ix. 4. 5. the external privileges and call which they had enjoyed, and he affigns the reafon why thefe were not effectual to falvation. In the fourth chapter he had defcribed the faith by which men are juftified ; and tells us how it wrought in Abraham the father of the faithful, and was accounted to him for righteoufnefs ; and that it muft be

fays. *Not as though the word of God hath taken
none effect, for they are not all Ifrael which are of
Ifrael; neither becaufe they are the feed of Abraham, are they all children : but in Ifaac fhalt thy
feed be called.* That is, they which are the children of the flefh, thefe are not the children of God,
but the children of the promife are counted for the
feed. He alfo inftances in the cafe of Jacob and
Efau; God fays, *Jacob have I loved, and Efau
have I hated,* and affigns the reafon, *that the purpofe of God according to election might ftand.*

THE meaning of the above is this; that though
fome of the Jews are now rejected and loft, this
is no evidence that the word or promife of God
hath taken no effect, or all the effect that it was
meant to have; for all are not Ifraelites indeed
and fpiritually who are fo nationally. Neither
becaufe they are the offspring of Abraham, are
they all children of the promife, or perfons to
whom falvation is engaged. All the Jews were
feed according to the flefh, or natural pofterity;
but all of them were not children of the promife, or
perfons who are to be faved; and therefore God
may confiftently with his promifes and purpofes,
leave them to an utter rejection, and cut them off
from the benefits of falvation by CHRIST. The
Apoftle, in this place, in order to eftablifh the
righteoufnefs of God in rejecting the Jews, moft
plainly makes a diftinction between men. The
promifes made to Abraham, and to the ancient
church were as much gofpel promifes, though
under another difpenfation of grace, as thefe are
which we have received; and thofe promifes were
not to all the natural feed or pofterity; but to
a part of them, whom he calls children of the
promife—children of God according to the election of grace—and all fuch were faved. So
that it could not be faid the word of God was

without effect, though many of Israel were left in blindness and should perish, for the promise would have all the effect that it was designed to have. Either the Apostles reasoning to shew the righteousness of God in rejecting Israel is without foundation, or a part of men will not.be saved, and are not included in any of the promises of salvation through Jesus Christ.

That the above is a true construction of the Apostles words, and a proof that all men will not be saved, we learn from what follows. He foresaw an objection in the hearts of men, to such doctrine as this. The same objection as we often hear against eternal punishment. Verse 14. *What shall we say then ? Is there unrighteousness with God ? God forbid.* Can it be, that God should take some, and bring them to an abundance of grace ; and leave others wholly in mifery ? Is this just and righteous, and will the Lord of the whole earth do it ?

To this objection, he first gives an answer from the Jewish scriptures, the old Testament ; and then he makes his own remarks upon it. From the old Testament he repeats what God said to Moses ; also what he said concerning Pharoah.— Verses 15 and 16. *I will have mercy, on whom I will have mercy ; and I will have compassion, on whom I will have compassion ; so then it is not of him that willeth, nor of him that runneth, but of God that sheweth mercy.*—Verses 17 and 18. *For the scripture saith unto Pharoah, even for this same purpose have I raised thee up, that I might shew my power in thee, and that my name might be declared through all the earth. Therefore hath he mercy, on whom he will have mercy ; and whom he will he hardeneth.* Either Paul must have heard the objection which he states and answers ; and if he had heard it, this shows how uniformly in all ages,

the corrupt human heart rifes againft the fcheme
of divine government, for it is the fame objection
which we now hear made ; or he muft have ftated it prophetically, and if this be the cafe, it
proves that the reply is from GOD himfelf. In
verfe 19th he continues the objection, and makes
his own reply to it. Thou wilt fay then, unto
me, why doth he yet find fault ? For who hath
refifted his will ? That is, why doth GOD condemn and punifh fin, when it is according to his
own will and council, to leave men under the
power of it ? This is a perfect defcription of what
is often faid. That GOD could if he had pleafed,
prevent what is commonly called fin ; and as he
hath not prevented it, we may either determine
that it is not fin, or that GOD will not punifh it fo
awfully as is predicted. A further notice of this
point, will be taken in the next part, when we
come to confider fundry popular objections,
againft the doctrine of eternal punifhment ; at
prefent we are to attend to the Apoftles reply.
Verfe 20th to 24th. *Nay but, O man, who art thou*
that replieft againft GOD ? *Shall the thing formed*
fay to him that formed it, why haft thou made me
thus ? Hath not the potter power over the clay, to
make one veffel to honour and another to dishonour ?
What if GOD *willing to shew his wrath, and make*
his power known, endureth with much long-suffering,
the veffels of wrath fitted to deftruction. And that
he might make known the riches of his glory on the
veffels of mercy, which he had afore prepared unto
glory ? Even us whom he hath called, not of the
Jews only, but of the Gentiles alfo. The Apoftle
doth not attempt to evade the objection, but
comes out with that boldnefs, which becometh every friend of the fcripture fyftem of truth. He
afferts that GOD doth exercife this fovereignty.
Some veffels are by the predeterminate council of

GOD, appointed to holinefs and glory ; and fome, are appointed to fin and mifery. As the potter hath power over the clay, fo GOD hath a rightful power in the arrangement of the univerfe, fo to difpofe of every creature, as will make the collective whole, the moft holy, bleffed and glorious that it can be. In afferting this fact, he plainly afferts, the utter rejection of a part of mankind, from the benefits of the gofpel ; and being thus cut off, they muft be eternally miferable.

CONTINUING this fubject in chapter 11th, he adds, verfe 1ft. *I fay then, hath GOD caft away his people?* Verfe 2d. *GOD hath not caft away his people whom he foreknew.* In illuftration of this truth, he introduces the interceffion of Elijah, who told GOD that *he only was left to ferve him* ; to whom GOD anfwered, verfes 4th and 5th. *I have referved to myfelf feven thoufand men, who have not bowed the knee to images. Even fo now, there is at this prefent time, a remnant according to the election of grace.* The fame ideas are here repeated, that there is in every age, a remnant according to the election of grace, and the reft GOD will leave to perifh in their fins. Who the faved are, the fovereign wifdom of GOD will determine ; but whoever they be, they muft be fanctified ; and the only evidence which men can have, that they in particular fhall be faved, muft be deduced from a knowledge of their own fanctification.

IT would be pleafing to men, to have a way of deliverance from mifery, in confiftency with thofe fins which they love ; but it is as inconfiftent with the nature and fcheme of the gofpel to have it thus, as it is with the threatenings of the law. If men loved holinefs, as they ought to do, there would be no anxiety on the fubject, how many will be faved ; but every man in his place, would do all in his power, to promote holinefs, to open

the eyes of the blind, to alarm sinners who are now
of a temper which must end in misery, and leave
the event with GOD; knowing, that the unholy
remaining such, ought not to be made happy;
and that a GOD who is infinitely holy, will permit no more sin and misery, than infinite wisdom
and benevolence know to be best.   GOD will be
able to justify himself, in not appointing some to
that abundance of grace which the gospel reveals;
and show that his conduct is consistent with benevolence; it will also appear, that their misery
is just upon them, and their punishment is no
more, than their character, temper and practice
deserves.   Further on in the prosecution of my
plan, these things will be again noticed.   I have
been lengthy in remarking, upon this epistle to
the Romans; as we must suppose that it is consistent, with the other writings of Paul.   This is
the first of his epistles in the order of record; and
a just understanding of it, will serve as a key to
the remainder; and also, to that scheme of sentiment, which he supposed true for time and eternity.   Thus far, we find him explicit in the sentiments and testimony of our LORD JESUS
CHRIST; that there is a day of judgment, when
the wicked will be sentenced, according to their
character and works, to a state of misery; and
there is not a single intimation, that their misery
will ever come to an end.   This solemn doctrine, is
not only literally expressed, but necessarily implied in the other doctrines of his scheme.

SEC. 13. PAUL TO THE CORINTHIANS, EPIS-
TLE 1st.   The greatest part of the two Epistles
to the Corinthians, is employed in directing particular matters of practice in the church; and
whenever the scheme of Christian doctrine, and
of the divine government is brought into view,
the doctrine of future punishment is either direct-

ly afferted, or plainly implied. Chapter i. verfe 18. *For the preaching of the crofs is to them that perifh foolifhnefs ; but unto us which are faved it is the power of God.* Verfes, 23, 24. *But we preach* Christ *crucified, to the Jews a ftumbling block, and to the Greeks foolifhnefs ; but unto them which are called, both Jews and Greeks,* Christ *the power of God, and the wifdom of God.* Verfes 26, 27, 28. *For ye fee your calling, brethren, how that not many wife men after the flefh, not many mighty, not many noble, are called ; but* God *hath chofen the foolifh things of the world to confound the wife ; and* God *hath chofen the weak things of the world to confound thofe which are mighty : and bafe things of the world, and things which are defpifed, hath* God *chofen, yea, and things which are not, to bring to nought things that are.* It is here faid, there are fome who perifh and to thofe the gofpel appears as foolifhnefs ; and that fome are faved, to whom it appears the power and wifdom of God. That in the choice which God makes he means to humble the pride of human wifdom, and fhow that the whole glory belongs to himfelf.

Ye fee your calling, brethren, how that not many wife, mighty or noble are called, &c. What is meant by calling in this place ? It is conceived, that it means effectual calling to eternal life, by fanctification of the holy fpirit. We know, that the earthly-wife, the mighty, and the noble, are called by doctrinal inftruction, as much as any other men. They have the fame advantages for knowing their duty, and the value of falvation ; the fame doctrinal light and warnings ; and doubtlefs the fame admonitions, by the fpirit and providence of God. Their earthly fituation, places them in the moft advantageous ftate, to

H

be inftructed, and to ufe the means of religion.
We alfo know that the earthly-wife, the mighty,
and the noble, have as generally belonged to
what hath been called the vifible church of
CHRIST; as the poor and defpifed part of mankind have : fo that if a doctrinal or vifible calling
be meant, they have had it. The vifible church
hath been in their hands, under their influence,
and open to their receiving all the benefit that
can be derived from it. The calling meant, muft
therefore be, an effectual calling by the fanctifying power of the Holy Ghoft ; which is the only
fcriptural evidence of attaining final falvation.
But why is it, that the earthly-wife, the mighty,
and the noble are not effectually called ? is it becaufe GOD hath any prejudice againft his creatures, who are endowed with thefe worldly advantages? By no means. The reafon why they
are endowed with thefe worldly advantages is becaufe they have no tafte for religion, and that
holinefs which prepares men for heaven ; and their
unpreparednefs for heaven, is not becaufe they
have thefe worldly advantages. Men fucceed
in gaining that which they are moft diligent in
feeking ; and they feek that moft diligently,
which they love beft. Had the poffeffors of worldly advantages, felt the fame relifh for the enjoyment of GOD and religion, as they did for the
world ; they would have been as diligent in feeking religion, as they have been in feeking what
the world can give; and would have been as eminent in religion, as they now are for worldly advantages. GOD hath not paffed them by, becaufe
they are mighty, and noble ; but they are earthly-wife, mighty and noble, becaufe they have paffed by GOD, and religion, and preferred other
things. Had thefe perfons been as folicitous for
the pleafure of honouring GOD, as they have been

for the pleafure and dignity of the world; they would have been in the place and circumftances, that meek and world weaned chriftians are. On the other hand; had thofe chriftians, who have little worldly greatnefs, been governed by the paffions of ambition, fenfuality and avarice, and condefcended to the means which fuch paffions fuggeft for felf-gratification; they might have been in the place of the worldly-wife, the mighty and the noble. This digreffion hath been indulged, to juftify the divine equity, in what the apoftle fays, that not many wife, mighty, and noble are called. We have before feen, that ·the calling meant by the apoftle, muft mean effectual calling, or real fanctification; for if the word be ufed in any other fenfe; the wife, the rich, the mighty, and the noble are as much called as any other men. If calling in this place means effectual calling, and I do not know how we can put any other conftruction upon the word, confiftent with what is fact; then the apoftle's defcription, is proof enough, that fome men, will not be faved: for thofe cannot be faved, who are not effectually called. In the end it will appear, that thofe who depend on their own reafonings concerning the divine government, in oppofition to the plain word of revelation, are left to the greateft folly; and the fupereminence of divine wifdom above all created wifdom will appear. We have many modern Greeks and Jews, who ftumble at the doctrines of GOD's word; and unholinefs of heart is at the bottom of all their objections. If they had a holy love of GOD they would be willing to give up, both their own righteoufnefs, and their fuppofed knowledge of the beft manner of governing and rewarding the univerfe.

CHAPTER ix. verfe 24 to 27. *Know ye not that they who run in a race, run all, but one recciveth*

*the prize? fo run that ye may obtain. And every
man that ftriveth for the maftery is temperate in all
things. Now they do it to obtain a corruptible crown,
but we an incorruptible. I therefore fo run, not as
uncertainly; fo fight I, not as one that beateth the
air: but I keep under my body, and bring it into
fubjection; left that by any means, when I have
preached unto others, I myfelf fhould be a caftaway.*
None will difpute that eternal happinefs and life
are the gofpel prize; and could fuch an exhortation as this have been proper, if all men are abfolutely to obtain it? Or could the Apoftle with
any honefty have faid, that he kept under his body
left he fhould be a caftaway, if there are to be no
fuch men? In the 10th chapter he continues the
exhortation as to perfons who were expofed to
be rejected. He refers them back to the ancient
fins and punifhment of Ifrael, by which they were
cut off from entering the earthly Canaan, and fays,
that all thefe things happened for examples unto us.
We know, that in the holy fcriptures, the earthly
Canaan is made a type of the heavenly Canaan.
Some of the Jews not entering into the earthly
Canaan, was a type of fome mens not entering
into the heavenly Canaan; and it is folely on this
principle that there is any propriety in the Apoftle's exhortation, and in referring us back to the
deftroyed Ifraelites, as a warning and example to
us. It does not appear, that there is any difference between not entering into Heaven and
being caft into Hell.

Sec. 14. Paul to the Corinthians Epistle 2d. Chapter ii. 15, 16. *For we are unto God
a fweet favour of Christ, in them that are faved,
and in them that perifh: to the one we are the favour of death unto death; and to the other the favour of life unto life.* The evident meaning of
thefe words is this. That God will be glorified

by the preaching of the gospel, whether the hearers be saved or lost. If they be saved, it will be a favour of life unto life, and magnify the riches of divine grace in their redemption. If they be lost, a *favour of death unto death,* that is, their rejection of the gospel will increase their sin and misery, and make their eternal wretchedness more awful, than it would have been without gospel light. And the unholiness of those aggravated sinners, who transgress against abundant light, will justify the righteousness of God, by showing the unreasonableness and true nature of sin. That sin is so malignant in its nature; neither light, nor love could persuade it, and must therefore deserve the punishment God hath prepared.

CHAPTER v. 10, 11. *For we must all appear before the judgment seat of* CHRIST *; that every one may receive the things done in the body, according to that he hath done, whether it be good or bad. Knowing therefore the terrors of the* LORD *we persuade men.* Here is a promise of the day of judgment, when we must be rewarded according to our character and practice in life. Is there not a difference in men's characters and practice? do not some appear to live much for God and his glory; and others wholly to forget and dishonor him? doth not this difference of character appear to continue to the end of life? Though a man through fear, should at his death, say he repents and will reform; yet is that, considering his enervated state both of body and mind, any evidence that he is become of another character and disposition? do we not, in most instances of this kind, on a release from fear, see that the man returns to his former course? and are there not very many, in whom, even on a death bed, there appears to be no sense of sin, and no repentance?

muft not thefe perfons have an end, as different
as their lives have been?

Knowing the terrors of the Lord *we perfuade
men.* It is the terrors of the day of judgment,
and of appearing before the bar of Christ, of
which the Apoftle is fpeaking. But if all men
are to be faved in that day, why did he fpeak of
terrors; or what terrors can there be in the moment that all mankind are commencing a ftate of
everlafting glory and peace? Why did not the
Apoftle fay, knowing the joys of the Lord and
the final falvation of all, we perfuade men; for
this would have been more agreeable to the fcheme
of Univerfalifm?

Paul to the Philipians. Chap. i. 28. *And
in nothing terrified by your adverfaries : which is
to them an evident token of perdition, but to you of
falvation.* Chap. iii. 18, 19. *For many walk of
whom I have told you often, and now tell you even
weeping, that they are the enemies of the crofs of*
Christ : *whofe end is deftruction.* It will be
agreed, that falvation means the bleffednefs of the
world to come. Salvation and perdition are ufed
as terms of oppofition, and fome men are to come
to each of thefe ends. Some men are enemies of
the crofs of Christ, which is proved by their
bad converfation, *whofe end is deftruction;* and if
their end, or the laft ftate in which they are found
be deftruction, there can be no following falvation; for there can be no other ftate after the
end or laft ftate of any being.

Sec. 15. Paul to Thessalonians, Epiftle 1ft. From chapter iv. 13, to chapter v. 4,
the Apoftle gives a defcription of the day of judgment. He tells them not to mourn as without
hope, for thofe that are afleep or dead, for that
thofe who fleep in Jesus (real chriftians) God
will bring with him. That thofe who are then

alive on the earth will not prevent the refurrection
of the dead ; for the dead in CHRIST fhall rife
firft, and then chriftians who are living in the
earth at that time, fhall be caught up together
with them in the clouds, to meet the LORD in the
air ; and fhall be ever with the LORD. This will
be the glorious deliverance of the faithful ; but
the Apoftle proceeds, in the beginning of chapter v. to tell a different end for fome of mankind.
*But of the times and the feafons, ye have no need that
I write unto you. For you yourfelves know perfectly
that the day of the LORD fo cometh as a thief in the
night. For when they fhall fay, peace and fafety ;
then fudden deftruction cometh upon them as travail
upon a woman with child ; and they fhall not efcape.*

I THINK it cannot be denied, that the Apoftle
is in this place giving a defcription of the day of
final judgment, when an end will be put to the
earthly ftate. He, firft, informs what fhall happen
to the faints, both thofe which have died and fuch
as are then living, and fays, that they fhall be
caught up together, and be ever with the LORD ;
and then tells chriftians, to comfort one another
with thefe words. After this, he fpeaks of thofe
whom this day fhall overtake as a thief in the
night ; on whom fudden deftruction fhall come,
from which they cannot efcape. Who can be
meant by thefe unlefs it be finners who are not
faved ? On them fudden deftruction fhall come,
and they fhall never efcape. It feems as though
infidelity itfelf could not demand a more plain
declaration of what fhall happen.

EPISTLE SECOND TO THE THESSALONIANS.
In this epiftle, the day of judgment and the rewards then to commence, if poffible, are more
plainly expreffed than in the firft epiftle. From
what Paul wrote in the firft epiftle, the Theffalo-
nians had conceived a falfe opinion, that the day

of judgment was near at hand.   To correct this mistake, was the probable reason why he introduced the subject again so explicitly.   For he writes chap. ii. verse 1. *Now we beseech you, brethren, by the coming of our Lord Jesus Christ, and by our gathering together unto him, that ye be not soon shaken in mind, or be troubled, neither by spirit, nor by word, nor by letter as from us, as that the day of Christ is at hand.*   And he tells them *there must be a falling away before this day come.*   Concerning the certainty of the event and its consequences he adds, chapter i. verse 6—10. *Seeing it is a righteous thing with God to recompense tribulation to them that trouble you ; and to you who are troubled rest with us, when the Lord Jesus shall be revealed from heaven with his mighty angels, in flaming fire, taking vengeance on them that know not God, and that obey not the gospel of our Lord Jesus Christ : who shall be punished with everlasting destruction, from the presence of the Lord, and the glory of his power ; when he shall come to be glorified in his saints, and to be admired in all that believe.*

From this very particular account we learn, that in the day when Christ shall come to judge and reward men, he will be glorified in the abundance and riches of that grace which saves his saints, and admired in their holy conformity to God which is given by the spirit ; also, at that time, the wisdom of his whole dispensation, in every event of nature, providence and grace, will appear in greater clearness, than can be seen at present.   But these saints in whom God will be glorified and admired, do not include all men ; for there will be those, who know not God ; and obey not the gospel.   Can there be more strong expressions than these, which mark their utter ruin and misery ? *God will take vengeance on them. They are to be punished with destruction.*   With ev-

erlafting deftruftion. Away from the prefence of God *and his glory;* the direct reverfe of being ever with the Lord.

In the fecond chapter, there is a large defcription of the character of fome of thofe miferable ones, who are to be deftroyed. The Apoftle fays, Verfe 10. *That becaufe they receive not the love of the truth, that they might be faved; and for this caufe* God *fhall fend them ftrong delufion, that they fhould believe a lie; that they all might be damned who believed not the truth, but had pleaf-ure in unrighteoufnefs.* Many fimilar threatnings are found in the holy fcriptures, fhowing that thofe who long refift fufficient light, are left by God to their own lufts. His fpirit is withdrawn, and they appear to lofe all fenfe of divine things. In fuch inftances, God doubtlefs leaves the guilty to a ftrange unbelief, that the true nature of fin may appear.

Sec. 16. *Paul, in his Epistle to the Ga-latians,* where he is defcribing the impoffibility that men fhould be juftified by any obedience that they will render, either to the moral law, or cer-emonial law of Mofes; and the neceffity of faith in Christ for juftification; alfo fhows, that the faving grace of God in the gofpel plan, extends only to thofe, who walk by the fpirit of God; and after enumerating many fins of heart, and life, fays exprefsly, *that they who do fuch things fhall not inherit the kingdom of* God. Gal. v. Paul to the Ephesians. The church of God under the ancient difpenfation, appeared to have very contracted ideas, of the extenfion that fhould be given to the church under the gofpel. The Jews and thofe who were profelytes to their religion, fuppofed, that moft of the Gentile na-tions lay under a perpetual rejection. They did

I

not apprehend that the coming of the Messiah, would break down the wall of separation, that had subsisted between the members of the Jewish communion, and other nations; or that the visible privileges of God's church, should be extended to all who would receive them. To convince them of this fact was very difficult. This truth, that the Jews and Gentiles should be united in one church, is one of those mysteries, so often mentioned in the sacred pages, which had been hid from ages. This is the mystery meant in Rom. xi, 25. xvi, 25. Col. i. 26, 27. Chap. ii. 2. One chief purpose of the Epistle to the Ephesians, was to enlighten men in this subject, and teach them that JESUS CHRIST is the head of all holy intelligencies, in the universal kingdom of God. Of Gentiles as well as Jews; of Angels as well as Gentiles; and that the whole holy Church, of whatever rank or order of existence, would be gathered together as one in him. This truth is the mystery meant in Eph. i. 9, iii, 3, 9. A view, of this design in the Epistle, explains the universality of many expressions, which are used in it. Such as this: *That in the dispensation of the fulness of times, he might gather together in one, all things in CHRIST, both which are in Heaven, and which are on Earth, even in him.* Chap. i. 10.

THE subject must explain the universality of expression; and the subject is the gathering of all holy creatures under one head; and not the gathering of all sinners into heaven. Lest an improper use should be made of these general truths, which the Apostle had been disclosing; he largely describes in the last part of the epistle that holy character, to which the gospel salvation is promised; and shows that none but those who were possessed of it might hope. After enumerating a number of vicious characters, he says, chapter v. 5. *That thefe have no inheritance in the king- dom of* God *and* Christ*;* and as if it were of fet purpofe, and in forefight of the abufe that would be made of fome expreffions in the epiftle, he adds the caution is verfes, 6, 7. *For becaufe of thefe things, cometh the wrath of* God*, upon the chil- dren of difobedience. Be not ye therefore partakers with them.*

Paul to the Colossians. In feveral refpects, there is a great fimilarity between this and the Epiftle to the Ephefians. The fame myftery is mentioned and explained. That Chrift is the head of the holy body, the church. Not the Meffiah of the Jews only; but of the Gentiles al- fo. And to make this more credible to thofe who had ftrong prejudicies againft the admiffion of the Gentiles, into the true church of God ; alfo to inftruct them in the unity of the holy uni- verfe of creatures, he defcribes Christ as the head of the whole; whether things in Heaven or things on Earth. But becaufe all holy beings are united in one body, and made of one fpirit, and placed under one head ; it doth not follow that all creatures will ever be made holy beings. In this Epiftle alfo there is a guard againft miftake, fimilar to that in the Ephefians. The neceffity of holy affections and mortification to fin, in or- der to fhare in this falvation, are abundantly ur- ged; and after mentioning the moft common vi- ces of men's hearts and lives, the Apoftle faith Chapter iii. 6. *For which things fake the wrath of* God *cometh on the children of difobedience.*

Sec. 17. Paul the Apostle to the He- brews. A great fcope of divine truth is inclu- ded in this Epiftle. It is addreffed to the He- brews, and its defign is to prove the diffolution of the Mofaic difpenfation, and convert them to the

chriſtian faith and practice. The divinity of
CHRIST, and the glory of his nature; his mediatorial offices ; the perfection of his prieſthood ;
and the efficacy of his atonement and interceſſion
for the ſalvation of all guilty ſinners, who come
to him are fully eſtabliſhed.   Having proved the
above-mentioned important points, from the Old
Teſtament in which the Jews believed ; he introduces in the 5th and 6th chapters, a ſerious re-
proof of their ignorance, and warning of the con-
ſequences of their infidelity.   In chapter v. xii.
he reproves them. _ *For when for the time ye ought
to be teachers, ye have need that one teach you again,
which be the firſt principles of the oracles of* GOD *;
and are become ſuch as have need of milk, and not
of ſtrong meat.* In chapter vi. 4, 6. he warns them
of their danger, and the difficulties they were
putting in the way of their own ſalvation.   *For it
.is impoſſible for thoſe who were once enlightened, and
were made partakers of the holy Ghoſt, and have
taſted the good word of* GOD*, and the powers of the
world to come, if they ſhall fall away, to renew them
to repentance : ſeeing they crucify to themſelves the
ſon of* GOD *afreſh, and put him to open ſhame.*   The
attainments, mentioned in this paſſage, are doubtleſs all of them ſuch as fall ſhort of holineſs or
love.   For in the 8th and 9th verſes, where the
Apoſtle contraſts the character of real chriſtians,
with thoſe who thus fall away, *he ſpeaks of things
which accompany ſalvation,* that is, attainments
which cannot miſs of ſalvation ; and theſe attainments were *their work and labor of love ;* ſo that
all the attainments before-mentioned, were ſuch as
fall ſhort of love.   But though men may differ
in opinion what theſe attainments are ; it is moſt
evident, that the Apoſtle means ſome kind or degree of apoſtacy ; and that this is an apoſtacy

without remedy, *for it is impoſſible to renew them to repentance.*

THAT the apoſtle meant an utter ruin, by the impoſſibility of renewing them to repentance, is illuſtrated by his compariſon in verſes 7, 8. *For the earth which drinketh in the rain that cometh oft upon it, and bringeth forth meat for the uſe of them by whom it is dreſſed, receiveth bleſſing from* GOD : *But that which beareth briers and thorns is rejected, and is nigh unto curſing ; whoſe end it is to be burned.* Doth not ſuch a compariſon as this, in deſcribing the condition of thoſe who cannot be renewed unto repentance, teach us, that they are rejected of GOD, nigh unto final curſing, *and that their end or laſt ſtate is to be burned.*

PAUL had a benevolent deſire to reſcue as many of his nation as poſſible, from the infidelity into which he ſaw them falling. He therefore introduces another warning, in chapter x. 26—31. *For if we ſin wilfully after that we have received the knowledge of the truth, there remaineth no more ſacrifice for ſins, but a certain fearful looking for of fiery indignation, which ſhall devour the adverſaries. He that deſpiſed Moſe's law, died without mercy, under two or three witneſſes : of how much ſorer puniſhment, ſuppoſe ye, ſhall he be thought worthy, who hath trodden under foot the Son of* GOD, *and hath counted the blood of the covenant, wherewith he was ſanctified an unholy thing, and hath done deſpite unto the ſpirit of grace? For we know him that hath ſaid, vengeance belongeth unto me, I will recompence, ſaith the* LORD. *And again, the* LORD *ſhall judge his people. It is a fearful thing to fall into the hands of the living God.* What can all this mean, unleſs there be a moſt awful puniſhment for ſin in another world? do not theſe deſcriptions imply, that there is ſuch a wilful ſinning againſt CHRIST, as may cut men off from the benefits of his facrifice, and that there is no other facrifice through which they can be forgiven? Either, this is an imaginary reprefentation, and who will ferioufly charge the fpirit of God with this; or all Apoftates do actually fuffer a fiery indignation in this life equal to this defcription, which it is prefumed no candid perfon will pretend; or there is a punifhment of mifery in the world to come.

CHAPTER xii. 15—17. *Looking diligently, left any man fail of the grace of God; left any root of bitternefs fpringing up, trouble you, and thereby many be defiled; left there be any fornicator, or profane perfon, as Efau, who for one morfel of meat fold his birthright. For ye know how that afterward, when he would have inherited the bleffing, he was rejected: for he found no place of repentance, though he fought it carefully with tears.* Verfe 25. *See that ye refufe not him that fpeaketh. For if they efcaped not that refufed him that fpake on earth, much more fhall not we efcape, if we turn away from him that fpeaketh from heaven.* This is a folemn warning of the danger of unbelief, whether it be by a doctrinal or practical rejection of JESUS CHRIST. Muft not thofe, who fail of the grace of God, be miferable in the world to come? Can thofe be faved to whom there is no place for repentance?—By him that fpeaketh on earth, is meant Mofes in the Jewifh difpenfation; and by him that fpeaketh from heaven, is meant CHRIST in the chriftian difpenfation. The fact is afferted that fome efcaped not, who finned againft the light and grace then manifefted; and the confequence is inferred that an efcape under the greater light and advantages of the chriftian difpenfation is much more improbable. Who can reconcile this reprefentation with the fact, that all men, all finners, of every defcription and every degree of guilt, will efcape ?

SEC. 18. JOHN's firft Epiftle.   Chapter v. 16, 17. *If any man fee his brother fin a fin, that is not unto death, he fhall afk, and he fhall give him life for them that fin not unto death. There is a fin unto death : I do not fay he fhall pray for it. All unrighteoufnefs is fin, and there is a fin not unto death.* Here is a direction to pray for the brethren, with a promife that prayer fhall be heard for them, who have not finned fatally or paft recovery. But the Apoftle faith *there is a fin unto death ;* and adds thefe remarkable words, *I do not fay he fhall pray for it.* Doth not this imply that there are fome fins which GOD will never forgive, and for which the finner muft fuffer the pains of eternal damnation ?

THE whole Epiftle of Jude might be recited as proof of eternal punifhment. In the 14th and 15th verfes he repeats a prophecy of Enoch, the feventh from Adam, of which we have no account but this, that may be fully relied on. *The Lord cometh with ten thoufand of his faints, to execute judgment upon all, and to convince all that are ungodly among them, of all their ungodly deeds, which they have ungodly committed, and of all their hard fpeeches, which ungodly finners have fpoken againft him.* This is doubtlefs a prophecy of the day of judgment, which fpeaks its own meaning fo plainly, as to need no comment.

EPISTLE GENERAL OF JAMES. It is faid by fome, that in the epiftle of James there is no intimation of future punifhment; but this is a great miftake. The defign of his writing did not lead him, particularly to confider this fubject. His object was to defcribe and enjoin chriftian holinefs, and to forbid fundry fins, which are inconfiftent with a gofpel temper. Many of the principal gospel doctrines are not particularly mentioned by him ; though they are strongly implied in his whole writing ; and it is thus with the doctrine of future punishment. There are however several passages, which plainly imply a punishment to come, and there is not a single intimation of universal deliverance. The several parties in this enquiry, agree that men are exposed to eternal punishment, and must suffer it ; unless God delivers them by his mighty power and grace. Therefore to place a sacred writer on the side of universalism, it is not sufficient, that he be silent concerning what is agreed to be just ; but it is necessary that he give a positive testimony for the contrary event, through the grace of God ; and it is certain that James gives no such intimation, but wholly the reverse. Chap. i. 15. *Then when lust hath conceived, it bringeth forth sin : and sin when it is finished bringeth forth death.* In such a place as this, where the Apostle is describing the rise, progress and end of sin, it certainly was incumbent on him, to give some intimation that all men shall be freed from this death, if it is to be the case; but the intimation is directly contrary. Chapter ii. 13. *For he shall have judgment without mercy, that hath shewed no mercy ; and mercy rejoiceth against judgment.* Must not the future state of that man be miserable, to whom no mercy is shewed, and it seems there are to be such ? What must be the state of those persons, who have no mercy in their own conduct, for an evidence that they have right to rejoice, in the day when *your flesh as it were fire : ye have heaped treasure together, for the last days.* This is a most solemn threatning to those who misuse the blessings of time, and dishonor GOD the giver. Of what na-ture is the evil threatened ? It is not the loss of their riches ; for through abundance they canker and rust in their possession. Also their garments are so many, that they are moth-eaten through want of use. Their treasures by a misuse of them, shall increase their wretched-ness in the last days. The miseries mentioned, are not these now felt; but miseries to come, and shall eat their flesh as fire. An attentive pe-rusal of this Epistle, will find many other impli-cations, of a future judgment and punishment.

SEC. 19. TESTIMONY FROM THE REVELATION OF St. JOHN. This book contains a prediction of events which should take place, from the time in which it was written, to the end of the world, and final day of judgment, when the holy shall be fixed in a state of eternal blessedness, and the wicked in eternal misery. The descriptions are in a language highly figurative. The purposes of divine goodness in giving this revelation, were to support the faith and patience of christians, under those calamitous things which were to happen to the church ; also to serve as testimony of the truth of the scriptures, when the events predicted should have a manifest accomplish-ment ; whereby there is an accumulating fund of evidence, that the Holy Bible is the word of that GOD, who governs and will judge the world.

No wisdom but that which is infinite, could so express scripture prophecy, as to answer the ends designed by it. In the first place the prophecy must be so expressed, that the church will see a promise of final preservation and triumph ; and

K

of destruction to their enemies, who do not fear and obey God; also that they may see the accomplishment of the prediction, when it takes place. The prophecy must also be so expressed, as not to be an intelligible history of all the facts and particular events by which it is fulfilled. For if it were thus particularly expressed, the prediction would frustrate itself. The church of antichrist, would never have acted out the principles by which it is governed, if the particular actions, proving their principles, and the punishment that is to follow their actions, had been so described as to be understood by the actors themselves. Prophecy is not written to keep bad men from their bad actions; but to support the good under their persecution, and to assure the friends of Christ, that in a proper time, his enemies shall be overthrown, and their reign come to an end.

These remarks on the design of prophecy, show the reasons why this book was expressed in that figurative and enigmatical language, which the prophets often used; and nothing but the inspiration of infinite wisdom could have done it. The obscurity concerning particular events, actors and actions, in which these prophecies are cloathed before the fulfilment; and the plainness with which they appear after fulfilment, prove God to be the author of them.

The prophecies of John assure us that the reign of wicked men, and of a corrupt church shall be destroyed, and that the enemies of Christ's cause and of pure humble christianity, shall come to a fearful worldly end. Also that a pure and very prosperous state of the earthly church shall succeed. Many of these prophecies have been fulfilled, to the astonishment of those who compare them with the history of nations, and of mankind; and they are now fulfilling in a more rapid succeſſion of events, than was ever known before. Every accompliſhment of God's vengeance in this world, gives credibility to his threatning of vengeance in the world to come.

I before obſerved, that this prophecy reaches to the final fixation of things, in a bleſſedneſs and miſery that is to be eternal. In the beginning of this book, it is ſaid of Jesus Christ who appeared in viſion to John; *Behold, he cometh in clouds ; and every eye ſhall ſee him, and they alſo which pierced him : and all kindreds of the earth ſhall wail becauſe of him.* Rev. i. 7. Theſe words, appear to have a direct reference to Christ's ſecond coming to judgment, which will take place after the prophecies of the whole book, are fulfilled. *Every* eye ſhall ſee him, and *all kindreds*, all nations of the earth ſhall wail becauſe of him. This doth not appear, as though he would thus come to give a final and glorious ſalvation to all men. Chapter iii. 5. *He that overcometh, the ſame ſhall be cloathed in white raiment ; and I will not blot his name out of the book of life, but I will confeſs his name before my father, and before his angels."* In ſundry other paſſages, as in this, mention is made of the book of life, and thoſe whoſe names are written in it. Christ himſelf ſpeaks of confeſſing and denying men before God and the holy Angels. Theſe, with many other repreſentations of holy writ, are entirely unintelligible; unleſs men are in the end to be divided into two claſſes. Some written in the book of life, and ſome not ; ſome confeſſed and ſome denied ; and that they are reſpectively to meet with very different treatment. Chapter xiv. 10, 11. " *The ſame ſhall drink of the wine of the wrath of* God, *which is poured out without mixture, into the cup of his indignation ; and he ſhall be tormented with fire and brimſtone, in the preſence of the holy Angels, and in the presence of the Lamb: and the smoke of their torment ascendeth up forever and ever.*" It does not appear probable, that these words describe any punishment, which the adherents of Antichrist are to receive in this world. Their worldly punishment, which is indeed awful, is expressed in very different language. *This is a punishment in the presence of the holy Angels, and in the presence of the Lamb,* denoting that it is to be in the invisible world, and it is to be forever and ever.

The conclusion of this prophecy, furnishes a most explicit testimony for the eternal punishment of some men. After the prophet had described, according to the visions presented to him; both the adverse, and the prosperous or millenial state of the church; together with a rebellion against God, which is to happen immediately before the general judgment; he proceeds to give an account of that awful and interesting day, which will end the probationary state of mankind, and place them all, in happiness or misery eternal.— From chapter xx. 10, to chapter xxi. 8. *And the devil which deceived them, was cast into the lake of fire and brimstone, where the beast and false prophet are, and shall be tormented day and night, forever. And I saw a great white throne, and him that sat on it, from whose face the heaven and earth fled away, and there was found no place for them. And I saw the dead, small and great, stand before God; and the books were opened; and another book was opened, which is the book of life; and the dead were judged out of those things which were written in the books according to their works. And death and hell were cast into the lake of fire. This is the second death. And whosoever was not found written in the book of life, was cast into the lake of fire. And I saw a new heaven, and a new earth: for the first heaven and the first earth were passed away; and*

*there was no more sea. And I John saw the holy
city, the New Jerusalem, coming down from* God *out
of heaven, prepared as a bride adorned for her huf-
band. And I heard a great voice out of heaven, faying,* Behold the tabernacle *of* God *is with* men, and
*he will dwell with them, and they shall be his people,
and* God *himself shall be with them, and be their*
God. And God *shall wipe away all tears from their
eyes : and there shall be no more death, neither forrow, nor crying, neither shall there be any more pain:
for the former things are paffed away. And he that
fat upon the throne, faid, Behold, I make all things
new. And he faid unto me, Write : for thefe things
are true and faithful. He that overcometh shall inherit all things ; and I will be his* God, *and he shall
be my fon. But the fearful, and the unbelieving,
and the abominable, and whoremongers, and murderers, and idolaters, and all liars, shall have their
part in the lake that burneth with fire and brimftone : this is the fecond death."*

On this paffage we may remark, that it defcribes a new era and ftate of things. Satan the
firft deceiver of mankind, and who had been immediately acceffary to many of their crimes, is
caft into the lake of fire, an emblem of extreme
mifery and torment. The beaft and falfe prophet
are with him. Thefe are prophetic names of
certain numerous claffes of mankind, who had
oppofed God's truth and committed great fin ;
and muft mean the individuals who compofed
thefe claffes. A day of judgment is particularly
defcribed. A great change in the natural ftate
of the univerfe is predicted ; there are to be new
heavens and a new earth ; all things are to be
made new ; in order to adapt them to the moral
character of creatures, and whether this character be good or bad, it will be perfect and fixed in
its kind.

WHEN all men become, either perfectly good or perfectly bad, it is reasonable to suppose, such a change in the natural structure of things as is described will be made; that all parts of the universe, may be accommodated to a fit treatment of their different characters, and dispositions. Two states, one of exceeding happiness and the other of exceeding misery, are promised as plainly as language can do it; also the characters of the persons consigned to them are drawn, that it may appear, GOD doth not act capriciously in their different destinations. The perpetuity of this state is also plainly expressed. There is to be no more death, sorrow or crying, and no more pain to the godly; and the evil are to be punished day and night forever.

WE have considered the writers of the New Testament, and the respective testimony they give to the doctrine of eternal punishment. The testimony of JESUS CHRIST alone, ought to be esteemed sufficient; for he is the omniscient GOD; the government of the world is in his hands; and he is to be the final judge of the state of men. The eternal punishment of part of mankind, and exhortations founded upon the danger of coming to that awful end, are often introduced in the discourses of JESUS; and he seemed to consider, a plain warning of these truths, to be a principal part of his business as a teacher of Religion. We have also examined all the other writers of the New Testament, and find them explicit in describing the same scheme of divine government, and the same end to the probationary state of men, as their divine master before them had taught; and their testimony of a future punishment, is not deduced from obscure intimations and far fetched consequences from other doctrines; but asserted in the most plain language, and used as an argument to receive and obferve other doctrines; inftead of being obfcurely founded on them. And it does not appear, that CHRIST and his Apoftles could have told this truth, in terms more plain, than thofe which they have ufed.

SEC. 20. IT is in the writings of the New Teftament, that we muft expect to find the point in confideration moft explicitly decided. It was referved for him, who came from the other world, and is to be the judge of all men, to tell moft plainly what he fhould do, acting as judge of all the earth. This collection of fcripture teftimony, with the remarks made upon it, hath already fwelled into much larger compafs, than was firft intended; and only a fmall part of what might be mentioned from the New Teftament, hath been adduced. The difficulty of my defign hath not fo much confifted in finding evidence of eternal punifhment in the fcriptures, as in making a felection from the proofs, which are too numerous to be all of them recited. Left it fhould be faid that the Jewifh fcriptures are filent on this point, a few paffages will be adduced from them. Job xxi. 30. *That the wicked is referved to the day of deftruction, they fhall be brought forth to the day of wrath.* Pfalm ix. 5. *Thou haft deftroyed the wicked, thou haft put out their name forever and ever.* Verfe 17. *The wicked fhall be turned into Hell, and all the nations that forget GOD.* xi. 6. *Upon the wicked he fhall rain fnares, fire and brimftone, and an horrible tempeft; this fhall be the portion of their cup.* xxxvii. 20. *But the wicked fhall perifh, and the enemies of the Lord fhall be as the fat of Lambs; they fhall confume, into fmoke they fhall confume away.* lxviii. 2. *As wax melteth before the fire, fo let the wicked perifh at the prefence of GOD.* xciv. 12, 13. *Bleffed is the man whom thou teacheft out of thy law; until the pit be digged for the wicked.* cxlv. 20. *The Lord preserveth all them that love him ; but all the wicked will he destroy.* Prov. xi. 7. *When a wicked man dieth, his expectation shall perish.* How can a wicked man's expectations perish at death, if he is to be saved? Prov. xvi. 4. *The Lord hath made all things for himself ; yea, even the wicked for the day of evil.*— xxiv. 19, 20, *Fret not thyself because of evil men, for there shall be no reward to the evil ; The candle of the wicked shall be put out.*—Ezek. iii. 19. *Yet if thou warn the wicked, and he turn not from his wickedness, he shall die in his inquity ; but thou hast delivered thy soul.* Dan. xii. 2. *And many of them that sleep, shall awake, some to everlasting life, and some to shame and everlasting contempt.* Job xi. 20. *But the eyes of the wicked shall fail, and their hope shall be as the giving up of the Ghost.* xx. 5, 7. *The triumphing of the wicked is short, and the joy of hypocrites but for a moment, yet he shall perish for-ever.* Psalm xxxvii. 38. *The end of the wicked shall be cut off.*—cxii. 10. *He shall gnash with his teeth, and melt away ; the desire of the wicked shall perish.*

Job xxxi. 3. *Is not destruction to the wicked ? and a strange punishment to the workers of iniquity?* Mal. iv 1. *The day cometh, that shall burn as an oven, and all the proud, shall be stubble ; and the day that cometh shall burn them up, saith the Lord of Hosts, and leave them neither root nor branch.*— Psalm i. 5. 6. *The ungodly shall not stand in the judgment, the way of the ungodly shall perish.* The whole of the 73 Psalm, is a description of the difference between the godly and ungodly, and the awful end to which the latter shall come.—Proverbs i. 26, to the end, *I also will laugh at your calamity ; I will mock when your fear cometh : when your fear cometh as desolation, and your destruction is a whirlwind ; then shall they call upon me, but I will not anfwer; they fhall feek me early, but they fhall not find me. Therefore fhall they eat of the fruit of their own way, and be filled with their own devices.* ' *For the turning away of the fimple fhall flay them, and the profperity of fools fhall deftroy them.* Thefe are a few, from many paffages in the Old Teftament, fhowing the future and utter deftruction of finners.—They are referved to the day of deftruction and wrath.—Their name is to be put out forever.—They are to be turned into Hell.—The portion of their cup is fnares, brim-ftone and an horrible tempeft.—They fhall per-ifh.—Confume into fmoke.—Confume away.— Melt as wax before the fire in the prefence of God.—A pit is digged for them.—Be deftroy-ed.—Their expectations perifh.—God made them for the day of evil.—They fhall have no reward of good.—Their candle fhall be put out.—They fhall die in their iniquity.—They fhall arife to fhame and everlafting contempt.—Their eyes fhall fail.—Even their hope fhall be like the giving up of the Ghoft.—Their triumphing is fhort.—Their joy is for a moment.—Their end is cut off.—They fhall gnafh with their teeth.—Their defires per-ifh.—There is a ftrange punifhment for them.— A day that burns as an oven, fhall burn them up, and leave them neither root nor branch.—God will laugh at their calamity, when their deftruc-tion comes as a whirlwind.—They fhall feek God and not find him.

HAVING thus collected in one point of view, a number of the expreffions ufed in the Old Tef-tament, to defcribe the future and eternal pun-ifhment of wicked men; I will join in the fame view, thofe from the New Teftament, which have already been more largely repeated. CHRIST faith there are thofe, for whom he doth not pray.—

L

That there is a Son of perdition who is loft.—
That many fhall feek to enter into Heaven and
fhall not be able.—That they fhall be fhut out
from Abraham and all the prophets.—They are
children of the Devil, and the judge at the end of
the world, fhall fend forth his Angels, and gather them out of his kingdom, and caft them into
a furnace of fire.—They fhall be fevered from
among the juft.—They fhall be bound hand and
foot and caft into outer darknefs.—The doors of
Heaven are fhut againft them, and God anfwers,
I do not know you.—They are caft away as unprofitable fervants.—They are called curfed ones,
and fentenced to everlafting fire, prepared for the
Devil and his Angels.—They receive their good
things, their portion in this life, and are tormented in the life to come.—An impaffible gulph is
placed between them and the bleffed.—They die
in their fins.—Where Christ is gone they cannot come.—They commit fins which fhall not be
forgiven either in this or the world to come.—
They never have forgivenefs.—They are in danger
of Hell fire.—Both foul and body fhall be deftroyed in Hell.—They fhall loofe themfelves.—Shall
be denied before God in Heaven.—The judge
will be afhamed of them when he comes in the
glory of the Father.—They cannot efcape the
damnation of Hell.—They have received their
confolation in this world.—They fhall come out of
their graves to the refurrection of damnation.—
They are caft forth as ufelefs branches and burned.—They are burnt up as chaff with unquenchable fire.—They are reprefented as fpirits in prifon, referved for future punifhment.—Perfons in
damnable herefies going to fwift deftruction.—
Their judgment and damnation flumbereth not.—
They are referved to the day of Judgment to
be punifhed.—They are utterly to perifh in their

own corruption.—The mift of darknefs is referved to them forever.—The heavens and the
earth which now are, are kept in ftore, referved
unto fire, againft the day of judgment, for the
perdition of ungodly men.—They treafure up
wrath againft the day of wrath, and the revelation
of the righteous judgment of GOD.—GOD will
render to them indignation and wrath, tribulation and anguifh.—They are veffels of wrath
fitted to deftruction, that GOD may fhow forth
his power in them.—The preaching of the crofs
is to them foolifhnefs, and therefore they perifh.—
All the means of grace are unto them a favor of
death unto death.—They are to receive in another
world according to the things done in the body.—
They are enemies of the crofs of CHRIST, and their
end is deftruction.—When they fhall fay peace
and fafety, fudden deftruction fhall come upon
them, and they fhall not efcape.—When CHRIST
comes in flaming fire, taking vengeance on them
that know not GOD, they fhall be punifhed with
everlafting deftruction, from the prefence of the
LORD.—GOD fhall fend them ftrong delufions,
that they fhould believe a lie that they all might
be damned.—They cannot inherit the kingdom
of GOD.—The wrath of GOD cometh on them.—
It is impoffible to renew them to repentance.—
They are nigh unto curfing, and their end is to
be burned.—For them there remaineth no more
facrifice for fin, but a certain fearful looking for of
fiery indignation, which fhall devour the adverfaries.—Though they feek repentance there is no
place for it.—There is a fin unto death for which
we are not to pray.—When CHRIST cometh in
the clouds of heaven, they fhall wail becaufe of
him.—Their names fhall be blotted out of the
book of life.—They fhall be tormented with fire
and brimftone, in the prefence of the Lamb and

his angels.—The smoke of their torment shall ascend up forever and ever.—They are consigned over to the second death.

Sec. 21. There is a wonderful variety of expressions, in both parts of the holy volume, representing the awful and ceaseless misery of sinners ; nor are they like the expressions of men. Neither any single man, nor any combination of men, without the holy spirit of God, could have produced such a diversity of descriptions on this subject and all of them forcibly depicturing the utter ruin, and misery without end of impenitent sinners. On this multitude of expressions and images varying in kind, but all uniting in a clear assertion of the same great and awful event, we may remark :

1st. That the diverse wording of the threatnings, is a presumptive proof, that they were given by the spirit of God. Parties and sectaries of every kind, fall into modes of expression peculiar to themselves ; and have only one or a few ways of describing facts which are past, or which they expect in future. On this subject, the whole known universe, natural and intellectual, is searched for images, and these images are used to aid the description of a future ruin to the sinner, that will be compleat and without end. And in all this variety of descriptions, there is not a single circumstance that is puerile, or sinks the dignity of that awful and glorious God who speaks and will execute his own judgment ; but the whole is expressed, as we might expect it would be by omniscience.

2dly. Doubtless one design of this variety of expression, was to teach us the greatness of eternal punishment, and effectually warn men, that the misery threatened to disobedience and impenitence is not small. Another design of this, was to teach us its certainty. Infinite wifdom knew how hard a thing it is for men to part with their fin, and own the righteoufnefs of his law and its penalties; alfo how inclined they would be to accommodate the gofpel call to a life of fecurity, in purfuit of pleafurable vices. He knew how apt they are to deceive themfelves, on imaginary grounds of fafety; and what mighty efforts would be made, to blot from the confcience a fenfe of judgment and wrath to come. And he therefore hath threatened the event in fuch a multitude of forms, that the certainty and clearnefs of his word might not be evaded; or its power on the confcience be loft. If only a few forms of expreffion were ufed, the ingenuity of thofe who oppofe the doctrine, might obfcure them by falfe gloffes; but in this multitude of varied expreffions, fuch a thing is not poffible, and the variety adds force to the truth expreffed. The humble chriftian, who heartily believes the whole bible; and the man who reads it without prejudice, will find fufficient evidence, that fuch a doctrine is there maintained; and the very variety of expreffions will be no fmall circumftance giving fuch a conviction.

3dly. If the attempts which are made fhould obfcure a few of the defcriptions ufed on this fubject; ftill they are fo many and fo varied, that the weight of evidence would not be effentially injured. The words moft naturally conveying, in our language, an idea of duration without end; are *eternal, everlafting, forever, and ever.* Pains have been taken by feveral writers, and are often ufed in converfation, to fhow that thefe words, do not certainly mean punifhment without end, when applied to this fubject. But if we fhould yield up all thefe expreffions, the fcripture teftimony would not be at all fhaken. Perhaps, many of us who teach in the church, have erred in our public ministrations by very much confining our scripture proofs, to those passages, where the words eternal, everlasting, and forever are used; which hath led our hearers to think, there are no other proofs; and that if these can be in any degree weakened, the doctrine is in the same proportion made uncertain. But this is far from being fact. All those expressions which deny any future good to the sinner; which deny a future forgiveness; which deny an end to his sorrows; which speak of his end or last state as miserable; which deny him those blessings that compose heaven; or that represent his character fixedly an evil one, without any change to take place; and many other besides these, are as strong proof of endless punishment, as the words eternal and everlasting would be, in the endless sense of them. To disprove the endless punishment of sinners, it is necessary, not only to explain away the natural meaning of the words eternal and forever; but also to prove that a creature's end or last state, is not his last state; that though he hath no future good, he still hath infinite good; and that though he never can have the good of heaven, he still has it through all eternity.

SEC. 22. FURTHER, all the promises of final salvation, which are made to persons of a certain character, and to certain graces, most strongly imply that some shall not be saved. Why are the gospel promises made in this way, if all men indiscriminately are to share in the benefits?

THE scripture exhortations, to diligence, watchfulness, perseverance, and striving to the end, imply, that some men will conduct in such a manner, as not to obtain. Final redemption in another world is the gospel prize, and if men cannot miss of this, there seems to be no propriety in such exhortations.

IT is the general tenor of fcripture, that men are in a dangerous fituation, and that there is fome evil to be avoided. The defcription of thefe evils cannot apply to any thing which happens in this world; they muft therefore be evils and mifery to be endured in another world.

THE word of GOD defcribes two kinds, or claffes of men; differing in moral chara&ter; of different temper and actions; engaged in different interefts; and having different pleafures. It reprefents GOD as preferving fome, and punifhing others; meaning good to fome, and evil to others; that his government will be propitious to fome, and dreadful to others; that all the afflictions of this world are a bleffing to fome, and a curfe upon others. Almoft half the Bible might be adduced to fhow the truth of this reprefentation. How can thefe things be, if all men are coming to the fame end? If his providence and grace mean the fame good to all, and if all are equally his children?

WHOEVER reads the holy fcriptures with any degree of attention, muft be fenfible, that they inculcate fomething neceffary to be done by us, and fomething to be believed by us in this life, for falvation: but the fcheme of thofe univerfalifts, who fuppofe happinefs at death, wholly blots out the neceffity of this; for the man who never prays, or meditates, or thinks of GOD, who is cruel and unjuft in all his actions, who hath fpent his whole life in tormenting mankind, who is a complete infidel refpecting all divine revelation, and dies in the very act of fome great fin, will go as directly to heaven on their principles as if he had done every thing which the word of GOD directs. If it be faid that the commands, and advice of the fcriptures in thefe things; only mean that it is much for the intereft of men in this life, to be holy just and pure ; it will follow, if this be their whole meaning, that the scriptures are very improperly expressed .—and the text which is now written " *For we know that no whoremonger, nor unclean person, nor covetous man, nor idolater, hath any inheritance in the kingdom of* Gᴏᴅ *and* Cʜʀɪsᴛ" ought to have been thus written " For we know that unclean persons, and covetous men, and idolators, are acting much against their worldly interest and pleasure." The reader can judge for himself, whether such advice would have much influence, either upon the adulterer or covetous man. If this be the real meaning of Gᴏᴅ's word, it is truly unfortunate for mankind, that great part of holy scripture, is most improperly expressed ; and that among all who were instruments in penning the sacred canon, there was not one universalist, by whose assistance the scriptures might have been expressed with propriety.

Sᴇᴄ. 23. Tʜᴇ infinite wisdom and goodness of Gᴏᴅ, designed that the holy scriptures should contain full information, concerning every point of faith or practice, that is necessary for us to know. We therefore find, that important doctrines, duties, and events, are many times repeated —in varied expressions—by different writers— and placed in many points of view ; so as to show their connection with other doctrines, duties, and events. The most important doctrines and duties of revelation, might have been expressed in much less compass, than the holy canon now contains ; but it would have cut off those varied views of truth, which we now have ; by which its reasonableness is proved, and its certainty made clear ; and by which, the final end of the divine government in the treatment of rational creatures, is placed beyond a doubt, to those who

make a thorough examination. As thefe remarks, may in fome degree be applied to all the
important doctrines and duties of revelation; fo
they apply eminently to the doctrine of future
punifhment. It is not only told in the moft plain
language, but interwoven with the whole fcheme
of divine revelation; with other important doctrines; and with other reprefentations of God's
character and government; and unlefs this be
true, a great part of fcripture becomes inexplicable and unintelligible.

CONSIDERING what human nature is; confidering how much men love their own fafety;
confidering alfo, how little they examine the
word of God; it is not ftrange, that fome embrace an opinion, which they think will be favourable to them; unlefs this be ftrange, that
any creature can rifk his eternal all, a heaven and
a hell, on the opinion of others, and without a
thorough, long and prayerful examination of the
word of God.

THE truth or falfehood of an important doctrine, ought not to be determined by any fingle
text of fcripture. It is very eafy, for frail and
prejudiced creatures, to miftake the meaning of
fingle paffages. And if we find a few paffages,
which to us feem to convey an idea of univerfal
falvation; but ftill on further examination perceive, that thefe few paffages, if thus underftood;
militate againft the great body of fcripture teftimony, there is reafon to fuppofe that we
mifunderftand them. We will make a fuppofition, (though I allow it only as a fuppofition,)
the moft favourable to the univerfalifts, which
they themfelves can demand.—That there are a
few paffages, which will bear the conftruction
they wifh to put upon them; it is alfo true, that

M

all fuch paffages will bear another conftruction. If the univerfal conftruction, appears either to be a conftrained one, or contrary to the general tenor of fcripture ; and the other conftruction be perfectly confiftent with the general tenor of fcripture ; common fenfe and candor will determine it to be the true one. Reforting either to a fingular or conftrained fenfe, fhows the defperatenefs of the caufe in which it is done.

. It is alfo worthy of remark, and very ftrange, confidering the neceffary ambiguity of language, and the laborious endeavors of fome to explain away the truth, that more evidence of univerfal falvation, fhould not be found, than its moft avowed and ingenious defenders are able to adduce. This fhows that infinite wifdom has taken particular pains, to make the truth plain, and to guard againft error.

Sec. 24. Some who deny eternal punifhment, have laborioufly criticifed upon a few particular words, both in our own and in the original languages, in order to eftablifh their opinion. When recourfe is had to fuch means, the friends of truth muft follow them ; but it cannot be fuppofed, that in a revelation defigned for the great body of mankind, a right underftanding of any important truth, fhould depend upon fuch critical and grammatical knowledge of a few words, in the original languages, as but few of mankind can ever attain. The very fuppofition of fuch a thing, cafts a great reflection upon divine wifdom, and fuppofes that the key of knowledge is ftill in very few hands. Wretched indeed would the cafe of mankind be, if the important doctrines of revelation, and the queftion, whether we are to be eternally happy or miferable, depends upon a nice, critical and grammatical knowledge of a few words, in the Hebrew and Greek languages.

That GOD, who was good enough to give us a revelation, hath alfo been good enough to exprefs his truth, in fuch a multitude of forms, that tranflators of the holy bible who have common honefty, without vaft grammatical attainments, will lead a ferious inquirer to the truth. If we were to found the doctrine of eternal punifhment, upon ftrained conftructions and grammatical niceties I am certain the univerfalifts would make an outcry againft us ; and they would do it with good reafon ; and if they, in their turn, are difpofed to rifk their falvation upon a few grammar rules, and the poffibility of fome little miftakes in tranfcribing, they muft bear the confequences.

SEC. 25. STILL it may be proper for me, to make fome remarks, upon the words ufed in the original languages, defcribing the punifhment of finners.

· 1ft. IT is a well known fact that the Hebrews and Greeks, in whofe refpective languages the Old and New Teftament were written, underftood the punifhment defcribed to be eternal ; and the defcendants of thofe nations who now have the beft knowledge of the power and meaning of words in thefe languages, underftand them fo to this day. It is conceived, this is a fufficient reply to all modern criticifms on this ground, againft the doctrine of eternal mifery. It is very abfurd to fuppofe, that half a dozen moderns, who call themfelves learned in the ancient languages, fhould be better judges of the power and meaning of words in thefe languages ; than the learned who fpake them from their infancy, and were the very perfons who fixed their meaning.

2dly. ANOTHER fact, as certain as the former is this ; that of all the learned, of all other nations, who have taken the greateft pains in acquiring a thorough knowledge of the Hebrew and Greek languages ; more than nine hundred and ninety nine out of a thousand, have understood the descriptions of the holy scripture to mean eternal misery. They have been as learned, as persevering in enquiry, as apparently honest as the few who have supposed differently. And is not such an uncommon unity of sentiment, a clear evidence for the fact ? In some of the most plain cases where the interests of this world in civil policy are concerned, do we not find, as much as one man in a thousand, who judges differently from the great body of the candid, the impartial and the judicious ; on some unaccountable grounds that no men but themselves can discover. This happens in politics, and in most cases of earthly concern. It is not of importance to determine on what principles the opinion of such persons is founded ; but the reason why God permits this, is to promote inquiry, and thereby bring the evidence of truth into public view. In the present question, the evidence of eternal misery from the holy scriptures, is doubtless in much more plain view of mankind, than it would have been, if none had been permitted to deny it. *Great is the power of truth and it will prevail.* I now ask ; in a great political question, on which mens whole worldly interest depended, and in which they did not suppose themselves to be competent judges ; how would a judicious man form his opinion ? Would he rely on the opinion of one in a thousand, against the judgment of all others, or would he be governed by the vast majority of opinion ? I think it is not difficult to determine how a wife man would act, in such a case. And why will not men be as wife for eternity, as they be for time ? There is but one reason to be assigned, and that is, the disaffection of their hearts to the truth.

3dly. A THIRD fact on this subject, is the following. That if eternal mifery be not afferted in the Hebrew fcriptures of the Old Teftament, and in the Greek fcriptures of the New; then there are no words in thefe languages, by which abfolute eternity and duration without end can be expreffed. Every one will perceive the improbability, that abfolute eternity and endlefs duration cannot be expreffed in thefe languages. But if they can be expreffed there is no other way of doing it, than by the fame words and phrafes, which are ufed to defcribe the future mifery of finners. If GOD meant to teach us the fact by language, that fome men will be miferable through an endlefs duration; he could not do it by any language now in the world, more plainly than it is afferted in the original fcriptures. So that either fuch a future event is certain, or the certainty of it is not a thing which can be told by any revelation made in the language of men.

4thly. IT is well known, that the human judgment is liable to be biafed by the wifhes of felfifhnefs. So great is the power of felf-intereft in biafing the judgment, that in all worldly matters, we take the greateft pains to procure difinterefted judges; and we fcarcely allow a man to be a competent judge, who hath any intereft depending on his own judgment. In fuch cafes, we do not fuppofe that all men will villainoufly judge againft their own confciences; but we fuppofe there is great danger that the bias of felfifhnefs, will work fecretly and unperceived by themfelves, to the corruption of their judgment. My reafon for mentioning this is to fhow, the common conviction and confent there is among mankind, of the danger that the human judgment will be biafed, and vitiated by the felfifh wifhes of the heart. This danger takes place, as much in judging of religious truths and the evidence that supports them, as in worldly interests.

Now let us propose the question. In judging of the doctrine, that some men will be eternally miserable, of the evidence in support of this doctrine, and of the meaning of words used in the holy scriptures on this subject; on which side of the question is the danger of a selfish prejudice found? It appears to me, that it must be found on the side against the doctrine. Suppose a man had a certain knowledge of his own freedom from the danger, he might be malicious enough to wish the doctrine true, that his neighbour whom he hates might be damned. But there is no such general knowledge among men of their own exemption from the danger. Though many may hope for their own safety; they have not, and do not pretend to an infallible certainty of their own safety, and it is hardly conceivable, that a man should have a selfish bias in favour of the doctrine of eternal misery, thinking calmly on the subject; when the doctrine brings his own eternal well being, unto the smallest degree of danger. Any man will certainly think, if the doctrine of universal salvation be true, I am certainly safe. And if we suppose him to be the most malicious conceivable, so that he should say, I wish the doctrine true that some whom I hate may be punished; yet as universal salvation, would place me and mine in a state of safety, I wish that may be true. So that all the influence of selfish prejudice must lie on the side of universal salvation. This prejudice will extend to the evidence by which the doctrine of eternal punishment is supported; also to the scriptural use of words on that subject, as much as it doth to the doctrine itself. A general concurrence of opinion in the christian church, directly in the face of a felfifh prejudice, which from its nature muft be general, is ground to fuppofe, that the doctrine of a future punifhment is revealed in the ftrongeft manner poffible.

FURTHER, this fhows the danger of miftaking felfifhnefs for benevolence. Benevolence is a pleafing, it is alfo a fafhionable word. It is often faid, how pleafing! to a benevolent mind is the thought of univerfal falvation. This may be faid honeftly; but ftill there is room to have it faid very felfifhly; when the pleafure to the mind arifes, not from thinking all men will be happy; but from thinking, I am one of all men, and if all men are happy, my own bleffednefs and glory is fixed.

LET thofe who pleafe themfelves fo much, with an idea of their own benevolence, on the principles of univerfal-falvation, faithfully examine their own hearts in this point; and it is poffible that fome may find their benevolence to be nothing but felfifhnefs; and if felfifhnefs in diftinction from the general good, it is the very fin for which they deferve to be punifhed. I fhall hereafter give a defcription of the nature of benevolence. I have now introduced thefe remarks, to remind the reader of the danger of a felfifh prejudice in judging of evidence, and the meaning of fcriptural words and phrafes.

SEC. 26. THE greek words that have been moft criticifed, and which are tranflated, eternal, everlafting, and forever; or which mean the ftate of exiftence that is to fucceed the prefent life, are the fubftantive αιων, and its derivative adjective αιωνιος. They are derived from αει, always, and ων exifting. The moft natural fignification of thefe words from their derivation is exifting always.

THESE words, apply more pertinently than any other in the greek language, to duration without end. Thofe who endeavor to underftand them in another fenfe, muft ftill allow that this is their natural meaning; and muft recur to a figurative ufe, to accommodate them to their own fcheme. Is it probable that in a fubject of this nature, which is moft interefting to men to know, that the infinite wifdom of the divine fpirit, would ufe words fo much in a figurative fenfe, as thefe are on the univerfalift's fuppofition. It will doubt- lefs be conceded, that thefe words when applied to any other thing, being or event that is to take place in the invifible world, or ftate to come, mean endlefs duration; except it be in the cafe of finners punifhment. It will be allowed, that when they apply to the happinefs of the faints, endlefs happinefs is meant. That they are ufed to exprefs the eternity or endlefs exiftence of GOD—the endlefs duration of his kingdom and government—a duration of futurity that fhall not ceafe to be—and alfo to exprefs every circum- ftance, of an eternity of glory and bleffednefs to GOD and his people. Doth it appear probable, when thefe words applied to every other be- ing, thing or event, that is to take place in the invifible world or ftate to come, mean endlefs du- ration; that they fhould mean only a limited du- ration, when applied to the punifhment of finners? Why fhould the holy fpirit ufe words on this point, differently from what they are ufed on ev- ery other point? and efpecially, this appears to be improbable, when we confider how important it is to be known by men, for their wife conduct refpecting eternity.

THE adjective αιωνιοσ, ftill more determinately means endlefs duration, and this is moft com- monly ufed on the fubject of future mifery. To

confirm what I have said, I may notice, the words,
eternal, everlafting and forever, in the Englifh
language. All who understand the Englifh language know that they mean endlefs duration, in
their natural fenfe. At the fame time, thefe words
may be ufed in a limited fenfe. I may fay fuch a
man is an eternal talker, though he paufes to fleep.
That another is an everlafting honor to his country, though there be the higheft probability, that
in a few centuries he will be forgotten. In thefe
cafes, men will underftand what is meant, for they
are limited by the fubject. Words ought never
to be ufed figuratively, or out of their natural
fenfe; except in thofe cafes, where the nature of
the fubject infallibly explains them, to thofe who
are acquainted with language. In the folemn
fubject which we are now confidering, there is nothing to limit the words ufed and turn them from
their natural meaning; there is nothing in the
nature of God, who governs the univerfe; nor
in the nature of thofe created beings who have finned; nor in the nature of fin, and the words
muft of courfe be underftood in their natural
fenfe.

Dr. Jonathan Edwards in his reply to Dr.
Chauncy, hath largely confidered the ufe and
meaning of thefe words, in every place where
they occur in the Greek New Teftament. My
own attentive examination hath led me to agree
in every material circumftance with Dr. Edwards,
and with his permiffion I have made an extract
from his book on this fubject.

PAGES 251, 252 of Dr. Edwards's reply to Dr-
Chauncy. " Aιων reckoning the reduplications
" of it, to be but fingle inftances of its ufe, occurs
" in the New Teftament in one hundred and four
" inftances; in thirty-two of which, it means a

" temporary duration.* In feven, it may be ta-
" ken in either the temporary or endlefs fenfe.†
" In fixty-five, including fix inftances in which it
" is applied to future punifhment, it plainly fig-
" nifies an endlefs duration.‡ How then could
" Dr. C. fay, that it is *commonly* if not *always* ufed
" in the facred pages, to fignify an age or difpen-
" fation only? And that this is *almoft the perpet-*
" *ual* ufe of it?

" But if αιων ufed abfolutely did generally fig-
" nify a mere temporary duration: it would not
" thence follow, that it has the fame reftricted fig-
" nification, when governed by the prepofition εις.
" It is never applied to future punifhment, but
" in this conftruction. In the whole New Tef-
" tament, it is ufed in this conftruction, fixty-one
" times, in fix of which it is applied to future
" punifhment.§ That in all the remaining fifty-
" five it is ufed in the endlefs fenfe, I appeal to
" the reader. If in thofe fifty-five inftances it
" be ufed in the endlefs fenfe; this furely is a
" ground of ftrong prefumption, that in the fix

---

* The places are, Matt xii. 32. xiii. 22, 39, 40, 49. xxiv. 3.
xxviii. 20. Mark iv. 19. Luke i. 70. xvi. 8. xx. 34, 35. Acts
iii. 21. Rom. xii. 2. 1 Cor. i. 20. ii. 6, twice, 7, 8. iii. 18. x.
11. 2 Cor. iv. 4. Gal. i. 4. Eph. i. 21. ii. 2. vi 12. 1 Tim. vi. 17.
2 Tim. iv 10. Tit. ii. 12. Heb. i. 2. ix 26. xi 3.

† The places are, Mark x. 30 Luke xviii. 30. John ix. 32.
Eph. ii. 7. iii. 9. Col. i 26. Heb. vi. 5.

‡ The places are as follows; Matt. vi. 13. xxi. 19. Mark
xi. 14. Luke i. 13, 55 John iv. 14. vi. 51, 58. viii. 35, twice,
51, 52. x. 28 xi. 26 xii. 34. xiii. 8. xiv. 16. Acts xv. 18. Rom.
i. 25. ix. 5. xi. 36. xvi 27. 1 Cor. viii. 13. 2 Cor. ix. 9. xi.
31. Gal. i. 5. Eph. iii. 11, 21. Phil. iv. 20. 1 Tim. i. 17,
twice. 2 Tim. iv. 18 Heb. i. 8. v. 6. vi. 20. vii. 17, 21, 24, 28.
xiii. 8, 21. 1 Pet. i 23, 25. iv 11. v. 11. 2 Pet. iii. 18. 1 John
ii. 17. 2 John 2. Rev. i. 6, 18. iv. 9, 10. v. 13, 14. vii. 12. x.
6. xi. 15. xv. 7. xxii. 5.——*The fix inftances in which it is applied to*
future punifhment, are, Mark iii. 29. 2 Pet. ii. 17. Jud. 13.
Rev. xiv. 11. xix. 3. xx 10.

§ In this conftruction it is found in all the texts mentioned in
the laft marginal note, except Acts xv. 18. Eph. iii. 11, 21.
Once in 1 Tim. i. 17, and 2 Pet. iii. 18.

" inſtances, in which it is applied to future pun-
" iſhment, it is uſed in the ſame ſenſe.

" THE adjective *αιωνιοσ* is ſtill more unfavoura-
" ble to Dr. C's ſyſtem.   It is found in ſeventy-
" one places in the whole New Teſtament ; ſixty-
" ſix, beſide the five in which Dr. C. allows it is
" applied to future puniſhment.†   In every one
" of the ſixty-ſix inſtances, except two, 2 Tim. i.
" 9 ; and Tit. i. 2 ; it may, to ſay the leaſt, be
" underſtood in the endleſs ſenſe."

SUFFER me here to adjoin, what Dr. Huntington, an author held in great veneration, by ſome,
hath ſaid on this ſubject.   Calviniſm Improved,
page 47.   " Now does the Bible plainly ſay that
" ſinners of mankind ſhall be damned to inter-
" minable puniſhment ?   It certainly does, as
" plainly as language can expreſs, or any man, or
" even GOD himſelf can ſpeak.   It is quite
" ſtrange to me, that ſome who believe, that all
" mankind ſhall be ſaved in the end, will trifle
" as they do, with a few words and moſt of all
" with the original word and its derivatives
" tranſlated forever, &c. page 48.   They there-
" fore who would deny that the endleſs damna-
" tion of ſinners is full yaſſerted in the word of GOD,
" are unfair in their reaſonings and criticiſms.

SEC. 27. THE words in the Hebrew language
which are moſt commonly tranſlated eternal, everlaſting, forever, &c. are from the root *Olam*.

_____

† The places are, Matt. xix. 16, 29. xxv. 46. Mark x. 17, 30.
Luke x. 25. xvi. 9. xviii 18, 30. John iii. 15, 16, 36. iv. 14, 36.
v. 24, 39. vi. 27, 40, 47, 54, 68. x. 28. xii. 25, 50. xvii. 2, 3.
Acts xiii. 46, 48. Rom. ii. 7. v. 21. vi. 22, 23. xvi. 25, 26. 2 Cor.
iv. 17, 18. v. 1 Gal. vi. 8. 2 Theſſ. i. 16. 1 Tim. i. 16. vi 12,
16, 19. 2 Tim. i. 9. ii. 10. Tit. i. 2, twice. iii. 7. Philem. 15.
Heb. v. 9. vi. 2. ix. 12, 14, 15. xiii. 20. 1 Pet. v. 10. 2 Pet. i.
11. 1 John i. 2. ii. 25. iii. 15. v. 11, 13, 20. Jude 7, 21. Rev.
xiv. 6.——*The five texts mentioned by Dr. C. are*, Matt. xviii. 8.
xxv. 41, 46. Mark iii. 29. 2 Theſſ. i. 9. *To which is to be added*,
Jude 7.

It hath been faid, that there is nothing in the Hebrew root *Olam* and its derivatives, which imply endlefs duration ; and that it can be thus underftood only when the nature of the fubject neceffarily requires it, as when it is applied to GOD. This matter deferves attention. The word in the Hebrew fcriptures is applied both to duration that is endlefs and that which is not endlefs. The queftion is ; doth this word mean fimply duration without any regard to its continuance ; or is its natural meaning endlefs duration, and ufed figuratively when applied to a fhorter term ; or is its natural meaning limited duration, and applied figuratively to that which is endlefs ? And it appears to me that a knowledge of the nature of language, and how words by the confent of mankind are originated and pafs from one meaning to another, will give a probable folution. It is known that one meaning of this word is *hidden* or *obfcured* ; and I have no doubt but this was its original meaning, as all words were firft applied to fenfible objects. Some have from this infinuated, that when applied to duration the word only means, there is a total uncertainty how long it will laft ; but there is no ground to fuppofe the infinuation a juft one. A finite mind cannot comprehend infinite ; fo that infinite or eternal duration, is in its nature hidden or incomprehenfible by men. But no limited duration, be it ever fo long, is in its nature incomprehenfible or hidden. A limited duration may be hidden from us, becaufe depending on the fecret will of GOD; but it is not hidden or incomprehenfible to men in its own nature, as is the cafe with endlefs duration. The original application of this word to duration, in the Hebrew language, was doubtlefs on the ground I have mentioned; and its natural meaning is duration in its nature incomprehenfible; and none but endlefs or eternal duration is fuch. There is great beauty and energy, in applying the word in this manner to the exiftence of God, and to other things which are eternal in the endlefs fenfe. In the Greek language, abfolute eternity is expreffed by the quality of exifting or continuing always. In the Hebrew, from its being hidden, or incomprehenfible in its nature, by a finite mind. In the Latin from its being without end or limit; and in the Englifh by a derivation from the Latin, in the fame manner. To eftablifh the natural and original meaning of the word *Olam*, when applied to duration is of importance in this fubject. The original word being as I have reprefented; it is not ftrange to find it applied alfo in a figurative fenfe, to long periods of duration, which are not abfolutely endlefs; neither is there any danger of error to a candid and unprejudiced mind, by its being thus applied. The moft facred words are thus ufed in fcripture. Jehovah, fpeaking of men, fays, *I have faid ye are Gods ;* but who in his fenfes, fuppofes from this that men are real deities; and there is little lefs reafon to fuppofe, that becaufe *Olam* is fundry times applied to long but limited duration, that its original and moft natural fignification is not endlefs duration. I have before fully expreffed my opinion, that this important fubject is not to be decided by criticifm on a few words, in the original Hebrew and Greek languages; but as fome refort to this method, thofe who oppofe their fentiments, are under a kind of neceffity, to meet them alfo on this ground.

Sec. 28. Having feen the teftimony of divine revelation on this fubject, it may not be amifs, in this place to inquire; whether, the dictates of reafon, and natural confcience do not teach the same as the Holy scriptures? or in other words, whether there be not something in the human mind, which forebodes the same as revelation threatens? and let this be called reason, conscience, or by any other name, it amounts to the same thing. It is known, that the heathen, of every age and country, have had ideas of happiness and misery, in that invisible world to which men go at death. They have had their good and evil deities; demons delighting in happiness and others delighting in misery. Many of them have described the kinds of happiness and misery, that will be experienced; and the characters of those who are destined to these different ends. They have also represented these two states to be eternal. Such a general opinion, among nations in a state of heathenism, must either come by traditionary accounts, which first originated in a revelation; or they must arise from some principle in the human mind, which forebodes such an event to good and bad men.

If we make the first supposition; that such a general opinion, was derived by tradition from an original revelation; it then proves, that revelation has been thus understood from the beginning; and that the doctrine of future punishment, is not a novel one.

The dissemination of nations was a very early event; and long before the christian æra: If all these nations have a uniform opinion; and this opinion came from those early revelations, which are handed down to us in a concise form, in our holy books; it not only proves what was the early understanding of them; but is also, a probable evidence of the opinion of those holy men, who were the instruments of communicating them to mankind. The general understanding and sense, that men have had of the meaning of revelation, for nearly fix thoufand years, muft have a confiderable degree of authority. And though heathenifm may have mingled much fuperftition, and many weak conjectures of the manner in which punifhment is inflicted; the truth for which we are enquiring, that there is future punifhment comes down unimpaired.

2dly. IF we fuppofe that the general opinion of the heathen, hath arifen from fome principle in the human mind, which forebodes future happinefs to the good, and evil to the wicked; it muft then have great weight, to fupport our underftanding of the holy fcriptures; and fhows an agreement between revelation and this principle in the mind, whatever it may be. Thefe forebodings, of which I now fpeak, have moft commonly been called natural confcience. Whether this natural confcience, be nothing but the judgment of reafon, upon a collection of evidence prefented before the mind; or whether it be a monition immediately from deity, warning of future danger; or whether it be compofed of both, may be difficult to determine, and is not neceffary to be known. All we need to know in the prefent cafe, is this; that by fome means common to the minds of men, whether they be heathen or poffeffed of revelation, there is a foreboding of punifhment to wicked men in another world.— This is found, where we cannot trace it back to revelation; it is alfo found, where revelation is enjoyed; and perhaps as generally in one cafe, as in the other. To fhow that this is the cafe, I afk the following queftions. Doth not that dread of death, which is common to men, appear to come from fomething more than an unwillingnefs to part with the pleafures of this world? Are not men afraid of coming into the prefence of God? Do they not anxioufly inquire, to what ftate am I going, and who knows but it may be a wretched one? and though at some moments I hope much; at others I fear much. Do they not feel the need of some preparation to fit them for coming before God? Are they not urgent in the use of preparatory means? Doth not conscience appear more alive in the hour of death, than at other hours? If these things be so, it proves a foreboding of wrath to come upon some part of mankind. On these forebodings, it may be remarked. First, that considering how general they are, we must ascribe them to some source of information in the nature of things and of the human mind, through which the creator of the universe warns them of their duty and their danger, and of the consequences of being good or bad. 2ndly. They teach us that men, being their own judges, know they are worthy of future punishment. 3dly. That men's natural notions of the divine character, are not inconsistent with the future punishment of the wicked. And when men argue against it, from the perfections of God, they go directly abreast, to those forebodings of the human mind, which have been common in every age and country.

It will not evade these observations to say, that natural conscience only predicts the penalties of the law, and that our hope of salvation is by the gospel. Natural conscience, whether it be the judgment of reason, upon the collected sum of evidence set before the mind ; or whether it be a more immediate monition from God, is as ready to forebode good, as it is to forebode evil, when there is a sufficient ground for doing it. The Apostle Paul speaks of natural conscience in the Gentiles, excusing as well as accusing. Conscience can give peace, as well as fear. The christian, who feels the sanctifying power of God, is by the testimony of his own conscience, made as willing to come before God, as the sin-

ner is unwilling. There is no reafon to fuppofe,
that fuch a caufe of fear would have been found
in the human mind ; if it be inconfiftent, either
with the nature of God, or of his government, to
make men eternally miferable. The truth is,
that God informs us of his nature and purpofes
in many ways : by reafon, by confcience, and
by revelation. Thefe dictates, of reafon and confcience, prepare us to receive a revelation. The
forebodings of natural confcience, correfpond to
the open threatenings of eternal death in God's
word. The gofpel pronounces thefe threatenings, with as much explicitnefs, as the law doth.
There is as much propriety, in faying there are
gofpel threatenings ; as there is that there are
gofpel promifes. A knowledge of the gofpel revelation, doth not remove the forebodings of natural confcience; and thofe who continue to fin
againft both, will have a moft miferable end. It
is conceived that thefe forebodings of confcience,
greatly confirm the doctrine of eternal punifhment.

SEC. 29. IT ought further to be confidered,
that the minds of men are fo conftructed by their
creator, as to be powerfully moved by addreffing
the paffions of hope and fear. Thofe who deny
this, or who think that it is a confideration of little weight in the prefent inquiry, betray great ignorance both of themfelves and of human nature.
This is one principal means, by which God governs his univerfe of intelligent beings. In order
for this, there muft be objects of hope and fear.
And we find them in the conftruction of nature :

thing harmonizes with another. The fact, that our minds are so made as to be powerfully moved by hope and fear, and that an address to these passions runs through the whole scriptures; is a strong indication that natural good and evil, which are the objects of these passions will be eternal. The principles of an Atheist, who denies the being of a GOD; and of that kind of infidels who suppose that the death of the body is an end to the creature's existence, are in the highest degree dangerous to society; because they remove the objects both of hope and fear. Men are thus left without restraint upon their evil appetites and lusts. The modern prevalence of Atheism, or of a kind of infidelity that in its nature approaches very near to it, is a principal source of those miseries, which a considerable part of mankind are now suffering. And while these principles increase, misery must increase with them. If GOD should in a great measure give men up to infidelity, as many circumstances indicate that he will; their passions, unrestrained by hope and fear, will execute upon themselves, the vengeance threatened in his prophetic word. I do not mean to rank those universalists, who profess to be so on the evidence of revelation, in the class of infidels. Still it is conceived, that their principles are dangerous to society, in a lower degree. Though they leave to us the objects of hope; they take away the objects of fear, and these are necessary to be combined in the present state, both for self-government and for public order. And though some who embrace these sentiments, may be persons of irreproachable conduct and very useful at present in society; their good conduct and usefulness may arise from other causes, while their sentiments in this point, have a corrupting influence upon the manners of the world.

PART II.

In which sundry popular Objections against the Doctrine of Eternal Misery, are considered.

SECTION I.   WHEN GOD hath informed us by the strongest evidence, which the nature of the case admits, of certain future events; it becomes us as creatures, to rely on the information, and to use our reason and powers of inquiry, in reconciling such promised events with the infinite moral rectitude of JEHOVAH; that we may thus be enabled to adore him in all his works. The invention of men hath been greatly exerted, in raising objections against the doctrine of eternal punishment, and in representing it to be inconsistent with the divine goodness. Inquiry ought not to be discouraged; for it hath uniformly ended in the vindication of doctrinal truth, and GOD will always provide that this shall be the case. At the same time, our inquiries ought to be conducted with great respect to the word of revelation, and a deep sense of the imperfection of human reason, compared with infinite wisdom. I doubt not but the objections raised against the doctrine in question, will lead to such researches as shall end in its more full establishment; and that the representation of its inconsistency with GOD's goodness, will be the means of fixing more definitely in human knowledge, the nature and objects of infinite goodness; and thus of unfolding the glory of GOD in the government of the universe, and the depths of his wisdom in many scenes that appear surprising to frail and sinful men.

I shall now take notice of several popular objections, against the doctrine I am considering. And to prevent misconception, I ought to acquaint the reader; that in the following pages, the terms *public good*—*general good*—the *good*, or *glory* or *blessedness of the whole*, with other similar expressions will often occur. By these expressions, the greatest glory and blessedness of God, and his holy intelligent kingdom are meant; and this eminently comprizes the glory and blessedness of God. As God is infinitely greater than all creatures, and as all creation is an existing emanation from his will; his glory and blessedness, and the greatest glory and blessedness of the whole, cannot be considered as distinct things.

Sec. 2. Objection. The eternal misery of individuals is inconsistent with benevolence.

Answer. Among all the objections on this subject, that which I have now mentioned, is perhaps the most common; and it is not strange, that many honest minds should find difficulty in solving it. But I conceive, that the whole difficulty arises, from their not having just and accurate ideas of the nature of benevolence, and in what it consists. It is agreed by all, that the supreme Jehovah is a being of infinite benevolence; and that no event will take place in his government, that is inconsistent with the most perfect goodness. Doubtless it is also true, that God hath wisdom to contrive, and power to execute a scheme of existence and government, that contains the greatest possible quantity of happiness; and which every benevolent mind will say is the most perfect scheme, and wholly the fruit of goodness. Those who believe in eternal punishment, found their belief, in consistence with the infinite benevolence of Godhead.—They suppose, that benevolence is the sum of all his glorious perfections—

that it is a comprehenſive name for his whole moral rectitude—that there is no ſeparation to be made, between punitive juſtice and benevolence—that it is his benevolence which moves him to puniſh now and eternally—and that if he did not puniſh he would not be an infinitely benevolent God. They alſo ſuppoſe, on the teſtimony which God hath given of what he will do, that thoſe who argue againſt a future puniſhment, however awful it may be to individuals, or however honeſt they may feel to themſelves ; are oppoſing the beſt, the greateſt, and the eternal intereſts of God and his kingdom.

It here becomes neceſſary to obtain true ideas of benevolence, goodneſs, or holineſs. 1. The exiſtence of miſery is a fact which cannot be denied. This miſery hath exiſted under the direction of God, was cauſed by his will, and is executed by his providence. It therefore appears, that the exiſtence of miſery is not inconſiſtent with benevolence. One of three things muſt certainly be true. Either 1ſt. That God is not a benevolent being ; and if he is not, his promiſe can be no ſufficient foundation for expecting the certain happineſs, either of all, or of any part of men ; for a being who hath no benevolence, would take delight in deceiving.—Or 2dly. God hath not been able to prevent miſery ; and if he hath not been able for ſix thouſand years paſt to prevent it, I do not know what evidence we can have, that he will be able to do it, in the future ages of eternity.—Or 3dly. Infinite benevolence is conſiſtent with the exiſtence of miſery, and this is doubtleſs the truth.

2. Benevolence is conſiſtent with immediately appointing, and producing miſery. The judge who condemns a criminal, and the officer who executes the ſentence, may be very benevo-

lent men.   They have a love of the greateſt happineſs in ſociety, and know that this is the direct
means of promoting it.   The criminal hath loſt a
real good ; but ſociety would loſe a greater good,
if he were not puniſhed and made miſerable.
Hence it appears that benevolence hath no reſpect
of perſons ; or in other words, hath regard to the
greateſt quantity of happineſs in ſociety, and doth
not require the happineſs of every individual.   It
appears therefore that the following things are
true concerning benevolence : Firſt, That it is a
love of the greateſt quantity of happineſs.   Secondly, that it is conſiſtent with the exiſtence of
miſery, and with being the inſtrument of executing it.   Thirdly, that it has regard to the greateſt quantity of happineſs in ſociety, and not to
the happineſs of every individual.   Benevolence
thus defined, is that goodneſs or holineſs, which
directs the ſupreme God in creating, governing
and rewarding.   The good of the whole or the
greateſt happineſs of intellectual being, is the object of benevolence.   If two different ſyſtems of
being are preſented before a benevolent mind,
one admitting a much greater quantity of happineſs than the other poſſibly can ; that ſyſtem will
be choſe, which admits the greateſt.   If benevolence were to chooſe that ſyſtem which admits
the leaſt happineſs it would be acting againſt its
own nature, which is a delight in happineſs.
We may therefore be aſſured, that the infinitely
benevolent, all-wiſe and all-powerful God, will
eternally execute ſuch a government, as will make
bleſſedneſs in the univerſe the greateſt that is poſſible.   It is doubtleſs on this principle, that he
hath admitted moral and natural evil into his government.   Not becauſe he delights either in ſin
or miſery ; or views them as good in their own
nature ; but becauſe they are the neceſſary means

of producing the greateſt good. The happineſs
of every individual, and the greateſt happineſs of
the whole, are conſiderations entirely ſeparate ;
and the benevolence of GOD will chooſe the latter. GOD will as effectually prove himſelf the
friend of good, by puniſhing the unholy ; as by
glorifying the gracious. It is not conceived, that
on any principles different from theſe, the divine
benevolence can be juſtified, in admitting the ſin
and miſery that have already taken place.

3. A REGARD to the happineſs of the whole, is
the very thing which diſtinguiſhes benevolence
from ſelfiſhneſs. It is the important criterion of
diſtinction, and the whole which makes the difference between holineſs and unholineſs. Selfiſh-
neſs delights in happineſs as truly as benevolence
doth ; ſeeks it as diligently ; and is as ready to
allow its excellence. The difference is this ; ſelfiſhneſs is ſeeking individual, private and ſeparate
happineſs ; and hence it ſets up intereſts, that are
ſeparate from the intereſt of GOD, and contrary
to the greateſt good of his kingdom. The baſeneſs of a ſelfiſh temper, ariſes from its being a love
of a ſeparate, a private, and an individual happineſs; and not from its being a love of happineſs.
When men ſay, that GOD is under obligation
from the benevolence of his own nature, to make
every individual happy ; they are arguing from
their own ſelfiſh feelings, and not from divine benevolence juſtly underſtood. If the happineſs of
every individual, coincides with the great happineſs of the whole ; then the benevolence of GOD
obliges him to make every individual bleſſed ;
if theſe do not coincide, his benevolence forbids
him to do it.

4thly. IT appears therefore that thoſe, who
attempt to reconcile the preſent miſery of individuals with the goodneſs of GOD, by ſaying, he

will make it the means of increasing their future
happiness, so as to compensate for present suffering; have entirely departed from the nature of
benevolence, and are judging of the dispensations
of God, on the principles of selfishness. They drop
general good out of the question. They draw rules
of righteousness in the divine government, from
the nature of individuals; and not from the nature, good and happiness of the whole. They
set up so many distinct grounds of equity, and so
many distinct and separate interests in the divine
government, as there are distinct existencies in
the intellectual universe. Let these selfish principles be once admitted, and there is an end of all
moral union and obligation in the kingdom of
God. On these principles, the most wicked sinner in the world may be reconciled to present
misery, without any exercise of love or obedience
to God. While his heart is filled with enmity,
he may still rejoice that God reigns, by supposing; that he shall hereafter gain two degrees of
bliss, for every degree of pain now endured.
Christian submission under present sufferings, is
drawn from another source. Though the christian cannot promise himself any personal benefit
from what he endures, except it be that of thinking God is glorified; his confidence that infinite
wisdom will make all events redound to the divine
honor and happiness, and the general good, ex-
cites his benevolent resignation; and he rejoices
that God reigns, because he will glorify himself
and make a universe of the greatest blessedness.

5. A BENEVOLENCE limited by the law of individual happiness, is so far from the true benevolence of God, and of holy creatures, and from
making all creatures blessed in its operation; that
it is not holiness, neither can it ever give perfect
happiness to any mind. There is no middle way,

between felfifhnefs and a fupreme regard to the
good and glory of God and his kingdom. The
heart muft have an object of its fupreme regard.
If felf be this object there is a neceffary oppofition to the public good; and all the meafures of
divine government, will be approved or difappro-
ved by this rule, am I benefited or not. Selfifh-
nefs will look with a jealous and an afflicted eye
on the emolument of every other being, that cannot be made fubfervient to its own purpofes.
The human heart, wifhes that every thing may
confpire to the advancement of that intereft, which
it prefers to all others. A felfifh creature wifhes
that every thing may confpire to the advancement
of felf, and puts himfelf in the place of God and
the univerfe; and he muft either be unhappy or
the divine government muft bow to his individual
interefts. It may be determined from the nature
of an intelligent mind, that perfect happinefs muft
arife from fuch benevolence, as hath the good
and glory of the whole for its fupreme object, and
to which all individual interefts are fubordinated;
and this is what divines mean by holy or difinterefted affection. No other moral ftate of the heart
will make any being perfectly happy. No other
ftate of the heart is that holinefs and evangelical
obedience, to which are made the gofpel promifes
of bleffednefs. This is the chriftian happinefs, and
it is a happinefs, refulting both from the fatisfaction
of perfonal wants, and feeing God and his kingdom
infinitely bleffed. We hence fee why God requires
a benevolent temper in his creatures. For firft,
the happinefs of others is as valuable as our own
happinefs. Neither exiftence or happinefs, are
any better or more deferving of our good wifhes,
becaufe they belong to ourfelves; and if our
hearts were right, we fhould inftantly fee that fyf-

P

tem to be the beft, which admits the greateft happinefs without any regard to the felfifh confideration who receives it. I know that this is directly
contrary to all the feelings of a proud and finful
mind ; but it is not contrary to reafon ; and however ftubbornly the wicked heart may rife againft
the truth, there is a GOD who will prevail, and
will continue his glorious government on thefe
principles. A fecond reafon, why GOD requires.
this benevolence in his creatures, is that it
will make thofe individuals who comply with
their duty and exercife it, the moft bleffed they
can be. They will have the happinefs of feeling
every want of their own minds fatisfied ; and the
additional happinefs of enjoying the bleffednefs of
GOD, and of all the fubjects of his holy kingdom.
The increafe of general bleffednefs will neceffarily carry with it, an increafe of happinefs to every
member of the holy body, and thus an infinite
good will become the object of his enjoyment.

6thly. BENEVOLENCE is a favorite word, and
much ufed in prefent religious difcuffions. Almoft all parties will agree in the word, while they
widely differ in the meaning affixed to it. Benevolence as I have explained it ; confifting in a
friendlinefs of the heart to the general good, to
which all private, feparate and individual interefts are fubordinated, is a moral ftate of the heart,
entirely different from what many mean by the
word. According to the above explanation, the
infinite benevolence of GOD is no proof of univerfal falvation ; for if the juft and eternal mifery
of fome, be a neceffary means of the greateft happinefs, it will doubtlefs be preferred in his government, by a holy GOD. Benevolence, applied
to the divine character, in the loofe fenfe that many ufe the word, means the fame as that all creatures will be made happy. In this fenfe of the

word, it will be denied that God is a benevolent being ; and thus uſing it, is only taking that as granted, which is the real matter of diſpute. This looſe ſenſe of the word will be very agreeable to ſinful minds, and hath a fatal tendency to fix them in the ſecurity of death.

SEC. 3. BENEVOLENCE is of the ſame nature in creatures, as it is in God. Holy affeétions in the chriſtian, will be like the benevolent exerciſes of the deity ; ſo far as a finite knowledge, powers, and ſphere of aétion permit. Every good mind, wiſhes the greateſt poſſible happineſs in the univerſe of being. He wiſhes the greateſt poſſible number of individuals to be made happy, that can be with the greateſt happineſs in the whole ; and that each of theſe individuals ſhould be the happieſt poſſible. If God had made a revelation concerning any one or number of perſons, that their ſalvation would be inconſiſtent with the plan of his benevolent government ; and that their being made happy would neceſſarily alter the ſcheme of ſocial exiſtence, in ſuch a manner, that the univerſe would looſe more than they could gain ; in ſuch a caſe, it is not ſeen that benevolence could wiſh their ſalvation, at the expence of a greater good. Benevolence never can wiſh a diminution of real good in the univerſe, for this would be aéting againſt an eſſential quality of its own nature, which is, a delight in good or happineſs. Theſe are the reaſons, on which a well informed chriſtian temper, acquieſces in puniſhing juſtice ; and not becauſe vindiétiveneſs, revenge, or delight in miſery can belong to a good heart. With reſpeét to mankind, it is ſuppoſed that ſome of them will never come to final ſalvation. Who ſuch individuals are, is wholly a ſecret of the divine counſel, and there is a fitneſs it ſhould be thus retained. Benevolence doubt-

less wishes, concerning all men now living in the
world, that they may be saved; if it be the will
of God, who is the guardian of the interests of
the great whole.   Though we may think such an
event improbable concerning all men now living,
and greatly fear that many will be lost, we have
no certain knowledge of what is best on the whole,
or of what God will do.   With this limitation,
christian love will desire salvation to every creature on earth, and express that desire. . Wherever there is christian holiness, there will be a strong
desire for the salvation of souls.   *There is joy in*
Heaven over one sinner that repenteth.   The man
who is unconcerned for the salvation of others,
gives no evidence of his own real christianity.
A love of souls, is one of the most essential, ani-
mated, and active exercises of a holy heart.   We
know that men must become holy before they
can be saved ; or rather, that personal holiness is
a most essential part of salvation.   What then is
the most wise method, of manifesting a concern
for the salvation of others ?   Is it by disseminating
an idea, that all are safe and will be saved ?   Is it
natural to suppose, that men will be quickened in
escaping sin, by telling them there is an infinite
certainty their sin cannot hurt them in the end ?
When they love sin for the present life, and believe that it cannot hurt them in the life to
come ; what motive that can be offered in human
address, is left to arouse them from the sensuality
in which they delight, to a life of watchful sobri-
ety and godliness ?   Is is not a more fit method,
to tell them you never can be saved in your sins ?
Doth it not look more like a love of souls to exhort them away from their sin, and show them the
natural, the indissoluble connexion between sin
and misery ; than it doth to be constantly declaim-
ing there is no danger ?   Sin is the fire that burns

and makes mifery. It burns in all who are unholy, making them miferable now; and fo long as it burns, mifery will continue. If the cry of fire were made and men were gathered round the enkindled building, would it be proper to fay; the houfe is truly fired, but be perfectly eafy for it will certainly be faved, and no poffible event can hinder its prefervation. Would it not be more proper to fay? The building is fired, but not paft remedy; fuitable exertions may fave it, and without them it is wholly loft. The two cafes are fimilar. The building cannot be faved, unlefs the fire is extinguifhed; neither can the finner be faved unlefs his fin is extinguifhed, and God hath given him the moft folemn warning, that this is the cafe.

SEC. 4. THE obfervations that have been made upon the nature of benevolence or holinefs, fhow us, why fome whofe doctrinal belief is right; whofe vifible converfation is regular; and who live in a punctual attendance on gofpel ordinances, may ftill be very unholy perfons, and entirely unprepared for heaven. They may perform all their vifible duties, and maintain all their regularity of manners; they may attend God's houfe and ordinances, and do kind things to men; they may have a great zeal in their own way, and give their bodies to be burned; all from felfifh motives. People of this character, though they may be much better members of civil fociety, than the openly immoral can be; have ftill no preparednefs for heaven. There are the fame immoral principles in their hearts, as are found in the hearts of the profane; only thefe principles are exercifed in a different way. It is on this account, that thorough felf-examination becomes fo difficult a work, and that fo many are deceived. Even thofe wifhes of the heart, which men call benevo-

lent; and which they esteem evidence of their
own good estate, may be the highest evidence a-
gainst them.   I may instance in the very subject,
of our present consideration.   If the supreme motive of those, who suppose that they benevolently
wish the salvation of all, and who please themselves
much with their benevolence ; be, that on this
principle their own safety is secured ; there is no
real benevolence in the wish, and selfishnefs is at
bottom.   In this case, the desire of universal happinefs is built, entirely on the previous and all-
governing desire, of individual, private and separate happinefs.   Should GOD say to such an one;
your own eternal happinefs depends, on having
a universe which is infinitely greater than your-
self eternally miserable; on the selfish principle
above-mentioned, the unholy heart would answer;
then let this universe be miserable, and GOD the
creator forever dishonoured.   A benevolent love
of GOD and the truth produces a visibly good
and regular life; but the same visibly good actions, may originate from very contrary motives;
and it is therefore wise to use great circumspection in judging.—Men ought to be grateful when
urged to this circumspection, because they must
live and die for themselves.   The good or the
evil will be their own.   The corruption of human nature never appears more unreasonable,
than when men become angry, by being exhorted
to look well to their own eternal well-being ; and
in a case, where those who give this advice, can
have no selfish purpose to serve.

SEC. 5. OBJECTION.   GOD is a being of infinite power and wisdom, who can do every thing
that he pleafes, and can therefore make every individual happy, in union with the greatest happinefs of the whole.

ANSWER. A LIMITATION of divine power ought always to be made with reverence, and
when made ought not to be confidered as imperfection in GOD ; but as arifing from the perfection of his nature, and of the fyftem he hath created.   I believe it will be allowed, that there are
certain things which no power can effect.   Such
as thefe.   Can any power make twice two, to be
ten ?   Can infinite power make a thing to be, and
not to be; or to be both true and falfe, at the
fame time?   If expreffed with ferious intentions,
it doth not feem to be any irreverence of the deity, to fay, that thefe things are impoffible even
to infinite power.   When CHRIST faid, all things
are poffible with GOD ; he only meant fuch things,
as do not in their nature imply a contradiction.
We are told that it is impoffible for GOD to lie.
A wilful falfehood would be a contradiction
to his infinite holinefs, and they cannot be
made by any power, to exift together.   This
impoffibility arifes from the perfection of the fupreme GOD and his works.   If the power of numbers adds perfection to the works of GOD ; a poffibility of making twice two to be ten, would deftroy that perfection.   If the power of making
things to be, is a perfection of GOD's nature ; a
power of making them not to be, at the fame time,
would be an imperfection.—It would only be a
power of deftroying his own agency, council, and
the attributes which make him to be GOD.

IT is conceived on thefe principles, there is no
room to fay; that becaufe GOD hath infinite
power and wifdom, he can unite the happinefs of
every individual, with the greateft poffible happinefs of the whole.

IT may be a thing, implying that kind of contradiction or impoffibility, which is contained in
the fuppofition of *being* and *not being* at the fame

time. The poſſibility of ſuch a union between individual and univerſal happineſs, is one of thoſe matters, which men never can determine, without information from GOD himſelf ; and we muſt not ſuppoſe it, on the poſſibility, that infinite power can do all things. GOD only knows the nature, connexions and capacities in his own univerſe ; and what is neceſſary to make it the moſt bleſſed. If the happineſs of every individual is compatible with the greateſt happineſs in the whole, then doubleſs every individual will be made happy ; but if not, the contrary will take place. We ought to have ſuch confidence in the wiſdom and goodneſs of GOD, when he tells us ſome creatures ſhall be always miſerable under puniſhment, as to believe ; that the eternal happineſs of every creature, and the greateſt happineſs of the whole are incompatible ; and cannot come together into that plan or ſcheme of exiſtence and government, which is the beſt poſſible.

FURTHER, If there be any force in this objection, it goes as much to prove that there never was, and never will be any miſery ; as it doth to prove that there will not be eternal miſery. Partial miſery, according to its quantity, is as undeſirable and as inconſiſtent with benevolence, as eternal miſery. If GOD could have made every individual as happy without ever taſting miſery as he can with it ; then benevolence would have forbid it. If he could not make every individual the moſt happy, without ſome miſery, this ſuppoſes the ſame limitation to almighty power, with which the objection contends. If there be any ground, on the infinitude of GOD's power, to exclude eternal miſery, there is the ſame ground to exclude partial miſery. We may as well ſay, there hath never been any miſery ; becauſe GOD is a benevolent being, and almighty benevolence

, can make the greateſt happineſs without any miſery ; as we may that he can do it without eternal
miſery.   The poſſibility from infinite power applies alike in both caſes.   The exiſtence of partial
miſery no one will deny, which reduces us to the
following concluſion, either, that God did not act
benevolently in the miſery which hath already taken place ;   or that the poſſibility ariſing from the
infinite power of God, is no ſecurity againſt miſery without end.   It is preſumed none will pretend, that the miſery which hath taken place, is a
proof againſt the benevolence or goodneſs of God.
. Sec. 6. Objection. The ſolution to the former objection, ſtands upon the principle, that God
appoints ſin and miſery to take place for the public good.   How is this juſtice in God, or juſt to
the ſinning, ſuffering creature? Will God give
up one to miſery forever, to make the univerſe
more happy, and is this conſiſtent with equity to
individuals ?

ANSWER. This objection, leads us back to ſome
fundamental principles in God's moral government of the rational univerſe, and in the nature
of holineſs or moral virtue.   Here it becomes neceſſary, that we ſhould form accurate ideas of the
nature of juſtice, as it exiſts in God, and is exerciſed in his government of the univerſe.   To aſſiſt in this, I make the following remarks :

1ſtly. JUSTICE in God is but a branch, or exerciſe of his love, benevolence or goodneſs. God
is love.   His whole moral character is love, benevolence or goodneſs ; and juſtice is always an
exerciſe of that moral character, which is deſignated by theſe words.

2dly. THE object of benevolence or goodneſs ;
or the end to which it is directed, in all its exerciſes, is the public or general good.   The object

Q

of justice and its exercises in GOD; and the sole
end which he means to promote is the general
good. What we call the vindictive or punitive
justice of GOD, has in all cases the public benefit
for its ultimate end. We have no reason to suppose, that any end detached from the general
good, is GOD's ultimate end in any thing that he
does. For if we once admit this, it introduces
into the divine government two opposing principles ; public good, and individual or separate
good. I call these opposing principles, because
they are thus in their own nature. While individual or separate good is the object of supreme choice and love ; the general good cannot
be. And when the general good is the object of
supreme choice ; individual or separate good cannot be. This doth not militate against individual
happiness, because the greatest possible happiness
of individuals, is when they give up their own
private interests and make the public interest
their supreme and governing object in all their
actions and wishes. Though GOD hath forbid
his creatures, making their own interest a supreme
object ; he hath so constructed their nature, that
they are the most happy they can be, when they
supremely love the public interest, happiness and
glory. It is in this way, that infinite wisdom
hath united, the highest possible public good and
the greatest individual or personal blessedness.

3dly. IT hence follows that the punitive, or
vindictive justice of GOD, as it is sometimes called,
doth not delight in misery or punishment for its
own sake. Even punitive or vindictive justice
hath no approbation of the misery of punishment,
only as it is the necessary means of a happiness
to the whole, greater than the misery is to the individual. This must be the case, if justice as it
exists in GOD, is only a branch or exercise of be-

nevolence, acting under certain circumstances. The notion of punitive or vindictive justice, as a perfection which delights in the misery of punishment, in any other sense than infinite goodness or benevolence delights in it, is conceived to be utterly a misconception. An insidious misrepresentation of some, whose sentiments I am now opposing, has been this; that the believers in future punishment suppose the justice of God to be a devouring perfection which delights in torment, for its own sake, and on this they declaim most laboriously; when in fact it is a phantom of their own creating, and abundantly proves their ignorance of the true nature of benevolence, and of justice as included in it.

4thly. THE public or general good, is the true and the only measure of justice in the treatment of a sinner. The public good, in the large sense of the expression as I have before explained, is the reason which makes sin to be sin, or wrong and unfit; it is the reason which annexes guilt to the exercise of a sinful temper; it is the reason why God ordained the moral law, and annexed a penalty to the violation of it; it is the reason why this penalty consists in misery; and the quantity and duration of misery must be determined by the same reason. If the public good did not require it, there would be no fitness, in following moral evil with natural evil or misery; and there is no perfection in God that delights in misery for any other reason, but its necessary subserviency to the interests of general being. This is the rule, by which the most holy God limits himself, in creating and in governing; and agreeable to which his whole agency in the treatment of individual creatures is regulated. He creates so many individuals as the public good requires; and when created, he treats them according to this rule. If this requires him to make them happy, he doth it; if this requires him to make them miserable, he doth it. A disposition to do this is holiness,—is benevolence,—is justice, for justice as it exists in GOD is not distinguishable from benevolence. The reason, that we use the different names of goodness and justice, is from the different effects, wrought in the condition of the creature who is the subject of them; and not from any thing different or distinct in the nature of that moral principle, according to which the supreme GOD acts.

The consequence follows, that whatever treatment of the individual creature is required by the good of GOD and his kingdom, is just in GOD to execute. Having endeavored to explain the nature of justice as a perfection existing in GOD, and why it is justice in him to punish the sinner, I observe further.

There is but one law of holiness in the universe. GOD prescribes the same law of benevolence or holiness both to himself and his creatures, and requires nothing from them, but what is consistent with the moral principles, by which he directs himself. There is the same reason, that the creature, should seek and endeavor to promote the public good, in his temper and in all his actions; as there is that GOD should govern for this end. When the creature's temper becomes opposed to this good, he is sinful. If it be just in GOD to treat him as a sinner; then it is but justice and equity to him to be thus treated; for certainly the same reasons which vindicate the justice of GOD, must vindicate the justice of the treatment which the sinner receives, and their equity is inseparable. If it be fit, that GOD should punish such a temper as the sinner possesses; then for the same reason, it is fit the sinner should be punished ; becaufe the fame law of holinefs, is a law both to God and the creature. The finners charaĉter is in its nature bafe and odious. It becomes the moral governor of the univerfe to exprefs his fenfe of it, and for this reafon, a punifhment of mifery is applied. A delight in the greateft happinefs is the ground of application.

FURTHER, with refpeĉt to the degree and duration of the finners punifhment, thefe alfo muft be determined by the fame rule. I may in this place, mention fome things to be confidered, as evidential that eternal punifhment is not greater than the general happinefs requires, and confequently not greater than the demerits of fin.

1. THE finners temper and praĉtice, is direĉtly oppofed to the glory and bleffednefs of God, and his intelligent kingdom. This objeĉt, is a good in every fenfe infinite. By its quantity it is infinite for the time being.—The glory and bleffednefs of God and his kingdom are uniform in their nature through eternity ; fo that the finner's temper is oppofed to a good that is infinite both in quantity and duration.

2. THE finners temper and praĉtice is a violation of infinite obligation. Whatever other caufes may enter into the nature of moral obligation ; the excellence of the objeĉt to which our duty is due, is certainly one of them ; and our obligation is in proportion to the excellence and value of the objeĉt. The excellency of God is the ground of our obligation to love him. Our obligation is in proportion to his excellency compared with other beings ; and as this is infinite, fo alfo is that obligation refulting from it, which the finner hath violated.

3. THE tendency of the finners temper and praĉtice is to banifh infinite bleffednefs from the univerfe, and to introduce infinite evil or wretch-

edneſs. The malignity of a ſinful diſpoſition or action, is not to be eſtimated, by the wretchedneſs it actually doth produce ; for it may be arreſted by a ſuperior wiſdom, and the evil prevented. No thanks are however, in ſuch a caſe, due to the ſinner ; but his temper and intentions remain equally baſe, as if ſuch effects had not been prevented. Common ſenſe makes this judgment of a ſinful temper. Certainly the tendency of an immoral diſpoſition is to produce infinite evil. It is aimed againſt the bleſſedneſs of GOD himſelf, and of all the holy intelligencies of his kingdom. It is aimed againſt that vaſt, eternal and bleſſed univerſe, which almighty power, wiſdom and goodneſs mean to form. The ſinners temper, give it ſcope, would dethrone a GOD and unmake a univerſe, to build up himſelf. Thus inſatiate are ſelfiſhneſs and pride. They go through this world carrying deſolation ; and if they had power would go through a univerſe, either deſolating or engroſſing the whole. Theſe principles, left without controul would do the ſame eternally. How evil they are is not for men to deſcribe —words cannot tell—human imagination cannot conceive. GOD alone can comprehend the evil of ſin, and the enormity of its baſeneſs ; and therefore he alone can tell the greatneſs of deſerved puniſhment.

IT appears therefore that ſin is oppoſed to an infinite good ; is a violation of infinite obligation ; and hath a natural tendency to introduce infinite and eternal wretchedneſs. Theſe things cannot be denied ; and in contemplation of them many eminent divines, have called ſin an *infinite evil.* With this deſcription of ſin, as an infinite evil, ſome have been diſpleaſed, and oppoſed it with this argument. That ſin is the act of a finite creature, and the act of a finite creature cannot be infinite. To wrangle about words, is difingenuous, and fhows an indifpofition to come to the truth. It is well known, that thofe venerable divines who have called fin an infinite evil, did not mean, that the act of a finite creature can be infinite in its nature ; and thofe who have ufed the argument above mentioned had reafon enough to know, that they did not mean this. But the confequence doth not follow, that a finite act may not tend to evil effects that are infinite ; or that the guilt and demerits of fin are not to be judged by this rule. Suppofe a moral evil or fin, that is oppofed to an infinite good; a violation of infinite obligation ; and tending in its very nature to infinite wretchednefs, (and this is a juft defcription of every fin men commit) I think it may fairly be called infinitely evil, unfit, and unreafonable. And how can God in any proportionate way difcover his fenfe of this evil, but by an infinite and eternal punifhment. This I conceive to be the force of the argument for eternal punifhment, from the infinite evil of fin ; and it fhows that the finner may be eternally punifhed in juftice.

Ir is certainly fit, that God fhould exprefs his fenfe of the evil of fin, as a means of making his own character known. It is fit, that he fhould make a true expreffion of his own fenfe of the evil of fin ; or in other words, that this expreffion fhould be in proportion to the real bafenefs of the finners character. There is no conceivable way in which this can be done, but by punifhment. Words alone will not do it. It is a maxim of common experience, *that actions fpeak louder than words.* All poffible prohibitions or verbal condemnation, would not exprefs to the minds of creatures, the divine fenfe of the evil of fin, if God's actions or treatment of the finner acquitted him. If the finners temper be aimed against the greatest possible good ; then the divine expression ought to be the greatest possible. If this temper be aimed against an eternal good, the expression ought to be commensurate with infinity or eternity.   It must be one also, that by finite means displays the energy of feeling in an infinite mind.   In all views of this subject, it runs into eternal misery, and both the nature of things and the moral obligation of God to himself and his kingdom seem to require it.

The use God will make of sin, and the cause, manner and means by which a sinner becomes such ; are not in the least connected with his demerits, and the treatment he may justly receive after he is become a sinner.   In determining the demerits of a sinful temper or action, we never stand to inquire ; how did the man come by this temper ?   We look directly upon the temper itself and judge of its baseness and just demerits from its own nature and tendency.   This is the dictate of common sense, and all men act according to it. In the present argument, the divine motives in appointing sin and misery ; the use God makes of it ; and the manner in which men become sinful, are one thing ; and God will doubtless be able to justify his own holiness, and take care of his own honor.   The baseness and just demerits of a sinful temper are entirely another thing ; and the treatment that is just to a sinner, depends not at all on the manner of his becoming sinful.   It is just, it is glorious in God to treat the transgressor according to what he is, let his corruption come how it may, and whatever use God may make of it in happifying the universe.   God is just in punishing ; because he treats him according to what he is, and in such a manner as public good requires.

I will give an example, by way of suppofition, which may carry conviction on this fubject ; and I fhall endeavor to ftate one of the ftrongeft kind. The reader will obferve, it is merely a fuppofition. Suppofe that God fhould create a man, more wicked than any one ever yet exifted ; and by his own power immediately infufe into him, the moft perfect enmity and vice. Suppofe this wicked creature placed in fociety, and perpetrating all the crimes natural to fuch a temper. What would men judge of fuch a creature, and what would their treatment of him be ? Would his character appear amiable becaufe he was made as he is? Would men patiently bear with his fin, and indulge his violence, becaufe it is his nature to fin and do violence? Would it be any excufe for his enmity and murders, for him to fay, by my creation I was fo made as to delight in wickednefs, and vice is the element in which I am moft happy ? It is prefumed that his character would not appear lefs deteftable, or lefs worthy of punifhment, on this account. This fhows that the juftice of punifhment arifes from the nature of men's temper and actions, in relation to the rational univerfe ; and is not in the leaft, connected with the caufe, or manner in which they became finful ; nor with the end for which an infinitely holy God appoints fin.

In purfuing the fubject we are brought to thefe two points. 1ft. That God is juftified to himfelf and to the univerfe, in appointing fin and mifery, by his defign of making them the means of the greateft poffible good. 2dly. He is juftified in his punifhment of the finner, by his treating him according to what he is—a creature with a temper that is unfit, unreafonable, hateful in its nature, and oppofed to the greateft good ; and to neglect pun-

R

ifhment, would hide the glorious holinefs of his own nature, and fecrete from the intellectual fight of good beings his character, which is the object of their blifsful enjoyment. GOD acts from the fame benevolence or holinefs, through the whole; and he will be glorious in the whole. In the end, it will appear that in him there is nothing like what we call enmity or revenge; and that he both creates and punifhes in benevolence. Every mouth will be ftopped before him; and guilty finners, who now cavil againft his government, as an excufe for their fin, and to quiet their own confciences in an evil way, will be totally felf-condemned; and they muft alfo be eternally miferable, unlefs they are renewed by his fpirit and forgiven through the blood of CHRIST.

THE very excufes, which finning creatures make for their bad hearts and practice, is often an evidence of the excefs of their wickednefs; and inftead of excufing, proves them worthy of being punifhed. GOD will need nothing more in the day of judgment to convict finners, than their own confciences and their own excufes. Their excufes will prove the criminal nature of fin, and their confciences will prove that they have committed it. Thoufands of finful fouls, fpend their time which ought to be filled with repentance and amendment, in endeavoring to excufe their corruption; and to contradict the fitnefs of punifhment; either on the ground that GOD is a good being and therefore will not punifh; or that he holds the reins of government, and all things are according to the purpofes of his counfel, and that therefore it is not equitable he fhould punifh. Both thefe excufes overlook the truth, that fin is worthy of punifhment by its nature, and not from the caufe and means which introduced it.

However eafy it may be to prove on rational principles, the juftice of inflicting eternal mifery on finners; it will be hard to filence thofe, whofe hearts do not love the juftice of God, as it hath been defcribed. The higheft rational evidence never filences an oppofing heart. Nothing but the gracious power or God, giving a holy temper, will do it; for as it belongs to the nature of fin to delight in felf and felfifh interefts; fo it does, to deny God's juftice in condemning and punifhing. The writer doth not expect to make one unholy mind acquiefce in divine juftice; or feel a love of God for exercifing it; or fee the moral beauty of that holinefs which governs the univerfe. If finners feel their hearts rifing againft the doctrine, they muft apply to the gracious power of God, and not to men, to heal their hearts. They alfo ought to confider, that the rifing of their hearts, will never ftop God in his government. He will go on fteadily and glorioufly, doing that which he knoweth to be juft, for his own glory, and the good of his kingdom.

Sec. 7. Objection. The original threatning pronounced by God, was this. *In the day thou eateft thereof thou fhalt furely die.* This threatning is abfolute. Divines generally fuppofe that it includes eternal death or mifery. If any men are faved, (which all parties allow will be the cafe) then that threatning is not fulfilled, and if the original threatning was not fulfilled, what certain evidence can we have, that any other threatning in the bible will be?——To enforce this objection it hath been faid; that it is God's manner to reveal one difpenfation at a time.—That he firft revealed the law, and told thofe effects of tranfgreffing it which muft fucceed; if men were left under the law.—And that as he was under no obligations, fo he did not at that time intimate any thing of a gofpel.—That God did not mean

by the legal threatning to exclude a gospel; also
that by the threatnings in the gospel dispensation,
he doth not mean to preclude some new and future dispensation, which may deliver those from
misery, who reject the gospel salvation.

ANSWER. 1st. IT is not allowed that the stating
in this objection, or that the reasons to enforce it
are true. But making the supposition that they are
true, it is no evidence of universal salvation. The
most that it makes in favour of that doctrine is this,
that GOD hath once omitted to inflict on some
part of men, all the misery that he might in justice have executed; and that he hath placed them
by sovereign mercy in a situation to retrieve their
ruin. But doth the consequence follow that he
will do this the second time? doth his having
done one unmerited favor, lay him under obligation to grant a second or a third?——Common
sense, in all transactions of men, certainly argues
directly opposite. When the immediate and rig-
orous execution of punishment deserved by a criminal, hath been once delayed or remitted by a
good sovereign, on condition of future good conduct, and the criminal abuses this favour by a
repetition of sin; do we in this case judge, that
the first undeserved favour is an evidence of a
second? Do not all impartial people say, now let
the criminal suffer the utmost extent of the penalty! Having a chance for deliverance, and having wantonly and against warning abused his
sovereign and himself, he must now endure the
consequence. Miserable indeed, is the foundation of hope for all men, that stands solely on the
expectation of some new and unknown dispensation in favour of gospel impenitents, because the
gospel succeeded a condemning law.

2ndly. THE momentary supposition, which I
granted in my first answer to the objection, must

now be taken back, and I will consider the matter more particularly. It is said in the objection, that divines generally suppose the threatning, "in the day thou eatest thereof thou shall surely die," means eternal death or misery. It is incumbent on me to describe what is meant by this threatning, and how it hath been generally understood, with respect to eternal misery. It hath not been understood, that all men actually will suffer eternal misery; for this would be inconsistent with the salvation of any by the gospel.——It hath not been understood, that any partial period of duration will ever be compleated, in which it can be said the sinner hath suffered eternal death. There must be the suffering of an absolute eternity, to make the death eternal.——Much less hath it been understood, that the sinner could suffer a death that is strictly eternal, within the limits of that natural day in which he fell. The meaning of the threatning, must be such an one as is consistent with the nature and possibility of things, and I conceive it to be this. In the day thou eatest or sinnest, a death of misery shall commence with thee ; it will be just to thee if thou art left in this situation ; and being thus left the misery must be eternal. The very words, in which the penalty is expressed, seem to be designed for two purposes. First, to express the sinners desert, and what must take place according to the nature of unholy minds. And Secondly, to leave room for a gospel to follow. There was a literal fulfilment of the threatning. The creature did eat and become a sinner. In that very day death commenced.—A death that would be just on him, extended through an absolute eternity.—A death that must continue, according to the very nature of an intelligent mind, so long as he continued unholy. That the original threatning meant the desert of eternal misery to all sinners, is not learned wholly from the words in which it is expressed; but more abundantly from the general tenor of scripture, and even from the gospel which followed the law; for if the threatning of the law did not mean a desert of eternal misery, there would have been no need of an infinite Saviour. But we may observe on the original threatning; that though it is so worded as to express a desert of eternal misery, and to excite an expectation of it unless some revelation of grace should commence, it did not preclude a method of deliverance. It did not say there shall be no grace—no Saviour. Had the threatning been in the following words, " in the day thou eatest thereof thou shalt die, and remain in a state of death through endless duration," or " in the day thou eatest thou shall die, and there shall be no forgiveness," this would have totally excluded a gospel recovery, and have made it inconsistent with God's truth to forgive any sinner.

3dly. There is a most observable difference between the original threatning of the law on the one hand; and the threatenings against those who neglect the gospel, and the description of future judgment given by Christ and the sacred writers, on the other. The former asserts misery begun, and a desert of misery eternal; the latter assert the actual existence of misery eternal. The former asserts what is strict justice to the sinner, and the commencement of its execution, leaving a possibility, without any contradiction of the divine threatening, for God to interpose by sovereign grace, and rescue so many as he seeth fit. The latter assert, there shall be no forgiveness either in this or the world to come—that they shall be punished forever and ever—and that they shall go into eternal or endless punishment. A vaſt multitude of expreſſions, implying endleſs miſery, may be found among the latter or goſpel threatenings, which totally take away all ground to expect, that ſome new and unſeen way for the deliverance of goſpel impenitents, may hereafter ariſe.   And it is conceived, that if the original threatening of the legal penalty,. had been expreſſed as theſe latter threatenings are, all poſſibility of a goſpel to ſave any, would have been excluded by the truth of God.—Thoſe therefore who make themſelves quiet on this ground, are acting againſt the dictates of common ſenſe, and the expreſs teſtimony of ſcripture.

Sec. 8. Objection. Allowing that benevolence requires God ſhould govern for the greateſt good of the whole, and that there will be more happineſs in the univerſe with the eternal exiſtence of ſin and miſery than could be without it; ſtill how is this conſiſtent with creating goodneſs? Can God be acting the part of a good being, in making a creature, who he knows will be eternally miſerable; even though juſtice allows the deſert of the creatures miſery?

Answer. This hath been a very popular objection againſt the doctrine of eternal puniſhment. I think a very little attention will diſcover that it is utterly without force.   The objection derives its whole appearance of weight, from an idea that creating goodneſs and governing goodneſs are two things; whereas in fact, they are but one and the ſame.   Creating goodneſs, is governing goodneſs begun; governing goodneſs, is creating goodneſs continued.   The eternal wiſdom and goodneſs of God fixed on an object to execute. The execution was begun in creation—is continued in governing, and will be continued through eternity.   Every part of creation was exactly fitted for the benevolent purpoſe, of producing the greateft poffible degree of happinefs. Infinite wifdom had this end in view, as much in creating as he hath in governing. In both, he was the fame benevolent GOD, uniformly carrying his own vaft purpofe into effect. The objection makes a total feparation between creation and government; it reprefents GOD as acting on different principles in one cafe from what he does in the other; it defcribes him creating with a private view of the higheft happinefs of every individual, and governing with the public view of the greateft happinefs in the whole. GOD is hereby reprefented as having two fchemes of action; one to make every individual the moft happy; the other to make the greateft happinefs in the whole : but it is not fuppofable that GOD created the univerfe on one fcheme, and governs it on another. If it be rectitude in the Deity to govern the univerfe, with reference to the greateft happinefs; it was certainly right in him to create it with that view. The queftion which he would propofe to himfelf, in order to act with benevolence in creating any individual; would not be, whether this creature will have more happinefs than mifery; but whether the making of this creature, will add to the quantity of univerfal happinefs; and if it will, then benevolence requires the creation. It was doubtlefs with this view that GOD created every being who exifts. Creating goodnefs in GOD does not imply a regard to the happinefs of the individual created, but to the happinefs of the whole; and he will make creation fubferve this end, though many individuals may be miferable. We depraved mortals have fo many felfifh, partial and private feelings; that it is very difficult for us to reafon on the things of GOD, in which fuch feelings have no place. It is hard for us to feel and reafon on the benevolent plan of GOD ; ef-

pecially when we think it will turn againſt ourſelves. It appears that the argument for the ſalvation of all men, derived from the particular
creating goodneſs of God, is founded on a diſtinction between creating and governing goodneſs,
for which there is no manner of foundation.
God is hereby repreſented as a changeable being,
beginning with one ſcheme and ending with a-
nother; whereas there is every reaſon to ſuppoſe,
both from the nature of an infinite being, and ⋅
from the word of revelation; that the ſcheme of
his counſel is uniform throughout, and from eternity, and that he hath had a perpetual regard to
it both in creating and governing.

Sec. 9. Objection. The doctrine of the eternal ſalvation of ſome, and the eternal miſery of
others, repreſents God as exerciſing an odious partiality, in the choice of thoſe who are to be the
ſubjects of happineſs and miſery.

Answer. It here becomes neceſſary for us to
form true ideas of partiality and impartiality.
The common feelings of mankind fix an odium on
partiality, and it is doubtleſs juſt thus to do; but
we ought very exactly to know in what it conſiſts,
before we apply the odium, either to a ſcheme of
belief or to a particular truth. A confuſed manner of thinking is one cauſe of the objections
brought againſt the truths of revelation, and in
no inſtance more eminently than in the preſent.
It is preſumed that the following things will be
conceded:

1ſt. Impartiality did not require that God
ſhould originally create all beings exactly alike.
As there were different purpoſes to accompliſh in
the univerſe, there muſt be creatures of different
capacities and characters, adapted to the part which
they were deſtined to act, and to the uſe which is

S

to be made of them.   God cannot be charged
with partiality in creating beings very unlike each
other, when different purposes are to be effected
by their existence.   A father is not partial in
giving a very different education to two sons, one
of which is destined to one employment, and the
other to another employment.—A prince is not
partial in appointing one of his subjects, to an
employment much more honourable than is af-
signed to the other, and all expected of him is that
he assign each one, in the manner that will most
promote public good.   God did not create two
beings for the same purpose ; and if created for
two purposes, they must be made different, or
else not be made in the best manner, for the purposes to which they were destined.

2dly. Impartiality doth not require that all
beings be treated alike.   There is no maxim to
which the common sense of men more universally
assents, than this ; that all ought to be treated
according to what they are.   To treat two beings
in the same manner, who are of different characters ; instead of being impartial, would instantly
be called the most odious partiality.

It appears therefore, that partiality in the odious sense of the word, doth not consist ; either in
creating beings very unlike to each other, or treating them differently.   Justice and public good require this, and we must look to some other cause
to know in what an odious partiality consists.
And I think it consists in acting from private and
selfish motives, and in nothing else.   If a man in
judging between his neigbour and himself, judges selfishly, his judgment is partial.   If he be called to judge between two neighbours, and shows
more favour to one than to the other, on account
of some interested connexion with one of them ; in
this case he is partial, and his partiality arises

from his acting on a private and selfish motive, and on this account an odium is affixed to his conduct. If a prince in the appointment to a public office, appoints his son to the exclusion of a good subject ; when it is evident that the subject would execute the office in a better manner, in that case we call him partial ; that is, he acts on private and selfish motives, and the odium of partiality is the same as the odium of selfishness. If it be evident that the son will execute the office in a better manner for the public than the subject ; we still call the prince impartial, though a son be appointed. I might go on in a thousand instances, and show that the odium of partiality, arises from selfishness or acting on private motives to the exclusion of a greater good ; and that impartiality, which is allowed to be the glory of a governor, and the thing which entitles him to confidence, consists in such principles and actions, as will promote the general benefit. Having fixed with some degree of precision, what is meant by partiality and impartiality ; and whence the odium of one, and the honor of the other arises ; we are now prepared to consider the objection, *That the doctrine of the eternal salvation of some, and the eternal misery of others, represents God as exercising an odious partiality, in the choice of those who are to be the subjects of happiness and misery.*

If in the choice of these persons respectively, God acts wholly on principles of the greatest good, there is no partiality in the matter. In treating this subject, it has commonly been said that God acts as a sovereign. In a sovereign manner he chooses one and leaves another. The meaning of his acting as a sovereign, is not that he acts without reason ; but only that there is no meritorious cause in the person chosen to salvation, why he should be chosen in preference to another. He draws the motive of his choice from the nature of that fyftem, which he means to bring to the higheft condition of bleffednefs; and this fyftem, is the infinite wifdom and goodnefs of his own nature acted out, in producing the greateft quantity of good in the whole; fo that it may fairly be faid, the motive of his fovereign acting is drawn from within himfelf; but though drawn from within himfelf it is not without reafon. It is God's holy nature from which he cannot deviate to regard the public good, and do every thing in fubferviency to that. Acting out his own nature, is feeking the general benefit; and through eternity there will be no feparation between them. We, through the fcantinefs of our underftanding, cannot tell who ought to be chofen to eternal happinefs and who paffed by, on the principle of promoting the greateft good. Infinite wifdom can tell; and on this principle, made the choice what beings to create; how to create them; what capacities and what moral character to give them; whom to choofe to falvation; and whom to leave in their fins. All was done by God from love to the greateft good, directed by infinite knowledge and fkill; and with a defign to produce the moft bleffed univerfe.—Suppofe that myfelf and my neighbor are two finners, of a bafe character and deferving nothing but evil. Infinite wifdom, fees, that it will moft promote the good of the whole, to have my neighbour chofen to holinefs and happinefs, and myfelf left to fin and mifery; and the choice is accordingly made. In this cafe, can I charge an infinite God with partiality, or any thing that is private, felfifh, odious or cruel? Very far from this, for he is acting in the higheft perfection of goodnefs. My neighbour muft forever afcribe his falvation to unmerited grace; I muft afcribe

my being left to my own bafenefs, and God's regard to a greater good than mine, and we muft
both confefs, that Jehovah has in the whole been
an impartial God. The univerfe will forever
applaud, both the wifdom and goodnefs of his
choice.

Let us now view what would be the effect of
a contrary conduct in God. Suppofe, he had
alfo chofen me to falvation, when he knew I had
no claim of defert, and alfo that the choice would
leffen the glory, perfection, and happinefs of the
univerfe. Would not this choice bring him directly under the charge of partiality, and of acting
with reference to a private and feparate intereft,
and not the intereft of the whole? Here is the
place in which the charge of an odious partiality
would arife, and not in paffing me by. Thus
ends the loud-mouthed charge, of a God odioufly
partial in appointing fome to happinefs, and others to mifery. The odious partiality is not in
God, but in the objector himfelf. He is fo felfifh;
he acts, and feels, and judges fo much on interefted motives, that he cannot fee the beauty and
fitnefs of the divine conduct, in acting on motives
different from him. Thus will end almoft every
objection againft the fcripture doctrine of eternal
happinefs and mifery. The very objections a-
gainft the doctrine, on being examined terminate
in its eftablifhment; and fhow God's rectitude
to be more glorious than would have been known,
if fuch objections had not been made.

Sec. 10. Objection. How are the gofpel invitations, many of which are expreffed in very
general terms, confiftent with the eternal mifery
of great numbers to whom they are made? God
faith, look unto me all ye ends of the earth and
be faved. (Ifaiah xlv. 19.) Are fuch invitations
as thefe confiftent with fincerity, if God doth not

intend effectually to save all those to whom they are made? Is there not some sense, in which salvation is offered to all men, and how can the offer be an honest one, if GOD doth not intend effectually to assist all sinners in complying with it; and does not an invitation, in such a case as the sinner's is, imply a promise?

ANSWER. IN attending to this objection, we ought very carefully to inquire, what is meant by a gospel invitation. Some seem to conceive, that a gospel invitation, is something different both from the commands and from the promises of GOD; and that though it be not an absolute promise, it does in some sense lay GOD under an obligation, to exert his whole infinite power in saving the sinner to whom the invitation is made. But it is conceived there is no such thing, and that all those addresses of GOD to men, which have commonly been called gospel invitations; are direct promises; or direct commands; or partaking of both. The greater part of what have been called gospel invitations, are direct promises. The prophet saith, *ho! every one that thirsteth, come ye to the waters,* and he adds the promise, *I will make an everlasting covenant with you, even the sure mercies of David.* This invitation is a promise; the character to which it is made, is described by the word thirsteth, meaning one who desires holiness, and a real desire of holiness, is being holy. Thirsting, in the scriptural use of the word, means a very sensible degree and exercise of holy desires. David used that word to describe his highest longings after GOD. CHRIST says, *come unto me all ye who labor and are heavy laden, and I will give you rest.* This is a promise. Who are the persons heavy laden with sin? They are truly gracious persons, and no other. Those, whose hearts are changed, to loathe every wrong thing,

The unfanctified finner, may be heavy laden with a fear of mifery, and with thofe fruits of fin which he finds in himfelf; but he is not heavy laden with fin itfelf, for if he were, he would loathe it, become a penitent, ferve God with delight, and this would entitle him to the promife. God hath multiplied his promifes to all holy and penitent perfons, that they may have ftrong confolation in his grace. He hath made particular promifes to every particular grace. But how the promifes, made to thofe who have complied with the terms of falvation, fhould be confidered as invitations to thofe who have never complied with the terms of falvation; or how they are an invitation, of fuch a nature as lays God under an obligation to fave all men, it is believed can never be fhown. All that can be gathered from thefe promifes which are exprefled by way of invitation, is this; that God will treat as being gracious, thofe who have become gracious. So far are they from an encouragement of all men being faved; that they are a ftrong implication of the contrary; for if God had defigned falvation for all men, what need would there have been of thefe particular promifes, to a gracious ftate of the heart. God's having confined his promifed bleffings to a particular character, ftrongly implies, that thofe who are not of this character can never have them.

It was faid, that what have been called gofpel invitations, are either direct promifes; or direct commands; or comprehending both. We have confidered them in the nature of promifes, and find that they give no encouragement for the falvation of all men; but imply the contrary.—— Some of the gofpel invitations are direct commands; do thofe lay God under any obligation, or give any encouragement to the perfons to

whom they are made, that GOD will fave them?
Look unto me all ye ends of the earth and be faved.
Hearken unto me, O ye children. Hear *inftruction*
and be wife, and refufe it not. Thefe are ftrictly
and literally commands, as much as the precepts
of the law, *thou fhalt not kill, or thou fhalt not fteal.*
The nature of our relation to GOD is fuch, as does
not admit of any invitation from him to us, unlefs by invitation we mean the fame, as a command. In tranfactions between men, there may
be a difference in the meaning of the two words ;
but it is not fo in the addrefs of GOD to finners.
If I exprefs a defire to my child that he fhould
walk with me, this is to all intents and purpofes
a command ; for the expreffion of my defire
brings the child under a moral obligation to comply. If I exprefs a fimilar defire to my neighbor ; this may be confidered as no more than an
invitation, for it does not appear, that my neighbor is under any moral obligation to comply with
my defire. There is this difference in the meaning of the two words when applied to tranfactions
between men ; but this is a difference which does
not take place in the expreffion of GOD's will to
finners. Every expreffion of his defire carries
with it the force of a command. Believe thou
in the LORD JESUS CHRIST ; or I befeech thee to
believe in the LORD JESUS, coming from GOD,
amount to the fame thing in all refpects, and are
both of them as pofitive commands, as the ten
commandments. To repent of fin through
CHRIST ; to believe in CHRIST ; to come to him
and truft in him for falvation ; together with all
evangelical exercifes, fince the publication of the
gofpel, are become moral duties incumbent on
every finner ; and are as proper matter of command, as the moral duties of loving GOD or of
fpeaking the truth were in the original moral law.

So that thefe gofpel invitations are commands, and in no effential refpect to be diftinguifhed from them.---The queftion recurs, do GOD's commands to all men, lay him under any obligation, or give any encouragement, that all fhall be faved? I will begin my anfwer to this queftion, by afking fome other queftions. In the beginning GOD doubtlefs commanded the angels who are now fallen, to continue in holy love and obedience; and did that command lay him under any obligation to preferve them in rectitude? If it did, it appears that the moft holy GOD is a breaker of his obligations, in not preventing their fin. GOD commanded our firft parents to obey the whole law; but they difobeyed, and in confequence of their fin, all their pofterity are finners. Can it be fuppofed that GOD violated obligation in this matter? This fuppofition would indeed be fhifting the fcene. It would remove fin from earth to heaven, and arraign infinite majefty at the bar of a worm of the duft.

THE commands to evangelical obedience do not imply any more obligation on GOD, to affift the perfon to whom they are made, than the original commands of the moral law did.—GOD's commands are not the origin of obligation. The origin of obligation, is in the infinite nature of God, our own nature, and the relation we bear to him and his creatures. Obligation had its origin antecedent to any precept of the law or gofpel. Moral and evangelical precepts only exprefs our obligations. They exprefs GOD's holy character; our duty to that character; and the awful confequences of not doing our duty: but they are no expreffion of any obligation in GOD to affift us fpecially in doing our duty. Further, the notion, that GOD's commands carry with them

T

an obligation on his part, specially to assist the
commanded persons in obedience; will totally
exclude sin from the universe, or make the infinitely holy GOD himself the only sinner. All holiness is matter of command; all unholiness is
matter of prohibition; if commands and prohibitions carry with them any obligation on GOD,
it is he who is blameable for the want of holiness,
and for the commission of crimes.

ON this subject, in order to vindicate the divine
sincerity, in what have been called gospel invitations to those who never repent, I ought to observe
further. That these invitations, if that word be
the most pleasing to any, are exactly the same in
all respects, to those who do repent, and to those
who never repent. They hold forth the same
truth to each; they give the same assistance to
each; and produce no effects in one, which they
do not produce in the other. So that from GOD's
sovereign grace to those who repent, there is no
evidence of any insincerity to such as do not repent.

IT is not the gospel invitation which saves the
redeemed. They go on resisting it like other
sinners; and they treat it as others do, until GOD
in sovereign power renews their hearts. It is
not the gospel call, but the holy spirit who changes
their heart, and we might as well say that GOD is
insincere in the gospel invitation to those who
are saved; because he did not renew them sooner,
as we may that he is insincere to those whom he
never renews. The gospel command, and the
renewing power of GOD are two things; one
does not imply the other; and they may go together or they may be separated, as infinite wisdom sees best. The gospel command expresses
the character of GOD, with our duty and obligation to him, and no more. Every invitation ex-

presses the same, either with or without a promise ; and men have no right to suppose concerning themselves or others, that they shall be saved, until they come within the limits of a promise. Adam or the fallen angels after their apostacy, had as much right to charge GOD with insincerity in not preserving their rectitude, as impenitent sinners have for not bringing them to eternal salvation. GOD is therefore in the highest degree sincere, in every part of his word which can be called gospel invitations to sinners. For such invitations are either ; first, promises to a certain character, which will be eternally fulfilled to all who become of that character. Or secondly, these invitations are commands, and GOD is as sincere in commanding those who never do their duty, as he is in commanding those who do it. There is equal propriety that he should command in the two cases. GOD never could be a faithful moral governor in this sinful world, unless he did command sinners and express his sense of their duty, and it is a most unfounded consequence that because GOD is faithful all men will be saved.

I HAVE dwelt so long on this point, because many conceive· there is something in the scriptures, which they call gospel invitations or encouragements to sinners, which are not promises, but still bring GOD under some kind of obligation to save men, and that make the state of the sinner more safe. But there is not one encouragement, that is different in its nature from the words of Christ ; he that believeth shall be saved, but he that believeth not shall be damned. This is all the encouragement that ought to be, or that is necessary in such a case. Men are either holy or unholy ; if holy it is fitting they should have a promise ; if unholy it is fitting they should be threatened, and treated according to their character.

There is no half way character, between the renewed and unrenewed; and it is not therefore fit there should be any half way promises.—If thou believeſt thou ſhall be ſaved, is encouragement enough to a ſinner; for it declares what his duty is, and ſets before him a rational motive to compliance. Any other manner of treating ſinners, would be directly calculated to make them ſecure in their ſin. It is therefore a matter of high importance, that men have juſt ideas of what have commonly been called goſpel invitations, as conſiſting wholly in commands and promiſes. The promiſory part is moſt ſtrictly limited to evangelical holineſs, and implies an awful threatning to the want of holineſs. The commandatory or preceptive part declares the ſinners preſent duty, and contains no promiſe of future grace to the delaying ſinner, or of final ſalvation to the dying impenitent.

SEC. 11. OBJECTION. Thoſe who believe there will be eternal puniſhment, allow that the merits of JESUS CHRIST are ſufficient for the ſalvation of all men; and if ſufficient is it not juſt that all ſhould be ſaved?

ANSWER. This objection leads us to conſider the nature of the goſpel atonement by ſuffering; and on what grounds it was required by GOD, and is abſolutely neceſſary for the forgiveneſs of ſinners. By this we ſhall ſee the kind of ſufficiency there is in it for the ſalvation of all men, and whether it be ſuch a kind of ſufficiency, as makes ſalvation a matter of juſtice to them. The nature of holineſs or benevolence doth not admit that temper, which we commonly call revenge. Revenge is a delight in miſery, or a pleaſure in ſeeing another being wretched. It ſuppoſes the idea, that ſeeing another miſerable is a good to the mind; but there is nothing like this in the

divine mind. GOD takes no pleaſure in the nature of miſery, or in beholding it for its own
ſake. Seeing the pain of a ſinner, is no good to
GOD, or to any one mind in that holy univerſe,
the rights and privileges of which he protects.
The infinite wiſdom of GOD, never introduced
miſery into the ſyſtem, under an idea that the beholding of pain, would be a good, either to him or
any holy mind. GOD conſidered it as evil or undeſirable in its own nature, when he introduced
it; and he juſtified the introduction to himſelf,
on this reaſon, that there would be more happineſs in the univerſe with the exiſtence of miſery,
than there could be without it. The nature of
holineſs in GOD and in creaturès, is the ſame.
What it is in creatures we learn from the divine
commands. CHRIST ſays, *love your enemies, pray
for them—and do them good.* The meaning of
which is, take no pleaſure in the miſery of enemies; but on the contrary, take pleaſure in doing
them good, when there are no reaſons of a public
nature againſt it; and in a caſe, where doing
good to our enemies, would injure the public
more than it benefits them, the obligation to do
good to our enemies ceaſes, for our obligation to
the public body of intelligence, is greater than it
can be to any individual.

　The puniſhment of ſin, cannot therefore be
put upon a footing with the payment of a pecuniary debt: In the caſe of a pecuniary debt, the
debtor has received of the creditor, a real good;
and is under obligation to return a like quantity
of real good; and when a like quantity of real
good is returned the obligation ceaſes. But in
the puniſhment of ſin there is no ſuch thing.
When GOD gave the moral law, he annexed miſery as a penalty, and why did he do it? Will
the eternal miſery of the ſinner be in itſelf a real

good to God, the beholding of which will be the repayment of a good the sinner has received from him? This certainly can not be, because neither misery in itself nor the seeing of it can be any good to God.

If we can tell why misery was a proper penalty of the law; it will lead us to see why Christ's atoning sufferings were necessary, for the reason is the same in both cases. To bring this subject into view, I will attempt to explain the following things:

1st. Why misery was the proper penalty of disobedience to the law.

2d. Why the attoning sufferings of Christ were necessary in the gospel.

3d. In what sense Christ did stand in the place of sinners.

4th. Whether the sufferings of Christ and the sinner are the same in kind.

In order to see why misery was a proper penalty of the law, I will recur to the feelings of a penitent before God, when he comes to true repentance. The feelings of such a mind, under the sanctifying influence of the spirit of all knowledge, are a more sure guide, than all the philosophical researches in the world. I believe that every penitent will agree to the following description. " I am worthy of all this punishment. I am " justly condemned by the law of God, and it is " perfectly fit that he should make me miserable. " But why is it fit he should make me miserable, " and why did he annex misery as the penalty of ". the law which condemns me? Will my misery " be any good to him; will it make him happy; " will he delight in looking on my torment? " No! he is too good a God for this, and it en- " hances my guilt, that I have sinned against so " good a God. Will my misery be the repay-

" ment, or a reward to him for the good I have
" received at his hands? Neither can it be this.
" The good I have received of him is loſt out of
" my hands, and I can never repay it. My miſ-
" ery if it ſhould be eternal will never be a repay-
" ment to GOD of the good I have received.
" Why then ſhould GOD make me miſerable, and
" why do I deſerve it? The reaſon is this. My
" character and temper is a moſt unreaſonable
" and baſe one—I feel, I know it to be ſuch;
" and GOD in juſtice to himſelf, and to the whole
" holy univerſe ought to expreſs his ſenſe of my
" baſeneſs. He ought to bear a teſtimony againſt
" me and my practice, and the nature of things,
" doth not admit any other way under the law,
" but by making me miſerable. GOD infinitely
" abhors my whole character; my temper; my
" practice; my tranſgreſſion of a law that is per-
" fectly juſt; and he is glorious in thus abhor-
" ing me. The happineſs of the holy univerſe
" depends on having a juſt view of GOD's char-
" acter. Therefore in juſtice both to himſelf
" and his kingdom, he will expreſs his ſenſe of
" ſin and its turpitude; and puniſhment is the
" natural way of manifeſting this expreſſion."
Such I think will be the ſentiments of a penitent on conſidering himſelf expoſed to the penalty of the law. Theſe are the reaſons which
ſhow him the rectitude of GOD in ordaining and
inflicting eternal miſery. And I alſo believe theſe
penitential feelings, without the aid of philoſophy,
reach the whole truth in this matter; and ſhow
the grounds, on which it is infinitely reaſonable
that eternal miſery ſhould be the penalty of the
law. Not becauſe GOD or the holy univerſe delight in miſery; not becauſe the miſery of the ſinner is the refunding of that good he had received
from GOD, or of any equivalent to it; for it never

can be repaid. The finners mifery is the only expreffion or manifeftation, admitted in the ftructure of nature, of God's fenfe of the finners bafenefs; of his guilt in violating a holy obligation; of the importance that the law be obeyed; and of the holy difpleafure that arifes in every good mind againft fuch a character as the finner poffeffes.

SUFFER me to inquire, in what other way could thefe truths be expreffed, but by the finners mifery? Doth nature without a gofpel admit of any other; and the penalties of the law were ordained according to the exifting nature of things, and without reference to a gofpel which has fucceeded. God's forbidding fin, or his faying it to be wrong after committed, would be no evidence of thefe truths; if he treated the holy and the unholy alike, and made one the fubject of as much happinefs as the other.

WE fee therefore, that the reafon why mifery was annexed as the penalty of the law, was not becaufe God delights in mifery; it was not becaufe any repayment would be made to God for a good which he firft beftowed on the finner; but folely as an expreffion of certain moral truths (which have been mentioned above) and thefe could not in the nature of things, be fo well expreffed by any other means.

2dly. WE are hereby prepared, to fee why the atoning fufferings of CHRIST were neceffary in the gofpel fcheme, and how they become efficacious for the falvation of repenting finners. The atoning fufferings of CHRIST, were neceffary in the Gofpel fcheme, for the fame reafon, as the eternal mifery of the finner was under the law; to make a difplay of God's moral character—of his righteoufnefs as king of the univerfe—of his fenfe of the turpitude of the finners principles and practice—and also the nature of benevolence, in its high and infinite source, Godhead himself. If God had been governed by revenge or personal resentment against the sinner, there would have been no possibility of a gospel ; and the transgressor must have borne the necessary misery himself. But as the divine motive, in this matter, was solely the public benefit; and as the sinners misery was solely to answer a public and governmental end, God might accept as a substitute, whatever would answer the same purposes in government, and equally conduce to the blessedness of the universe. Whatever would make an equal display of the same truths, might be accepted in the stead of the sinner's eternal misery. The sufferings of Christ, who was both God and man, would in a limited time make this display in a higher degree than the eternal sufferings of the whole universe ; and therefore his sufferings might be accepted by God in justice to his government, in the stead of so many sinners, as infinite wisdom saw it would be best to sanctify and forgive. By the suffering of Christ, all those truths which relate to the divine character, the support of his government, and the unchangeable obligation of the law, are seen in a brighter manner, than they could be by any suffering of the sinner under the law. It is thus that the gospel opens a greater view of God and the holy system, and prepares the way for higher happiness.

3dly. In what sense did Christ stand in the place of sinners ? By coming into the place of guilty men, he did not become a sinner ; for it is said that he was *without sin,* that he knew no sin ; he was the lamb without spot and without blemish ; he was the fathers son with whom he is well pleased.—There was no sense in which any

moral turpitude or baseness was found in him.——
His own nature had no moral turpitude in it.——
Neither did GOD, as some seem to conceive, by
a sovereign act of power transfer the whole moral
turpitude of sinners, and make it the moral turpitude of CHRIST. There are two reasons why
this could not be the case. First, it is impossible in the nature of things. It is just as impossible
to make the moral turpitude of one being, the moral turpitude of another being ; as it is to make
a thing to be, and not to be, at the same time ;
and is indeed the same kind of impossibility. After the utmost pains, we cannot bring our minds
to conceive the possibility of it.——Secondly, if we
were to allow, that the moral turpitude of sinners
might become the moral turpitude of CHRIST ;
it is conceived that he would thereby become totally disqualified to act the part of a Saviour ;
and that it would be as inconsistent with the infinite holiness of GOD, to negociate the great work
of redemption with him, as with the sinner himself. The turpitude of the sinner must forever
remain his own. If he be sanctified, forgiven and
brought to Heaven ; he must look back upon his
own sins, and say, " These sins are mine—the
" turpitude of them is mine—and though I am
" now in Heaven, I am unworthy of being here.
" CHRIST stood in my place to suffer, and de-
" liver me from eternal misery. He purchased
" the spirit to change my base temper, but he
" never made my sin his own, for that was in the
" nature of things impossible, and on my own ac-
" count I have no claim to Heaven." If the
saint in Heaven, cannot claim his place there as
an act of justice to himself. even after he has
complied with the Gospel by fai h and repentance ;
it is hard to conceive, how all men may say, it
is just they should be saved, because there is a

fufficiency in the merits of Christ for the falvation of a whole world.

The true fenfe of Christ's ftanding in the place of finners is this. According to the will of the father and with his own choice, he hath by obedience and fuffering made a difplay of certain moral truths before mentioned, which the eternal mifery of thofe who are forgiven was neceffary for difplaying ; fo that their mifery is not now neceffary for the good government of the univerfe. The reafon that their eternal fuffering was fit under the law, was to make this difplay ; the neceffity of which hath now ceafed, if God be pleafed to fanctify and forgive through Christ ; but if he be not pleafed to fanctify them through Christ, the neceffity doth not ceafe. The meritorious caufe on which he forgives is the atoning fufferings of his fon ; the moving caufe in his own mind, to provide the gofpel atonement and pardon the finner on account of it, was his own goodnefs and the general good. So many as the general good requires he will fanctify and pardon, and no more.

If the fufferings of the finner under the law, or of Jesus Christ in the gofpel, be not confidered as the repayment of a good to God, in the ftead of one he had beftowed on the finner, but only as a difplay of truth ; it is not apprehended that the finner can have any claim to falvation becaufe of the infinite fufficiency of Christ's merits. There does not feem to be any other claim of juftice in this cafe, than man had before a Saviour was promifed. Suppofe that after the apoftacy, man had been informed ; God can make fuch a difplay of himfelf, of his government, and of all truth, as will render your falvation poffible in confiftency with the general good ; but this difplay muft be made by himfelf, and you can

have no part in making it. Would such information have given man any right to expect salvation as a matter of justice? I think it certainly
would not. And are not the cases similar? God
has made the display—it is all his own work—
devised by his wisdom and executed by his power
and sufficiency; but what sinner can in justice
claim a right to the benefits of what God hath
done. So far as respects the sinner, God had a
perfect right to make the provision or omit
making it; and when made, he has a right to
extend the benefit of it to whom he pleases; either to one man, or to all men, as his wisdom
judges best. And the rule by which he will be
directed in the extension of these benefits is the
general good. If he sees that the extension of
it to all men will make the greatest quantity of
happiness in the universe, it will be thus extended; if he sees that it will be better to take part,
and leave part, as we suppose his word informs
us, part will be omitted, and in the omission no
injustice is done to them.

4th. It does not appear that the Saviour endured the same kind of sufferings, in all respects,
as those who are saved by him, must have endured, if they had been left to perish. Sundry
things which we must suppose will be essential
parts of the sinner's suffering, Christ never did
endure. He never felt the stings of an accusing,
condemning conscience. He never felt a pain of
heart in seeing the holy government of God tri-
umphant and glorious. He never looked upon
God with awful and tormenting fear. He never
felt that soul-piercing misery, which arises from a
conflict between reason and passion. He never
felt the anguish of despair. All these, which we
must suppose to be principal sources of misery to
the sinner, were never endured by Jesus Christ.

If there had been an actual transfer of the finner's turpitude to JESUS CHRIST; or if the finner's mifery was a real good to GOD, in repayment of one which had been beftowed; it feems as though it would have been fit, that CHRIST fhould fuffer the fame kind of mifery as muft have been endured by the finner to fatisfy the law. But on the principles, which have been mentioned in this difcourfe, there was no need of the fame kind of mifery. It does not appear, if thofe who are now faved, had fuffered in their own perfons; that they would all have fuffered mifery of the fame kind, in all refpects, in order to anfwer the end of punifhment. In fome refpects, all finful beings muft by the very laws of nature be miferable in the fame way; but there is no reafon to conclude, any particular mifery the fame in all refpects, is neceffary as a penalty to the law. The wifdom of GOD was abundantly able to determine, what kind of fuffering the Saviour fhould endure, in order to anfwer the end of fuffering. And whatever it may have been, it was fufficient to make all that difplay of GOD, and of truth, which was neceffary for the good government of the univerfe, and higheft glory of GOD. In defcribing the finner's liablenefs to punifhment, fome have ufed the phrafe, *of a debt due to divine juftice;* and have alfo fpoke of CHRIST as *paying that debt by his fuffering.* This hath led many to conceive, that CHRIST hath paid a debt for the finner in fuch a manner as to extinguifh the claim of juftice, in the fame fenfe as a claim is extinguifhed by the payment of a pecuniary demand, or the returning of one good for another which had been received. I do not wifh to criminate the manner of expreffion mentioned above; but only to caution againft an idea which is fuppofed to be falfe. The fenfe in which CHRIST hath paid the debt is this.

Through the obedience and suffering of CHRIST,
GOD may forgive so many sinners, as infinite wisdom seeth to be most for his glory and the good
of his kingdom; but no claim of justice is created
on the sinner's part, nor any obligation on GOD
to forgive unless his own glory require it. It depended on the sovereign pleasure of GOD whether he would accept the sufferings of another.—
Whether he would provide a Saviour.—On what
terms the benefits of CHRIST's suffering shall be
offered to sinners.—And whether he will by his
spirit assist those to whom the offer is made, to accept salvation. It is all sovereign mercy. No
demand of justice can be made by the sinner in
any stage of this glorious work.—We allow that
it is an act of justice to the Saviour himself, to save
so many as the father promised the son should be
saved in consequence of his undertaking and suffering; but this justice to CHRIST, is no justice
to the sinner; and it does not appear there was
any encouragement given to the son, that all men
should be saved through his atonement. Entirely contrary to this, CHRIST himself in praying to
the father, speaks of the world as persons distin-
guished from those whom the father had given
him. He says, that he does not pray for them;
most plainly intimating that he had no claim on
GOD for their salvation. Who the saved shall be,
and the number of them, are matters in which
the father and CHRIST the Saviour are most perfectly agreed. Infinite wisdom, from a regard to
the universal good, directs their united counsels.
The promise that CHRIST shall see of his seed until
he is satisfied will be most gloriously fulfilled; and
he will be satisfied when so many of the human
race are saved, as will bring the greatest amount
of glory to GOD, and of happiness to the universe
of created beings. Sovereign mercy doth not

act without reason and motive, and the motive according to which God determines this point, is the higheft happinefs and perfection of the great whole in holinefs. He will make the moft holy and happy univerfe that can be, and we can wifh no more!!!

Sec. 12. Objection. Allowing that the final falvation of all men, may not be determined as a thing of juftice to the finner, from the fufficiency of Christ's atonement; ftill may we not determine that the end propofed will be as extenfive as the means provided will admit ? Is it probable that infinite wifdom would provide in the atonement of Christ, means fufficient for the redemption of the whole human race, when God did not defign fuch an event fhould take place, and is it not more agreeable to God's ufual method to adapt the means and end one to the other ?

Answer. It may not perhaps be proper to call the atonement of Christ, means of falvation exactly in the fenfe that the objection fuppofes ; but omitting any further remarks on this, I obferve, that we ought in this cafe to confider the manner, in which Christ's merits became of infinite fufficiency. This fufficiency doth not arife from the quantity either of his obedience or fuffering ; but from the infinite nature of the perfon who fuffered. So that the fufficiency feems to be of the fame kind, as that of the divine power is to make more worlds than he has made ; and wifdom muft limit the application of this fufficiency. Nothing appears, but that the quantity of obedience and fuffering which was neceffary for the falvation of one, was fufficient not only for that one, but for millions more of finners than ever did or ever will exift. The fufficiency arifes not from the particular quantity of obedience and fuffering ; but from the infinite nature of him who obeyed and fuffered. If there be a fitnefs on this ground that all men be faved ; left fome of the fufficiency of CHRIST's merits fhould be loft, and left the means be over proportioned to the end ; there feems to be the fame kind of fitnefs that infinite power fhould go on forever, introducing finners into being and faving them, in order to prevent this lofs. There is in the natural world, a fufficiency of light from the fun, to give day to ten times more men than ever exifted ; but who ever from this confideration determined, that it was fit infinite power fhould create ten times the number of men that have been, to prevent this lofs of light.

IF GOD had made only ten creatures, the whole moral law would have been neceffary to inftruct and guide them to happinefs. The law is as fufficient for millions, as for ten. The moral law is as much the means of happinefs as the merits of CHRIST are ; and we may as juftly determine that it was fit GOD fhould create double the number of creatures, that he has created, becaufe the law is fufficient to guide and inftruct them in duty ; as we may that all men will be faved becaufe there is a fufficiency in the merits of CHRIST. In all thefe cafes, there is nothing to be determined, from what we call the fufficiency of means, how far there will be an actual application. Wifdom will determine how far the application ought to be made ; and infinite goodnefs and power by the fufficiency of CHRIST's merits will fave fo many men, as wifdom knows to be neceffary for the greateft good of the whole.

SEC. 13. OBJECTION. WAS not GOD the Son united to human nature ; does not human nature include all men ; and may not all to whom CHRIST was united expect falvation ?

Answer. This objection, which many profess appears to them of great force, derives all its plausibility from an inattention to the right use and meaning of words. In the strict meaning of words Christ never did unite himself to human nature.

1st. Human nature is only a general or abstract name. It doth not mean any individual, but only something that is common to all individual men. It appears therefore, that human nature doth not mean an actual being ; but is only an ideal existence or thing of our own imagination. To make this familiar to the reader I will give several examples. Snow is white ; milk is white ; and many other things. Observing this, we form the abstract or general name of whiteness to describe the quality, wherever it is found. But what is whiteness separate from all these particular substances, in which it exists ? It is only ideal, and not a real existence. Cicero, Paul, and Julius Cæsar possessed certain powers and qualities which are common to all men. These qualities, we separate or abstract from all the qualities, that were peculiar to Cicero, Paul, Julius Cæsar or any other individual ; and when thus separated, we call them human nature. But this human nature is an ideal and not a real existence ; because every individual hath some qualities or powers not included in it. Human nature is an abstract name, the ingredients of which are combined in an arbitrary manner, by the will and imagination of men ; and it is not a real existence. There is therefore no strict propriety, in saying that Jesus Christ was united to human nature. If it should be said, that this was done by a divine constitution ; this doth not help the matter : for a divine constitution cannot unite a real and an ideal exist-

W

ence.   Or if it fhould be faid, that this was done
ideally to anfwer a purpofe in law and government; neither doth this obviate the difficulty.
Though men fpeak of fictions of law, to anfwer
their own purpofes ; there is no room to fuppofe,
that an infinitely wife and holy GOD hath need of
thefe fictions in his government.

I DO not recollect any paffages of fcripture,
more defcriptive of the union of the GOD MAN
CHRIST JESUS, than the following. Phil. ii. 6,
7, 8. *Who being in the form of* GOD, *thought it no
robbery to be equal with* GOD ; *but made himfelf of
no reputation, and took upon him the form of a fervant, and was made in the likenefs of men ; and being found in fafhion as a man, he humbled himfelf,
and became obedient unto death, even the death of
the crofs.* Heb. ii. 16. *For verily, he took not on
him the nature of angels, but the feed of Abraham.*
Innumerable other paffages fpeak of him as being
a man, and as having the qualities of a particular
man.   But in all that is faid on this fubject, there
is no intimation of a general union to that abftract,
ideal thing which we call human nature ; and the
fcriptures feem to preferve the moft logical accura-
cy on this point.

IT is very probable, that many both in writing
and fpeaking, have ufed the defcription; of the
Son of GOD being united to human nature ; when
all they intended, was that GOD the Son by a
myfterious natural union, was joined to the man
CHRIST JESUS.   I do not know that it is to be
expected from men, always to ufe fuch caution
in their expreffions, that they cannot be perverted;
or that the imperfection of language will permit
it ; and the only remedy is, when particular expreffions are mifapplied, to explain the mifapplication, and to fubftitute, if poffible, fome other
defcription that is lefs liable to perverfion.

2dly. God the Son was united to the particular man CHRIST JESUS. The manner of union between the God and the man, is totally inexplicable; nor is it feen that any benefit would refult to us from comprehending it. The union of our own fouls and bodies is inexplicable, but this doth not prevent our receiving all benefits refulting from the union. The benefits which refult immediately and directly from this union between God the Son and the man CHRIST, will belong to him eternally and to no other. The benefits which come to the faved, do not refult immediately from that union itfelf; but from CHRIST's obedience and fufferings, which he was enabled to perform and undergo in confequence of a union between his two natures. The natural union between God the Son and the man CHRIST, was to prepare him to be and to do that, through which finners might be faved. The benefits immediately refulting from that union, were; that it enabled him in his own perfon and nature to make a fufficient atonement for fin; in confequence of which, in his own perfon and nature, *he was highly exalted and a name given him above every name, that at the name of Jesus every knee fhould bow.* God was pleafed to give him this perfonal reward for his obedience and fufferings. On the fuppofition that God the Son was united to human nature, in the manner I have endeavored to refute, the following abfurd confequences would arife. That · the God man Saviour was a real finner, and fuffered for his own fins. That all men are part of the mediator, fo that every finner is forgiven through an atonement made by himfelf. Alfo if CHRIST is united to human nature, the benefits juft now mentioned as refulting immediately from that union, and which have commonly been confidered as perfonal benefits acquired only by CHRIST himfelf, may fairly be extended to all mankind ; and we may fitly fay of them, they have a name given them above every name, that at their names every knee fhould bow, and that every tongue fhould confefs, that they are Lords to the glory of GOD the father ; in fhort, that all men are mediators and fhall reign as fuch.

THE truth is, the GOD was not united to human nature; but only to the man CHRIST JESUS, who was an individual, innocent, of miraculous birth, and perfonally diftinct from all the fons of men. GOD the Son was united to this innocent creature, preparatory to his acting the part of a mediator ; and after he had fuffered, he received his own peculiar and proper reward, in which no other creature will ever fhare.

3dly. IT is a fpiritual union between CHRIST and believers, which entitles them to falvation ; and this is a thing entirely different from the union of GOD the fon, to the man CHRIST JESUS. His union to the man CHRIST JESUS, was a work of his own wifdom and power, and neither the confent of men's wills nor the moral ftate of their hearts, had any thing to do in it ; for it was compleated and carried into full effect, before many finners had an exiftence. That union with CHRIST which entitles to falvation, is formed between him and every foul individually that is to be faved. It is a moral union, confifting in love, repentance and faith. Faith is that exercife of the renewed heart, which meets the promife, and on the part of the believer, forms a covenant relation. Promifes are alfo made to other gracious exercifes ; becaufe one grace implies all other graces in the heart. All the chriftian graces, are only branches or exercifes of love, in different circumftances of acting, and of beholding truth. The union of believers, to God and Christ is expreſſed many ways in the word of God. By their being one in God; denoting a oneneſs of deſign and intereſt, through a love of the ſame objects and truths. By Christ being in them; denoting the inward action and ſanctifying power of his ſpirit. By their abiding in Christ, and he in them; deſcriptive of the ſpiritual communication between him and the hearts of his children. By the union between the vine and its branches; denoting, that holineſs, light, and comfort, and their whole ſpiritual nouriſhment, is derived through Christ. By the union between huſband and wife; denoting the love and ſameneſs of intereſt there is between Christ and his people. By the union between the head and the other members of the body; intimating their agreement in council and action. By the foundation and the building erected upon it; denoting that chriſtians ſtand on Christ as the foundation of their ſafety and title to Heaven.

ATTENDING to all theſe, and many other images where they are uſed, we may ſee that a moral union or ſome of its effects is meant. The holy ſpirit is the agent in forming this union, and it is therefore called, the unity of the ſpirit. Its nature and effects are always repreſented to be holineſs and ſpiritual peace; which proves, that it conſiſts in moral character flowing out in holy exerciſes. God freely juſtifies all who are thus united to his ſon. The fruits of this union, which are found in the heart, are the ſame as the fruits of the ſpirit, and its end is everlaſting life. The final ſalvation of all men cannot be inferred, from the union between God the ſon and the man Christ Jesus. With reſpect to the ſpiritual union laſt mentioned; the diſcourſes of Christ ſhow that he did not conſider all men as having it ; or entitled to its benefits.   He fpake of thofe who did not believe, receive or come to him— of thofe who hated him—of thofe whom the father had not given him—and in many other defcriptions he continually kept in view, that he was fpiritually united, only to a part of mankind, and who are included in this part, muft be known by their love, faith, repentance, fpiritual peace, and holy lives.   If we could find any proof, that all men became holy, by the fpirit of GOD working in them faith and repentance, we fhould allow the falvation of all ; but as no fuch proof appears, and much to the contrary, we cannot conceive the poffibility of any kind of union to the redeemer, that will deliver all mankind from eternal mifery.   The objection I have been now confidering, is the foundation of Mr. Relly's book on union, from which he infers the falvation of all men.   I fhall be ready as any man, to acknowledge to divine power, the poffibility of uniting in a manner above our comprehenfion, thofe beings and fubftances which have a real exiftence.   Of this kind, is the union between GOD the fon and the man CHRIST ; alfo between the fouls and bodies of men : but to tell of union between Deity, who is the higheft poffible exiftence, and the abftract idea which we call human nature, is incredible myfticifm.

SEC. 14. OBJECTION. IT has been faid, that the eternal exiftence of fin and mifery, is the probable means of increafing the glory of GOD, and the good of the univerfe.   Is this mere conjecture, or is there any reafon from the ftructure of the mind to think, that it will be the cafe ? Have we any evidence that as great happinefs could not have been caufed in fome other way ?

ANSWER 1ft. FOR believing the doctrine of future punifhment, it is by no means neceffary that we be able to defcribe how it will increafe the general good. The grand evidence of the doctrine is in the word of GOD; and not in our fpeculations. That fin and mifery exift, is a fact which cannot be denied. We alfo have fufficient evidence that GOD is a good being, under whofe government thefe things happen. We infer from the moral nature of GOD, and facts which are feen; that fin and mifery are made to exift, to promote that in which infinite goodnefs delights; and the thing in which infinite goodnefs delights, is the greateft good of the whole. When we are called upon to fhow how this will take place, we may fairly refer thofe who make the objection, to the infinite wifdom of GOD; and in our turn, we may call upon them to believe, that infinite wifdom can bring light out of darknefs, and good out of evil, in ways which are above the comprehenfion of mortals.

ANSWER 2d. THOUGH we are under no obligation, to fhow the manner in which eternal mifery will promote the greateft good; ftill it is conceived, fome remarks tending to elucidate the point, may profitably be made. To vindicate the ways of GOD to man, is a defirable thing; neither do I believe, there is any want of evidence in this matter. The difficulty lies in collecting and methodizing the evidence, in fuch a manner, that truth may come into plain view. There is an evident progreffion in the fuccefs of human inquiry on the fubject, and we muft not defpair, that in fome future day, it will be well underftood even in the church here on earth. It is proper to begin this inquiry, with a definition of happinefs. Leaving to others to give a more accurate definition, I fhall give one which will fufficiently affift in exprefling what I wifh on the point.——*Happinefs is the confcious love and en-*

joyment of an object, that is agreeable to the moral tafte of the heart. It will be remembered that I am now confidering the fubject only in a moral view.

The three following things will have an influence on the degree of happinefs. Firft, the perfection or greatnefs of the beloved object.—Secondly, the ftrength of love there is in the heart.—Thirdly, the knowledge which the mind hath of the object.

If the object of love and enjoyment, be in its nature lefs than the capacities of the mind; the happinefs muft be fmall. If the object be in itfelf fufficient, but the knowledge of it imperfect, the happinefs will ftill be fmall in degree. Or if love be weak, it will diminifh happinefs.——If the object be infinite; if a knowledge of the object be as great as the mind can receive; and if love be as great as the heart can exercife: the happinefs of that mind is great as it can be, or in other words, it is perfect.

God himfelf is the object of a holy love, and he is an infinite object. In him is included, the natural and moral fyftems of finite being; for they are only his will acted out, and brought into view; fo that a holy love of God, and of the univerfe come to the fame thing, and cannot be feparated. As God is infinite there can be no want in the object of happinefs, to thofe who know and love him.

A love of God is produced in the heart by his own fpirit, and will always be in fuch degree, as he in fovereign wifdom is pleafed to excite. The production of love, is that divine renewing by the Holy Ghoft, which the fcriptures of truth defcribe as the beginning of true religion. No means will either produce or keep it in exercife, without the fpirit of God.

THE third thing neceffary for happinefs, is a knowledge of God, who is the object of holy love. Other things being equal, the greater knowledge there is of God, the greater happinefs will be; and the exiftence of fin and mifery are neceffary, to give creatures the moft perfect conception which they can have, of moral rectitude in the deity and in the univerfe of created beings.

1ft. THE introduction of fin and mifery, hath been the means of difplaying or giving creatures a greater knowledge of God, than they could have attained without fuch an event.

God's wifdom has taken occafion from fin, to bring his love, truth, goodnefs, and juftice, indeed the whole of that infinite virtue, which fits him to be the governor of a rational univerfe; into much plainer view of creatures, than ever would have been without fin. Had creation taken place, and no apoftacy and mifery followed, it does not appear probable half as much of God could have been known by any means which the nature of things admits, as may be now known.—God's juftice in guarding the rights of the rational univerfe, againft all attacks, would have been wholly out of view. There would have been little room, compared with what there now is, to fhow his own love of that moral fyftem which he hath inftituted. Juftice is an amiable part of his rectitude, and that would have been in a great meafure out of fight—nothing of his patience and forbearance with finners could have been feen. His pity and compaffion to the miferable could not have been known. His love of holinefs and happinefs, is manifefted in a higher degree by the work of redemption than it could have been by creation and the giving of the law. The love of the father in giving his fon; the

X

the love of the fon in dying ; the love of the holy
fpirit in fanctifying, exhibit divine goodnefs
above all other defcription. The love of the fon
to the fathers honor, to the law, and to guilty
creatures, manifefted in the gofpel, which
could not have been without an apoftacy and
mifery, is unparalleled; and it is what, creation
without redemption never could have difcovered.
Indeed, the moft that men know of God's moral
nature and character comes in this way. No
one perfection of the deity can be mentioned, that
is not highly illuftrated, by the work of redemption ; for which the apoftacy and mifery of finners
was a neceffary antecedent. In this great work,·
the moral nature of God is highly acted out;
his character as a moral governor difplayed ; his
feelings in governing the univerfe unfolded;
and the end to which he is bringing all things revealed. This increafed knowledge of God, which
comes out of the apoftacy and mifery of fome part
of the univerfe is not limited to men. *The angels
defire to look into thefe things*—they come from
heaven to earth, to learn the character · and
the plenitude of perfection, which there is in
that God, whom they love and adore.

2dly. Such is the natural ftructure of created
minds ; that fin, and mifery its confequence, are
neceffary means of giving them the moft perfect
ideas of the nature and obligations to moral virtue
in fociety. The anfwer which fatan made to Eve
was very remarkable. *In the day ye eat thereof, then
your eyes fhall be opened, and ye fhall be as Gods,
knowing good and evil.* Though his defign was in-
fidious and vile, he perhaps told the woman nothing but what was in a fenfe true. That it fhould
increafe their doctrinal and fpeculative knowledge,
both of good and evil. The deceiver had made
the experiment, and though by a bad heart he was
rendered incapable of feeing the moral glory of

GOD; his knowledge of evil might be the means, of giving him greater doctrinal knowledge of the nature of good, than he had before his apostacy. And if this were the case, he would probably exult and use it as an argument in seduction.

AFTER their eating it is said, *and the eyes of them both were opened.*—Satan's prediction was fulfilled. By becoming acquainted with evil, its nature and consequences, they saw in a new manner, the nature, extensiveness and speculative fitness of that holiness from which they had fallen. ——*and they saw that they were naked.* They felt they were guilty sinners, and deserving of GOD's punishment. An increased doctrinal knowledge of their obligation to be holy, was a principal thing which gave strength to that condemning conscience, by which they knew themselves to be naked. The obligation to truth and its happy effects in society never can be known by a finite mind, so perfectly from speculation; as they may be known by actually seeing truth and falsehood and their effects. The detestable nature of vice, and the fitness of virtue in the social relations, are principally known to us by seeing their effects. We learn our moral obligation to holiness by its own effects; but perhaps still more from seeing the effects of vice or unholiness. Men cannot know in the most perfect manner the fitness of being a good neighbor, parent, child, ruler or subject, nor the wisdom of GOD in instituting these relations; until illustrated to their knowledge by the characters that are contrary to them. The value and fitness of civil liberty, is best felt by having suffered or seen tyranny. We may go through the whole system of holiness, in all its duties, and find that their nature and our obligation to do them, is obtained principally by seeing the contrary temper and its effects.

It does not appear, that in the nature of things, there is any other possible way of coming so perfectly to this knowledge. Though sinners, are by the badness of their hearts, rendered unable to see the moral glory of GOD, and in this sense are called ignorant, and will eternally remain so unless renewed ; still it is conjectured, that the sinners of this world have more doctrinal knowledge of GOD—of the moral and social system—of the nature and reasons for holiness—than the most holy angel or man could have had, without an apostacy and misery its natural consequence. The nature of men and angels is so made, that a sight of evil is the necessary means, of teaching them the nature of good. Men seem to have a general apprehension that a knowledge of evil, teaches them the nature and fits them for the enjoyment of good. If there be such a common apprehension, does it not go far to show the goodness of GOD in admitting eternal sin and misery into the system, and to prove that it was the most direct way for promoting the good of the whole.

3dly. THE natural structure of created minds is such, that a knowledge of misery, either by feeling it in themselves, or seeing it in others, is a necessary means for teaching them the nature and value of happiness; and of preparing them to enjoy in the highest manner, the good that GOD is pleased to bestow. Suppose three persons ; one of whom hath never felt or seen pain ; a second hath been in the uninterrupted enjoyment of bodily ease, but hath seen excruciating distress in others ; the third is just recovered from the long torture of a cholic or a gout. What estimate will these persons form of the value of bodily ease? The second, who hath only seen pain in others will have tenfold more sense of its value, than the first who never saw it. The third, a hundred fold more than the fecond, who never felt it; and thus animal eafe will appear of a thoufand fold more value to the third than to the firft; and he is made a happier being by the fimple enjoyment of animal eafe, than the firft would be by the addition of a whole world. If it fhould be faid, that both enjoy the fame good, and confequently the fame happinefs-; this is an error. They both enjoy the fame object; but not the fame good, or happinefs. The fact is, the torture of the cholic, hath brought the mind into a fituation, that bodily eafe which is the object of enjoyment to each, is a thoufand times greater good to the relieved perfon, than it could have been without the intervention of pain. Hence it appears, that mifery not only affifts us to eftimate the value of happinefs; but brings the mind into fuch a ftate that the object of enjoyment, though the fame in itfelf is a greater good than it could have been without mifery. This holds true of all the kinds of happinefs, which we ever feel, or are capable of enjoying. Darknefs prepares our minds to make light pleafant. Dwelling in a defert to enjoy the beauties of a well cultivated country. Solitude to enjoy the pleafures of company. The bitternefs of malice to feel the pleafures of love. The nature of man is fo made, and there does not appear any reafon to expect an alteration.

On this principle alone, there may be a thoufand fold more happinefs in the univerfe, than if mifery had never entered it. The elect angels never tafted mifery but they have feen it, and through the fight, variated as it is by the infinite wifdom of God, they may become more happy beings, than they could have been without it. Thofe who are redeemed from among men have both feen and tafted mifery, and according to the quantity of their intellectual being, will from this caufe be capable of enjoying higher happiness than the elect angels.

4thly. It further appears, from the structure of created minds, that the eternal continuance of misery, will be a probable means of increasing the quantity of final good. Such is the nature of created and finite minds, that a thing in present view, affects them more strongly and is more instructive, than the same thing can be when contemplated at a distance ; whether the distance be past or future. A sight of present misery is more instructive, and impressions made are deeper, than can be by recollection. Memory cannot be so vivid as present sight. And whatever effects, sin and misery may have in showing the rational fitness of virtue, these effects, will be most powerfully wrought, by having sin and misery in constant view. We are told that the wicked shall be punished in *the sight of the lamb and his redeemed.* The actual sight of their misery, will constantly teach the fitness of holiness ; as it will appear that the misery of the wicked arises from the very nature of that temper which they continue to choose and practise. All this doth not imply that God hath any delight in misery ; but entirely the contrary. When it is seen how beneficial this is to the universe, benevolence will acquiesce in the exhibition, and know that it is perfectly fit it should be made.

Further, it is highly probable, the very same reason which makes it fit, that misery should begin to exist ; will make it fit, that it should exist always. We have seen that neither sin or misery exist for their own sake ; but as necessary means, of bringing into the knowledge of creatures, the nature of holiness, and to prepare their minds to enjoy it. Infinite wisdom will doubtless so order, that the nature of holiness and sin shall be perfectly acted out. The more the nature of each of these is brought into the knowledge of creatures; the more room there is for happiness. As the exhibition of their nature grows; happiness will increase, and there will be a growing exhibition of both through eternity. It was not fit in the opinion of infinite wisdom that a state of trial should continue through eternity. The trial of some creatures is ended—the trial of all creatures will end at the day of judgment, and a state of continued retribution commence. But it doth not from hence follow, that new manifestations of the nature both of holiness and sin, will not be necessary for the greatest good; and be actually made. And doubtless, the sinful under the wise controul of infinite power, will be placed in such a state, as to be forever giving new manifestations of the nature of sin, and its inseparable effects. This will be a growing illustration of the nature, fitness and beneficial tendencies of holiness; and thus sin and misery will through eternity continue to be the means of promoting the good of the whole. It may be as necessary, millions of ages hence, that sin and misery should continue, in order to make the blessedness of the universe a growing one; as it is now in the beginning of the divine scheme. Some will allow that good may be brought out of misery, and seem reconciled on this ground, that it should exist for a season; but start back from the idea of its being eternal. This, they say, is incredible! That an infinitely good God, should suffer eternal misery in his universe is beyond belief!! But what creature knows this? The good of the universe is to be a growing one, and the continuance of sin and misery may be necessary to make it such. If God, consistently with his rectitude and with his own nature, may make use of misery for a short period, to in-

creafe the general good ; he may on the fame principles, make ufe of it eternally. The fitnefs or un-
fitnefs of the thing doth not arife from the period of
duration ; but from the ufe and effects which flow
from it. If infinite wifdom can make it ufeful
fo long, it will doubtlefs be eternal.

SEC. 15. OBJECTION. ALLOWING, that eternal fin and mifery are neceffary to make the moft
happy univerfe, it is ftill unreafonable that any
one creature fhould be made eternally miferable ;
and the end of divine goodnefs may be anfwered,
by a fucceffion of fin and mifery in different fubjects. This objection hath been virtually anfwered, in my reply to feveral other objections ; but
I will ftill attempt a further reply. The good of
individuals is not GOD's ultimate end in creating
and governing ; and if it were, it would make him
a refpecter of perfons and a partial being. He
cannot regard the happinefs of individuals, when
that comes in competition with the general good.
If his wifdom fees, that the eternal mifery of fome
individuals, will make the univerfe more happy ;
than the mifery of an eternal fucceffion of individuals, then a love to the whole will incline him
to make individuals forever miferable. We allow that mifery is undefirable in its own nature,
and no more of it will be admitted, than is neceffary for good in the great whole. But it is not lefs
evil or undefirable in its own nature, when thrown
into a fucceffion of individuals ; than it is when confined forever to a certain number of individuals.
The undefirablenefs of it does not arife, from its
falling on this or that particular perfon ; nor from
the number of perfons on whom it falls ; nor from
its duration ; but from its nature : and its nature
is not changed, whether one or many be the fuf-
ferers. GOD alone can determine, which is moft
for the public good ; either the fuffering of a cer-

tain number of individuals, or of an eternal fucceff-ion of individuals. Infinite wifdom hath made the choice; human wifdom ought to acquiefce; and benevolence does not fee any thing more unde-firable, in the eternal mifery of a certain number, than it does in the fame quantity of mifery, fpread through an eternal fucceffion of creatures. The probable reafon that it appears thus to any, is a lurking fear that eternal mifery will be their lot; and on their own partial and felfifh principles, they would rather take a turn in mifery, than to be forever wretched.

SEC. 16. OBJECTION. COULD not GOD have given to creatures, all that knowledge that is ne-ceffary, of himfelf, and of the nature of holinefs and fin, without the actual experiment of fin and mif-ery? Would not a direct, inftructive impreffion from GOD on the mind concerning the nature of thefe truths have anfwered all the fame purpofes, that are gained by the experiment itfelf; and thus the greateft good of the whole have been ob-tained, without fuch an immenfe quantity of mif-ery, as the doctrine of eternal punifhment fup-pofes?

ANSWER. THIS objection fuppofes fundry ab-furd things. It as much difproves the exiftence of fin and mifery, as it doth their eternity. That fin and mifery have exifted is a fact. If it would have been as well, or had been poffible for GOD by an inftructive impreffion on the mind, to give all that knowledge, which the actual experiment doth, then it was as unfit that fin and mifery fhould take place a fingle moment; as that they fhould remain through eternity. The objection, by denying a fact in the divine government, is an impeachment of GOD; but no evidence againft eternal mifery.

2ndly. The objection denies the fitness of the whole scheme and structure of creation, and even of the existence of such creatures as men and angels are; and supposes that another scheme and structure of existence, and other orders of creatures far different in their nature from men and angels, ought to have been made in their place. Certain ways of attaining knowledge, are as essential to the nature of men and angels as the capacity of knowing is. The nature of men is such, that it doth not admit knowledge in any way, but by the experiment of actual existence. A fight of what happens to others, and a feeling of what happens to ourselves are the means of all knowledge; and these imply the experiment of actual existence. If there be such a thing, which is not denied, as is meant in the objection, by direct, instructive impressions from God, still the power which impresses or communicates, acts through the medium of things seen and felt, or of knowledge first obtained by the fight and feeling of actual existence. And it doth not appear, that the nature of man is capable of being informed in any other manner. The gift of revelation, whatever special power God exercises in giving it, still comes in this way; and this method of attaining knowledge, is as essential to the nature of man, as the capacity of knowing is. If a creature were to receive knowledge in another way; he would not be a man; but a creature of entirely a different nature, and one of which we can form no idea. We have no reason to think it possible, in the nature of things, that such a creature should exist.

3dly. Those who make this objection, doubtless do it on the supposition; that it is an unfit thing in God and inconsistent with the rectitude of his nature, to make the existence of misery eternal. But if we allow, that the thing itself would be unfit ; would it not be equally unfit for God to give any such representation to our minds, as truth ; either concerning his own character, or the nature and effects of holiness and sin. It is conceived, that it would be totally inconsistent with the holiness of God to make any representations, on this matter, to the minds of his creatures ; which he could not carry into execution, consistently with the perfections of his nature.

4thly. It would be endless to mention all the absurdities implied in this objection. On beholding the scheme of natural existence, which infinite power and wisdom have produced, we see the whole to be an endless chain of causes and effects. It is the acting out of God, in an infinite succession of events. It is happiness produced by an infinite variety of means and views of the Deity. It is one immense whole composed of innumerable parts, in combination, connection, and depending on each other. In this whole, intermediate causes and means, are as much parts, as those things are, which we call ultimate ends and effects. This system, thus combined and connected is what we call created nature. The connections, powers, and dependancies of the several parts ; are what we call the particular nature of things. If we break in upon this system we know not where the breaking in will terminate. To say that God might give knowledge or give happiness, to any one mind, directly from himself, without the intervention of customary means ; is in fact an objection against all created existence. There is such a connection, between what we call creating and governing wisdom, that an objection against one necessarily implies an objection to the other. To say that God might give, all the knowledge of himself and of the moral system, that is necessary for the greatest good of the whole, without the experiment of sin and misery ; is in

fact faying, that creation might have been better
formed. That inftead of creating men and angels, a creation of quite another nature ought to
have been formed. It is faying, that infinite wifdom and power have been wrong through the
whole; and that fuch a conftruction of things, as
no one knows to be poffible, would have been
better than that which exifts. When men take
fuch grounds of argument, they are beyond converfing with creatures any longer; for they have
affumed the place of GOD, and challenged him
in all the vaft work of creation and government.
Yea more, they profefs to have fcanned his nature, and determined better than he hath, what
he may do in confiftency with himfelf. When
objections againft the divine government, are of
that kind, as to be equal objections againft the
original fcheme of creation; it proves the caufe
to be a very defperate one. If the prefent fyftem of
creation muft be removed to pleafe men, can they
promife to make a better one; to make one with
more happinefs and lefs mifery; or againft which
fewer objections will arife. The neceffity of holinefs and of fin, and of their effects, being brought
into view by a practical experiment; in order to
promote the greateft good of the whole; appears
to rife from the very ftructure and nature of the
creation. Can thofe who contend with ALL-GOVERNING WISDOM, ftep into his place and do his
work in a more unexceptionable manner!

SEC. 17. OBJECTION. IF eternal fin and mifery be neceffary for the greateft good of the univerfe; ftill may we not hope that men are exempted from this awful end? The finful angels
have fallen, and as there is no Saviour provided
for them, muft be forever punifhed; may we not
hope that this will be a fufficient manifeftation of
what infinite wifdom defigned by the introduction

ANSWER. GOD comprehends his own univerfe, and he only can tell, how far fin and mifery muft prevail for the greateft good. We may reft affured, he will not fuffer them to extend further, than is neceffary for the end defigned; alfo that none will be miferable but thofe who perfectly deferve it. We muft depend on revelation for our knowledge in this matter. Had the whole depended on finite wifdom, it is not probable creatures would have thought, that happinefs and holinefs could be promoted by fuch means; but *his wifdom is unfearchable, and his ways paft finding out!* This fin and mifery, which the proud wifdom of creatures calls a ftain on the government of GOD, will be the means of fhowing that it is a fcheme worthy indeed of infinite wifdom.

REVELATION informs us, that fome men as well as fome angels, muft be forever wretched. It appears to be the defign of infinite wifdom, to give the moft extended view of holinefs, fin and their effects; and to bring them out to the fight of creatures, in all their forms of exifting and acting. This was neceffary for bringing himfelf into the moft perfect view, and for difclofing both the nature and excellency of his chofen moral fyftem. The event hath proved that infinite wifdom judged it beft, fin fhould be manifefted both in angels and in men; and no reafon can be affigned, why *eternal* fin and mifery fhould not be neceffary in both. If fome men continue forever impenitent, they muft doubtlefs be forever miferable; and the eternal impenitence of fome men, will exhibit a quality in the nature of fin, which the eternal finfulnefs of fallen angels never can do. No Saviour is provided for the fallen angels, and though it be true, that the nature of fin will forever keep them from becoming holy; there are alfo other things which abfolutely prevent their salvation. They are under a condemning law, which stands in the way of their being restored ; and as they are left to make personal satisfaction, there is no possible way of this being done, only by their eternal misery. The case of sinful men is very different. The wisdom of God hath removed out of the way of men's salvation, every thing, except the sin of their own hearts. Here sin appears exceedingly sinful. The unreasonableness and malignity of an unholy heart, appears much more clearly, than it can in a fallen angel. The fallen angel may say, I cannot be saved from misery, if I would repent and love God. In the case of impenitent sinners it will appear that every impediment was removed from the way, but their own will and love of sin. This is a manifestation, which is to be made by the final impenitency of some of the human race. It will be an eternal and visible evidence before the universe ; of the nature of sin ; of the stubbornness of the unholy will ; and that all sinners do delight in their iniquity, whatever they may pretend contrary. Also that they do not choose God and holiness, and such a holy heaven as God offers ; because there is nothing but their own choice, which stands in the way of their coming to it. If the greatest happiness depends on having holiness and unholiness set in the eternal view of the universe ; we must suppose there are the same reasons, for some of the human race being left eternally in sin and misery ; as there are, that some of the angels should be thus left. God will doubtless cause sin and holiness to be acted out in all possible forms ; and so far as we can now look into the divine government, there is an astonishing foundation laid for this event. Sin hath appeared, both in the angelic and in the human nature. Sin is continued in those, for whom no Saviour is provided. Sin is found in creatures placed on probation for recovery; where an eternal heaven and hell are set before them as motives to repentance. There is sin in those who are to be actually saved, existing in a strange state of warfare with holiness, in the hearts of christians. Finally, sin and its companion misery existing both in the angelic and human natures through eternity. During the whole of eternity, the subjects of this bad temper, will be permitted in new and inconceivable ways, to show the baseness of their characters and the unfitness of a selfish heart. In a most astonishing degree, this will discover to innumerable holy beings, the rectitude of God; his wisdom in choosing holiness; the excellency of that scheme of holiness, which he has enjoyed; the impossibility of creatures being happy, on any other scheme of principles and practice; and the extreme misery that flows from the contrary.

This doctrine, fully vindicates divine wisdom in that immense number of sinful scenes, which are suffered to take place in this world. Their variety is strange—their number is beyond computation---the actors in them are many—the excess of sin is often so great, that even sinners through natural affection weep over it—christians sometimes wonder why their heavenly father will permit it to be thus, and their faith is shaken. Take courage ye friends of God, and let not your faith fail. Michael and his angels fight in heaven, and it is for the same reasons as call you to be bold in this warfare. The captain of your salvation hath infinite wisdom, and he will in the end, present to you a universe containing the greatest possible quantity of blessedness; and certainly you cannot desire more! you will for all these things, which you now see and feel, offer praises to God in heaven, which are ineffable in your state on earth,

The immense number of sinful scenes, which now take place ; are neceffary to act out the nature of fin in all its poffible forms and effects ; and if one of them were omitted, the univerfe would be lefs happy and God lefs glorious. I know your hearts. You will inftantly reply, if a change would make God lefs glorious, let things remain as they are ; for the leffening of his glory, would both injure him and diminifh forever the bleffed-nefs of all good beings.

May I not alfo addrefs thofe, who have no de-fire to be called faints of God and difciples of Je-sus ; and affure them, that on their own prin-ciples they have no caufe to complain.

To carry conviction to your confciences, I will for a moment grant, all that you can demand. That you have the fame right to judge in this mat-ter that God hath, and furely you can demand no more.

In a focial fyftem, there are but two poffible fchemes ; the benevolent and the felfifh. Either the good of the whole, or a feparate and felfifh good muft preponderate, and become a commanding principle in the heart. On the benevolent fcheme, which regards the good of the whole, it is per-fectly fit, that the unholinefs and mifery of finners fhould be permitted. This is the neceffary means of bringing into view of the intelligent creation, fuch truths as are neceffary for its higheft happinefs. With the knowledge of thefe truths acted out, there will be much more happinefs, than there could have been without a knowledge of them. That this is the cafe I have endeavored to fhow, from the ftructure of minds and things as they exift.

Further, it is fit and juft on your own prin-ciples that finners fhould be thus treated in the divine government, and they have no caufe to complain. Allowing to you all which can be demanded, that you have the moſt perfect right to determine your own temper and actions; allowing alſo, that a ſupreme regard to yourſelves, is the beſt and moſt fit ſtate of the heart; there is ſtill the higheſt propriety that you ſhould be treated as you are, in the divine government. If you have a right to be a ſelfiſh being, ſtill you have no right to ſuppoſe yourſelves privileged beings beyond all others. God and all creatures have the ſame right to be of this character, and to act on theſe principles, as you have. If you may ſeek a ſelf-exaltment, on private and ſeparate principles; all may do the ſame. If they ſuppoſe on any account, that it will promote their private intereſt in the ſmalleſt degree, to make you eternally miſerable, they may do it with as much fitneſs, as you may oppoſe them. The ſelfiſh and ſeparate ſyſtem of feeling and acting, really comes to the ſame thing in practice; as it would be to make power the ultimate rule of right. In practice it always has been the ſame thing, and will forever remain ſo. On this ſcheme, it will be a ſufficient juſtification of any action to ſay, *he has power to do as he hath done;* or, he has conſulted himſelf and has done right. The only conſolation which would remain to ſufferers would be this, *I could not prevent it,* and if it is ever in my power, I will treat him as he hath treated me. All this is fit, if your ſelfiſh principles of action are ſo, and you have no right to complain. Whichever ſcheme we aſſume, either the benevolent or ſelfiſh, it is fit you ſhould be eternally miſerable; on the benevolent, becauſe it will be the means of advancing the general good; on the ſelfiſh becauſe you cannot prevent it, and an Almighty God hath the ſame right to make you

Z

miferable as you have to refift him. There is therefore no way to efcape mifery, but by efcaping a felfifh, unholy heart. How much more wife it would be, for us to fpend our time in doing this, than in attempting to prove all men will be faved.

SEC. 18. OBJECTION. THOSE who believe and preach the doctrine of eternal punifhment, have a rigid fcheme of faith. They join this with fo many other doctrines; fuch as the neceffity of a renewed heart; a life of conftant holinefs and felf-denial; and a regard to the glory of GOD in all which men do, that if their fcheme be true there can be but few men faved. If only a few were to be miferable, to anfwer fome important purpofe in the univerfe; the idea would be more tolerable; but as things are now reprefented, it fpreads a great deftruction through the human race, and leaves but few for falvation; which is contrary to the reprefentations of fcripture, that the number of the faved fhall be innumerable, and that CHRIST fhall fee of the travail of his foul and be fatisfied.

ANSWER. WE often hear declamation on this fubject, including the ideas fuggefted in the objection, and perhaps fome others. Much that is faid in this loofe way, cannot be brought to a point of inveftigation. Much that is faid, is alfo addreffed to the interefted feelings and paffions of men, and will appear to them to have fome weight, until their feelings are changed, or their paffions cooled by rational inquiry. Thofe objections, which are incapable of being reduced to a point, or that addrefs nothing befide the paffions, are often found to be moft fuccefsful in bewildering men and leading them into error. The ftrictnefs of thofe who vindicate the doctrine of eternal punifhment, is no proper argument againft that doc-

trine, if there be fufficient evidence to fupport it.
The doctrine of the new birth, or a renewed
heart by the fpirit of GOD ; of the neceffity of
chriftian holinefs and felf-denial ; and of acting
in all we do for the glory of GOD, ftand on their
own evidence; and fo doth the doctrine of eternal mifery. The writer and many others believe
thefe doctrines, rigid as they are called, to be doctrines of CHRIST, and that they explain the nature and way of falvation. Some reject thefe doctrines, who are ftill firm believers of eternal punifhment, which fhows that there is a peculiar evidence, ftanding on its own ground, that this will
be the event. The queftion at prefent in debate,
is not what are the qualifications for falvation,
but whether all men will be faved.

THOSE objections againft eternal mifery, which
arife from the many or fewnefs of the number to
be faved, in the prefent conception of men, are
of little weight; and they are evidently brought
forward by the felfifh feelings of the objector.
Fear, and a finful love of himfelf have a great
fhare in the bufinefs. He would be willing that
fome few fhould be miferable, to promote important purpofes in the univerfe ; but fo many as he
thinks muft be condemned, on what he calls a
rigid fcheme, he fears would include himfelf ;
and he therefore intends to be rid of the doctrine
at all events. There is much reafon to fear, that
his rafh refolution comes from a knowledge that
he is not renewed by the fpirit of GOD, and from
a diflike of the holinefs, felf-denial, and devotednefs to GOD, required in the chriftian practice.
If he can free himfelf from the fear of eternal
punifhment, he can live quietly as he wifhes to do.
Such feelings of felf-love and fear, have a prodi-
gious influence in biafing the judgment of men
on this important point. In all this, there is no ar-

gument, but only interested and sinful feelings against the divine government. However men may think, in order to make their own state safe, GOD in his infinite and wise goodness, will go directly forward in his own plan, executing that which is for the greatest good.

As to the question, whether few or many will be lost, in comparison with the whole; or whether few or many of those who now live, or have lived in the world will be lost; they belong to GOD and not to man to determine. He has determined in wisdom and in goodness, and the end will give proof of his perfection.

THAT an innumerable number will be saved from among men; and that CHRIST will see of the travail of his soul until he is satisfied; are truths which cannot be questioned, for it is the uniform representation of GOD's word, that this will take place. It must be allowed, that an immense number of mankind in the present and in all past ages, have given too little evidence of a holy and heavenly temper, but this is no proof that there will not be many more saved, than are lost. Those who have studied the scriptures, are sensible that another state of things on earth is promised. The church, in dependence on these promises, is daily praying for their accomplishment; and though the present period be a dark one, there is abundant evidence that GOD is rapidly fulfilling his threatened judgments on mankind, and preparing the way to set up the redeemer's kingdom on earth, with a new degree of glory and success. Almost half the Bible is filled with promises and descriptions of that blessed day, when the earth shall be filled with holiness, and converts be multiplied as the sands on the sea shore. In that period of promise CHRIST will see of the travail of his soul and be satisfied.

ᴄ· Iꜰ it ſhould be objeſted that this is viſionary; we reply—That ſuch an opinion is confirmed not only from the prophetic promiſes of Goᴅ, who knows and can reveal his own ſcheme; but alſo from other principles which have been abundantly brought into view.

· ·Goᴅ hath permitted ſin and miſery, in order to caſt light on the nature of holineſs and of the moral ſyſtem, and this will be the means of aſſiſting his people to make ſwift advances in holineſs and happineſs. On theſe principles, it is reaſonable to ſuppoſe, that a great proportion of thoſe beings, who are to make a manifeſtation of the nature of ſin, will be among the firſt, who are called on the ſtage of being. The happy ſubjeſts of divine grace, who are yet to be called into exiſtence, will come forward with every advantage for a rapid improvement in the knowledge and love of Goᴅ, whom they will ſerve eternally. They will look back on the paſt ages of the world; and from the hiſtory of mankind, which will be faithfully tranſmitted to them, learn the nature, tendencies, conduſt, and effeſts of a ſinful temper; by all the ſins and wicked aſtions that have been perpetrated. They will learn the divine charaſter from his paſt government. The ſcheme of redeeming wiſdom and goodneſs is but beginning to unfold; and the inhabitants of that happy day, will in a very ſhort time, obtain more knowledge of Goᴅ and of the moral ſyſtem, than they could have done had they been firſt called into exiſtence, and the manifeſtation of ſin made afterwards; ſo that at the day of judgment, it is probable they will be much more holy and happy beings, than if the earthly ſtate of the church had been brought forward in a reverſe order. It therefore appears that one of the leading principles in our inveſtigation, corroborates the expeſtation of the church; that its laft days will be its moft profperous ones, and the period when the greateft part of CHRIST's people fhall be gathered in. Prophecy fpeaks of a great falling away near the end of the world; and it would be eafy to fhow, this is agreeable to the principles that have been advanced. In the days of the millenium there will be a great increafe of light. This will arife from an abundance of the influences of the holy fpirit; and from a prevalence of real religion, by which men will be difpofed to examine and collect evidence of truth, which now lies fcattered. A general practice of religion and godlinefs, will fhow their beauty, fitnefs, beneficial tendency in fociety, and the ftrength of moral and holy obligation on men to ferve GOD and obey his law. All religious duty will appear with great plainnefs. The evidence of the truth of the gofpel will arife to the higheft demonftration, and there will be the beft advantages for obtaining falvation. After the power of religion has prevailed for ages through the whole world, and the beauty of its fpirit and order is fhining in every place; to fee infidelity and all its train of vices rifing anew, in the face of fuch light and fuch benefits as men enjoy by means of religion, will be an aftonifhing evidence of the natural corruption of the human heart, of the bafenefs of a finful temper, and of its juft defert in the government of GOD. It will alfo fhow that all which is good in men, comes from the fovereign influence of GOD's fpirit; and that all the excellent orders and means, which will probably be eftablifhed in the millenial church, are infufficient to hold men in gofpel obedience, a fingle moment, when the fpirit is denied. Holy prophecy fpeaks of this great apoftacy, as immediately preceding the laft judgment. It will compleat the difplay and evidence of the nature of sin, and prove the judge to be infinitely holy and wise, in punishing impenitent sinners with an everlasting destruction. Though the gospel hath had less effect than short sighted men would wish; the whole is ordered by an infinite God, to make the most rapid advance towards the greatest possible quantity of holiness and happiness. The use which we should make of the present dark state of things, is not to determine there is nothing in religion, or that all men will be saved; but to excite our own fears of falling short. For if we are brought into being, at a time, in which there is reason to believe a less proportion of men will be saved, this is a motive to use the more diligence in making our own calling and election sure, and to fear that we shall fall short through some delusion. We should not wish to know how many will be saved in this dark period of the church. Enough will be effectually called to bear a witness for the truth, and to give the sinful world a practical view of the nature and effects of holiness; so that their inexcusableness will be perfect.

WHETHER in the most successful periods of the gospel, there may not be some few left in the deepest sin, in order to give others an ocular view of its nature and effects, the event only can show. That GOD who reigns will do all things wisely and for the best. When the divine government of the world is opened and explained at the day of judgment, he will be glorified in his saints and admired in all them who believe. The riches of divine grace will be magnified. Every mouth will be stopped, and all the works of the Lord appear to be right and good!!!

SEC. 19. OBJECTION. MAY not annihilation be the evil meant in the penalty of the law, and in the threatning of the second death?

1ft. ANNIHILATION is a total ceſſation and lofs of exiſtence. The creature is extinct, and is a ſubject neither of good or evil. Only a few who have the chriſtian ſcriptures have fallen into this notion. This few are much divided in their opinion, how annihilation is to be conſidered, as it relates to GOD, and the creature who loſes his exiſtence. Some ſeem to conceive, that annihilation is a kind of eternal puniſhment or evil on the annihilated perſon ; but it is difficult to ſee how this ſhould be the caſe. The proſpect of annihilation may be an evil, for in this caſe, there is a conſcious exiſtence to endure the apprehenſion ; but to tell of its being an evil, to one who hath no exiſtence is unintelligible to common ſenſe. If annihilation be the puniſhment meant by death, in the penalty of the law ; then the penalty is to be conſidered only as an inducement not to ſin, and not as an evil to be endured by the ſinner after his tranſgreſſion, for the ceaſing of exiſtence, muſt end all ſuffering.

2dly. NEITHER is it conceived that annihilation can bring any glory to GOD. The appearance of ſuch an event would be this; that GOD had created a being capable of doing his duty, and honoring his maker ; and this creature had become rebellious, irreclaimable and a real evil, from which his creator had no way of delivering himſelf, but by the deſtruction of that exiſtence, which his own almighty power had made. It is difficult to put any other conſtruction upon annihilation, as an evil that is to follow ſin. It looks like diſappointment in a plan of exiſtence and government, and ſuch a kind of diſappointment as infinite wiſdom and power will never ſuffer. It will not do to compare this to the caſe of eternal miſery. In that caſe, though there may be a diſappointment to the wiſhes of the creature himself, there is no difappointment to GOD; for the exiftence and fin of the creature, by a difplay of moral truth and its contrary, may be the means of increafing univerfal happinefs which was GOD's motive in creating, though it be not the means of the perfon's own happinefs. It is difficult to conceive how non-exiftence fhould difplay exiftence with its relations and duties. Therefore it is fuppofed, the glory of GOD cannot be advanced by the annihilation of a finner.

3dly. THE holy fcripture, in many places fpeaks of the laft punifhment of fin, as defigned to difplay the mighty power of GOD. Rom. ix. 22. *What if GOD, willing to fhow his wrath, and make his power known, endureth with much long fuffering the veffels of wrath fitted to deftruction?* Is annihilation an act of power in GOD, or the contrary? I think not an act of power, but the ceffation of all power. If it were an act of power which created, and the continuance of exiftence depends on the continued exercife of that power; then the difcontinuance of all exercife of power, would refult in annihilation; and there feems to be no fitnefs in calling this the making of power known.

4thly. THE few who plead for annihilation, as the final punifhment of impenitent fin, are profeffedly of opinion that eternal mifery is inconfiftent with the benevolence of GOD, and they choofe this as an alternative more confiftent with infinite Goodnefs. But it is not feen, how any principles can be affumed to make annihilation confiftent with infinite benevolence; which will not alfo reconcile eternal mifery with the fame benevolence. Benevolence is a love of happinefs, and though annihilation doth not in itfelf imply any pofitive mifery; it is ftill as inconfiftent with happinefs as pofitive mifery is.

Iｆ the happinefs of every individual, be the object of divine benevolence; then annihilation and eternal mifery are both againft it. If the general good be the object of divine benevolence, and annihilation be compatible with this; for the fame reafons, eternal mifery may be compatible with it likewife; becaufe annihilation is as really oppofite to individual happinefs as eternal mifery is. So that thofe who reject eternal mifery, and fall in with the idea of annihilation, in order to fave the benevolence or goodnefs of Goｄ from difhonor, feem not to have attained their end.

Fｕｒｔｈｅｒ, it is conceived that annihilation is lefs confiftent with benevolence than continued mifery is. Their beneficial ufe, in the hands of infinite wifdom are the only ground on which either of them are confiftent with benevolence; and it is very difficult to conceive, how fo beneficial a ufe in the purpofes of a holy government, can be made of annihilation, as may be made of continued mifery.

5th. Tｈｅ defcriptions of finners punifhment, which are found in Goｄ's word, are not confiftent with annihilation. They are to arife to everlafting fhame; and this implies everlafting confcioufnefs. The fmoke of their torment is to afcend up forever and ever. All the places in Goｄ's word, and they are very numerous, which defcribe punifhment to be eternal, directly contradict the idea of annihilation. Eternal fuffering and eternal punifhment, imply eternal and confcious exiftence, in order to be the fubjects of that fuffering. Annihilation prevents an eternal good, but it is not eternal fuffering; and there is no greater propriety in faying that an annihilated finner is punifhed or fuffers eternally, than there would be in faying; that all thofe poffible but not actual beings, which men fuppofe they can paint in imagination, are eternally punifhed becaufe they never received an exiftence.

In the next place, it becomes us to inquire whether any of the words, which are ufed to defcribe future punifhment, do naturally convey the idea of annihilation or extinction of being. And I think it is not bold to affert, that not one of them conveys fuch an idea either naturally or even in their moft figurative ufe. The words moft favourable to fuch a fuppofition, are perhaps the following. *Death, perifh, confume, deftroyed, end, burnt up, &c.* Neither of thefe words, naturally mean any thing more than a change in the manner of exifting, and that the change is for the worfe. When we fay a man is dead, no mortal underftands by this that the man is annihilated; but only that his manner of exifting is changed. There is no other reafon to fuppofe that the fecond death means annihilation, than that the firft doth, efpecially when we are told that the fecond death, is being caft into the lake of fire and brimftone. Or if we fay that a man hath perifhed; or is confumed; or deftroyed; or come to his end; or burnt up; no man by thefe underftands annihilation. This fhows that the natural meaning of the words implies only a change in the manner of exifting and not extinguifhment of being. The figurative ufe of thefe words certainly doth not countenance the idea of annihilation. In the figurative diction, we fay that a man hath fuffered deftruction, and there is an end to him; when all his profpects, and hopes of what the world call happinefs and greatnefs are cut off. None of the words or defcriptions ufed in the fcriptures of God, either naturally or figuratively mean an extinction of being; and as words are understood by mankind, there is not a single hint of such an event through the whole Bible. If it be said, that the meaning of such words when applied to matter, only means a change in the manner of existing ; but applied to mind must intend destruction of existence. On this I would observe—that all words in their original use, were applied to sensible and material objects and they are borrowed in describing moral and intellectual subjects ; but though borrowed, we have no right to use them in a borrowed or different sense from their original sense, except on the direct authority of revelation, or from the necessary nature of the subject. And in the present case, it is presumed there is no authority in revelation more direct than the words we are considering ; also that there is nothing discoverable by human knowledge, either in the nature of God or of a sinful mind that necessitates annihilation.

6thly. THERE is nothing in the analogy of nature so far as we can at present examine it, which intimates annihilation ; or that any existence either material or intellectual will be extinguished. There is a general uniformity in the works of God, which we call the analogy of nature. This is designed for the direction of creatures in truth, duty, and their expectations of futurity. On examination, we find that the truths of revelation are confirmed by the analogy of nature, as might be illustrated in innumerable instances, especially in those that relate to a reward consisting in happiness or misery. In all nature we see nothing that appears like annihilation. Substances change their qualities ; their manner of existing ; their capacity of being acted upon ; their place ; and they put on different appearances ; but they do not loose their being. There is nothing, either in nature or revelation that countenances the notion of annihilation ; and it appears to those who have most thoroughly examined the subject, like the fancy of a mind, which is ready to subordinate the counsels of infinite wisdom to its own weak invention ; or of one who loves sin, and with trembling guilt wishes to retire into the shade of non-existence to escape its consequences.

7thly. It is apprehended, that those who have embraced the opinion of annihilation as the final punishment of impenitent sinners, have been led to it, from an apprehension that the existence of sin and sinners, is a misfortune to the divine government ; and that God esteems them, as men do those natural or moral evils, from which they wish to be entirely delivered ; but it should be considered that nothing can in this sense be an evil to God. There is no more sin, nor any greater number of sinners than he originally intended to admit into that scheme of existence and government, which his wisdom most approved. The introduction of sin, though sin be detestable in itself, is no blemish to the divine plan ; no misfortune to the divine government. If God were to concert his own plan again, he would order it as it hath been from eternity; and would admit the same quantity of sin, and the same number of sinners as have existed. To suppose otherwise, would be to suppose that infinite wisdom had not done best, or was disappointed.

God views sin with abhorrence, because it is in its nature wrong, and in its genuine consequences mischievous ; but he doth not like his own plan the less because sin is in it. And though his whole nature be opposed to the nature of sin, he knows how to promote by it that in which his nature delights. Inattention to this truth, hath made some suppose, that God views sin and sinners in the same manner that men view the natural evils from which they wifh to be wholly exempted, and as a misfortune to his government, from which he wifhes to be delivered. They hence lead themfelves to think, that after he hath a long time unavailingly tried to reclaim the wicked and doth not find the effect produced; that either in defpair or the rafhnefs of angry impatience, he deftroys their exiftence. Such apprehenfions of GOD and his government are as difhonorable to a being of infinite power, wifdom and goodnefs ; as the event is improbable. Let finners therefore repent, or expect to meet fuch eternal mifery, as omnipotence can inflict.

Sec. 20. I HAVE repeatedly expreffed an opinion, that the great and folemn fubject we have been confidering, muft be ultimately determined by the teftimony of divine revelation. In the firft part of this work, I have endeavored to lay fome part of that evidence in a collected view before my reader. And though fome reafoning hath been ufed to reconcile future and eternal mifery with the infinite benevolence of GOD, I defire to be fenfible that his word is the fupreme light by which human judgment is to be guided ; and that what GOD faith to be juft and confiftent with his infinite goodnefs, cannot be contrary to it ; even though men are unable to comprehend their confiftency. I have hitherto fuppofed that thofe whofe fentiments I oppofe believe the fcriptures to be the word of GOD ; but there are fome who call themfelves univerfalifts (with what fairnefs they do it, is not for me to determine) who either totally deny the fcriptures, or difcard fuch parts of them as are not agreeable to their own notion.

Such I now addrefs, and requeft to know of them, on what evidence they can build a belief, that either all or any part of men will ever be perfectly happy. You fpeak in ftrong terms that all will be happy ; but how do you know it ? Or what evidence can you adduce to render the event in any degree probable? By rejecting the scriptures, you have deprived yourselves of all evidence immediately from God himself. You are left to the dim guidance of reason and experience. I will not tell you how weak your reason is, as I suppose it to be equal to the reason of any other men, and in the present instance, will allow it to be the greatest among mortals. Yet what is your reason, with all the accutenefs that is allowed to it? Is it an intuitive view of futurity? Not this certainly ; for daily events show that futurity is as much hidden from you as from others. Is your reason a faculty or power of looking immediately on the nature and counsels of God, without the inftrumentality of means? I think this will not be pretended. I will tell you what your reason is, and how far it will go in determining this point. Your reason is the power of judging, from evidence prefented before the mind, of the probability or improbability of certain suppofed facts that are prefent or future, and of the truth or falfehood of certain propofitions. The fact fought for is this ; will any or all men ever be perfectly happy? The only evidence from which you can possibly judge, is paft experience in nature, for you have no revelation to guide you. Your only evidence of duration or exiftence to come, is taken from duration or exiftence paft. Your only evidence what kind of a God the Lord is and what he will do in time to come, muft be taken from what he hath done in time paft, and the experience you have had of him in the works of nature and providence. Have you ever feen perfect happinefs, or such as is commonly defcribed by the name of heavenly? Is there reafon to fuppofe, that any man among all who have lived before us attained it? Doth there not appear to be in nature, so far as you can examine it, a foundation laid for pain, dissolution, sorrow, disappointment, grief, the vexation of passions, and the turbulence of opposing parties and opposing interests? Doth not natural good draw natural evil after it? Is there not in the nature of things, according to all you have seen and experienced, as much a time to decrease, to weep and to die; as there is to increase, to laugh and to be born? Say not that this is nature's childhood, and that something better may be expected from her hereafter; for if said thou knowest it not, and another with equal assurance, may say it is her old age, and something worse may be expected. Or if you tell me, that GOD is good; this I will not deny; I will allow him to be just as good as these things indicate, and no better; for this is all the evidence which you have, without a revelation, that he is good; If a good being hath dealt thus for six thousand years, why not the same forever?

WHEN you dismiss your friend on a journey, it may be to meet all the evils that he can endure in this manner of existing; and when you dismiss him in death, it may be to meet all the plagues of another manner of existing. Reason, judging from experience, instead of promising a heaven or state of perfect happiness to all men; cannot promise or even give probable encouragement, that any one creature will ever come to such a state. And reason is not to be faulted, for it judges the best it can from the evidence presented before it. How many come into a bitter existence in this world; live groaning; and die in torment. How many are there, whose whole lives are filled with sorrow; and why may it not be thus with the existence to come? Let those who deny divine revelation, beware how they tell of a goodnefs in God, which will bring all men to perfect happinefs; for the evidence from experience in nature, by which only they can tell what kind of a being God is, directly contradicts it. The beft that we can expect by this information, is that there will be an eternal mixture of pleafure and of pain; and a reward of enjoyments and curfes, on which the mind of man after it hath experienced them, even in their beft ftate, writes the motto vanity of vanities all is vanity.

If to this it be objected, there is a general perfuafion in the minds of men, of a benevolent goodnefs in God, which will make fome, if not all creatures perfectly happy; I allow that there is fuch a perfuafion, but it came from revelation and not from experience in nature, by which alone the rejector of revelation muft learn the character of nature's God. If there had been no revelation, there would have been no fuch opinion. If it comes from revelation, then let this revelation decide the point; whether only a part or all men are to be faved, and the way in which falvation is to be obtained. The point is determined in the holy fcriptures. The door is fet as wide open as it ought to be, by a promife to all who repent, believe in the fon of God, and live in holy obedience to the divine law.

B b

PART III.

Section. I. I NOW come to the third part of this work, containing some strictures on a late publication, entitled " Calvin-" ism improved, or the gospel illustrated as a sys-" tem of real grace issuing in the salvation of all " men."

This publication is announced to the public, as a posthumous work of the late Rev. Joseph Hun-tington, D. D.

It is always unfortunate, when posthumous publications discuss those subjects, which it is known will become matter of public controversy. It must be expected that some person will attempt a refutation of tenets which he supposes dangerous to the present and future interests of men. In most such cases, there are surviving friends who have a tender feeling for the reputation of their deceased. To conduct a controversial discussion with candor is very difficult, and perhaps was never perfectly done. In the present instance, some of the friends and connections of the deceased have committed his sentiments to the public; and they could not but know them so contrary to the ancient orthodoxy of this country, that a severe scrutiny would be excited. They also knew that their friend could speak no more in this world to vindicate his own opinions. The writer though a junior in years, and much inferior to Dr. Huntington, was suffered to number himself among his friends and acquaintance, and feels no disposition to injure his reputation. A refutation of his sentiments, and not a defamation of the man is

the object of the following remarks. Justice to
the truth will be attempted, and it is hoped without the appearance of party spirit, or personal ill-
will.

Dr. H. has chosen the name limitarian, to de-
signate those who believe that a part of men will
not be saved. I have no objection against any
name, if all who use it will carefully attend to the
sense in which it ought to be understood. If by
limitarian be only meant, one who believes that
some men will fail of salvation, I have no objection
to it. But in the Doctor's book, there are sundry passages which insinuate ; that those who
think different from him, limit or set bounds to
the infinite goodness of God. Such insinuations
are totally contrary to fact. It is the infinite
goodness of God, and not the limitation of his
goodness, which will incline him to administer
eternal punishment. The most perfect and eternal happiness of the universe, is his motive for
admitting partial evil. It has been necessary in
the periods past, and nothing appears but it may
be necessary in all duration to come. If it be a
fact, that there is more blessedness in the universe
with some evil, than could have been without it ;
then it is God's infinite goodness and not a limitation of his goodness, which ordains eternal punishment. The misery of some individuals who
deserve such an end, is no evidence against divine
love ; for his primary motive in governing, is
not individual but general good. All arguments
on this subject, which stand on the ground of individual creature happiness, are selfish and unholy. Dr. H. in various parts of his book expa-
tiates much on the infinite mercy of God in the
gospel, and seems to conceive such descriptions to
be arguments in favor of Universalism ; and that
his scheme represents God more good, than what

has been the common opinion of the christian church. But all this is quite away from the subject. God's goodness and mercy may be infinite, and the universe the most blessed, and still individuals may be unhappy.

Dr. H. as is right, professes to take revelation for his principal guide in this subject; but he has some recourse to human reasoning, and so far as he rests his opinion on this, he ought not to have supposed it sufficient to speak diffusely on the mercy and goodness of God, but to have proved that the eternal misery of an individual is inconsistent with his goodness; and I do not recollect through his whole book a single argument to prove that the eternal misery of individuals, is inconsistent with the greatest blessedness of the universe collectively.

To show my own opinion of the plenitude of divine goodness, I will express the following sentiment, That the universe will not only in the end contain the greatest possible quantity of happiness; but in every period of its duration this hath been, and will be the case. If this world of creatures, considered separately for the time they have existed might have been happier; this is no evidence that the universe could have been. We do not understand the connections between the parts of an immense whole. I do not know, that we have any right to suppose, infinite wisdom must diminish the quantity of happiness in the beginning to make it the greatest in the end. If this conjecture be true, and I think no man can disprove it; I also think it exalts the divine character; it will then follow, that eternal misery is as reconcileable with infinite goodness, and as probable on rational grounds, as the present misery is which we all feel. If we were filled with that benevolence which subordinates private to public

intereft, it would give us a new view of many divine truths, with which men have quarreled
from the beginning.

SEC. 2. IT will appear to thofe who have read
the Doctor's piece, that he was in the fulleft fenfe
a univerfalift, and this was his favorite doctrine ;
at the fame time, fome fundamental doctrines of
truth and the exprefs declarations of fcripture
ftruck his mind fo forcibly, that he could not give
them up even to carry a favorite point.

I WILL make a quotation of feveral paffages from
his book.* Page 144. " The doctrine of the
" total depravity of human nature, is fo plain a
" doctrine, that we cannot deny it without reject-
" ing the whole authority of divine revelation."
" Every power, every faculty of the foul was left
" without any degree of moral good : all dread-
" fully polluted," " every imagination of the
" thought of man's heart was evil only and that
" continually." The depravity was total, and
" there was nothing left in the foul of man, of a
" moral kind, but enmity againft GOD.

THE doctrine of depravity, confifting in enmity or an alienation of the affections from the moral character of GOD and from all holinefs, is denied by many, who call themfelves univerfalifts,
and they build on this ground.

THE laft quotation gives the Doctor's idea of
human depravity, as confifting in enmity or an
alienation of men's affections from truth and infinite holinefs.——The next will give his notion
of the deferts of fuch a character. Page 46.——
" To argue as fome do that it is not juft for GOD
" to punifh us eternally for tranfient fins in this
" world, is the perfection of abfurdity, and arifes

---

* As there may be future editions of Dr. H's piece, I ought to
give notice that my references are to the firft edition, printed
at New-London by SAMUEL GREEN, 1796.

" from a total ignorance of God and ourfelves
" in the true charaǎer and relation of each"—
page 45 " endlefs duration of torment appears
" obvioufly juft : no more than we deferve, and
" not in the leaft cruel for God to inflict. Should
" we, *in fact*, fall under it, every mouth would
" be ftopped, and every foul would be convinced
" of fuch guilt before God, as to render this
" punifhment equal in reafon and juftice."

There cannot be more exprefs conceffions
than the above, that men deferve endlefs punifhment—that it would be juft and reafonable in
God to inflict it ; and if it would be according to
juftice and *reafon* for God thus to do, as the
Doǎor fays it would, may we not infer that his
charaǎer will be glorious in doing it ? Are not
all his perfeǎions agreeable to reafon and
juftice ? And is not that which is agreeable to
reafon and juftice agreeable alfo to his perfections ? Why then does the Doǎor, very often
infinuate, that our notions are unworthy of
God, when we think nothing of him, or his government, but what he himfelf allows to be according to reafon and juftice.

The infinite evil of fin is another point, on
which I will recite his opinion. Page 45. " If
" our obligations to obedience are not infinite ;
" God is not a being of infinite perfeǎion and
" worthinefs. To affert which is equal to athe-
" ifm ; for if there is not fuch a God there is
" none. Our fin can be an infinite evil only in
" one fenfe, as oppofed to a being of infinite
" perfeǎion" " Our punifhment can be infi-
" nite only in one fenfe, viz. endlefs duration ;
" for finite natures are not capable of infinite pain
" in any given time. Thus, endlefs duration of
" torment appears obvioufly juft ; no more than

" we deferve and not in the leaft cruel for GOD
" to inflict."——The Doctor has here conceded the infinite evil of fin, and the juftice of eternal punifhment in the very fenfe which thofe who
believe future mifery mean to eftablifh. This con-
ceffion overturns moft of the arguments on which
many other univerfalifts depend.

IT is hoped that thofe gentlemen, who have
endeavored to criticife mifery out of the univerfe,
and furnifhed the world with many grammatical
remarks on the original words, tranflated, forever, eternal, everlafting, &c. will be convinced by
what Dr. H. fays in pages 46, 47, and 48, of his
book. " Now does the Bible plainly fay that fin-
" ners of mankind fhall be damned to intermi-
" nable punifhment? It certainly does as plainly
" as language can exprefs, or any man, or even
" GOD himfelf can fpeak. It is quite ftrange to
" me, that fome who believe that all mankind
" fhall be faved, trifle as they do with a few words,
" and moft of all with the original word and its
" derivatives tranflated forever."——" They
" therefore, who would deny that the endlefs
" damnation of finners is fully afferted in the
" word of GOD are unfair in their reafonings and
" criticifms."

BUT though Dr. H. allows that the Bible declares the interminable damnation of finners, as
plainly as language can exprefs, or any man or
even GOD himfelf can fpeak; he ftill profeffes to
believe, that all men will be forever happy;——
Now to have this a rational belief, it muft be built
on evidence greater than words can exprefs, or
than any man or even GOD can fpeak; becaufe
the counter-evidence that the mifery of finners
will not terminate, is as great as words can exprefs or GOD can fpeak. If therefore there be
not greater evidence of Univerfal Salvation, than

God can fpeak, it does not feem that the doctrine is yet eftablifhed. How this greater evidence appears, is among thofe dark things which men in general do not comprehend.

FURTHER, Dr. H. allows through his whole book, that finners deferve eternal mifery—that God was under no obligation to find a redeemer, and that if he had not found one, men muft have been miferable forever.———Let us make the fuppofition that a Saviour had not been provided, and then according to the Doctor's idea all would have been miferable. But how could God have affured them of it, more plainly than he now has affured us, that fome will be miferable though there be a Saviour. God hath now told us, faith Dr. H. as plain as he can fpeak and as words can exprefs; and if there had been no Saviour could he have told it more plainly? If we ought not to believe this plain fpeaking, neither ought men without a Saviour to have believed it.———Suppofe God had gone further, and placed the firft finners under the pains of damnation; neither would this be any evidence of interminable mifery according to the Doctor's fcheme; for he reprefents all as being now in a ftate of damnation and fuffering its pains.———If neither fuffering the pains of damnation nor God's affurance as plain as he can fpeak, are fufficient evidence againft the termination of mifery; it does not appear that any evidence of this awful fact, could have been given even if a Saviour had not been provided. Many other difficulties attending his fcheme of evidence and belief will appear in the courfe of examination, all of them tending to infidelity.

SEC. 3. THE beft view which I am able to obtain of what Dr. H. calls his capital argument is in the following paffages, fimilar to which many

C c

others are scattered through his work. Pages 27, 28. " It will abundantly appear in the sequel, " that we must keep our ear open to the voice " of pure justice to man as he deserves out of " CHRIST ; also to the voice announcing what " shall in very deed, through infinite grace, take " place with respect to man in CHRIST: or it " will be wholly in vain, for all the wit, and art in " the world, to make any thing better of the holy " scriptures than a long, solemn series of the " most palpable contradictions." Page 32. " GOD displayed in an absolute character without " any intimation of a mediator, this is moral law " and all glorious. GOD displayed to man in " a mediator ; this is gospel, pure gospel and " exceedeth in glory." " We find the law and " gospel displayed side by side through the whole. " The law every where sounds with awful terror " in accents of pure justice, towards man, without " a Saviour. The gospel is all mere news, good " news, glad tidings through a mediator." " The moral law every where speaks to man in " his own personal character ; the gospel in that " of the Messiah. The law tells what man de- " serves in his own personal character ; the gos- " pel what the son of man, the son of GOD de- " serves." " The divine law enjoining perfect " obedience, on pain of endless misery, runs " through the whole of divine revelation from " beginning to end ; and so does the gospel, ex- " hibiting a salvation fully tantamount." Page 34. " The gospel is all mere news and good news." " The gospel is pure tidings, and more it is good " tidings. Whatever is law in any part of the " sacred writ is founded on the nature and char- " acter of GOD, adapted to man's nature, and his " relation to GOD. Whatever is gospel in any part " of the bible is founded wholly on JESUS CHRIST

" his character and offices." Page 35. " The
" law fpeaks in righteoufnefs ; every where de-
" nounces what is juft and equal towards man.
" It thunders aloud the true defert of man. But
" it fpeaks not what fhall in fact take place on
" man, and his furety both ; or on man at all
" in faith and union with CHRIST, or any other-
" wife than in his furety." Page 42. " The gof-
" pel on whatever page of facred writ it is found
" either in the Old Teftament or New—knows
" nothing at all of mifery or torment or the pun-
" ifhment of any creature under heaven, I fhould
" have faid mere creature. Page 43. " The
" voice of the whole law and the voice of the gof-
" pel are exceedingly diftinct and diametrically
" oppofite. The law demands perfection ;
" curfes for want of it; and cries vengeance.
" The gofpel points out perfection, highly ap-
" proves of it and the imputation of it ; and pro-
" claims falvation. The law fays do well and
" thou fhalt live. The gofpel fays thou fhalt live
" becaufe CHRIST lives and fhalt do well. The
" moral law is no news at all, it is what our rea-
" fon dictates and approves. The gofpel is all
" news, it is all good news, and there is not one
" word of bad news in it. Page 191. " I read-
" ily grant, if this diftinction which I would ev-
" ery where keep in view between the voice of
" juftice and that of mercy, the difplay of law
" and that of gofpel, running through the whole
" word of GOD, is without foundation, my whole
" argument falls to the ground." This laft quotation is from the latter part of the book, after
Dr. H. had mentioned his principal arguments,
fo that he muft confider this as the pillar of his
fcheme.

THE Doctor's notion feems to be, that as the
law is a difpenfation carrying death to all men ;

so the gospel is a dispensation carrying life to all men—that between the law and gospel there is a direct opposition, and in their nature they tend to different ends in the divine government.

To confute these representations, the following things will be attempted.

1st. To show, that the gospel contains threatnings of death, and impenitent sinners will be as much condemned by the gospel as by the law.

2d. To show, that there is in no sense a contradiction or opposition between the law and gospel.

1st. THE gospel contains threatnings of death, and sinners who are finally impenitent will be as much condemned by the gospel as by the law.

NEITHER the law nor gospel give life or death, independent of the moral temper and actions of men. The law in itself, hath the same power to give life as to give death. To the obedient and holy the law gives life. It gave life to Adam so long as he was a holy being, and it now gives life to all those beings who have not sinned. To the disobedient, by means of their sin it gives death; and as all men have become disobedient, they are under a sentence of condemnation. Therefore Paul says in Rom. vii. " *The commandment which* " *was ordained unto life, I found to be unto death.* " *For sin taking occasion by the commandment, de-* " *ceived me and by it slew me. Was then that* " *which is good made death unto me? God forbid;* " *but sin that it might appear sin working death in* " *me.*"—It seems, the Apostle conceived it was sin carried death and slew him, and that the law in its own nature was ordained unto life.——So it is with the gospel, there are conditions on which life is offered, repentance towards GOD and faith in our LORD JESUS CHRIST; and if there be not a compliance with these conditions, the gospel becomes a difpenfation of death to finners, as much as the law is ; yea of a much more awful death, than the law threatened.

THOSE who are impenitent will be judged, condemned and eternally punifhed as much by the gofpel as they are by the law. In Rom. ii. chapter, after the Apoftle, had fpoken of indignation, wrath, tribulation and anguifh, he tells us when thefe fhall be, verfe 16. " *In the day when* GOD *fhall judge the fecrets of men, according to my gofpel.* Here it is according to gofpel, that indignation and wrath are rendered unto men. If men are to be judged according to the gofpel, the gofpel muft contain both a law and a penalty.——Paul tells us that a difpenfation of the gofpel was committed to him, and defcribes the effects of his preaching. 2 Cor. ii. 15, 16. " *For we are unto* " GOD *a fweet favour of* CHRIST *in them that are* " *faved and in them that perifh ; to the one we are* " *the favour of death unto death ; and to the other* " *the favour of life unto life.*" If this preaching of the Apoftle, which was a favour of death unto death was not gofpel preaching, how could he fay that it was a fweet favour unto GOD in CHRIST ? ——CHRIST's commiffion to his difciples to preach the gofpel, fays, Mark xvi. 15, 16. " *Go* " *ye into all the world and preach the gofpel to ev-* " *ery creature. He that believeth and is baptized* " *fhall be faved ; but he that believeth not fhall be* " *damned.*" Believing in CHRIST was not a duty originally enjoined in the law. The obligation to believe, and men's right to believe had their origin in the gofpel. *Believe in the* LORD JESUS CHRIST, is a precept of the gofpel, and it is enforced by a gofpel penalty. Damnation is as much a gofpel penalty for unbelief, as death was a legal penalty for eating the forbidden fruit. Thefe, with innumerable other paffages teach us, that both law and gospel contain threatnings of death. The law threatens death to all who sin, and saith nothing of a remedy. The gospel comes after the law, and reveals a way of recovery; but it also threatens death to all who do not comply with that remedy. The notion, that the denunciations of wrath to come are all merely law threatnings; and that the gospel supercedes them, is no where hinted in the scripture, and is directly repugnant to the general tenor of the evangelical writings. It may as well be said the gospel doth not require holiness; as it may, that it doth not threaten death. We know that the law requires holiness, and when the gospel exhortation to live in all holy conversation is urged on men; they may as well say, this and all other precepts of the same kind are law precepts, and we have nothing to do either with the holiness or death of the law.

Dr. H. seems to rely much on this, that the gospel is *good news*, and that there is not *one word of bad news* in it. Let me ask the following questions; is there one word of bad news in the law to a heart that is right? Was not the law good news to holy and innocent Adam? Did it ever become bad news to him until he was a sinner? Further doth it not often happen that the gospel is bad news to a sinner? " *If any man will come after* " *me let him deny himself and take up his cross and* " *follow me.*" Is not this bad news to one who is fired with lust, and determined to indulge his passions? When the young man inquired of CHRIST, what he should do to inherit eternal life, he was told, "*go and sell that thou hast and come follow me.*" This was gospel, but it proved bad news to the young man, and he went away sorrowful because he had great possessions. The truth is, that both law and gospel are in their nature good news; or in other words, they are a reasonable ground for rejoicing; but whether they be in fact such to those who hear, depends on the moral state of their own hearts. It is well known, that the primary meaning of the greek word translated *gospel*, is good news; but this doth not appear to be any argument that all men shall be saved. Might not the salvation of only one sinner, if that had been the divine purpose, have been called good news with the greatest propriety? Tidings of joy are brought to sinners on condition of their repentance, but this is no proof that they will repent and believe. Their own unbelief may change gospel good news into a law of condemnation. In page 44 of his book, the Doctor rejects the idea of gospel law and says the phrase is not according to scripture. But in 1 John iii. 23. we find " *This is his commandment, that we should be-* " *lieve on the name of his son* JESUS CHRIST." Is not this a gospel law?

As to the ridicule which he attempts by telling of the condemning power of good news, I cannot feel the force of it. The law is good news to every good heart, and all will allow that it has a condemning power. Misimproved blessings may carry condemnation with them; light is a blessing, and it is good news, *but* CHRIST *says this is the condemnation, that light is come into the world and men choose darkness rather than light.*

Page 34. " WHATEVER is law in any part of " sacred writ is founded on the nature and char- " acter of GOD. Whatever is gospel in any part " of the bible, is founded wholly on JESUS " CHRIST, his character and offices."

IT seems to be a new discovery in divinity, that the gospel is not founded on the nature and character of GOD, as much as the law is. How strange the idea of a vast scheme of grace, which according to our author is to save all men, and is

the grand object of divine government; and
that this scheme not founded on the nature
and character of God. But what faith Christ,
John iii. 16. "*God so loved the world that he*
"*gave his only begotten son, that whosoever believ-*
"*eth in him should not perish but have everlasting*
"*life.*" Was not this gift of divine love, which
is the fountain and origin of all other gospel blessings, founded on the nature and character of
God? Or did God act in giving his son contrary to his nature and character? Or was the
Saviour a law gift and not a gospel gift?

2ndly. I am to show, that there is in no sense
a contradiction, or opposition between the law and
gospel. In the 43 page of the Doctor's book there
is the following passage. "The voice of the
"whole law, and the voice of the gospel are ex-
"ceedingly distinct and diametrically opposite."
In answer to which I observe, First.—That
the law cannot give salvation, and the gospel
can, is readily conceded; but that this argues
any opposition does by no means follow. Paul
expresses this matter much better, and calls it the
weakness of the law. Rom. viii. 3. 5. "*For what*
"*the law could not do in that it is weak through the*
"*flesh.*" And further on. "*That the righteous-*
"*ness of the law, might be fulfilled in us, who*
"*walk not after the flesh, but after the spirit.*"
We may very properly speak of the weakness of
the law, in point of salvation; but not of its being
diametrically opposite to the gospel, for it is said,
that the righteousness of the law is fulfilled in
them, who walk after the spirit of Christ and his
gospel.

Christ knew how prone sinful men would be
to think, on seeing him appear as a Saviour, that
he took their part in opposition to the law, and
early warned them "think not that I am come

" to deftroy the law and the prophets, I am not
" come to deftroy but to fulfil." He here fpoke
in the character of a gofpel Saviour, and on no
other ground, could he rationally have made himfelf a facrifice for fin. Had the gofpel been oppofite to the law he would haye faid, this law is
unreafonable, both in its precepts and its penalties
and muft be repealed.

2dly. The law hath no objection to the falvation of finners, who are in Christ and united to
him by a faving faith. Therefore the Apoftle
faith, (Gal. v. 23) againft fuch there is no law,
that is, no law oppofing their falvation. So far as
they are fanctified and reftored into a conformity
to God, the law approves their character; fo far
as they have been and ftill are finners, the law ac-
cepts of Christ's fatisfaction inftead of their eternal mifery. Both law and gofpel have the fame
view of finners, in every poffible fituation we
can conceive them to be. The law confiders
them while out of Christ as juftly condemned;
fo doth the gofpel, for its defign was to deliver
juftly condemned finners, and not thofe who are
unjuftly condemned. The law confiders them of
an odious character before their renewal by the
fpirit of Christ; fo doth the gofpel. The law
forbids all forgivenefs without fatisfaction; fo
doth the gofpel. The law knows not of any fafety
to the finner until united to Christ by a faving
faith; neither doth the gofpel. The law commands perfect holinefs; fo doth the gofpel, and
all the fins of chriftians are as much againft the
gofpel as they are againft the law. The gofpel
faith that God is juft, in juftifying the ungodly,
who have faith in Christ; the law alfo acknowl-
edges this truth in its fulleft extent, and both agree
in the juft and eternal punifhment of impenitent

D d

tranfgreffors. After the law hath condemned finners, it can provide no remedy.—The gofpel acknowledging the juftice of the law in all refpects, and affirming its fentence as a good one, alfo affirming all the principles on which the law is founded; ftill goes farther, and provides a remedy for the repenting finner. It furnifhes an atonement for the pardon of fin, and a fanctifier to deliver from its reigning power, and in both thefe refpects hath ftrength. Thus it appears that the law and gofpel harmonize in their nature and tendency as well as in CHRIST. The law was as much ordained unto life as the gofpel is. The law can give life to thofe who comply with its conditions, and it can do no more ; and in this way it doth give life to thofe who never finned. The gofpel can give life to thofe who comply with its conditions, faith and repentance; and it can do no more, and thus it gives life to all holy believers. The gofpel can give life to fome who cannot live by the law, but it doth not this on the principles of oppofition. It is fuppofed that on thoroughly canvaffing the fubject thefe ideas of contrariety between law and gofpel will all vanifh. Juftice is a branch of divine goodnefs and the fame act of juftice which punifhes a finner and thus makes him unhappy, may be the moft direct means of rendering the univerfe moft happy ; fo that what we call punifhing juftice to individuals is happifying goodnefs to the whole. To call law and gofpel two oppofing fchemes in the divine government, is either to fuppofe the everbleffed GOD in contention with himfelf and that there is no harmony between the great fcenes of his government; or that he has been difappointed in the effects of law, and to remedy himfelf had recourfe to an oppofing gofpel. Such fuppofitions are wholly unworthy JEHOVAH. There has been a perfect unity of defign in the divine government. The object of law and gofpel was to produce the greateft quantity of holinefs and happinefs in the univerfe. The legal and evangelical difpenfations, as we fometimes call them, are parts of one grand difpenfation tending to this important end. As means they are different ; as means they produce different effects on holy and unholy creatures ; but their general tendencies in the divine government are perfectly harmonious.

Sec. 4. Dr. H. has allowed, page 191, that if his diftinction between law and gofpel, which in other places he calls their oppofition, be without foundation, his whole fcheme falls to the ground. We ought therefore to fearch this matter to the bottom. The reafon, which he affigns for his notion, is what he calls the contradictions of fcripture if this be not the cafe. He fays, page 48, if this be not the cafe, " it will be wholly in " vain for all the wit, and art in the world, to " make any thing better of the holy fcriptures, " than a long, folemn, feries of the moft palpable " contradictions."

. From wit and art we appeal to common fenfe and common honefty ; and hope by the aid of thefe, to fhow that though fome men will be eternally miferable, there is no long, folemn, feries of moft palpable contradictions in the word of God.

The way the Dr. takes to fhow thefe palpable contradictions, is firft, to allow that the endlefs damnation of finners is fully afferted in the word of God ; and then (page 48) affert that " the " Bible plainly tells us, that all the human race " fhall certainly be faved." His proof that all mankind fhall certainly be faved are the following texts. John i. 29. " *Behold the Lamb of* God " *which taketh away the fins of the world.*" John iv. 42. John vi. 33. John xii. 47. 1 John iv. 14.

THE Doctor's argument from these passages, doubtless arises from supposing the word *world* to mean all individuals of the human race.———To this I reply.

ANSWER 1ft. The word *world* is often used for a part of mankind, John vii. 7. " *The world cannot hate you, but me it hateth.*" If the world means every individual, those disciples to whom CHRIST spoke are included, but no one will think that he meant to charge them with hating him. The Pharisees said, John xii. 19, " *The world is gone after him.*" The Pharisees were individuals of the human race, did they mean that they had themselves gone after CHRIST? John xvi. 20. " *The world shall rejoice and ye shall be sorrowful.*" Certainly in this case the world means only a part of mankind, for there were some left to mourn. John xvii. 14. " *The world hath hated them because they are not of the world.*" If *world* means every individual, then this text may be thus read, " every individual of the human race hath hated " them because they are not individuals of the " human race."

THERE are several other words and phrases used in scripture such as, *all, all men, all things, every, &c.* on which our author in the course of his work makes much dependence for proof. It is strange he should not have known, that these words and phrases do not necessarily imply universality, either in the holy scriptures, profane writers, or in conversation. Matt. x. 22. " *Ye shall be hated of all men for my name's sake.*" Did CHRIST mean that every individual of mankind even his disciples should hate each other for his sake? Luke xviii. 43. " *And all the people when they saw it, gave praise to GOD.*" The rulers of the Jews were certainly an exception in this case. When Paul said, " *all things are lawful unto me,* but *all things are not expedient."* *" I am made all things to all men."* Did he mean that all poſſible actions were lawful for him, but not one of them expedient; or that he aſſumed every poſſible character in the ſight of every individual of mankind? If in converſation the following deſcriptions were uſed, " all the town. come together—all " things are in confuſion—all men are aſleep— " the whole world is at war" would not the common ſenſe of the hearer limit the univerſality of ſuch expreſſions without danger of miſtake? Time, circumſtances, the nature of the ſubject conſidered, the conſiſtency of the writer or ſpeaker, and many other things muſt determine the univerſality or limitation that is deſigned. It is ſtrange the holy ſcriptures ſhould be charged with contradiction on this ground.

LET the reader turn to Mr. Cruden's Concordance of the Engliſh Bible, under the heads *all, all men, all things, world, whole world, &c.* and examine the various ſenſes in which theſe words are uſed in the Holy Bible, and I think he muſt be convinced that the argument is too weak to ſupport a doctrine of ſuch importance.

I CONSIDER theſe remarks on the uſe of the words, *world, all, all men,* as a ſufficient anſwer to Dr. H's argument; but as the minds of ſome may be conſcientiouſly perplexed on this ſubject, I ſhall endeavor to give the real meaning of thoſe paſſages which the Doctor adduces for proof, and of many others which are ſimilar to them, and to ſhow that they are perfectly reconcileable with the doctrine of eternal miſery; alſo that there was no other way, in which infinite wiſdom could expreſs the truth to men, in the language of common ſenſe, even on the ſuppoſition that part of them will never be ſaved.

Sec. 5. To show that Dr. H's opinion is wholly unfounded I add——

Answer 2nd. If we allow that the words and phrases, *world, all, all men, all things,* &c. on which he relies ; do really mean all individuals of the human race, there is still no proof of universal salvation. We must attend to the relative situation and moral character of men, to whom the gospel salvation is offered.   Considering men as sinners, two difficulties occured in the way of their salvation.

1st. The public good required their punishment, and for this reason, misery was the appointed penalty of the law.   This first difficulty is removed from the way of all men ; if they will comply with the gospel conditions of forgiveness. In this sense Christ died for all men and all the world ; still whether all men and the whole world will be saved, depends not on the amplitude of Christ's atonement, but on their own temper.

2. The immoral and unholy state of sinners hearts is another difficulty in the way of salvation, and there is no evidence that this will ever be removed from all mankind.   To show the nature of the first difficulty, let the following things be considered.

The happiness of the universe depended on the true character of God being brought into view. If he had by his law and government, treated the holy and unholy in the same manner, it would have hid, both his character and the nature and obligations of the moral system ; and thus lessened the happiness of the whole.   The manifestation of God's character was necessary for the highest happiness of the universe, because happiness consisted in the sight and enjoyment of God.   A display of his sense of the sinner's temper and conduct, was necessary to manifest his character ;

and punifhment was the only means in the nature of things by which he could difplay his fenfe of the finner's character. For this reafon eternal mifery was made the penalty of the law.

SINNERS never could themfelves remove this objection to their forgivenefs. Even if they were by any means to become holy, this would not remove it ; for it would ftill be fit they fhould be treated according to what they had been and done ; and not to treat them fo, would have been hiding the divine holinefs and taking away the object of happinefs. Hence came the neceffity that finners fhould remain unforgiven and in a ftate of punifhment ; unlefs fome other means could be devifed to anfwer the fame purpofe in the divine government, and in difplaying the nature of GoD and of the moral fyftem.

FURTHER, In this cafe, not only the happinefs of holy creatures depended on GoD's making a true difplay of his character. But his own happinefs alfo. GoD is a being of infinite benevolence and hath delight in happinefs. His own happinefs depended on making the greateft happinefs around him that can be made. If GoD's own happinefs depended on making the greateft happinefs around him that can be made ; and if the greateft happinefs around him is made by a difplay of his averfion to fin ; then his own happinefs alfo, as well as the happinefs of his kingdom, depended on fuch a difplay as would be made by the eternal punifhment of fin. Therefore the bleffednefs of the univerfe, depended on the penalty of the law being executed ; unlefs fome adequate means could be found to anfwer the fame ends.

THIS difficulty in the way of falvation, is removed from the way of all men by the obedience and fufferings of JESUS CHRIST, unlefs their own un-

holinefs prevents. CHRIST by his obedience and
fufferings, has made a difplay of the rectitude, holinefs, and all the moral perfections of GOD; alfo
of the moral fyftem and its obligations on every
rational mind, equivalent to what would have
been by the fuffering of thofe who are faved. As
GOD had no perfonal enmity or revenge againft
the finner, he might in juftice to himfelf, his law
and government, and in favor to the greateft happinefs, accept of what CHRIST hath done and fuffered, in the ftead of fo many as he pleafes to fave.

ON this ground ftands the gofpel command
for all men to believe in the Lord JESUS CHRIST,
that they may be faved. On this ground, the
fcriptures reprefent finners failure of falvation to
be their own fault. There is no difficulty in the
way of their falvation now remaining, but the oppofednefs of their own hearts to fuch a falvation
as is offered. They do not choofe a holy Saviour,
law and gofpel, and a holy kingdom.

IT is in this fenfe that *CHRIST gave himfelf a
ranfom for all*—*that he will have* or commands *all
men to be faved*—*that he is the Saviour of the world*
—*that the world through him may be faved*—*that
he is the propitiation for the fins of the whole world*
—*and that he came not to judge the world but to
fave the world.*—It is in this fenfe that a door of
mercy is really opened for all mankind. When
we fay that a door of mercy is opened for all mankind, it doth not imply that all will enter. It
only means that they may be faved, if they choofe
fuch a falvation as is offered; and that all difficulty, foreign to the moral ftate of their own
hearts is removed. If they choofe and their love
be right, they may be faved; but if CHRIST had
not obeyed and fuffered, even though their choice
and love had became right, they could not have
been faved from mifery, without a public injury.

It is this, which is meant, by all finners being brought into a ftate of trial and probation. Every thing is removed out of the way, but their own perfonal unholinefs; and when all foreign objec‑ tions are removed, God places their falvation or deftruction upon the proof of their own temper and choice. This is meant by the gofpel being preached to all the world, which Dr. H. (page 55) ufes as an argument that all men will be faved. Before the provifion of a Saviour, there was a neceffary oppofition between the beft good of the univerfe, and the forgivenefs of any finner. The wifdom of God in the gofpel hath provided fuch means as reconcile the forgivenefs of every penitent, with the beft good of his kingdom and the greateft glory of his own name; and no caufe but the finner's own perverfe heart can fruftrate the application.

This ferves to explain 2 Cor. v. 18. which Dr. H. fays is fo plain in favor of his fcheme that it cannot be any plainer. *Who hath reconciled us to himself by* Jesus Christ, *and hath given to us the miniftry of reconciliation; to wit, that* God *was in* Christ *reconciling the world to himself, not imput‑ ing their trefpaffes unto them; and hath committed to us the word of reconciliation.* Being actually re‑ conciled to God, as thofe chriftians were to whom the Apoftle wrote; doubtlefs means a holy ftate, and a certainty of falvation. By the miniftry of reconciliation given to the Apoftle; is to be un‑ derftood fuch means, as have a reafonable ten‑ dency to turn men from fin to holinefs. The means which he principally ufed, were to tell them of God in Christ, reconciling the world to himfelf; God in Christ, reconciling the in‑ terefts of his kingdom with the falvation of fin‑ ners; God in Christ reconciling and removing

all difficulties out of the way, except the sinner's
own enmity. All will concede, that the sinner's
enmity must be laid aside, before he can be actually saved. The phrases used, of *reconciling the
world to himself and not imputing their trespasses to
them*, are not in this place, descriptive of a fact,
that the enmity of all men either now is or ever
will be laid aside; but they are descriptive of the
ministration of reconciliation, of means used, of arguments set before sinners. The argument is
this. God is in Christ, using fit means to
bring you to such repentance, that the punishment
of your iniquity may not be executed upon you.
Therefore there is now no difficulty in the way
of salvation, except your own enmity. Lay that
aside and be reconciled. But there is not in this
place one intimation that all men ever will lay it
aside.

The words of the Apostle in Col. i. 19—21,
Dr. H. uses as an argument. If there be any argument for Universalism, in this passage, it lies
in the phrase " *reconcile all things to himself*," but
we have before showed that the terms *all, all men,
all things, every, &c.* do not mean every individual, either in the language of scripture or common sense; and this is conceived to be a sufficient
answer to the argument from this passage. But
I would observe further, it does not appear that in
this passage, the Apostle had any reference either
to the limitation or universality of salvation, in
fact. He was treating of the fulness and sufficiency of Christ; and it is allowed, there is a
sufficiency in the obedience and sufferings of
Christ, to reconcile all men, if their own hostility
doth not prevent. It is allowed he hath set on
foot a treaty of peace by his death on the cross;
the treaty is published; but if it be not ratified
by the consent of the sinner's will, the benefits

propofed will all be loft to him, and he muft endure the confequences of his own hoftile heart.
Still further, we know that God is ufing the moft
fit and rational means for reconciliation, and
nothing more than this is naturally meant by the
phrafes of *reconciling the world to himfelf*, and *the
fulnefs that there is in* Christ to reconcile. In
this paffage things in heaven are mentioned. This
doubtlefs is an intimation of a glorious union and
communion between all parts of the true church
through the univerfe, in Chrift; who will be in
fome fenfe a common head to the whole holy
body; but as this is a point not directly connected
with the prefent inquiry, no further remarks will
be made upon it.

Dr. H. and all who are in his fcheme of faith
make much ufe of 1 Tim. ii. The paffages they
ufe are thefe. *That prayers be made for all men—
who will have all men to be faved—and to come to a
knowledge of the truth—who gave himfelf a ranfom
for all.* The duty of prayer, as it is connected
with the doctrine of univerfal falvation will be
confidered hereafter.—The paffage we now confider is this " *who will have all men to be faved
and come to a knowledge of the truth.*" It will not
be difputed that compleat falvation includes deliverance both from *fin* and *mifery.* The expreffions, *falvation* and *being faved*, fometimes mean
both; fometimes one or the other of the two
parts; but moft commonly *falvation* and *being
faved* mean a deliverance from fin, and where this
takes place there will be a deliverance from its
confequences.

The will of God fometimes means his determination what fhall abfolutely take place. (Mark
i. 41.) " *I will be thou clean.*" Here it expreffes
God's abfolute determination what fhall take
place. Sometimes the word *will* is ufed as an

expreffion of what God knows to be the creature's duty, as in the following paffages. Rom. ii. 18. " *And knoweft his will,*" that is, knoweft the expreffion God hath made of thy own duty. 1 Theff. v. 18. " *In every thing give thanks, for this is the will of God.*" No one can underftand by this that all men do give thanks. Christ alfo faid of Jerufalem " how often I would have gathered " you, and ye would not." Suppofe, that after God had given the law to Adam or to Ifrael, he had added, it is the will of God that all men keep this law. Would any man in his fenfes, fuppofe from this, that Adam or all Ifrael did in fact keep the law. It was God's will, that is, his expreffion of their duty that they fhould keep the law; but the confequence doth not follow that they did keep it. So it is God's will, or his expreffion of men's duty, that they be faved from their fins, become holy, and forfake all iniquity; but this is no evidence that they will in fact forfake and be faved from their fins, for we know that men do innumerable things contrary to their duty, and fuffer the confequences.

" *Who gave himfelf a ranfom for all.*" It is a fact that Chrift hath given himfelf a ranfom for all, in fuch a manner that every difficulty except the finner's own bad heart is removed from the way of falvation. This is all that the words imply, and this underftanding of them is perfectly confiftent with eternal mifery. A confideration of the circumftances under which Paul wrote to Timothy will fully explain his meaning. Under the Mofaic difpenfation, the inftitutions of revealed religion had been confined to the Jewifh nation. By the gofpel thefe religious privileges were given to the Gentiles alfo. Timothy a young Jew was now made a gofpel minifter. Paul wrote to direct him in his duty, and teach him the na.

ture of the gofpel difpenfation. That prayer was now to be made for men of all nations.—That God had now placed all nations under equal advantages for falvation—and that Chrift was as much a ranfom for other men as for the Jews. The phrafes of *all being faved*, and a *ranfom for all*, are placed in oppofition, not to none being loft; but to the confinement of falvation to the Jews, in preference to the Gentile nations. Thus it appears, that there are feveral ways of making this paffage confiftent with the other parts of Paul's writings, without fuppofing a jumble of contradiction. Dr. H. (page 50) endeavors to prove that the inhabitants of ancient Sodom are faved. By attending to Ezek. xvi. from which he takes his proof, it may be feen that it is a mere play of names. There is not in that chapter one word concerning thofe inhabitants of ancient Sodom, who are faid by the Apoftle, to fuffer the vengeance of eternal fire. Ezekiel wrote 1300 years after ancient Sodom and its inhabitants were deftroyed, and he fpeaks of Sodom and her daughters as cotemporary with the time of his writing. Verfe 46, " *And thine elder fifter is Samaria, fhe* " *and her daughters that dwell at thy left hand,* " *and thy younger fifter that dwelleth at thy right* " *hand is Sodom and her daughters.*" The Samaritans had no being in the time of ancient Sodom. Thefe were people of whom the prophet fpeaks as then living, on the right and left hand of the Jews. By Sodom and her daughters, is probably meant the Ammonites and Moabites, the defcendants of the daughters of Lot and therefore Sodomites by defcent. The bringing again the captivity of Jerufalem, Samaria, and Sodom and their daughters, is a prophecy of that glorious day which is yet future, when the defcendants of all thofe people and the inhabitants of the countries

in which they dwelt, fhall with the reft of mankind be holinefs to the Lord.   After the prophet,
through the greateft part of the chapter, had denounced judgments which have been long fulfilling on the Jews and their neighboring nations, he
promifes a future day when the church of God
fhall fill the earth ; but left the Jews fhould expect this reftoration too foon ; he adds, that this
fhall not be done " *by thy covenant*" not under
the Jewifh difpenfation, but under the gofpel.

The whole of the xi Chap. of Ifaiah to which
Dr. H. refers, is a prophecy of the future profperity of the gofpel kingdom, when the vifible church
fhall fill the earth ; and there is not one verfe in it,
which hath any relation to the fubject we are
confidering, unlefs it be part of the 4th, " *with*
" *the breath of his lips fhall he flay the wicked.*"

Ezek. xxxiii. 11. " *As I live faith the Lord, I*
" *have no pleafure in the death of the wicked, but*
" *that the wicked turn from his way and live.*"
On this alfo Dr. H. relies. Page 51.   But what
doth it prove ? The death of the finner are his fin
and mifery.   Sin and mifery have both taken
place, and God never had any pleafure or delight
in either of them.   Death means fin as much as
it doth mifery, and its being faid, God hath no
pleafure in the death of the finner, will as much
prove that men never fell, as it doth that all men
fhall be faved.   But though God hath no pleafure in fin and mifery ; he may ufe them to
increafe the happinefs and holinefs of his own
kingdom.   He hath begun, and it is probable
will continue to ufe them forever.

If God delighted in mifery for its own fake,
the finner could have no reafon to fuppofe deliverance poffible.   The Lord hath affured us he
doth not delight in death, fin and mifery, and the
ufe of fuch an affurance is ; Firft, To teach us

there is room for pardon, on our repentance and faith in Chrift ; Secondly, This very declaration of God, that he doth not delight in mifery, when rightly underftood, is a moft folemn warning of danger to the impenitent. For certainly thofe threatnings, which come from a being, who inflexibly acts on the principle of promoting the general good, are more to be feared, and there is more probability they will be carried into execution ; than if they came from a being who is capricious and paffionate. The threatnings of God arife from his benevolence to univerfal being, and ftanding on this broad bafis, are more terrible to the tranfgreffor, than if they arofe from particular and private animofity. The benevolence of God which prevents him delighting in mifery, and caufes him to love happinefs, makes the fulfilment of his threatnings certain.

We often hear it faid ; it is incredible that a God who was fo good as to give his fon to die for finners, fhould after this make any of them forever unhappy. The very remark, fhows that thofe who offer it have not thoroughly attended to the fubject. The death of Chrift really adds an awfulnefs to the threatnings of the law. To fhow this I inquire, what was the object of that benevolence in God, which moved him to give his fon to die for finners? Men are apt to think it was a particular, private affection to thofe who are faved, which moved God to give his fon to die for them ; but it is conceived this was not the cafe. His wifdom faw it would be beft for the whole, that was his primary motive in giving Chrift to die for thofe who are faved, and the gift did not come from a private, partial affection to them in particular. Their f.'vation was neceffary for the beft good of the whole, and therefore it became a fecondary motive with GOD in giving his fon to die for them.

CHRIST himfelf was an example of this truth. the glory of his Father, which is the fame thing as the general good, was his principal motive in obeying and fuffering, and this he often expreffed. His tender affection to individual members of his fpiritual body, always appeared fubordinate to a greater intereft.

FROM this we may infer, that GOD's goodnefs in giving his fon to die for finners is no evidence againft the eternal mifery of fome. If GOD's benevolence induced him to give his fon to death, to promote the general good; it will certainly be confiftent with his benevolence, to punifh forever thofe finners who deferve it, if the fame end will be promoted by their punifhment. A fight of the crofs of CHRIST, when the reafons of his fuffering are juftly viewed, folemnly confirms the threatnings of GOD's word, and equally manifefts the glory of divine grace in forgiving, and of divine juftice in punifhing. The reafon that any fuppofe different, is becaufe they think GOD was moved to give his fon to die, by a partial and particular affection to the faved; whereas his real motive was a love of the greateft good, which would be advanced by the falvation of a certain part of finners.

DR. H. and thofe who are with him in opinion, place great dependance on Rom. v. as evidence in their favor. The paffage is from the 15th to the 18th verfe. *But not as the offence, fo alfo is the free gift. For if through the offence of one many*

be dead; much more the grace of God, *and the gift
by grace, which is by one man,* Jesus Christ, *hath
abounded unto many. And not as it was by one that
finned, so is the gift : for the judgment was by one to
condemnation, but the free gift is of many offences unto
justification. For if by one man's offence death reigned by one; much more they which receive abundance
of grace, and of the gift of righteousness, shall reign
in life by one,* Jesus Christ: *therefore, as by the
offence of one, judgment came upon all men unto condemnation ; even so by the righteousness of one, the free
gift came upon all men unto justification of life.* On
this passage I remark,

1st. It hath been sufficiently shown already,
that the phrase *all men*, neither in the scriptural or
common use, necessarily means all individuals of
the human race ; but is very often applied to numerous classes and bodies of men, not meaning the
whole of mankind.

2dly. It must be supposed that Paul is consistent with himself in his writings. In the first part
of this work, I have taken a general view of all
his canonical writings, and particularly of his e-
piftle to the Romans, from which this passage is
taken ; and collected a great number of places, in
which future and eternal punishment is asserted
in most express terms. From the remarks I made
on this epistle, to which I refer the reader, I
think it appears that such an event is implied
through the whole epistle ; and that it is one of
the doctrines most clearly told, and a necessary
branch of the scheme which the Apostle is endeavouring to establish. If we allow this passage to
mean universal salvation; we shall find several
hundred verses in the writings of Paul, which are
more irreconcileable with universal salvation, than
this passage is with everlasting punishment. If

F f

we were reduced to the alternative, either of saying this passage means universal salvation ; or of saying, we know nothing of its meaning, the last must be chosen to preserve any consistency in the writings of this Apostle.

3dly. But it is happy we are not reduced to this difficulty. A strict attention to the passage, in connexion with the subject the Apostle is considering, will explain it in consistency with eternal punishment to come. After he had stated the doctrine of justification by the righteousness of Christ through faith, in the fifth and succeeding chapters, he mentions a great number of benefits which come to justified persons by the grace of God through Jesus Christ. In enumerating these benefits, together with the greatness and richness of them, the passage under consideration is found. Paul is describing the benefits which come to the justified ; and it doth not appear, that he had any reference to the particular number or proportion of mankind that will be justified. He begins with the fifth chapter to enumerate these benefits. They are, peace with God ; access to him through Christ ; rejoicing in hope of glory with him ; glorying in tribulation, because of its beneficial effects ; pardon of sin and reconciliation to God ; and then comes the passage we are noticing, and it is indeed a glorious one. To show the infinitude of divine grace in pardoning those who believe, he introduces Adam and Christ as federal heads. Adam the federal head of all sinful men. Christ the federal head of all who believe and are sanctified. One offence, the eating of the forbidden fruit, brought condemnation on those whom Adam represented ; but those whom Christ represents, have through him the forgiveness of many offences—of a heart and life full of sins. For the judgment was by one offence to condemnation, but the free gift of forgivenefs, is of many offences unto juftification. In this cir-cumftance, that many fins are forgiven to the be-liever, confifts the abounding of grace which the Apoftle mentions. The abounding of grace doth not apply to the number of the faved ; but to the number of the fins which are forgiven to thofe who are faved. If the abounding of grace applies to the number who are faved, the whole defcrip-tion is wrong ; unlefs more perfons in number are forgiven through CHRIST, than fell through A-dam. Forgiving grace through CHRIST the fpir-itual head of all true believers, abounds or ex-ceeds condemning juftice through Adam ; as much as the number of fins forgiven to the be-liever, are more than the one fin by which Adam fell, and brought mifery on himfelf and his pof-terity. It is a matter of importance, that we un-derftand to what the abounding of grace in this paffage applies, for the fubject which the Apoftle is confidering, and the point to which the aboun-ding of grace applies, are the keys to a right un-derftanding it. The fubject is the privileges, which are through grace to the juftified ; and not the number of the juftified. The point to which the abounding of grace applies, is the forgive-nefs of many offences to the faved ; and not how great the number of faved fhall be. In recount-ing the privileges of the juftified, Paul might well mention the forgivenefs of many offences, as this is both a ground of fure confolation to them, and a difplay of GOD's infinite love in their falvation.

4th. IF Paul meant in this paffage to affert the final falvation of all individuals, the 17th verfe would have been expreffed very different. *For if by one man's offence death reigned by one ; much more they which receive abundance of grace, and of the gift of righteoufnefs, fhall reign in life by one*

Jesus Christ.—If univerfal falvation was meant, there is reafon to fuppofe the Apoftle would have faid, " much more all men receive abundance of " grace and of the gift of righteoufnefs and fhall " reign in life," but inftead of this, he is careful to fay, " they which receive abundance of grace, " &c." intimating that it is only a part, and not all the human race, who fhall receive thofe benefits of juftification which he is defcribing. And in the fingle place where he fays all men, it doubtlefs means all of that great clafs of men, who by a holy faith become federal members in CHRIST's fpiritual body.

CONSIDERING, that the phrafes, *many* and *all men* are often in fcripture applied to great bodies or claffes of men, not meaning all mankind ; that we muft fuppofe this paffage confiftent with the other writings of the Apoftle ; confidering the fubject he is defcribing, the privileges and number of the faved, and how pertinently it applies to this as has been explained ; confidering that the abounding of grace, muft apply to the number of offences forgiven, and not to the number of men who are faved, unlefs we fuppofe more men are faved in CHRIST, than fell in Adam ; it appears plain the Apoftle did not mean the falvation of all men. The application of thofe words to the doctrine of univerfal falvation fhows the danger of detaching particular paffages, and conftruing them by themfelves, without regard to the fubject of the writer. In my former remarks on this Epiftle, mention was made of the care taken by the Apoftle, to limit the abounding of grace which he had mentioned, by very largely defcribing the holy and fanctified character of thofe to whom grace abounds ; and if men would read thefe parts of his Epiftle with felf application, it

would cut off their vifionary hope from the paffage, on which I have been remarking.

Sec. 6. The unholy ftate of finners hearts, is
a second difficulty in the way of their falvation, and there is no evidence that this will ever
be removed from all men. The finner doth not
choofe a God, a Saviour and a gofpel of fuch holinefs. He could love a God according to
his own heart, but for fuch a God as the gofpel exhibits he hath no love and choice. Christ's
character as a Saviour from mifery he perfectly
approves ; as a fanctifier he fees no excellency in
it. While he loaths punifhment ; he delights in
his own felfifhnefs, pride, and lufts which are the
very things that deferve to be punifhed. With a
gofpel, which is *mere news, good news,* and no *bad
news* in it, and no law of holinefs in it ; a gofpel
that is in all points oppofite to the moral law of
holinefs, he will be delighted. On fuch grounds,
he will be ready to love Christ becaufe he thinks
Christ loves him. It hath been already fhown,
that the firft difficulty is removed from the way
of falvation, fo that no men will perifh merely by
that obftruction. The death of Christ was a
great governmental tranfaction ; not defigned to
make God good, for if he had not been antece-
dently good, he would not have given his fon to
die ; not making it a matter of perfonal juftice to
the finner that he fhould be forgiven, for he is
perfonally as worthy of punifhment fince the death
of Christ as he was before the promife of a Saviour. It was a governmental tranfaction, making
it confiftent for God to forgive fuch and fo many
finners as he pleafes ; and the good of the univerfe will be the rule of his benevolent pleafure.
Hence the neceffity of a renewal and of fanctification by the fpirit of God, which are fo much
fpoken of in the holy fcriptures. Though eter-

nal mifery be the threatened punifhment, no man will come to Chrift to efcape it, until he is changed by the Holy Ghoft, and made to love the Saviour's character. Therefore Chrift faid, "*Ye will not come to me that ye might have life.*" "*If I had not come and fpoken unto them they had not had fin, but now they have both feen and hated me and my father.*" The firft objection to finner's falvation lay out of themfelves, and arofe from their relative connection with the intelligent fyftem of beings, in which GOD defigned to produce the greateft poffible happinefs. This fecond objection lies in the finner himfelf; and will continue until he is made a holy creature.

WE know that the firft difficulty implies the fecond, and that it muft be removed before GOD can confiftently act to remove the fecond; but ftill they are of diftinct confideration, and the removal of the firft doth not imply the removal of the laft.

THE gift of Chrift, his obedience and fufferings, muft go firft to make it confiftent for GOD to give the fpirit, by whom finners are renewed and effectually inclined to choofe the gofpel falvation; ftill the gifts are diftinct. The gift of CHRIST was to remove a general difficulty which lay in the way of all mankind. The gift of the fpirit is to remove a particular difficulty from the hearts of individuals.

THOSE to whom he doth not give the fpirit will never leave their fins; and not leaving their fins will never be faved.——Of what benefit then will the gofpel be to them? Of no benefit, and through their mifimprovement a great evil. As Paul faid of the law in his own cafe, that though it was good in its nature and ordained unto life, ftill by means thereof fin became death unto him. So with the gofpel, though ordained unto life to

all repenting finners; to thofe who do not repent, it will be the means of an aggravated condemnation, through their own unbelief. In
another place this apoftle faith, that it will be
death unto death to fome. And Christ fays, if
I had not come and fpoken unto them, they had
not had fin. Their rejection of the gofpel by
unbelief made them more guilty than if there had
been no gofpel.

Is the gofpel then a difpenfation of goodnefs
in God, when it will probably be the means of
increafing the unhappinefs of many finners? truly it is not the lefs a difpenfation of goodnefs on
this account. The law was a difpenfation of
goodnefs; but if there had been no law we had not
known fin. The goodnefs of God in his difpenfations to creatures, is not to be determined from
the ufe which they make of them ; for the beft
difpenfations may be the worft improved. God's
goodnefs in his difpenfations, is to be determined,
Firft, From their influence upon creatures, who
make a rational and right ufe of them. Secondly,
From their eventual effect in promoting the greateft happinefs of the univerfe, which is the ultimate object of God in his whole government.

Sec. 7. It was faid a little back that the fcripture
expreffions of Chrift's dying for *all men, the world
&c.* were not only reconcileable with the doctrine
of eternal mifery, but that there was no other way
in which infinite wifdom could exprefs truth to
men in the language of common fenfe, even on
the fuppofition that part of them will never be
faved. And I now put the queftion, how could
infinite wifdom have expreffed the truth in all
refpects, more perfectly than is done in the holy
fcriptures, even allowing that part of men will
never be faved? Do they fay that Chrift died for
all men, and gave himfelf a ranfom for the world?

And is not this true? Is it not true that he hath removed every objection, but the choice of men's hearts? When we addrefs men, on any fubject whatever, exhorting them, and telling them there is no difficulty in the way, doth not this always imply an exception of their own choice and will? If we tell them there is no objection in the way, do we not mean to be underftood, notwithftanding what we fay, that their own will may be an objection, and even an infurmountable one? It is thus in this cafe. Chrift hath died for all men, in fuch a fenfe that there is no difficulty but their own choice, and this may prove an eternal obftacle. If it doth, GOD will not be difappointed, but fhow the nature of fin by means of their unbelief, and thus make it the caufe of promoting general happinefs.

Do not the fcriptures tell us " he that believeth not fhall be damned?" Do they not give us reafon to think that fome will not believe? They certainly do. And they affign as a reafon; that the wickednefs of men's hearts prevents their believing and choofing fuch a falvation as is offered, and going to heaven through the fovereign mercy of GOD. It is not conceived, how the fcriptures, could in all refpects, have told us the truth better and more plainly than it is done. Though we believe in as diametrical oppofition to Dr. H. as he fuppofes the law and gofpel to be to each other; there is ftill no reafon to charge the word of GOD with being a volume of contradictions. Not attending to the relation of the law and gofpel to each other in GOD's government, and in his difpenfations to finful men, is the fource of innumerable errors. In this fource Dr. H's fcheme begins, which we fuppofe to be a fyftem of error; and that moft of the premifes from which his final conclufion is drawn, are as erroneous as the conclufion itfelf. I have endeavored to fhow, that there is not in any fenfe, an oppofition between the law and gofpel ; and if I have fucceeded, the Doctor's fcheme falls ; for he tells us, that if his ideas of " the difplay of law and gofpel running " through the whole word of GOD is without " foundation, his whole argument falls to the " ground."

SEC. 8. DR. H. in the moft important part of his argument, hath made a digreffion concerning the progrefs of light. (From page 35 to 42.) As I mean to follow him in his own order, I fhall notice it in this place.   He intimates, that the point on which light hath been increafing, is the falvation of all men.   It is well known there hath been an increafe of light in the church, but to what hath it tended ? Not to prove that all men fhall be faved.   There hath been an increafing light in the manner and means of falvation, and in the nature of that holinefs without which no man can fee GOD.   From an increafing knowledge of the nature of holinefs, it hath been becoming more and more apparent that all men will not be faved. The doctrine of future and eternal punifhment is much more clearly revealed in the New, than it was in the Old Teftament.   By an increafing knowledge of the true meaning of the fcriptures, the evidence hath been growing from Chrift's time down to the prefent ; and it will continue to grow as the fubject is examined on fcriptural grounds.

IT is ftrange Dr. H. fhould fay, as he doth in page 39, that the reafon the Jews were fuch malicious perfecutors of Chrift, was becaufe he fet the gofpel door open to all the nations.   It doth not appear that either the friends or enemies of Chrift, had an idea in the time of his life, that this would be the cafe; neither was it a fact. No door was opened to the Gentiles, until after the death, refurrection and afcenfion of our bleffed Saviour. He told the Syrophenician woman, *that it was not lawful to take the childrens bread and caft it to the dogs.* His miniftration was confined among believers in the law of Mofes. He exprefsly faid, *I am not fent but unto the loft fheep of the houfe of Ifrael,* Matt. xv. 24. He directed his difciples, *Go not into the way of the Gentiles, but go rather to the loft fheep of the houfe of Ifrael.* Matt. x. 5, 6. The caufe affigned for the perfecution of JESUS by the Jews, is directly contrary to known matter of fact. CHRIST affigns in many places (which a gofpel minifter ought to have noticed) the reafons of Jewifh enmity. He reproved their vices—told them truth which they hated—difplayed the character of himfelf and his father, which they did not love—and overturned their felf-righteous hopes of heaven.

WHEN the Apoftles of CHRIST were afterwards perfecuted, it was not for preaching to Gentiles, but for overturning the Jewifh difpenfation. Glad would the Jews have been, if the Apoftles had gone among the Gentiles never more to return, and threaten the overthrow of the Mofaic difpenfation. They had no prejudice againft fuch Gentiles as would become profelytes to Judaifm. Chriftianity and not Gentiles was the object of Jewifh enmity. It is eafy to fee, that Dr. H. fell into this idea of Jewifh prejudice, in order to infinuate, that pride and a felfifh defire to monopolize, as he expreffes it, the benefits of the gofpel, are the reafons that any difbelieve the falvation of all men. I think real chriftians will not feel any force, either in his argument or defcription.

Sec. 9. From the 57th, to the 71st, page of his book, Dr. H. attempts an argument, from what he calls the nature and office of faith. I moſt ſincerely wiſh if poſſible, to ſelect his argument from an extent of words; and if I have not done it, the fault is not intentional.

By ſeveral quotations, I will endeavor to place his idea of faith and its office before the reader. Page 70. " Faith, agreeably to every juſt idea we " can form of it, never had, never can have, any " other province than this; to give ſenſe and en- " joyment of an unalterable fact or object, if " comfortable; or diſtreſs, if the reverſe." Page 57. " The Apoſtles, in all their preaching, com- " manded every one of their hearers to believe " ſaving truth, on pain of damnation, knowing, " at the ſame time, that their belief, or unbelief, " would not in the leaſt alter that truth. Yet their " comfort in the truth, depended on their belief " of it." Page 59. " Faith is in the nature of " things neceſſary to an experience and enjoy- " ment of the benefit." Page 102. " He did " juſtify us not as penitent; but as impenitent; " not as believers, but as unbelievers; not as god- " ly in the leaſt degree; but as wholly ungodly; " and then brings the knowledge and comfort of " this previous tranſaction to our ſouls, by giving " us a heart prepared to have light and full evi- " dence operate properly upon."

In the deſcription that Dr. H. gives of faith we ſee the following things.

1ſt. " That it never had, nor ever can have " any other province than this, to give ſenſe and " enjoyment of an unalterable fact or object." Though Dr. H. ſpeaks much of being a Calviniſt, his idea of ſaving faith is eſſentially different from the calviniſtic, and he leaves out all exerciſe of the heart and affections. The calviniſtic ſaving faith, includes a holy choice of God, of Christ, of the gospel and its doctrines; and this choice is not grounded on expected personal benefits, but on the excellence and worthiness of the objects chosen. A person may have the calvinistic saving faith, and still have no hope that he hath become a christian indeed. The primary office of faith, is not to give sense or enjoyment of the certainty of salvation; but to form such an evangelical union with Christ as entitles to the promise; and whether the believer hath sense and enjoyment of the title or not, his faith is not the less effectual.

2nd. Dr. H. professes to agree with us that sinners are justified by faith, still he saith that " they are justified not as penitent but as impen- " itent; not as godly in the least degree but as " wholly ungodly; not as believers but as un- " believers." So that in his faith there is no penitence, no godliness, yea even no believing. The calvinistic idea, is this, that the unholy soul is regenerated, or born again by the holy spirit, giving a new moral principle, relish or nature. That from this holy principle or nature will spring the holy exercises of faith and repentance. The calvinistic faith is an exercise of evangelical godliness; but Dr. H's faith hath no godliness in it, because we are justified, according to him as wholly ungodly and impenitent. The calvinistic faith supposes a begun sanctification, but his faith supposes no sanctification. Enough hath been said to show the nature of his faith, and that it is neither more nor less than this, *believing that all men shall be saved.* Some enthusiasts have gone into the opinion that the essence of faith consists, *in thinking that Christ died for them in particular, or that they in particular shall be saved.* This does not seem to be the Doctor's notion, for he tells us page 135. " We

" do not confider affurance of falvation to be of
" the effence of faving faith, but merely confe-
" quential even as hath been ufual with protef-
" tants. The faith we contend for hath nothing
" immediately and directly to do with ourfelves"
that is, it is not believing that we in particular
fhall be faved; but it is believing all men will be
faved, and we of courfe as part of all men. According to him the office of faith, is to give us
enjoyment. " It never had nor ever can have any
" other office but to give us enjoyment" that is,
comfort us with the idea that we fhall efcape all
mifery, and come to everlafting felicity.

I DO not find any argument fhowing this idea
of faith to be a right one, except the Doctor's own
affertion, that he was a Calvinift. In page 55 it
is faid " all who hear the gofpel are command-
" ed to believe it—all who believe it have eternal
" life." To thefe maxims we affent. He adds
" their belief doth not make the foundation of
" their faith and falvation more true than it was
" before." This obfervation is calculated to
miflead. The foundation of men's falvation,
and on which a faving faith ftands, is the mercy
of GOD through the merits of JESUS CHRIST. It
is true, that this cannot be made any more fure
by the faith of a creature; but the foundation on
which a believer's faith ftands and his own title to
falvation, are two things. Faith is neceffary for
the title, but doth not lay the foundation, and
without faith there is no title. It is only to faith
that the promife of juftification is made, and the
Doctor's pofition that GOD juftifies finners, " not
" as believing but as unbelieving" is wholly unfcriptural. He alfo fays, " all who believe have
" a witnefs of their title to eternal life on their
" believing," this is true or not, according as we
underftand the word witnefs. If by witnefs be

meant, that they have a knowledge of their own eternal falvation it is not true, for many who have a faving faith, are not confcious of their faith. If by witnefs be meant, there is that in them, which in the fight of omnifcience is evidence of their right to the promifes, it is true.

NEXT follows an argument, which is faid to be founded on 1 John v. 10 to 13. " If we do " not believe that to be true, the belief of which " centers in a fure title to eternal falvation, we " make GOD a liar. But if GOD had not laid a " fure foundation for the fure eternal life of all, " fome would make him true in not believing, " and a liar in believing it."

THE femblance of argument in this paffage, arifes from a wrong idea of the nature of faith. Through all he fays on this matter, he goes on the fuppofition (though he does not exprefsly affert it) *that faith is believing all men fhall be faved.* This is begging the queftion, or taking for granted the very matter in difpute. All agree that thofe who have faith and believe fhall be faved. Saving faith or believing, doth not confift in thinking that I myfelf, or another man, or all will be faved; but it confifts in *receiving and depending with love,* on the object of faith. The object of faith, is CHRIST and the holy truths of the gofpel.

LET us take Dr. H's argument, and fubftitute *receiving with love,* in the place of the words *belief* and believing. " If we do not *with love receive* that as truth, *the receiving* of which *with love* centers in a fure title to eternal life, we make GOD a liar. Any man in the world does this who does not *receive with love.* But if GOD had not laid a fure foundation, for the fure eternal life of all, fome would make him true in not *receiving with love,* and a liar in *receiving with love.*"

By thus fubflituting a defcription of faving faith in the place of the words belief and believing, all appearance of argument for univerfal falvation vanifhes.

Page 4th. "It is clear that neither our faith "or hope can have any influence on the previous "objeƈt of our faith or foundation of our hope, "both thefe are immutable and eternal." I here perfeƈtly agree with Dr. H. and the confequence is this, that his faith and hope that all men fhall be faved, will have no influence to that event. The foundation which he often mentions is this "*the* Lord *knoweth them that are his.*" But the queftion ftill returns are all his in a faving fenfe? Or all his by fanƈtification? The expreffion knowing them that are *his*, is a ftrong intimation that fome are not his favingly. The foundation on which all men are commanded to believe, is an atonement that is adequate to the falvation of innumerable finners. The foundation of real falvation to men's fouls, is the renewing of their hearts in love and faith; and God hath no where faid, that he will remove a finful heart from all thofe in whofe way there remains no other difficulty. In order to fhow the nature of fin in the moft effeƈtual manner, and to prove that there is in it, an intentional oppofition to holinefs; it is probable he determined that he never would remove it from fome men.

Page 57. "Regeneration, fanƈtification and "perfeverance to eternal life are as abfolutely "from God as the atonement was." This is doubtlefs true; but is no evidence that God will give regeneration and fanƈtification to all. The fufficiency of the atonement is not God's rule in forgiving fin, but the repentance and faith of the finner.

PAGE 59. "They (the Apoſtles) excluded "every thing in man from having the remoteſt "ſhare in the matter of his juſtification or recon-"ciliation to GOD: every thing I ſay, good as "well as bad, grace after the implantation of it as "well as enmity before." Every thing in man ought to be excluded as the meritorious matter or ground of juſtification; ſtill this doth not prevent the need of a holy faith, as the means of being entitled to juſtification. The meritorious matter, is the atonement of CHRIST: the means entitling to juſtification, are the holy exerciſes of the believers heart.

FROM Dr. H's parable in page 60, we learn his idea of faith. That it is believing all men will be ſaved; alſo, that the reaſon they do not ſooner believe, is an apprehenſion that GOD is their enemy on account of ſome paſt ſin; and not becauſe there is a preſent oppoſition of their hearts, to the divine character and law.—Is this conſiſtent with what CHRIST ſays, *they have both ſeen and hated me and my father,*" or is the enmity of the carnal mind of which the Apoſtle ſpeaks, as natural to man, agreeable to this repreſentation?

WE may further learn our authors notion of gracious exerciſes, from what he ſays of repentance, from page 126 to 134, where he tells us that the certain ſalvation of the human kind, may be argued from repentance. He no where expreſsly defines repentance; but the only kind of repentance that is conſiſtent with the obſervations he makes upon it, *is a mourning for ſin becauſe it is againſt our own intereſt,* and this is not that repentance to which the promiſes are made.

PAGE 128. "The gift of repentance as well "as faith and every other grace, is only that the "ſure pardon and ſalvation may be enjoyed by the "ſoul." Here it appears that his repentance, in whatever it confifts, hath the fame office as his faith, to make the perfon know and enjoy the expectation of being faved.

. He informs us page 128, that the command to repent implies that repentance is made fure and all the benefits connected with it. But why is repentance made more fure by this command, than obedience to the law was? God's right to command doth not arife from the certainty of a compliance. If a command implies certain obedience, there would never have been any fin in the univerfe; for all fin is a violation of fome command.

. In page 131, we are told concerning " regen-
" eration, faith, love, and every good work
" wrought in us and exercifed by us, that there
" is ftrictly no propriety in preaching any of them
" as gofpel, that is, as truth founded in fact that
" ought to be believed, unlefs all is made true
" and fure before we have any acquaintance with
" the tidings or any operation from them."
The truth is, we have no right to preach any of thefe graces, as news founded in fact, until they really become matter of fact. All thefe graces are gofpel duties incumbent on all men, but they are not gofpel facts until they have an exiftence, by the real love, faith and repentance of men.

That kind of preaching which reprefents regeneration, repentance, &c. as founded in fact and made fure, and ftill without any operation on men's own felves, will be very agreeable to the libertines of the world. Thefe men will doubtlefs be contented with regeneration and repentance in Christ, fo long as they can keep perfonal repentance at a diftance. Though Dr. H. talks much about regeneration, faith, love, repentance, and being like other men who were right

H h

in fentiment, as he fays, yet when he comes to defcribe thefe graces and their office, it appears that the reality of chriftian holinefs is dropped from his fcheme, and only the name of particular exercifes retained. He retains calviniftic names and phrafes without the things fignified by them.

THAT my defcription is not uncandid, I think muft appear by a quotation from pages 132, 133. "They who would make repentance, faith, re-"generation, or any other grace, means neceffary "to our falvation fay right, but they who make "them terms of diftinction in us, to give us a "fure title to falvation, put our fafety now on the "fame footing or ground, on which Adam ftood "at firft, as to the general nature and reafon of it. "Adam muft have had a good heart and a good "life and then he would have been fafe, yet all "would have been of GOD's grace, or free gift, "as every body will allow : for his whole being "was fo. Now, fay they, we muft have *good,* "*penitent, believing,* and *holy hearts,* in a good de-"gree, *all of GOD's grace,* and then we have a ti-"tle to his favor, and not otherwife. We need "not be quite fo good as Adam muft have been, "but our fafety ftands on the fame general "ground, and in a good degree too. The degree "alters not the nature or ground of our fafety : "The general reafon is wholly the fame. Both "ftand on perfonal qualifications. But the truth "is, Adam ftood wholly on his perfonal qualifi-"cations : we ftand wholly on thofe of CHRIST, "and enjoy the comfort and operation of them by "regeneration, faith, repentance and every vir-"tue." On this paffage I remark :

1ft. DR. H. fpeaks of the benefits received by Adam in a flate of innocence, as the fruits of grace. He doth not diftinguifh between goodnefs and grace. A favor done to a holy creature is goodnefs ; but grace is a kind difpofition, or benefits done, to a creature that is finful and undeferving. There is no propriety in faying, that grace was exercifed to Adam, in his holy ftate.

2d. Though Dr. H. often mentions regeneration, he blends it in with thofe graces that are exercifes of the regenerated heart, fuch as faith, repentance and hope. He certainly knew that divinity writers confider regeneration as the implantation of a holy temper, and that the chriftian graces are exercifes flowing from that temper and conformable to its moral nature. This mingling of names tends to confufion of ideas.

3d. He tells us that repentance, faith, regeneration, are not terms of diftinction in us neceffary to give a title to falvation ; but only to give a knowledge of it ; that is a knowledge that all men will be faved, as he treats the fubject. So that a man who, moft fixedly believes that all men will be faved, is regenerated, is a penitent, is a believer, notwithftanding the moft abandoned wickednefs of heart and life. According to his idea of the chriftian character, a man may be moft eminent in wickednefs ; and a moft eminent chriftian at the fame time. This totally abolifhes holinefs from the chriftian falvation, and heaven on thefe ideas of the chriftian character, may be the moft wicked place in the univerfe. If " by terms of diftinction in us" he meant the meritorious ground of falvation, it would be right enough ; but he goes further, and difcards regeneration and perfonal grace, as neceffary for a fure title to falvation, and this was neceffary on his fcheme. What kind of repentance, faith and regeneration are neceffary in fuch a fcheme as his ? They need only be fomething, which gives us affurance that we fhall be forever happy ; and the comfort confifts, in fuppofing we fhall be delivered from eternal torment. Only convince the devils that they will be faved, and they may have all this comfort and all their malice in union; without any comfort in loving God and his law. Would this be chriftian comfort?

4th. The argument by which he rejects perfonal qualifications from being neceffary to a title for heaven, is, that this would make our ftanding fimilar to the ftanding of Adam. Doubtlefs in fome refpects the chriftian ftanding is fimilar to the ftanding of Adam; while in others it is totally diffimilar. It is fimilar in this refpect, that perfonal holinefs was abfolutely neceffary for both. Christ's Heaven requires holinefs as much as Adam's Paradife did; and his law requires holinefs as much as the original moral law. The benefits enjoyed by Adam and by the chriftian were both a fruit of divine goodnefs, and to the chriftian a fruit of grace; but God hath a different manner of exercifing his goodnefs; and the manner of exercifing, in both cafes required the perfonal holinefs of thofe who are the fubjects of it. God is a holy being, and the happinefs of the univerfe depended on having the higheft evidence of his holinefs. His creature Adam was alfo holy, and fo long as he continued of this character, there was a fitnefs that God as evidence of his own character, fhould beftow benefits upon him! After Adam fell, God did not beftow benefits upon him, not becaufe he delighted in mifery or was not good; but if he had treated him, being now become a finner, as he would have treated him if he had continued holy, it would have taken away the evidence of his own holinefs.

Though it would not be wife to fay, that the perfonal holinefs of Adam merited happinefs, it is ftill true that his holinefs made it fit God fhould treat him as a holy being, and as one holy being will treat another holy being.

Next, to come to the cafe of the finner. Christ's atonement was neceffary to ftand in the place of his eternal mifery and anfwer the fame ends. This atonement was the *meritorious ground* of his title to falvation. The free and efficacious grace of God the spirit, is the applying ground of his title to falvation. And his own fanctification or gracious exercifes, are the preparatory ground of his title to falvation. Though Christ purchafed forgivenefs, and purchafed the fpirit to fanctify, this doth not deftroy but confirms the need of perfonal holinefs. It is juft as fit, with refpect to the creatures relation to God, and as neceffary in the nature of things, that a finner faved by fovereign grace fhould be holy, as it was that Adam ftanding in divine goodnefs by the law fhould be holy. In the cafe of Adam, perfonal qualifications or holinefs gave a title to divine favor only on the ground of fitnefs, and not on the ground of merit ; and this is all that can be meant by his title to heaven or ftanding in the divine favor, by his own righteoufnefs. There was no reafon againft Adam's having his maker's favor ; and there was the reafon of fitnefs, but not of merit that he fhould have it. In the cafe of the finner, there is an actual reafon againft his having his maker's favor, which can be removed only by his union with Jesus Christ ; and it is unmerited mercy, in all refpects, which forms that union. Perfonal or meritorious diftinctions in us is not the reafon of its being formed, but folely the good pleafure of God. Still there is as much and the fame reafon, that the creature who hath his maker's favor through the grace of the gofpel, fhould have the perfonal diftinction of holinefs ; as there would be if he had it through the law.

The gospel, therefore as carefully provides for personal holiness, which Dr. H. calls *personal distinctions in us*, as the law did. And though the atonement of CHRIST is the meritorious ground of mens title to eternal life, in all respects, yet personal holiness, regeneration, faith and repentance, are as necessary for a gospel title to heaven as holiness was for a legal one. So far as the expression *title to heaven* is proper in this matter, the truth is this; Adam's title was in GOD's goodness by holiness; and the believer's title is in GOD's sovereign grace through holiness. Personal holiness is in both cases equally necessary, and there is the same need or fitness that the sinner should be renewed and have a holy temper given to him, in order for the gospel salvation, as there was that Adam should be created with a holy temper in order to be treated as a holy being. The new birth or new creation is as necessary as the first creation was. There can be no heaven for sinners without, nor any title to heaven. Dr. H's idea, that the only need of regeneration, faith and repentance is to give us comfort in the apprehension we shall be saved, falls wholly short of the office of holiness and grace in the christian salvation. GOD cannot, even through a Saviour, accept the sinner without personal holiness.— Christian comfort, is the comfort of enjoying GOD and CHRIST; and for this also, personal holiness is necessary. He is as erroneous in his whole scheme of the nature and necessity of grace or holiness in the soul, as he is in his apprehension of future rewards. It is conceived, that in order to establish his doctrine he hath taken away from the gospel all holiness and morality of character. Much more of this will be seen in the sequel.

Sec. 10. In the courfe of Dr. H's defign, he found the fcripture doctrine of election, as it hath been commonly underftood by chriftians, ftand directly in his way. For if part of men are e-lected, and part not elected to eternal life; the confequence follows that all men will not be faved.

To fupport his fcheme, it became neceffary to make the fubjects of a divine election co-exten-five with the human race.

Dr. H. gives the following defcription of the divine decrees, " every thing moral and natural, " every being and mode of being, every circum- " ftance, every connection and confequence " throughout the whole fcale or fyftem of being, " did originally, abfolutely depend on the choice, " decree or predeftination of the eternal, immu- " table Jehovah. And all things, in actual be- " ing, have now the fame entire, abfolute de- " pendence, and ever will have to all eternity." While I agree with the above defcription of God's decrees ; I can by no means fuppofe that they en-fure the falvation of all men. The firft ftep which Dr. H takes to eftablifh his opinion, is to fit the meaning of words to his own purpofe. Page 78. " It is a miftaken apprehenfion in fome, that " election, decree, predeftination, &c. neceffarily " implies diftinction. The words do not even " *naturally* imply any fuch thing." In feveral pages preceeding this quotation the Doctor largely infifts that thefe words imply great diftinction in the worldly ftate of individuals and nations, and gives us many examples. But if none of thefe words *naturally* imply a ftate of diftinction they muft be unnaturally ufed in the fcriptures where they def-cribe fuch diftinctions in men's worldly ftate.

In page 78, we find the following. " When- " ever election or predeftination, in facred fcrip- " ture, doth diftinguifh one perfon, or one com-

" munity, or one defcription of perfons from a-
" nother, it never hath the leaſt regard to any
" thing beyond the grave, excepting a difference
" in degree of felicity." Page 80. " The divine
" will, purpofe, election, decree, predeftination,
" or by whatever term you would fignify the e-
" ternal, immutable plan of JEHOVAH, does, ev-
" ery where in his word, fully fecure the certain
" happinefs of all the human race, after death.
" This affertion is bold the reader may fay, I
" therefore now appeal to GOD's own word for
" the truth of it.   The words decree, predeftina-
" tion, purpofe and election (which the learned
" will bear me witnefs, are terms promifcuoufly
" ufed in tranflating the fame original Hebrew
" and Greek) with their derivatives, are brought
" to our view one hundred and twenty four times
" in the Old and New Teftament."   Here is a
folemn appeal to the word of GOD, and alfo an
appeal to the learned.   Haft thou appealed unto
the learned? Unto the learned, judging from
GOD's word, thou fhalt go.

DR. H's affertion is this, " the words decree,
" predeftination, purpofe and election (which the
" learned will bear me witnefs, are terms promif-
" cuoufly ufed in tranflating the fame original
" Hebrew and Greek) with their derivatives.
This is not a fact. To *determine* or *predeftinate* is
expreffed by the Greek verb οριζω with its com-
pounds, from the theme ορος, which fignifies
bounds or *limits*. The meaning of the Greek verb,
is to fix the bounds or limits of any thing before-
hand, and very exactly correfponds with the Englifh verbs. *predeftinate* and *predetermine.*

THE Englifh noun *purpofe* meaning a *fixed determination* or *decree*, is expreffed by the Greek
noun προθεσις, which is derived from the verb
τιθημι. This verb fignifies to lay the foundation's

of any scheme either of counsel or practice.
Words, from one of these derivations are used in
the Greek of the New Testament, to express the
fixed purpose, counsel, predetermination, or predestination of God. The words translated elect,
elected, and election, are from another theme.
They signify both fixed determination, and choice
between two objects. They invariably mean that
some are *chosen* and others not *chosen*. The words
used in the Greek Testament for *elect*, *elected*, and
election, are from the compounded verb εκλεγω,
which signifies to collect, choose, or separate from.
The verb *eligo* and its derivatives, are used in the
Latin language with the same signification. From
the Latin, it hath past into most of the European
languages, still with the same signification. In
English, *to elect*, and *election* invariably signify a
determinate choice, by which some are taken and
others left. We hence use these words for choice
to public offices, and designation to a condition or
duties, from which other men are excluded.

In the Old Testament, to *counsel*, *determine*, or
purpose, in the manner of a decree, with their corresponding nouns, are from the Hebrew word
yangatz, which signifies to *deliberate* or *determine*
what to do. The word elect is little used in the
English Old Testament. The Hebrew word corresponding to it, is *bachar*, and signifies to choose
by a particular choice, or in the way of selection.
These are the facts, concerning the words predestination, purpose and election, and the Greek and
Hebrew words, from which they are rendered into our language. From which facts, I suppose
Dr. H. to be mistaken, when he says, the words
decree, predestination, purpose and election, are
terms promiscuously used in translating the same
original Hebrew and Greek.——Dr. H's argu-

ment reduced to a short compass stands thus.
All things are predestinated; election means the
same as predestination; therefore all men are e-
lected to eternal life. If his assertion concerning
the use of words had been right, the consequence
of which he is tenacious would not follow; for
as things are predestinated to different uses and
ends, so it might be with men; some appointed
to happiness and others to punishment. The original and natural signification of the words, elect
and election, is that some are chosen in such a
sense, as implies that others are not chosen.

2d. ANOTHER of Dr. H's arguments, is taken
from the word Ben Adam, which he says is an appropriate name of CHRIST, either in his own person or in his types. The meaning of Ben Adam,
is son of man; he tells us that this name being
given to CHRIST, implies he is the elect head of
human nature, or of all the individuals in the human
race. Suppose that JESUS CHRIST was in fact
called Ben Adam or son of Adam, I do not see in
this, any argument, that he is the elect head of
all men. Or if this phrase, in its structure carries evidence of being an elect head, I see no reason why the prophet Ezekiel is not the person;
for the name Ben Adam or son of man, is applied
to him oftener than to all other persons mentioned in the scriptures, and it doth not appear
that he is to be considered even as a type of
CHRIST, in any other sense, than all good men
may be thus. On examination, I cannot find
that the name Ben Adam is applied to JESUS
CHRIST in the whole bible. In the English Old
Testament, the phrase *son of man* is used in the
following places. Num. xxiii. 19.—Job xxv. 6.
—xxxv. 8.—Psalms viii. 4.—lxxx. 17.—cxliv.
3.—cxlvi. 3.—Isaiah li. 12.—lvi. 2.—Jer. xlix.
18.—li. 43.—Dan. 7. 13. and in a multitude of

places in the prophecy of Ezekiel. Ben Adam or son of man, was the appellation by which GOD uniformly called his prophet Ezekiel. The phrase son of man, hath three corresponding phrases in the original Hebrew. One is *Ben Adam.* Adam being a general name applied to the human race, from their common ancestor. Another is *Ben Ænosh.* Ænosh is a name applied to man, from his being liable to pain and misery. A third is *Bar Ænash.* Bar is the Chaldaic for son, and Ænash is of the same derivation and meaning as Ænosh mentioned above. The only place in the Old Testament in which the phrase son of man clearly applies to CHRIST, is in Dan. vii. 13. " I saw and behold, one like the son of " man, came with the clouds of heaven, and came " to the ancient of days, and they brought him " near before him. And there was given him " dominion and glory and a kingdom." In this place, son of man, means JESUS CHRIST. The original is *Bar Ænash* and not Ben Adam as Dr. H. asserts. The meaning of the description is this. I saw one like the son of affliction, come near to the ancient of days, and there was given him a throne and a kingdom. A most beautiful description of CHRIST's humiliation, and his kingly dignity that was to follow.

In the Greek of the new Testament υιοσ ανθρωπου is the phrase translated, son of man. The Greek name of man signifies by derivation, a creature who walks erect, or looks upward; and has no relation to Adam. Thus it appears that through the whole bible, JESUS CHRIST is not called the son of Adam. The learned to whom the appeal is made are impartial judges. The names by which CHRIST most commonly called himself, were *the son*, by way of eminence, meaning the son of GOD; and the *son of Man*, intimating his human nature. When he spoke of his sufferings or humiliation, he generally used the name son of man; and it is evident that by the son, and the son of man he meant to intimate both his divine and human natures. Our author hath a notion, which to me appears like mysticism, concerning the sameness or identity of human nature, as though the human race formed one moral being, of which Christ is head, just in the same sense, as the trunk and the branches make one tree. He tells us that because there hath been no inter-marriages with any other order of beings, all human nature is identically one, just as much as it was, when all were in Adam; and that all human flesh is called *thy own flesh*, and all human blood, *one blood.* I leave the inconsistency of such a notion for the common sense of every reader to discover; only remarking, that if what he says were literally true of men's bodies, it is still in no way essential to the point. It is the spiritual part or soul of man, that commits sin, and whatever affinity of body there may be between the descendants of Adam, their souls appear to be distinct existences, and there is no evidence, that one soul is in any sense contained in and deri-ved from another. Further, our author's notion, is directly contrary to all the feelings of personal consciousness, and that distinct sense of moral obligation, and of merit and demerit, which all mankind possess.

3d. When Dr. H. comes to prove that all mankind are members of Christ's elect body, he doth not adduce any evidence from the holy scriptures which appear to relate to this subject. We have an instance in page 87, of his manner of reasoning on this subject. " The son of man " saith, all that the father hath given me shall " come unto me, &c. John vi. 36. The ques-

" tion is how many ? The anfwer is, *he fhall give*
" *the heathen for thine inheritance, and the utter-*
" *moft parts of the Earth for thy poffeffion.*" Pfalm
ii. 8. Both queftion and anfwer are taken from
the fcripture, but on confulting the context it appears, that the writers were confidering very
different fubjects, and the anfwer adduced is no
more pertinent to the queftion, than the firft verfe
in the bible would have been. Chrift was defcribing the certainty that all whom the father
had chofen, and given to him, would come to
him. Such a difcourfe as we find in this verfe,
and the context implies that fome will not come
to CHRIST and be faved, as pointedly as if he had
afferted the fact and faid, fome fhall not be faved.
If falvation is to be univerfal, why did not Chrift
fay *all men*, inftead of *all whom the father hath
given me.* The very manner of expreffion implies a rejection of fome, as a truth that was well
known. Innumerable fuch implications are found
in the difcourfes of Chrift. It is well known by
thofe acquainted with the holy writings, that all
the prophets fpoke of a time in the latter days,
when the gofpel kingdom fhall fill the earth, and
all thofe who then live, fhall be vifible chriftians.
The paffage adduced from the ii. Pfalm, hath a
clear reference to that event, and is no anfwer
to the queftion, how many of the human race
fhall be faved ? The paffages to which Dr. H. refers in the 11, 45 and 65 chapters of Ifaiah have
an evident reference to the fame latter glory, and
he might have collected a thoufand others, which
are to the fame purpofe. They prove there will
be a very happy and holy future ftate of the
church on earth ; but are no evidence that Chrift
is the elect head of all mankind.

4th. ALL which Dr. H. tells us of the words
elect and election, meaning only diftinctions and

differences in men's worldly flate, is mere affertion; and his whole proof is faying it in a pe-
remptory manner, and many times repeated.
The diftinctions made in men's worldly flate,
proves that it would be no injuftice to make diftinctions in their future flate. The greateft defign of the fcriptures was to teach us concerning
another flate, and to limit fuch defcriptions to this
world, is fubverting the main end of revelation.
To prove that the Doctor's affertion is wholly unfounded, I have only to refer my reader back to
all the fcripture teftimonies, mentioned in the
firft part of this work, of the eternal rejection and
punifhment of fome men. All fuch teftimonies
are moft pointed proof of a diftinguifhing election,
in the eternal condition of mankind. By carefully attending to all the paffages in the Englifh Bible, where the words elect, elected and election
are ufed, it is evident that in moft inftances they
have an immediate reference to a flate beyond
death; in thofe inftances where they imply or
defcribe different treatment in this world, it generally relates to fuch things as are a neceffary
preparation, or particular acts in the divine government, that will terminate in a glorious elect
kingdom in the world to come, to which fome
will not be admitted.

5th. Dr. H. attempts to fhow, from what Paul
fays of God's dealings with the Jewifh nation, in
the ix. x. and xi. chapters of Rom. that all that
nation fhall be faved. The whole of his argument depends on the following paffage, chapter
xi. 26. " *And fo all Ifrael fhall be faved.*"

To fhow the Doctor's mifapplication of this
paffage, I would refer the reader back to what
was faid on that epiftle in the firft part of this
work; it is alfo neceffary to take fuch a general
view of God's dealings with that people, for four

thoufand years paft, as is contained in facred and
profane hiftory; and of what his future dealings
will be, as is foretold in thofe prophecies which
have not yet been fulfilled. The prophets of the
Old Teftament predicted that CHRIST would be
rejected by the Jews; and that as a punifhment for
their fin, they fhould be difperfed over the earth,
ceafe to be the vifible church of GOD, and fuffer
innumerable miferies by the hands of the Gentiles; and that after this, in the latter days, they
with the fulnefs of the Gentiles fhould be con-
verted to the faith of the true Meffiah. The rejection foretold began to take place foon after the
days of Paul, and was compleated afterwards.
Their converfion hath not yet taken place; but
the figns of the times collected from holy prophecy lead us to fuppofe the event is not far diftant;
when Paul's prophetic promife, *all Ifrael fhall be
faved*, will have its fulfilment; and the remains
of that nation now fcattered over the earth, and
kept in a ftate of feparation from other people by
the wonderful providence of GOD, will be con-
verted to chriftianity. The phrafe all *Ifrael fhall
be faved*, doth not mean that all the individuals
of that nation, fhall come to final falvation in the
kingdom of heaven; but that there is a time
when that whole people fhall become chriftians,
own JESUS as the Meffiah, and enjoy chriftian
privileges. This is apparent from attending to
the courfe of Paul's reafoning.

THE Jews, forgetting the fpirituality of the ancient promifes, had applied them to the national
pofterity of Abraham; whereas they ought to
have been underftood of his fpiritual feed. This
falfe idea of the Hebrews, Paul began to correct
in the ii, iii and iv Chapters of this fame epiftle.
Chap. iii. 3. *For what if fome did not believe?
Shall their unbelief make the truth of* GOD *without*

effect? God *forbid.* Chap. ii. 28, 29. *For he is not a Jew who is one outwardly; neither is that circumcision, which is circumcision in the flesh: But he is a Jew, that is one inwardly, and that is circumcision that is of the heart, in the spirit, and not in the letter; whose praise is not of men, but of* God. Chap. iv. 12 to 16. *For the promise that he should be the heir of the world, was not to Abraham or his seed through the law; but through the righteousness of faith. For if they which be of the law be heirs faith is made void and the promise is of none effect, because the law worketh wrath. Therefore it is of faith, that it might be by grace, to the end the promise might be sure to all the seed, not to that only which is of the law, but to that also which is of the faith of Abraham, who is the father of us all.* Gal. vi. 15, 16. *For in Christ Jesus neither circumcision availeth any thing, neither uncircumcision, but a new creature. And as many as walk by this rule peace be on them, and mercy, and upon the Israel of God.* Conformable to the above sentiments we find in the ix Chapter of the Epistle to the Romans the following passage, which may be considered as the basis of all he faith concerning that people. Verse 7, 8. *Neither because they are the seed of Abraham are they all children, but in Isaac shall thy seed be called; that is, they which are the children of the flesh, these are not the children of God, but the children of the promise are counted for the seed."*

Still further, to illustrate the truth, lest we should suppose all the children of Isaac to be saved of the Lord, and the spiritual Israel to whom the promise is made, we find in the 11th chapter, *I say then, hath God cast away his people? God forbid. God hath not cast away his people whom he foreknew. Wot ye not what the scripture saith of Elias, how he maketh intercession to God against Is-*

rael, saying, Lord they have killed thy prophets, and digged down thine altars, and I am left alone, and they seek my life. But *what saith the answer of God unto him, I have reserved to myself seven thousand men, who have not bowed the knee to the image of Baal. Even so at this present time there is a remnant according to the election of grace.* The Apoſtle Paul is much guarded, through his writings againſt ſuch ſentiments as Dr. H. avows. The true Iſrael, are all thoſe who have the faith of Abraham ; and not all his natural ſeed. Jacob was choſen and Eſau left. In the time of Elijah, ſeven thouſand men were choſen, and the reſt left. In the time of Paul, there was a remnant according to the election of grace ; and the reſt of the nation were blinded in hardneſs of heart. After all this, as a prophet of God, the Apoſtle aſſures us ; that in ſome future day the poſterity of thoſe Iſraelites, who were then left, with the fulneſs of the Gentiles, ſhould become chriſtians. This is what he means by ſaying *all Iſrael ſhall be ſaved ;* neither is there any obſcurity in his reaſoning, to thoſe who will faithfully follow it through the epiſtle. Dr. H's argument from the topic of election appears totally unfounded through the whole, and the very ground which he aſſumes as evidence of univerſal ſalvation, is replete with evidence againſt his doctrine ; for there is nothing more expreſsly ſaid in the ſcriptures than this ; that ſome men are choſen to eternal life, and others left to the eternal puniſhment of their ſins.

Sec. 11. Dr. H's next argument in favor of univerſal ſalvation, is drawn from the nature of the goſpel atonement, and it is one on which he appears to place much dependance. He conſiders this ſubject, from page 94 to 121 of his book. No ſufficient

K k

evidence appears, that the great and good men whom he names, had thofe conceptions of the a-tonement which he advocates. Several of them lived in times, when the rationale of that great tranfaction in the fcheme of divine grace, was the fubject of little inquiry. Neither were there the fame attacks on fcripture doctrine as are now made; and feeling themfelves fafe againft a mifun-derftanding of their fentiments, they might often exprefs themfelves incautioufly, and without that precifion of words, as is proper on this fubject, at the prefent day. At the fame time, if all our chriftian fathers had thought concerning the a-tonement, as Dr. H. reprefents, it would not pre-clude prefent inquiry; nor if they were wrong in fome of their notions, would it be any argu-ment, either againft their piety or greatnefs. While error continues to make different attacks, it may drive chriftians, even though there be lefs of the power of religion in their fouls; to fuch refearches, as will caft new light, on the rationale of redemption by JESUS CHRIST.

MY own ideas of the atonement I have already explained from page 148 to 159 of this book; which ought to be read in connection with what will now be added.

THE following things will be attempted.

Firft. To ftate Dr. H's notion of the atone-ment.

Secondly. To fhow that his notion is naturally impoffible.

Thirdly. THAT it is morally wrong. And,

Fourthly. THAT the expreffions of holy fcrip-ture do not countenance it.

HIS opinion feems to be, that there is an ac-tual transfer of fin and guilt to JESUS CHRIST; and an actual transfer of his righteoufnefs to the

ſinner.   Page 98.   " The true doctrine of the
" atonement is in very deed this.   A direct, true
" and proper ſetting all our guilt to the account
" of Christ as our federal head and ſponſor, and
" a like placing his obedience unto death to our
" account.   In the covenant of redemption, and
" divine conſtitution, God regards both parties,
" juſt as tho' the ſon of man had perſonally done
" all man hath done : and man had done and
" ſuffered, all that the ſecond man hath himſelf
" done and ſuffered."

That Dr. H. by the word *transfer*, meant a
perſonal communication of guilt and righteouſneſs
from one being to another, is further evident
page 99.   " Here ſome will cry out and ſay, guilt
" and righteouſneſs is of a perſonal nature, and
" cannot be transfered.   But I now promiſe,
" that in its proper place, I will fully demon-
" ſtrate, that although both theſe are perſonal,
" they may be transfered, fully according to rea-
" ſon and common ſenſe, as well as agreeably
" to the divine conſtitution.

The proper place to which Dr. H. alluded, in
which he would demonſtrate that guilt and righteouſneſs could be transfered according to reaſon
and common ſenſe, I ſuppoſe to be from pages
107 to 117.   The only argument, which he uſes
to prove both the poſſibility and the lawfulneſs of
the thing is that all creatures, their powers, faculties, actions, righteouſneſs, ſin and guilt are
God's property, in the moſt abſolute and unlimited ſenſe, and that God may do what he will
with his own.   Though there appears to me, to
be ſomething that is unfit in repreſenting ſin and
guilt as the bad property of God, and in comparing
God's bad property as he calls it, to the bad property of men, and to a den of ſerpents in a field ;
yet I will let all this paſs, and concede if it be de-

fired, that all the fin, guilt and righteoufnefs in the univerfe are GOD's property, in the moft abfolute fenfe; as I do not conceive, this will have the leaft influence on the argument. The Dr's idea feems to be, that by an act of power, GOD made the fin and guilt of man, the fin and guilt of CHRIST; in the fame manner, as if he had perfonally done all that man did, for this is his expreffion; and concerning the transfer of Chrift's righteoufnefs his words are the fame.

2d. ON this notion of transfer, I remark that it is naturally impoffible. The thing is fo plain to common fenfe, that its very plainnefs, renders it difficult to illuftrate. It is hard illuftrating truths or facts, when none more clear than thofe we would illuftrate, can be found to compare them with. I call on all mankind, to defcribe how it is naturally poffible to make a fin of my commiffion, the fin of another man's commiffion. My thoughts, volitions, affections, and mental exercifes are necefiary for my fin and guilt, and without thefe I could have no fin and guilt. Is it poffible to make my thoughts and volitions, the thoughts and volitions of another man? and all thofe muft be transfered with the fin and guilt, becaufe without thefe, there is no fin and guilt to transfer. Can it be made poffible that my falfehood or violence committed many years ago, fhould be made the falfehood and violence of another being, who had no exiftence at the time of my committing them. I go further and fay, that the human mind cannot conceive of fuch a transfer. We may eafily conceive of the impoffibility of the thing; but are wholly incapable of conceiving the poffibility of it. Let the moft acute thinker try to conceive the operation of transfering the fin and guilt of one to another, and it will elude his attempt. Let him try to conceive what this transfered fin and guilt is, in the character of a perfectly holy being, and he will foon find that he is fearching for a nonentity.

FURTHER, fuppofe that Dr. H's notion of transfered fin, guilt and righteoufnefs, in the cafe of Chrift and the finner were poffible in the nature of things; ftill the following confequences would follow.

IF the tranfgreffor's fin and guilt were all transfered to Chrift; if they were taken from his character and placed in Chrift's character; then the tranfgreffor hath no longer any fin and guilt; and Chrift died for his own falvation and not for the finner's. If it be replied; CHRIST's death was neceffary to purchafe the right of transfer, in which the finner's falvation doth confift; then Dr. H's argument of GOD's right to transfer, arifing from his property in all things falls to the ground; for a purchafed right is not a natural right—a right derived from the death of CHRIST, is not a right derived from property.

FURTHER, if fin and guilt are transfered to CHRIST, then there is no grace in any favor done to man fince the firft transferal. There may be goodnefs but no grace. Grace is the granting of favor to the guilty and undeferving, but how can acts of favor be called grace, when all that guilt which made them undeferving is removed.

Thirdly. THE transferal of fin and guilt, in the manner Dr. H. fuppofes, would be morally wrong as well as naturally impoffible. I wifh to be fenfible of the deference due to the infinitely wife and holy Jehovah, when fpeaking of things right and wrong in application to him. But doubtlefs it will be allowed, that we may conceive of things, in GOD's government of the univerfe, which would be doing wrong to himfelf, if he were to perform them, and I wifh to take no other ground in this argument. GOD hath the higheſt property in his own exiſtence, and if the thing were poſſible, it would be morally wrong for GOD to injure his own exiſtence and happineſs. The univerſe of created beings is his property—the diſplay of his wiſdom, goodneſs and power; and he is happy in the perfection of his kingdom and works. It would be injurious and morally wrong towards himſelf, to mar the perfection of his intelligent kingdom. This kingdom is compoſed of many individuals, with moral and ſocial relations and obligations to each other—each of theſe individuals hath a diſtinct perſonality—GOD hath given them diſtinct rights which are the neceſſary appendages of ſuch a nature as they have received.—They have diſtinct merits and demerits, ariſing from the moral nature of their diſtinct volitions.—Guilt or a deſert of puniſhment, belongs to an unholy volition in the very nature of things. This is that ſtructure of nature, out of which moral obligation ariſes. Making the ſuppoſition, that it were a poſſible thing, ſtill would it not be morally wrong, under theſe circumſtances, to transfer a deſert of puniſhment from an unholy being to one who hath been always holy? Is it not a falſehood to ſay this is a guilty being and deſerves puniſhment, when in fact, according to the natural ſtructure of intelligent exiſtence, and the moral obligation ariſing out of that ſtructure, he is not guilty and deſerving of puniſhment? Would not this be deſtroying the benefits which infinite wiſdom propoſed to himſelf in giving diſtinct perſonality, and a natural capacity for merit and demerit? It is conceived, that no propoſition can be more ſelf-evident than the following; that the perſon who ſteals muſt eternally be the thief and guilty perſon; and alſo that if it were poſſible, to ſeparate the ſin and guilt from the act of ſtealing, it would be morally unfit to attribute them to the nature or character of one who never stole. In doing thus, GOD would destroy both the natural and moral system, which were created by his own wisdom and for his own glory; and thus do a wrong to himself. To suppose any thing in the divine government, contrary to the laws which GOD gave in creation, is to suppose him divided against himself, and dishonorary to his character. When he created he gave laws, agreeable to his foreknowledge of his own government.

IN the case of our blessed Saviour and the sinner; JESUS CHRIST never was guilty, either by his personal actions or an imputed transferal. Those who are saved, will be saved as sinners; as guilty and undeserving. The renewing power of GOD will change their hearts, so that they shall sin no more; but the sins they have committed and all the guilt appertaining to them, will as much remain their own sin and guilt through eternity, as they were before forgiveness. The creature who is once guilty, must be guilty forever. If any suppose that true believers in CHRIST, do by their union to him, loose a sense of their own guiltiness; it is to be feared, that such persons are experimentally ignorant of the nature of religion in the heart.

THE notion of a transferal of personal guilt and righteousness, is so alluring to those who wish to hope well of their own state, and to live still in their sins; that the error becomes extremely dangerous. Dr. H. challenges common sense as a judge in this matter. Let us see how common sense will judge, in an illustration which I will propose.

SUPPOSE the following case. A son for a most odious crime is sentenced to suffer death. Circumstances of public good forbid he should be

forgiven, without fome means, which will 'as effectually difplay the nature of the government
tranfgreffed, and the character of the legiflator
and judge, as the actual death of this wicked fon
would do.   A venerable father offers to become
a ranfom for the fon ; when it is judged, that the
lofs of a fingle limb of the parent, will as fully anfwer all good ends in government and the public
weal, as the death of the fon would do.   The father fuffers accordingly.   In fuch a cafe, could
any one look on the fuffering father, and think
him to be either a finner or guilty and deferving
of punifhment ! conceive the criminal fon, ftanding by the fide of the fuffering father in the very
moment of his pangs ; and every beholder, inftead of conceiving that the real guilt is transfered to the father, would probably look on the fon
as a more guilty creature than ever he appeared
before.   In fuch cafes as thefe, common fenfe,
common feeling and apprehenfion of fact (and
fact is truth) do not conceive any transferal of fin,
guilt or righteoufnefs.

Fourthly. THE general expreffions of GOD's
word do not countenance the opinion which Dr.
H. advocates,

BEFORE we attend to the expreffions of GOD's
word, it is proper for me to obferve; that to
make the fcriptural fcheme of redemption moft
glorious and perfect, there is no need of introducing a fact that appears impoffible in the nature
of things.   There are many kinds and branches
of evidence for the truth of the gofpel.   If it became neceffary either to reject the gofpel with all
the evidence that fupports it, or believe this thing
which appears naturally impoffible, it might be
proper for us to fufpect our own common fenfe ;
for on fuch a fuppofition, the whole quantity of
gofpel evidence would become evidence of a tranf-

feral ; but happily there is no such necessity.   The gospel can effect all the ends for which
it was intended, without this ; and if it had been
God's intention to save all men, he could as well
have done this, without a transferal of sin and
righteousnefs. as with it.   Men, without this may
receive every blessing that is needed, or that their
natures are capable of enjoying.   Without this
they may be forgiven—liberated from personal
punishment—entitled to all the blessings of eternity—sanctified, and thus rendered morally capable
of enjoying and serving God forever.   These
blessings contain all that creatures have a capacity
of receiving ; also these blessings may be bestowed
in a way glorious for God, and consistent with the
highest good of the univerfe.   The supposition of
a transferal is therefore needless ; and it appears
highly unreasonable to introduce into the gospel,
any thing which is at once, needless, naturally impossible, and morally wrong ; especially as there
is nothing in the holy scriptures to countenance it.
This is the point I shall next consider.

THE holy scriptures use the word righteousnefs
in various senses, and most generally in one of
the two following.

1st. FOR moral rectitude and personal holinefs.
In this sense the word is applied to God, and includes the whole moral rectitude of his nature,
and sometimes particular acts of justice.   Applied
to men in this sense, it means personal holinefs ;
or that temper which is given in sanctification by
the spirit of God, and the practice proceeding
from it.   In this sense of the word all the saved
must become righteous, or personally holy ;
though this is not the righteoufnefs by which any
are justified.

2dly. The word righteousness, in an appropriate gospel sense, means that, on account of which sinners are justified, forgiven and by the promise of God entitled to eternal glory. This is the righteousness we are now considering. That this righteousness was acted and wrought by Christ, in his obedience and sufferings, is a matter agreed. The question is, whether this righteousness remains, and will forever remain the righteousness of Christ, and sinners only receive benefits by means of it ; or whether this righteousness, though wrought by Christ, is transfered and communicated over to the sinner, so that though Christ was the author of it, the sinner now holds it as his own ; and holds it in such a manner, that when called to account by the judge, he may present it, as a debtor presents money in payment of a debt, saying, that this righteousness is now mine. If there be a transferal this must be the case.

Divines have generally agreed in saying, that we are justified by the righteousness of Christ ; and I fully believe, that though they have incautiously admitted some expressions, which will bear another construction ; it was still their idea, that this righteousness was as much the righteousness of Christ in every sense, after the sinner's justification, and after he had received all possible benefit from it, as it was before. In the scriptures this righteousness is called *the righteousness of faith*, Rom. iv. 13, because it is by faith, as a means appointed by God, that sinners are entitled to its benefits. It is called the righteousness of God, Rom. i. 17, both as it was appointed by the infinite wisdom of God, and as Christ the author of it was a divine person. It is called the law of righteousness, Rom. ix. 3, or a divine constitution, by which guilty sinners receive benefits, as they might do if they were perfonally obedient. In none of thefe paffages is there any thing which looks like transferal. Next let us confider a-nother manner of expreffion, as in the following texts. *The* Lord *our righteoufnefs.* Jer. xxiii. 6. *Who of* God *is made unto us, wifdom, righteoufnefs, fanctification and redemption.* 1 Cor. i. 30. Christ *is the end of the law for righteoufnefs to every one that believeth.* Rom. x. 4. If any fuppofe thefe paffages favor the idea, that Chrift's righteoufnefs is communicated over to men, they ought to no-tice that a rejection of the figurative meaning proves too much. It is not faid the righteoufnefs wrought by Chrift is our righteoufnefs, or is made our righteoufnefs, or is the end of the law for righteoufnefs to them who believe ; but that Chrift himfelf is fo. So that if thefe paffages be not figurative, and are to be underftood literally; it is not the obedience and fufferings of Chrift which conftitute a juftifying righteoufnefs ; but it is the whole Chrift, in his divine and human natures, with all his perfections, attributes and of-fices ; and the transferal muft be of all his per-fections, attributes and offices, and the juftified believer muft become God and Saviour to him-felf. Thefe paffages are figurative, and to under-ftand them literally will lead us into the great ab-furdity juft mentioned. Their meaning is doubt-lefs this. The Lord who is our juftification through what he hath done and fuffered, received by our faith. God, who in Chrift enlightens, juftifies and fanctifies. The end of the law is the execution of its penalty. Chrift hath done that, which anfwers in the place of this execution ; fo that the law doth not forbid the believers juftifi-cation, and his being treated as righteous. In this fenfe Chrift is the end of the law for right-eoufnefs.

THE words *imputed* and *imputeth*, are used in the fcriptures on this fubject. Hence arofe the expreffion, *imputation of* CHRIST's *righteoufnefs*, which is not a fcriptural expreffion. The words are forenfic, and have relation to a judicial decree, and in this cafe, to the juftifying or condemning fentence of GOD. To impute fin, means GOD's determination by which the finner is condemned to endure the penalty of the law in his own perfon. Not to impute fin, or to impute righteoufnefs is his juftifying act, by which he pardons the finner, and adjudges to him perfonal benefits. Imputation, in the fcriptural fenfe, cannot mean a transferal either of guilt or righteoufnefs. For in Rom. chapter iv. the believers faith is faid to be imputed for righteoufnefs, and the believers faith cannot be that righteoufnefs of CHRIST by which we are juftified. This fhows that the word has relation to the juftifying act of GOD: and the meaning of faith being imputed for righteoufnefs, is this; that GOD adjudges to the faith of a believer the benefits of juftification.

FURTHER, none of the terms ufed in the word of GOD naturally fignify a transferal of guilt or righteoufnefs.

THE word propitiation, means that, through which GOD may be favorable or propitious in his treatment of finners; and for this, it is not neceffary CHRIST's righteoufnefs fhould become their righteoufnefs.

RANSOM and *price* are words ufed. CHRIST is the ranfom and he paid the price. Thefe words mean the obedience and fuffering that is rendered to GOD by the Saviour, to open a door for the fafe exercife of his grace to the guilty, and cannot mean any thing done, adjudged or transfered to the finner himfelf.

THE words *redeemer, redeemed* and **redemption,** are much ufed in the fcriptures. They mean a deliverer and deliverance from fome evil. They are in a great number of paffages applied to the deliverance of Ifrael from Egypt, Babylon, and their other enemies, by the power of God. Deliverance from ficknefs, from famine, from temporal death, from various earthly troubles, from iniquity, and from eternal punifhment, are in the fcriptures expreffed in this manner, and there is nothing in thefe words that implies a transferal of righteoufnefs to the redeemed finner.

CHRIST is called our reconciliation. Both God and finners are faid to be reconciled. The natural meaning of this word is the making thofe to be friends, who were before enemies; but the word itfelf doth not imply either the manner or means of reconciliation.

ATONEMENT is alfo ufed, and it properly fignifies the means by which anger or difpleafure are appeafed, whatever thofe means may be. The word *purchafed* is ufed. The purchafe of falvation for finners, was from God and not from finners themfelves; and therefore doth not imply any transfer of the price of purchafe to them, but quite the contrary. Chrift is called our facrifice. He was facrificed for our fins. He gave his foul an offering for fin. The natural fignification of the word facrifice, is a thing confecrated and offered up to God; hence we are exhorted to prefent ourfelves a living facrifice to the LORD. Many of the Jewifh facrifices were typical of Chrift's death. The Jewifh facrifices, on the part of the offerer, fignified that it would be a righteous thing in God to punifh the finner eternally; on the part of God who accepted them, they fignified, that there was a way devifed in which he could be propitious to thofe who became obedient; but there is nothing, either in the name or nature of the transaction, that intimates righteousness and guilt to be negotiable from one being to another. The meaning of Christ's being a sacrifice is this; that he offered himself to GOD by obedience and suffering, which offering through the divinity of his nature, made such a display of moral truth and of the divine character and government, that it is safe to remit the personal punishment of the sanctified and believing. In this sense he made himself an offering for sin—was bruised for our iniquities—the chastisement of our peace was upon him—tasted death for every man—was made a curse for us—and died for us while we were ungodly and sinners. The meaning of all these, and many other expressions similar to them, is that Christ suffered under such circumstances, as makes it safe for the divine government, and for the general good to forgive repenting sinners. Common sense, judging from the nature and possibility of things, cannot give any other construction. As in the case before mentioned of a father suffering for a son, all men would say, that the father was broken for the iniquity of the son—that the chastisement of the son's peace was on him—that he tasted pain and was made a curse for the son; at the same time, all men would say there was no transferal or negotiation of guilt or righteousness.

FURTHER. The sin and guilt for which Christ died, are called our sin and guilt in the scriptures. Guilt means a desert of punishment. No man can read the scriptures, without perceiving that those whom God hath forgiven, are still considered deserving of punishment, and his treatment of them is according to his own grace, and not according to their desert. Sin after it is forgiven, is still called our sin.

THE words in 2 Cor. v. 21. are evidently fig-urative. "*For he hath made him to be fin for us* "*who knew no fin.*" Both the expreffions *being made fin, and knowing no fin,* are figurative, and the latter is defigned to limit and explain the former. If they are to be underftood literally they are a plain contradiction. Every man who is acquaint-ed with the fcripture may fee the true meaning to be this ; that Jefus Chrift, who was perfectly free from fin and guilt, fuffered, to open a way in which men who are finners may be forgiven, and that we by the application of fovereign grace, might have the benefits of righteoufnefs.

DR. H. tells us page 100, that types do not ad-mit a metaphor. I fuppofe by this he intends, there can be no metaphorical or figurative mean-ing in them. But if there be not a figurative meaning in them, there is none. All the types of Chrift are figures or fimilitudes pointing to him the fubftance. A metaphor in words, is a word applied out of its natural meaning, ftill in fuch a manner as to be intelligible. A metaphor in things or actions ; is a thing or action turned from its natural ufe, to convey fome inftruction. All types are metaphors or figures, and this is the meaning of the word type, both by derivation and common ufe.

IN the xxi Chapter of Exodus, a fine laid on a man for knowingly keeping a mifchievous Ox, is called the ranfom of his life. Alfo a certain tax for building the tabernacle, is called atone-ment- money. The fine and tax were paid in ne-gotiable money. From the words ranfom and atonement being ufed in thefe cafes, Dr. H. infers, that fin, guilt and righteoufnefs are negotiable. This argument may have weight with thofe who can fee no difference between money, and perfon-al merit and demerit. The following paffage is in

John xviii. 37. *To this end was I born, and for this caufe came I into the world that I fhould bear witnefs unto the truth*, that is, to make a difplay of truth. This was the great end of his incarnation, life, preaching, obedience, fufferings and death. The way was thus prepared, for God to forgive through fanctification fo many finners as he faw would be beft for the glory and happinefs of himfelf and kingdom.

I HAVE endeavored to fhow as was propofed, that Dr. H's notion of the atonement, is naturally impoffible; if poffible, that it would be morally wrong; and that it is not countenanced by the expreffions ufed in the fcriptures.

CHRISTIAN divines ought to ufe great care in explaining the doctrine of imputation, left they lay a foundation for the moft dangerous errors. The word imputation hath been ufed in the three following cafes. The finfulnefs of human nature through the apoftacy of Adam.—The fuffering of Chrift for finful men.—And the juftification of believers by Chrift's righteoufnefs; but in neither of thefe cafes is there any transferal of fin, guilt or righteofnefs. Adam's pofterity, were never guilty of that particular fin by which he apoftatized. By a divine conftitution, which was founded in wifdom, if Adam fell, all his pofterity were to come into exiftence finful beings. The fin for which they are condemned is their own, the guilt is their own, and not a guilt of their father's making.

CHRIST endured fuffering by the father's appointment, and his own choice. He fuffered as an innocent, and not as a guilty being; and was not confidered as made guilty, by a transfered guilt from thofe who fhould derive the benefits of his fuffering.

To the believer there is a remiſſion of puniſhment and the poſſeſſion of great privileges, given
on account of Chriſt's righteouſneſs, which will
forever remain his own righteouſneſs. It is not
conceived, that we have either ſcripture example,
or a right to uſe the word imputation in a ſenſe
contrary to theſe explanations.

In page 117, Dr. H. mentions an objection to
his ſentiment, and endeavors to obviate it. He
thus ſtates the objection. " Some have imagin-
" ed that this idea of juſtification by a true and
" proper atonement, ſubſtitution or ranſom, is
" inconſiſtent with free juſtification by grace ſo
" often ſpoken of in ſcripture." By a true and
proper atonement and ſubſtitution, he means
transfered or negotiated righteouſneſs. To obviate the objection he tells us, that grace abounds
more in this, than it can in any other way; and
ſays, that the father's gift of the ſon, the ſon's acceptance, his death, the ſinner's pardon, and every
ſtep in this great work until final glorification are
all grace. A little attention to the meaning and
juſt uſe of words will ſhow that the objection is
not obviated by any thing the Doctor hath ſaid.
Goodneſs ſignifies benevolence or holineſs.
Favors granted either to innocent or guilty creatures are acts of goodneſs. Grace ſignifies favor
to the guilty. Mercy ſignifies favor and help to
the miſerable. Juſtification is a favor granted,
but it is not grace, if all guilt is negotiated away
from human nature and centered in Chirſt. By
attention to the juſt uſe of words, it appears that
all thoſe ſcriptures which ſpeak of juſtification by
grace, or of any perſonal application of goſpel
benefits by grace, are directly in point againſt Dr.
H's repreſentation.

M m

THE Dr: appears exceedingly attached to the word vicarious. All know that it is not ufed in the fcriptures, and its application to this fubject is human invention. Men who have made the word and its application, will give it a meaning, as pleafes them. It is as applicable to one fcheme as to the other.

IN page 97 Dr. H. fays, if that notion of the atonement which he oppofes, be true, it fhows that the eternal happinefs of all finners is made fure. The reafon affigned is in the following words. " For what will not infinite love joined with infi-" nite power do, when there remains not the " leaft claim of juftice, or any other divine attri-" bute in the way?" Further on it is added, " That the moral nature of GOD is infinite love " is moft certain, that this love pleads infinitely " for fparing every finner from eternal death he " hath often faid, and confirmed by folemn oath. " Ezek. xviii. Now what can any defire more " than the folemn oath of GOD, that his whole " difpofition is infinitely oppofed to the final def-" truction of any man." On the firft of thefe paffages I remark; that according to a true idea of the atonement, the claim of juftice remains in full force upon every unfanctified finner. If the claim of juftice were removed, the danger of punifhment would doubtlefs be removed with it. The only way in which the claim of juftice can be removed, is by repentance, faith and a holy obe-dience, to which the promife of forgivenefs is made. Every finner, until he believes and re-pents, is under a fentence of condemnation pro-nounced by juftice. The atonement of Chrift hath no effect upon this fentence, and juftice holds all its claim, until there is a juftifying act of GOD remitting the punifhment. The pretence of juftice having no claim is unwarranted by the word of God.

As to the moral nature of God, I know that it is infinite love. The greatest general good is the object of infinite love. There is no evidence that the " holy love of God pleads infinitely for sparing " every sinner from eternal death" or " that " God's whole disposition is infinitely opposed to " the final destruction' of any man" on the contrary; if the destruction of any be necessary means of the general good, his whole disposition will plead infinitely for that punishment, to which justice will have an eternal claim. But I have before been sufficiently explicit on this point.

I shall conclude this subject with a single remark more. The notion of a righteousness transfered from Christ to the believer, so as to be his in the same sense, as if he had done what Christ hath done, appears to me inconsistent with the doctrine of Christ's intercession. *Wherefore he is able also, to save them to the uttermost, that come to* God *by him, seeing he ever liveth to make intercession for them.* Heb. vii. 25.—*For* Christ *is not entered into the holy places made with hands ; but into heaven itself now to appear in the presence of* God *for us.* Heb. ix. 24. It hath been generally supposed, that all benefits granted to believers, are a fruit of Christ's intercession with the father; and that his righteousness presented by himself in intercession, is the ground on which God bestows. But if Christ's righteousness be transfered by an act of divine power, to the believer, to be his own in the same sense, as if he had wrought it ; what need is there of the divine intercessor ? Or what propriety in Christ's appearing in heaven to solicit for his people, when they have already received that, which is the ground of all benefits bestowed. In the same manner it will be found, that the suppofition of transfered righteoufnefs, fin and guilt, is inconfiftent with almoft every doctrine in the chriftian fyftem.

Sec. 12. Another of Dr. H's arguments is exprefled in the following words, page 121. " If " we attend to the threefold office of our Sav- " iour, as prieft, king and prophet ; we fhall " find the final falvation of every human crea- " ture, made fure in him." Dr. H's ideas of the prophetic, facerdotal, and kingly offices, feem to be very indiftinct. As proof of what I fay, I will recite a paffage from page 123. " *Paul* " reprefents the offices of Christ as co-extenfive. " Effectual *calling* is by virtue of the prophetic " and kingly office of Christ. Juftification " pertains to the facerdotal or prieftly office by " the atonement. The fanctification, perfever- " ance and glorification of finners refult from all " the offices of Christ alike. This Apoftle tells " us that where one of thefe offices is exercifed, " the other two are in every inftance." For proof of this he adduces, Rom. viii. " Whom he " did predeftinate, them he alfo called ; and " whom he called, them he alfo juftified ; and " whom he juftified, them he alfo glorified."

The feveral parts of falvation which Dr. H. here mentions are effectual calling, (and it is well known that effectual calling, means regeneration and fanctification,) juftification, perfeverance and glorification. All thefe are wrought by his kingly, and folely by his kingly power. As a prophet he gives doctrinal inftruction ; but all the inftruction in the world will neither regenerate, juftify, nor glorify a foul. As a prieft he hath made an atonement which is fufficient for the falvation of all who repent ; and this atonement hath long fince been compleat. There is no power in it either to regenerate or glorify. Regeneration is a work of his kingly power, changing and making the heart holy. Sanctification is a work of his kingly power by his spirit, increasing the holiness of his people. Justification is an act of his kingly power as God and Judge, pardoning the sinner, and giving him a right to eternal life. Glorification is a work of his kingly power, putting the believer in possession of the glory and blessedness appointed to him by sovereign wisdom. Predestination, which was antecedent to all these, was also an act of God's kingly and sovereign wisdom, appointing whom he would save.

CHRIST's prophetic office consisted wholly in teaching men their duty, and the way of salvation. His priestly office was wholly in making it consistent by an atonement, for God to forgive those, whom his power should bring home to himself. The whole application of salvation, in all its parts is a work of his kingly authority. He was a prophet and a priest, only to prepare the way to save as a king. If he had not been a prophet and a priest, he could not have consistently acted as a king to save. Neither doctrinal light nor the atonement, given by him as a prophet, and made by him as a priest, make any alteration in the sinner's personal state, until he works as a king; and when he thus works his chosen ones will become willing, and be saved. So that calling, or effectual calling, justification, perseverance, and glorification, the whole chain of applied salvation, which the apostle beautifully mentions in connection, are all the work of Christ's kingly power. And by the quotation I made from Dr. H. it appears he thought indistinctly on this subject.

THE next quotation I shall repeat from him is in page 122. '" Christ is just so far, and as ex-" tensively a king over mankind, as he is priest " and prophet." This I conceive to be true if properly understood, then follows " and as far as " he doth exercise these offices at all among the " human kind, he doth exercise, and engage to " exercise them all unto perfection." This latter clause needs a particular explanation.

CHRIST is king, priest and prophet to all mankind in the following sense. Much doctrinal instruction hath come to mankind in general by Christ's mediation ; also to the angels both holy and apostate. Doctrinal knowledge will be diffused throughout the universe by Christ's prophetic ministration. Through heaven as well as earth ; through eternity as well as time. Christ's prophetic office is to give doctrinal or intellectual light and knowledge, which may be possessed in the highest finite degree, without any holiness or righteousness of the will and affections. In this sense, Christ is a prophet to all mankind, and like other prophets his ministration may be either unto life or unto death.

THE atonement he hath made is sufficient for the pardon of all sinners, and in this sense he is a Priest for all mankind ; the consequence however will not follow that all mankind shall be saved, for some may reject such a salvation as he offers, and thus cut themselves off from the benefits of his atonement. He is king of the whole earth ; of the good and the wicked. His government is over all. It is as much the part of a king to condemn and punish the wicked, as it is to justify and glorify the holy. The exercise of a kingly power over all, carries no implication that all will be saved ; so that though there is a sense in which CHRIST, is king, priest and prophet for all mankind, this might be the cafe, without the falvation of a fingle creature ; if fovereign mercy and wifdom had not determined, that fome fhould be effectually called to obedience. With refpect to the faved, they will love the truth that is taught by the divine prophet ; they will receive and depend on the atonement in fuch a manner as to be delivered from the curfe ; and joyfully fubmit to Chrift's kingly government in all things. The unholy do not choofe and love fuch truth as Chrift reveals, nor receive his right-eoufnefs nor rejoice in his government.

DR. HUNTINGTON reprefents thofe who differ from his opinion, as limiting the regal power of Chrift. This I conceive to be a mifreprefenta-tion. In what he fays on this fubject, he alludes to a paffage in Philip. ii. 9, 10, 11. *Wherefore God alfo hath highly exalted him, and given him a name above every name : that at the name of JESUS every knee fhould bow, of things in heaven, and things in earth, and things under the earth ; and that every tongue fhould confefs, that JESUS CHRIST is lord to the glory of God the father.*—On this paffage I remark,

1ft. The word *every*, may be ufed in this paf-fage, as the words *all* and *all men* are in other paffages, meaning all the holy, and not all crea-tures.

2dly. Chrift will reduce all things, but not in the fame manner. His power will bring fome to a willing obedience, and others will be crufhed under its weight. Some knees will bow with love, and fome with trembling fear. Some high thoughts will be brought down by humility, and others fink under the weight of punifhment. His regal conqueft will be equal in both cafes.

3d. THE 12th verfe immediately follows as a confequence from verfes 10 and 11, before reci-

ted, which I think fully difproves univerfal falvation, and fhows the true meaning of the paffage,
*Wherefore, my beloved, as ye have always obeyed;
not as in my prefence only, but now much more in my
abfence; work out your own falvation with fear and
trembling.* The exhortation in the 12th verfe,
work out your own falvation with fear and trembling, is introduced as a confequence, from the
previous defcription that every knee fhall bow to
JESUS, and every tongue confefs that he is LORD.
What propriety would there be in faying, all men
will be faved, therefore be filled with fear and
trembling when you think and act on this great
fubject.   Is not this much more natural, all men
muft bow, either in love, or under the weight of
his punifhing juftice, therefore with trembling
fear feek a falvation from your fins.

So with refpect to his prophetic office, he gives
doctrinal light to all men, and the more doctrinal
light finners receive, the more they will be oppofed to it.   Their oppofition to the true light is the
very ground on which they will be finally condemned.   The enlightening of chriftians is not a
difcovery of new truths; but of the glory and excellence of truth, that was feen before.   The
glory or difagreeablenefs of truth depends entirely on the moral ftate of the heart.   A truth
which is loved appears glorious; a truth which
is hated appears difagreeable.   The fame truth is
feen in both cafes, producing different effects, as
the heart and its moral relifh is either good or
bad.

In 1 Cor. xi. 3, is the following paffage, " *the
" head of every man is* CHRIST.   From this paffage Dr. H. infers, page 125 " that in the cove-
" nant of redemption all mankind were given to
" the fecond Adam, as they were once included
" in the firft."   Or in other words, that Chrift

is the federal head of all men. To know the meaning of this text we have only to get juft ideas of the word *head*, as it is ufed in this place. The whole paffage is this. " But I would have you " know that the head of every man is Chrift ; " and the head of the woman is the man ; and " the head of Chrift is God. Every man pray- " ing or prophefying, having his head covered, " difhonoureth his head. But every woman that " prayeth or prophefieth, with her head uncov- " ered, difhonoureth her head, for that is even all " one as if fhe were fhaven." Now let us fup- pofe that the word head in this place means fede- ral head or Saviour ; then the paffage would run thus. But I would have you know that the federal head of every man is Chrift ; and the fed- eral head or Saviour of woman is the man; and the federal head or Saviour of Chrift is God. The abfurdity of fuch a meaning is apparent. The Apoftle, in this place, is confidering certain points of decency, that flow from the fubordination of fociety. The headfhip he intends is that of fu- periority and not of a gofpel union entitling to faving benefits.

In the fame place the following texts of fcrip- ture are mifconftrued. John i. 7. *The fame came for a witnefs, to bear witnefs of the light that all men through him might believe.* The witnefs here fpoken of is John the baptift ; and it is through him that all men are fpoken of as believing, which fufficiently teaches us that *all men* in this paffage cannot mean all mankind. John iii. 16, is alfo mentioned by Dr. H. A careful attention to the context, will abundantly confute his application. Under this branch of argument, and in various other parts of his book, he adduces the prophetic promifes of a future ftate of profperity to the

church in this world, as evidence of univerfal falvation; but if men follow his advice, and apply to
the fcriptures as they read, there will be no need
of an anfwer to difcover fuch mifapplications.

Sec. 13. It is very fingular, that in a matter
of infinite importance, Dr. H. fhould place fo
great dependence on metaphors and emblems, and
even ftrain them beyond the bounds of judicious
application. Page 135. " The univerfal extent
" of Christ's faving power and grace, is further
" taught us by metaphors and emblems which
" the divine fpirit hath made ufe of in the word.
" As that of the dew, the wind and the rain,
" which are known to be of univerfal extent o-
" ver the earth"—" perhaps no emblem is more
" fignificant than that of the fun often made ufe
" of in the fcriptures." After many pages to
fhow that the natural fun is of fome benefit to all
mankind; the confequence is infered, becaufe
God is compared to the fun and Christ called
the fun of righteoufnefs, therefore all men fhall
be faved.——God is alfo compared to a devouring and confuming fire—to a man of war—to a
deftroying conqueror—to a king ruling with a
rod of iron—and many other things of a like
nature, denoting his difpleafure againft fin, and
the deftruction he will bring on his impenitent
enemies. I might from thefe images, as well infer that no men fhall be faved. Such images are
beautiful and perfectly intelligible, but never were
defigned to build fyftems either of univerfal falvation or of non-falvation.

If Dr. H. fuppofed fuch metaphors to be all-
comprehending arguments, he ought to have
proved that there is rain in Egypt; which is a
natural emblem of the fpiritual Egypt, on which
none of the refrefhing influences of the divine

spirit fall; also that the shining sun cheers the deserts of Barca and Arabia.

CHRIST is.the fountain of religious doctrinal instruction to mankind, and on this account compared to the natural sun. It is probable that all men have received some degree of doctrinal light, either directly or indirectly from the sun of righteousness. But what is the consequence? not surely that all men shall be saved. CHRIST *tells us, this is the condemnation that light is come into the world, and men choose darkness rather than light.* Doctrinal light will not save men. The law was full of light; the gospel hath followed with greater light; but the doctrinal light of both law and gospel will not save men. The light instead of saving will increase their condemnation, unless GOD is pleased to sanctify; for the more a man knows of his duty, the more certainly and justly he will be condemned for not doing it.

THE following passages from page 141 show Dr. H's ideas of the nature of light, and that he made no distinction between doctrinal and saving light. " All mankind have some religion, which come " to them through CHRIST; though many have " never heard of his name. All people know " the truth in some degree. All are orthodox " in some points, and right in some measure. " GOD manifests himself and gives knowledge " and instruction of all kinds to the inhabitants " of this world, and indeed to all intelligent creat- " ures, only in and through CHRIST. All com- " mon sense, all extraordinary endowments of " mind, all science and learning, all new inven- " tions of every kind, all acquaintance with " moral and spiritual things, are by CHRIST. " Hence he is called the word of GOD; because " as men convey knowledge and instruction by " their words, so doth GOD by the mediator,

" When man fell he was then immediately in to-
" tal darkness, as to any impressions on his mind,
" or mental exercises that might profit him.
The mediation of Christ began that very moment.
" The guilty pair were immediately put in better
" circumstances by the son of God than other-
" wise they would have been." " None have
" been nearly so bad as if there had been no me-
" diator. Common grace, as we term it, having
" always been an unspeakable favor to all the fall-
" en race, and this is as really and truly by and
" through Christ as eternal salvation is." Thus
far Dr. H. In this passage, natural, intellectual
and moral powers, qualities and attainments are
thrown into one common mass, and the distinction between holiness and unholiness entirely broken down.

I am not disposed to deny that doctrinal light
may come to every creature in the universe
through Jesus Christ, but this is quite aside from
the question. The question is, doth holiness
come to all men through Christ, for without holiness there is no salvation? The apostacy did not
destroy the powers of natural understanding, wit,
memory, and invention. All these powers are
retained by those apostate spirits, who have no
benefit by the mediation of Christ. He might as
well have said that our rational existence is a gospel benefit. It is doubtless true that all things in
this world, and the state of all individuals are
subordinated by the controuling wisdom of God,
to the grand scheme of gospel probation. The
exercise of intellectual powers, even in those who
are lost, may differ in many respects, from what
it would have been without a gospel; still there is
no propriety in describing men's natural powers
and faculties as gospel blessings. If men had not
possessed these powers and faculties, they could
not have been proper subjects of gospel revelation

and command. Dr. H's idea that common grace as we term it, is as really and truly through Christ as eternal salvation, doth not prove any thing on this subject; for doctrinal light, God's powerful restraint on men's vicious temper and actions, and placing them in a situation that they might do their duty if they were disposed, do not imply holiness. Satan hath knowledge enough to do his duty if he were disposed; and men may if they please, call his knowledge and restraints, common grace, and thence infer that he will be saved; still it is conceived, that such reasoning would be thought inconclusive.

PAGE·141. "None have been nearly so bad, "as if there had been no mediator." This is an assertion that cannot be proved. To form and then apply a scale of wickedness, to men left without a mediator, and those who are in a state of probation is impossible. It is probable that GOD in subserviency to his own designs, and to preserve the world in sufficient peace for a state of trial, hath restrained the excess of visible iniquity more than would have been, if he had not designed grace for some; still this is not sufficient ground to determine, that all men are less wicked than they would have been without a mediator. An increase of doctrinal light by the gospel, increases the wickedness of mens unholy temper; and GOD who looks on the heart, may see much more wickedness in some, than if no Saviour or gospel had been provided.

ANOTHER of Dr. H's assertions which needs to be explained, is the following. Page 141. "All "mankind have some religion that comes to them "through CHRIST. All people know the truth "in some degree. All are orthodox in some "points, and right in some measure."——On this I observe; what is religion? If religion means some degree of moral conformity to the divine holiness, then there are many who have no religion. The same observations may be made upon, *knowing the truth, being orthodox*, and being *right in some things*, which are applied to all men. A doctrinal rightness of the understanding doth not imply any moral rightness of the heart; neither is there any power in an increase of doctrinal light to change the will and affections. Wicked beings will forever grow in knowledge, unholiness and misery; and an increase of knowledge will be the means of their increasing misery.

In all the Doctor's remarks on this subject, there is no distinction made between doctrinal or speculative light, and saving light. I am ready to allow, that all receive from JESUS CHRIST, either directly or indirectly, some degree of doctrinal or speculative light, and to illustrate this fact, Christ is called the sun of righteousness; but all men do not receive saving light. It may be here proper to describe the difference between them.

1st. DOCTRINAL light, is a natural or rational knowledge of truth. I will exemplify, in the divine perfection of justice. A doctrinal knowledge of the divine perfection of justice, consists in seeing what justice is, and that GOD actually possesses it, in the most perfect degree. This will be seen by all creatures, both good and bad. Both good and bad possess natural reason and understanding, by which the thing called justice, its nature, and in what it consists, are seen. Both have the means to know what justice is, and will have them eternally; and GOD will doubtless through all duration to come, set the nature of justice, and in what it consists, as fully before the minds of the punished, as he will before the minds of the blessed. They will know what the duties of holiness are; that they ought to perform them; and also

the righteoufnefs and wifdom of God, in punifhing them for not performing. It is by this light,
that the devils now believe and tremble, and that
awakened men, in contemplation of their own
character, are afraid of God's future judgments.
An increafe of doctrinal light, will increafe happinefs or unhappinefs ; holinefs or unholinefs, juft
as the moral ftate of the heart happens to be.
And perhaps the moft direct method, which infinite power can take, to increafe the mifery of the
wicked, will be to increafe their doctrinal light or
knowledge of himfelf, his law, and his holy kingdom ; without giving them any fanctification, or
laying any reftraint on their paffions. God hath
not inftituted the means of gaining doctrinal or
fpeculative light in this world, expecting they will
make men either happy or holy, if all the influences of his fpirit be denied. It is God's ufual
method, when men are ferioufly faithful, in ufing
the means of doctrinal inftruction, to give his
fpirit alfo ; and on this, depends our encouragement to ufe what we call means ; but in thefe
means of inftruction or light, there is no direct tendency or power to change the heart.

2dly. Saving light fees the fame truth, as is
feen by doctrinal or fpeculative light ; but with
this difference. Speculative light fees the object
or truth with its nature, and in what it confifts,
without any perception of its beauty and excellence ; but in a faving light, both the object itfelf
and in what it confifts are feen, together with a
fenfe of its beauty and excellence. A faving light
fees what juftice is, and the infinite beauty of juftice. God's character, and the infinite beauty of
that character.——The law, with its excellence.——
The gofpel with its moral glory.——There may be
a fight of truth and in what it confifts, without
any delight or happinefs to the mind, and perhaps

with mifery.   It is a fight of the moral beauty of
truth, and not of truth itfelf, which gives pleafure
to the good heart;   and   a   faving light is that
which difcerns the beauty and excellence.

3dly. HENCE it appears, that the difference
between doctrinal or fpeculative, and faving
light; arifes not from the truth feen; nor from
the evidence, nor from the means ufed; but folely
from the moral ftate of the heart, will, or affections.   It is the heart which difcovers, moral
beauty, amiablenefs, and excellence.   Two perfons may look on the fame truth, through the
fame means;   one difcovers an infinite beauty in
the truth, and by this beauty is drawn to it; the
other fees no beauty, but the contrary, and wifhes
to retire from it.   In this cafe, the difference
arifes entirely from the different ftate of thofe perfons hearts.   One is holy, and his holy tafte enables him to fee beauty in a holy object; the other
is unholy, and fees no comelinefs in it.   It is
thus that unholy men fee nothing in God that is
amiable.   With refpect to all moral objects, the
heart of the perfon who beholds them, folely determines whether they appear beautiful, excellent, and glorious;   or the contrary.   Thefe obfervations, concerning moral tafte and difcernment, might eafily be illuftrated by natural and
animal tafte and difcernment.   The animal tafte
of one, perceives goodnefs, in that which the tafte
of another loathes.

4thly. THROUGH the whole Bible, ignorance,
blindnefs, not feeing, want of perception, want of
underftanding, want of knowledge and wifdom,
are attributed to unholy men.   Their fin is reprefented as confifting effentially in this.   This
is faid to be the caufe of God's anger againft
them—the ground of their guilt—their mifery
&c.——The things of which they are ignorant,

are the moral beauty and glory of God's character and of the truth. All the doctrinal inftruction in the world cannot give them this light; becaufe doctrinal inftruction doth not change the heart. A man may fit forever at the feet of Gamaliel, and not have this light; unlefs he fits at the feet of Jesus alfo, who by his fpirit, changes unholy hearts; and when changed the light of the knowledge of the glory of God, in the face of Jefus Chrift, will fhine into the mind. This want of light is a fin, becaufe it arifes wholly from a finful ftate of the heart, a love to that which is wrong, and hence that which is wrong appears beautiful to the evil mind. In the great day of judgment, God will need no other evidence that finners deferve to be condemned and punifhed, but this, that they fee no glory in his character, law, and government; but difcover a beauty in fin. This proves their hearts to be wrong, and fuch as a holy law condemns.—When unholy creatures, for felf exculpation and to quiet con-fcience argue within themfelves, God cannot be fo hard as to condemn me for that which appears to me fo excellent and pleafing; they argue di-rectly contrary to what God will in that day. The very circumftance, on which they depend to exculpate, will criminate them in his fight. He will fay, the more pleafing thefe perfons fins ap-peared to them, and the more beauty and excel-lence they perceived in a finful life and objects; the more wicked their hearts are proved to have been—the more remote they were from a love of God and their duty—the more remote from that temper which makes heaven—and therefore the more worthy to be caft out of heaven.

HAVING defcribed the different nature, and the different fource of doctrinal or fpeculative, and of

O o

faving light; I now return to Dr. H. When he fays that all men have fome light, fome knowledge; it can be true only that all men, have fome doctrinal or fpeculative light and knowledge. But as the greateft quantity of this, will not fit or bring a man to heaven, or enable him to enjoy it, if he were introduced there; as this is common to the angels of glory, and the angels of the miferable world; I do not fee, how all men's having fome doctrinal light through Chrift, is any evidence of the final falvation of all. The whole which it proves, is that thofe who mifs of falvation will be more miferable, than if there had been no gofpel, and this I am very ready to concede.

LET us now alfo go back to Dr. Huntington's argument, " that Chrift is called the fun of right-
" eoufnefs, being compared to the natural fun;
" and as all men derive fome benefit from the
" natural fun, fo all men will be faved by Chrift."
The healthy and found eye is made happy, by beholding the natural fun; but to the difeafed, wounded eye it gives the moft extreme pain, and is a caufe of mifery.—Such an eye cannot behold the light without affliction, and it will continue thus, until the eye is cured. Such a perfon cannot fay, " *truly the light is fweet, and a pleafant thing it is for the eyes to behold the fun*" but the fun is the moft wounding object which can be feen. So with refpect to Chrift the gofpel fun. The heart is difeafed, and fo long as this remains the cafe, the perfon is wounded and made miferable by the doctrinal light which fhines from him. Where the gofpel doth not give comfort by its regenerating power, forming the foul to behold the moral glory of GOD, it muft give pain by prefenting fuch truths as are difpleafing to an unholy heart.

· I HAVE no doubt but many, not attending to the diftinction that hath been ftated, depend on their doctrinal or fpeculative knowledge, as evidence of their being in a fafe ftate; and though they are under all that ignorance and blindnefs, which the fcriptures defcribe to be men's fin and mifery, when they read fuch defcriptions, apply them to others; either to the heathen who never had doctrinal light, or to other perfons in chriftian lands, whofe doctrinal ignorance is very great. Concerning the fpiritual ignorance or want of faving light, I may add,

5thly. THAT it is always in proportion, to the finfulnefs of the heart. The more finful a man's temper and difpofition are, the more blind he becomes, and the greater his diftance is from feeing any beauty, glory or excellence in God. If he fpeaks of God as a glorious being, he only means that God is a great and terrible being; and his apprehenfion is fuch as difpofes him to retire from the light. But when a chriftian fpeaks of God as glorious, in his apprehenfion, there is beauty and excellence united with greatnefs. A great intellect, or great doctrinal attainments, will not give the leaft degree of faving light, or knowledge of the beauty of holinefs. Hence, eminent genius—an underftanding enriched with earthly fcience—thofe whom the world call the greateft of men—politicians—heroes—and the leaders in vaft earthly fcenes, may be perfectly ignorant, through an unholy heart, of the light of the knowledge of the glory of God, in the face of JEsus CHRIST. If Satan have the greateft intellect of any mere creature in the univerfe, though his doctrinal knowledge be doubtlefs very great by a long obfervation of what God is doing; he is ftill the moft blind fpiritually, of any being in the univerfe. It is on this account, that many who

have the beft advantages, appear to have no fenfe
of the reality, importance, and truth of that religion in the heart, which is given by the fpirit of
God. Therefore it is very natural for them to
give the name of enthufiafm, to the effects of a
fpiritual enlightening ; and the more blind they
are, the more fafe they feel concerning their own
condition.

6thly. It is this faving or fpiritual light, which
completes the chriftian's evidence, that the holy
fcriptures are a fcheme of truth directly from
God, and every way worthy of him. We therefore fee chriftians, who have fmall intellect—little
power of reafon—few advantages for knowing—
and but a low degree of doctrinal knowledge,
ftanding firm againft all the attempts which are
made to bewilder them, and fhake their faith.
They often meet cavils and objections againft
their belief, which they cannot anfwer, and ftand
filenced before their adverfaries ; while their
faith is not in the leaft fhaken. In fuch cafes,
the reafon of the firmnefs with which they ftand,
is their fight of the fpiritual beauty and glory of
truth ; and they cannot offer this in argument to
thofe who never faw, and have no conception of
it. When they are poorly able to defend their
doctrinal fentiments, a fight of the glory of truth,
convinces them it is all they need for bleffednefs
in time and through eternity ; that the God of
this glorious character, is the true God ; and that
what they have received as his truth, is every way
worthy of him. On the other hand, fpiritual ignorance or not feeing the glory and beauty of
truth, as it is feen by a good heart, expofes many
who have once had a rational conviction, and a
right education ; to fall into error. Error is
more pleafing, and they have not that evidence
which comes to the mind, from difcerning the

glory of truth. According to this idea, we always find a multitude of doctrinal errors, springing up in the church, when experimental religion and vital piety, are declining.

SEC. 14. As further evidence that I do not misreprefent Dr. H. let us attend to what he fays concerning a diftinction of character in refpect of perfonal holinefs, between the beft and worft of men. We have his opinion of thofe whom he fuppofed the moft wicked men, from page 144 to 151 of his book.—Of good men, pages 193, 194, 204 &c.—He begins with acknowledging the total depravity of human nature. But obferve how! It was in the firft man, that human nature was deftitute of all moral good and as bad as the fallen angels. But it does not feem, that he fuppofed any other man fince Adam was in a ftate of perfonal, total depravity, for he tells us, page 144. " That the mediation of CHRIST, in favor " of all human nature, began the moment after " the fall," and that then all human nature was included in Adam. And in confequence of this, that no men have been half as bad as they might have been. He gives as much approbation to Cain, Judas, and other mifcreants of the human race, whom he mentions, for not having been more wicked ; as he doth to the moft juft and pious for the holinefs they poffeffed. On the other hand, he takes pains to lower down the holinefs of the moft eminent faints, and the way he takes, to bring their holinefs to a level with the wickednefs of Judas, and others, is defcribing their own fenfe of remaining fin, page 198. " Much is faid about being fit to die. There is " one fitnefs and but one, and that is by no " means perfonal ; but in the perfect character " of a covenant head, a vicar or furety."—Here, and in what follows in the fame page, the perfonal Holinefs of chriftians is excluded from giving any fitnefs for death ; from which it is eafy to fee, that the Dr. fuppofed what hath commonly been called grace or holinefs given to the hearts of men by the fpirit of God, is not effentially different from the moft abominable fin. He tells us, page 145 "none in this life, are ever found " without fome degree of grace and favour from " the mediator, fuch as preventing goodnefs, " reftraining grace, checks of confcience, hu- " manity and kindnefs to their fellow men." He, alfo fays, that though this unrenewed grace may be felfifh, and worthy of damnation in point of deficiency, and fpecifically different from re- newed grace; yet there are fo many particulars in which they agree and are the fame, that the excellency of the one above the other, doth not in the leaft, militate againft his argument.

Dr. H. hath no where given an exprefs de- finition of holinefs, grace in the heart, depravity, total depravity, or what felfifhnefs is, or what the conceded fpecific difference is between the grace of a renewed and an unrenewed heart. Though he readily grants, page 148, that, " there is a " *fpecific difference* between common and faving " grace, or that grace which the renewed have " and that which is common to men." In the very fame page he goes on to fay, " there are " innumerable good things of a nature fpecific- " ally different, that are equally the gift and grace " of the mediator, as wifdom and wealth ; health " and a good name, and all the five fenfes."

We here have a guide, to find what Dr. H. means by fpecific difference, that is, not the fame things, and this is *all* that he appears to mean by it. Who ever fuppofed that felfifhnefs, holinefs and the five fenfes were the fame things ? Ac- cording to his meaning of fpecific difference, there is a fpecific difference between faith and repentance; for they are not the fame thing. And he gives us no reafon to fuppofe, that there is not as much fpecific difference between repentance and faith, as their is between repentance and felfifh-nefs, for they are all three different things.

FURTHER, whcie he allows, that his reftoring grace, and checks of confcience, are merely from felfifh motives, deftitute of moral goodnefs; and that there is fin in them worthy of damnation; he is careful to add, that this worthinefs of damnation, is in regard to deficiency; and doubtlefs he would allow that repentance and all holy exercifes are worthy of damnation, in regard to deficiency.

DR. H's fcheme of total depravity and of grace in the heart feems therefore to be this. That human nature, or all men became totally wicked in Adam. That GOD began immediately to reclaim all men in Adam. His words are " the mediation " of Chrift in favour of all human nature, began " the moment after the fall. In Adam and Eve " was all human nature included, or in Adam " alone; for the woman was from him"—that God gives different degrees of grace, but all have fome—to fome the grace or holinefs of a renewed, and to others that of an unrenewed heart—to fome the grace of faith, repentance and hope—to fome the graces of checks of confcience, which though they be felfifh, and worthy of damnation in point of deficiency, yet are grace, becaufe they prevent men's being and doing worfe.—To fome the grace of wealth and the five fenfes.—To Cain the grace of not murdering his parents as well as his brother—to Judas the grace of not nailing Jefus to the crofs after he had betrayed him—and to all men, the grace of being lefs wicked than they might have been. Between all thefe graces, there is a fpecific difference, that is, they are not the same things. Having stated what appears to be Dr. H's scheme, I shall make some remarks which are due to the truth.

1st. Though all men have received some benefits from God, this is no evidence that all men shall be saved. The object of the divine government in this world, is as much to bring into view the nature of sin, as it is to save some. God hath removed every difficulty from the way of all men, except the unholiness of their own hearts. The atonement of Christ laid as compleat a foundation for the tryal of all men, as it did for the final salvation of a part. The love of God hath a general object, the good of the whole. He hath no love to individuals opposite to this. Health, wealth, the five senses, doctrinal instruction, and checks of conscience, will all eventually appear to be goodness to the whole; but this is no evidence they will be eventual benefits to those who receive them. All these things, may be called favours or benefits in their own nature; that is their natural tendency is to promote the happiness of those who improve them rationally and wisely; but if improved unreasonably, they become causes of misery. Intemperance will make the five senses inlets of misery—wealth may be the means of pain—checks of conscience may be a torment—The restraints of providence may fill the soul with distressing rage.

We shall find this to be the case, with all Dr. H's graces of the unrenewed heart. Whether a holy God designs to use them as means of sanctification, or as means of showing how sinners will act, remains yet to be known by us; and he can probably make as good use of them in the latter, as in the former way. Things which are in their nature blessings, or have a tendency to promote happiness by a reasonable improvement, will be

continued to finners through eternity. This is
the cafe with their exiftence, reafon, underftanding, and confcience. A fight of GOD's charaƈter
is the greateft of all bleffings, but through the finner's temper it is a caufe of mifery to him. Let
not finners therefore think, becaufe bleffings are
granted to all men fince the apoftacy, this is any
evidence they fhall be faved.

2. NOTWITHSTANDING all Dr. H's endeavors
to make the charaƈter of good·and bad men a-
like, it remains true, that holinefs and fin are effentially oppofite in their nature. There is no degree of holinefs in the unrenewed finner, neither
is there any thing that approaches towards it.
He allows, that his unrenewed grace is all felfifh·;
and this is granting all I wifh, and all that he
could concede. There never was, nor ever will
be in the manfions of eternal mifery, any thing
worfe than felfifhnefs, or capable of greater crimes,
or of more black enmity and refiftance to GOD.
Satan tempted, Adam fell, Cain murdered, Judas
betrayed through felfifhnefs, and the human mind
is not capable of any vice that doth not concen-
ter in a felfifh temper. Whatever pleafing names
may be invented for mens felfifh difpofitions and
aƈtions, in order to quiet confcience, they are all
fin. Holinefs, in its nature, is diametrically oppofite to felfifhnefs. The glory and happinefs of
GOD and the good of his kingdom, are the only
motives to aƈtion and the only meafure of delight,
with which holinefs is acquainted. There is no
fuch motive to aƈtion or meafure of delight in finful men, before their hearts are renewed by the
fpirit of GOD, and for this reafon we fay they are
totally depraved. The implantation of a holy
temper is the new birth; the new creation; the
being renewed by the fpirit; fo much fpoken of

by CHRIST and his Apoftles, as being neceffary
for falvation, and without which men cannot inherit the kingdom of heaven.

3d. I HAVE here a remark to make on the expreffion *reftraining grace*. The Doctor ufes this
phrafe, but he did not invent it, for it has been
too long in the church. It is not a fcriptural expreffion, and it tends to convey fome very falfe
ideas. Grace fometimes means the exercife of
GOD's goodnefs to the guilty.—It fometimes means
that real holinefs or goodnefs in the creature's
heart, which is produced by the divine fpirit.
The expreffion, *reftraining grace*, has been ufed
by fome, meaning a divine reftraint on mens
wicked paffions and actions. This doth not imply any holinefs or goodnefs in the perfon reftrained, but only a curb on the apparent exercife
of that depravity with which his heart is filled.
Neither doth it with any certainty imply, that the
reftraint is any eventual benefit to the reftrained
perfon. It may be folely an exercife of goodnefs
to GOD's own kingdom, and thofe who compofe
it. The devils are doubtlefs under reftraint.
Reftraint is no indication of a beginning holinefs
in the reftrained individual, or that GOD will finally give him holinefs. This very reftraint,
may be the means of exciting his higheft rage,
and all the inward torment of hell.

4thly. As to what Dr. H. fays, concerning the
imperfection of good people, and the mixture of
fin there is with their grace; if he had faid it to
humble them, to make them more watchful, or
to extol the grace of GOD in fparing ungrateful
backfliders, his conduct would have been com-
mendable. But when he does this, with a defign
to remove the diftinction between holinefs and
unholinefs, I cannot commend him.

THAT chriftians have a great degree of remaining fin, and are very unfit for heaven, no true chriftain will deny. They are always ready to confefs this imperfection before God, and to acknowledge it to man in a prudent way. When fuch expreffions of unworthinefs are improved to argue away the reality of the chriftian temper, it becomes us to inquire, what chriftians mean by their acknowledgement of fin. They do not mean that felfifhnefs and holinefs are the fame thing; or that they have not a principle of grace in their hearts, which is effentially different and in all refpects oppofite, to what was their reigning temper before they were renewed. One of the fins of which they fpeak, is a dependance on their own, vifible duties and attainments, which are the fame as the goodnefs of finners. The fin confeffed by the unfanctified, when their confciences crowd them to confefs, is hating God, enmity to his law and oppofition to his government. The fin moft commonly meant by chriftians, in their confeffion, is a want of more love to God, more delight in his law, and a more perfect pleafure in his government. I faid moft commonly, for I am fenfible chriftians may backflide into pofitive difobedience; but when this is the cafe, we can hardly expect to hear them making any acknowledgement of fin. No chriftian arrives to perfect holinefs in this life. Perfection contains two things; firft, a freedom from exercifes of pofitive fin, fuch as enmity; fecondly, a ftrength of holy exercifes, proportioned to the natural capacities of the mind, and to the advantages under which it acts. The chriftian may be imperfect in both thefe refpects. He may have exercifes of pofitive fin, and in thefe exercifes there can be no holinefs. Alfo all his good exercifes may be deficient in ftrength and degree. His love, faith and repentance may be lefs than they ought to be.   An exercife of the heart may be holy, and ftill be defective becaufe it is not more holy.   I make this remark to prevent the notion of fome, (and I prefume this was Dr. H's notion) that the fame exercife may be in its nature, part holy and part pofitive fin.—That in the unrenewed, unholinefs almoft entirely preponderates, though there may be a little that is right, which is his grace of *checks of confcience or not doing worfe.* —That in a better fort of people, the holy part of the exercife comes nearer to preponderation, and at a certain point of increafe the perfon becomes renewed.   Such apprehenfions as thefe totally confound the nature of holinefs and unholinefs; and are as unphilofophical as they be inconfiftent with the purity of moral virtue.   However imperfect chriftians may be, holinefs or grace in the heart remains entirely different in its nature from fin.   Sin cannot by any melioration of its nature grow into holinefs; and when any heart becomes gracious, it poffeffes moral qualities of a new kind, and of which there was no degree before.   Hence arifes the neceffity of regeneration by the fpirit of GOD.

FROM page 151 to 155 Dr. H. attempts an argument from the tendency of his fcheme to exclude *all boafting.*   I remark on thefe pages, not becaufe they contain any argument, but to call the reader's attention to his notion both of human nature, and of holinefs.   He tells us, "*good diftinctions,* are the *only* things of which men boaft or are proud, and if thefe are confered upon them in the way of mere grace, they feel more pride than if they come by their own efforts."   This was defigned, to inform us that the tendency of particular electing and fanctifying grace is to make men proud; and that the only direct way GOD can take to preferve his creatures from pride, is to fave them all. In page 152 he fays " that the pride of family, genius, beauty and other natural gifts, arifes from the confideration that fo great a being as God, has fingled out the poffeffor as a fpecial favorite." This is entirely a new difcovery! We did not know before that thofe who are proud of their faces and purfes, were thinking fo much about God, the giver. The old fafhioned opinion has been, that family defcent, and the purfe and face themfelves were the objects of pride; and that the ground of pride was becaufe they are *mine* and not *another's*. Future experiments in human nature, muft determine between the two opinions.

We readily allow that *peculiar diftinction* is one thing promotive of human pride; but it is becaufe peculiar diftinctions advance felf, and not becaufe God or any other being is the author of thefe diftinctions.

Having noticed Dr. H's difcovery concerning human nature, let us next obferve his notion of grace in the heart. Page 154. "You will fay " then, that from this view of things, eminent " advances in grace and favor in this life are " ftrong incentives of pride, in the moft exalted " faints on earth. They are fo. They always " were and always will be, fo long as any moral " depravity remains." The argument brought to prove that grace in the heart is an incentive to pride, is the buffeting of Paul left his abundant revelations fhould exalt him above meafure. Left the incautious fhould be deceived by this reprefentation, I obferve—The revelations made to Paul were not grace or holinefs. The gift of prophecy was fometimes given to unholy men. King Saul was among the prophets. The prophecies of Balaam, who was a wicked man, are fulfilling until this day. Knowledge of future

events in whatever way it be obtained, is not holinefs. Holinefs hath its feat in the heart and
not in the underftanding. A prophet may diflike
that truth, which he utters. It hath been GOD's
ufual way to ufe good men as his prophets, though
fometimes he hath improved bad men. When
good men were employed, the gift of prophecy
was no part of their holinefs. It was the remaining fin of Paul, and not his grace which expofed
him to be exalted above meafure, through an
abundance of revelations. If he had been more
good than he was, and GOD had more diftinguifhed him than he did by fanctification ; there
would have been no need of his being buffeted.
Grace always humbles men, and mortifies pride,
and there is no tendency in it to felf-exaltation.
By the real grace of GOD in the heart, creatures
are emptied of themfelves and brought to the
deepeft abafement, on a comparative view of
themfelves with GOD and their brethren.

It is only thofe *good diftinctions*, which are Dr.
H's graces of an unrenewed heart that feed
pride ; and even thefe have in themfelves no
natural tendency to pride, for it is the unrenew-
ednefs of the heart which caufes the effect. Thefe
graces of the unrenewed heart do indeed need
buffeting, and for this very end the miferies of e-
ternity are prepared.

He felt a difficulty on his own ideas of grace,
how to keep pride out of heaven, but endeavours
to efcape it, by telling us that " the fuel for pride
will then all be taken away." This is however
a retreat and not an anfwer. For holinefs in
heaven and in earth are doubtlefs of the fame nature, though not in the fame degree ; and if the
grace of the moft exalted faints on earth has a
tendency to pride, heaven will unqueftionably be
the moft proud place in the univerfe.

IN page 134, we find the following. "It is a
"further symptom that the way of life I am plead-
"ing for, is agreeable to the gospel; that believ-
"ing in it will certainly make us hate all sin."
Dr. H. tells us abundantly that his ideas of the
gospel are entirely like other men, only they think
it includes the salvation of part and he of all men.
The thing then that is to make us hate sin is a
belief that all men will be saved. But why do
men love sin ? Is it because they think that part
of men shall be punished for it ? If this be not the
cause that men love sin ; it is not seen how a belief that all men will escape punishment, can have
any peculiar tendency to make man hate sin.

MEN love sin because it is agreeable to their
temper and taste. Let common sense then determine, whether, if they will not turn from it when
punishment looks them in the face, they will turn
and repent on being told there is no punishment.

DR. H. says page 134, "The infinite loveli-
"ness of GOD and salvation by grace through JE-
"SUS CHRIST, are essential objects of the faith I
"maintain. This wholly agrees with the old Cal-
"vinistic doctrine of saving faith." When the
sinner considers GOD as a being, who he thinks
will make him eternally happy, the divine character will doubtless appear lovely on this account.
But what is this different from the sin CHRIST reproved, "*If ye love them that love you, what re-*
"*ward have you ? Do not even the publicans the*
"*same?*" That sense of loveliness in the divine
character, which attends true holiness, doth not
arise from thinking that he will make us in particular or all men happy. The infinite holiness
of his character is the object of affection, and the
christian swallowed up in the view of what GOD
is in himself, thinks little whether all men or even
whether he himself shall be eternally saved. It is

presumed that this is the sense of lovelinefs in God
with which heaven is filled, and which is the only
preparation for heaven that can be attained in
this world.   Thinking God is lovely, because he
will make us or all men happy is not true holiness.

FROM page 155 to 158, also 195 to 198, Dr.
H. assures us that his scheme hath a tendency to
produce practical holiness, and esteems this an argument in his favour.   He also supposes, (pages
206, 207,) himself to be right on this ground, because fear and torment have no tendency to change
the heart ; but on the contrary excite more hatred against the being who inflicts them.   His
argument to prove that his scheme hath the beft
tendency to promote practical virtue, is, that acts
of benevolence have more influence than objects
of fear have to make men holy and good, and that
this arises from the nature of the human mind.

RESPECTING this matter it may be said, that
neither acts of benevolence nor objects of fear
will ever change the human heart, or make a
wicked man turn from sin, without a divine sanctification.   The objects both of fear and hope,
are motives to those who act rationally to turn
from sin to God.   The misfortune is, that sinners
hearts lead them to choose and act irrationally ;
and neither hope nor fear will change their hearts.
No one supposes that the fear of punishment will
make men love God.   The experience of ages
hath proved the contrary ; and the same experience hath also showed, that benefits from God,
instead of renewing the heart have often been
improved as the means of licentiousness.   When
the threatenings of God are not speedily executed, and his long-suffering bestows favors, the
hearts of men are most fully set in them to do
evil.   We hence find, that times of prosperity are
times of the greatest visible wickedness, if the

fanctifying influences of God's spirit are denied. The doctrine of univerfal falvation, will therefore be fo far from leading men to repentance, that it will be the means of hardening their hearts. God hath not threatened punifhment, with any expectance that finners difpofition and tafte will be hereby changed; ftill there may be good reafon for the threatening. The paffions of hope and fear are implanted in the human mind—In the divine government, there are objects calculated to act upon them; but the confequence doth not follow that either hope or fear will change the moral tafte of the heart. Even Dr. H. allows that fear hath an excellent influence in preventing vifible crimes, and preferving the peace of the world. Certainly this is an important object to be obtained. Fear alfo teaches the finner his need of a Saviour, though it will not make him love a holy God and law. It is the means of his acquiring fuch doctrinal knowledge, as is neceffary for the exercife of a holy heart after God is pleafed in fovereign power and mercy to give it. With refpect to future punifhment; though as Dr. H. fays, " Ages of torment will " not have the leaft tendency to change one " heart" there may ftill be reafons for it. The punifhment of another world will not be defigned to change hearts, as the period of forgivenefs will be paft. The end propofed will probably be to keep up an eternal manifeftation of the divine character and his oppofednefs to fin, and the genuine nature and effects of an unholy temper.

Sec. 15. I have now confidered Dr. H's principal arguments, and endeavoured to fhow them unfcriptural, and inconfiftent with reafon and fact. —That his notion of oppofition between law and gofpel is wholly unfounded—his ideas of the at-

onement impoffible—his faith and graces not holy—and that his whole plan totally deftroys the
neceffity of holinefs, and confounds moral virtue
with fin. If my remarks have been juft, his
fcheme falls to the ground, and there is not in
ftrictnefs, need of faying any thing more for his
refutation. But as he appears very perfevering
in his defign, and hath drawn into the queftion a
great number of circumftances and topicks, which
really have very little or no connection with the
fubject; and as his manner of writing hath a
certain plaufibility, of its own kind, calculated to
allure the incautious and thofe who wifh to believe in him, it may be proper for me to purfue him
further. On a fubject fo important it is better to
fay too much than too little.——Dr. H. reprefents, page 158 to 161, the prayer and preaching
of thofe who think different from him to be contradictory. He fays, " We all agree in thefe
" particulars. We in the name of CHRIST, offer
" falvation to all on the purchafe of his blood.
" In the name of CHRIST we command all to
" believe. We tell all men that they have a
" good warrant to believe. That a fufficient
" foundation is laid for them all to believe ; and
" and that if they do believe they fhall certainly
" be faved ; and that not at all on the merit of
" their faith, but the merit of CHRIST"—" In
" the name of CHRIST, we promife them full
" pardon and life eternal when they repent and
" believe and obey the gofpel : and this not in
" the leaft for their repentance faith and obedi-
" ence."——The reader will obferve that this
quotation is Dr. H's own words, and not fcripture. If we allow him to affix his own ideas to
thefe words, they will doubtlefs be inconfiftent
with eternal punifhment. But even the Doctor's
own manner of preaching here expreffed, allow-

ing the common fenfe of mankind to be a fufficient judge of the meaning of words, would not
perhaps be thought inconfiftent with a belief of
future mifery. As a proof of what I fay, I may
adduce the people among whom he miniftered.
They are refpectable judges of the meaning of
language, and great numbers of them know the
principles of God's word. For thirty years they
heard this manner of preaching the gofpel without any general fufpicion that the preacher was a
Univerfalift. Is not this a fufficient proof that to
make fuch expreffions inconfiftent with the doctrine of eternal punifhment, there muft be a la-
tent meaning to them, different from what is common in the churches, and among thofe who fpeak
of gofpel truths. It now appears fince our fufpicion is awaked, there is a fingular joining of words
in Dr. H's fpecimen of gofpel preaching, to accommodate it to his own plan.

I WILL therefore tell in my own words, what
I conceive to be the common method of preaching the gofpel, which is not in the leaft inconfiftent with final punifhment. We in the name of
CHRIST offer falvation to all, telling them this
falvation means holinefs, as the firft thing by
which they can be partakers in it. We tell them,
that by the offer of falvation is meant, there is no
difficulty in the way of their eternal happinefs but
the moral ftate of their own hearts, their own
choice, their own love; the death of CHRIST
having put every other difficulty from the way of
all men. We entreat them to believe in the
Lord JESUS CHRIST; and we explain believing
in him to be, a receiving of him, his law and
kingdom with love.—That if they do thus believe
they are pardoned.—That if they do not thus believe, the wrath of GOD abideth in them.—We
tell them that faith and repentance are not the

meritorious ground of acceptance, but neceſſary in the nature of things and by God's ſpecial appointment, to give any title to final ſalvation.— We tell them that a rejection of the holy goſpel by unbelief, will leave them in ſin and everlaſting miſery.—That the ſin of their own hearts is the only thing which can prevent their being ſaved.— That ſin cannot be its own excuſe, and therefore a failure of ſalvation will be their own fault.— We plainly let them know God is under no obligation to renew their hearts, and that they are in the hands of a ſovereign God, who will do to every individual as is beſt for the whole.

At the ſame time we tell them, though they are in the hands of a ſovereign God, there is more probability of his giving them a new heart, in one way than in another.—It is more probable the contemplative, convinced ſinner will be ſanctified by the ſpirit of God, than the ſinner who is profane, thoughtleſs, and inſenſible that his heart is oppoſed to his duty. We urge on them the uſe of means, as being in the nature of things neceſſary to inſtruct them in the natural enmity of their own hearts ; and alſo to aſſiſt in the exerciſe of grace when God is pleaſed to give it ; at the ſame time, we caution them againſt thinking that means render them more worthy of divine mercy. I need not ſpend time to ſhow this manner of preaching the goſpel to be perfectly conſiſtent with the eternal miſery of ſome.

Dr. H. tells us, we pray for all men, and ſeems to think this an argument in his favour. Others before him have uſed it ; and if there be an argument it ariſes from ſome falſe ideas of the nature and duty of prayer ; and in what ſenſe we pray for all men. The duty of praying for ſalvation, ariſes from a divine permiſſion and command. We ought not to pray for any event, that is directly contrary to what GOD hath told us shall take place. We have no right to pray that every man, from Adam down to his last born child, shall be saved; because GOD hath told us, they shall not all be saved. When it has been conceded, that we ought to pray for all men, this was not meant. Many are dead and their state is fixed, and by conceding that we should pray for all men, these were never intended. When Paul to Timothy, directed that supplication should be made for all men, all kings, and all in authority; it is very evident he meant men of all nations and not Jews only, as I have before explained. CHRIST, tells us there are some for whom he did not pray. The Apostle John tells us some have committed the sin unto death, and releases us from an obligation to pray for them. So that we have no right to pray for the salvation of all men, from Adam to his last born child.

FURTHER, in prayer there is always an implied limitation to the request, and this limitation is, if the thing requested be agreeable to the will and designs of GOD. All our requests in prayer, ought to be under this limitation. If there be any event which GOD hath told us shall not take place, there would be high impiety in praying for it. When a rational believer in divine revelation, in his prayer for salvation, uses the expression *all men*, this limitation is implied. In praying for deliverance from sickness, war, or any other evil; we mean if it may be agreeable to GOD's council and for his glory. Prayer for the salvation of all men; thus limited and understood is most fit. It is an expression of the benevolent feelings of our own hearts, and that it would please us to see all we know, and all who now live made holy and happy, if the infinite wisdom of GOD sees best. In this way, doubtless, christians often pray for the falvation of thofe, who never will be faved. Not becaufe their benevolence is greater than the benevolence of GOD; but they pray in ignorance of what his infinitely wife benevolence will determine to be beft for the whole. If they had GOD's knowledge the very benevolence which now caufes their prayer, would prevent their praying; and there are many reafons, which determine it beft they fhould be held in this ignorance during their earthly life.

THE fame remarks hold true refpecting our defire for the falvation of men, which Dr. H. mentions page 200; for prayer is only the expreffion of our defires. If GOD hath faid falvation fhall not extend to every individual of mankind, we have no right to defire fuch an event. The perfect, holy, and wife will of GOD ought to limit our defires. Benevolence, from its very nature, defires the greateft happinefs to GOD and his univerfe; and if the falvation of all men will abridge this happinefs, fuch falvation is not an object of holy defire.

DR. H. frequently infinuates, that the doctrine of eternal punifhment implies the lawfulnefs of hatred; but this is mere infinuation. Every man who will attend, is able to fee the difference, between an approbation of mifery juftly inflicted as punifhment to promote the general happinefs; and a delight in mifery on motives of private and perfonal refentment. The firft of thefe is benevolence; the laft is hatred, and is unlawful in all cafes whatever.

FROM page 161 to 164, Dr. H. informs us the ground of his own comfort. No one is difpofed to difpute his knowledge of himfelf, or to difbelieve that his comfort was built on the grounds he fuppofed. At the fame time, he had no right to afcribe the comfort of others, fome of whom he

hath named and fome are pointed out by the period in which they lived, to any fuch fyftem as
that he hath publifhed to the world. He fays
concerning thofe worthies among our fathers,
" that they could make no foundation of hope
" in all that God had wrought in their fouls, but
" praife his glorious name that he had been
" pleafed, in mere, fovereign mercy, to work thus
" effectually on them, only to lead them to the
" fenfe and comfort of what was immutable truth
" before, viz. the all-fufficiency of Christ for
" the chief of finners." Doubtlefs Dr. H's real
fentiments were as much difguifed from many of
our venerable fathers now in the grave ; and alfo
from many of the refpectable, furviving clergy
who furrounded him, as they were from the people of his charge ; and on this account they may
not have ufed that pointed caution in converfation
with him, which they would otherwife have chofen. Yet as to all thefe fathers and chriftians,
public teftimony avers, that their fentiments and
profeffed grounds of comfort were as follows.
The fovereign mercy of God through the merits
of Jesus Christ, was the foundation of their
hope. That it was God who had fanctified them by
his gracious power, and this fanctification did not
merit eternal life. Still they fuppofed the effectual working of God on their fouls was neceffary
not only to give them fenfe and comfort of the
truth, but alfo as preparation for heaven, and a neceffary means of their title to heaven. That they
could have no title, without a faith and repentance,
in their nature holy. In confiftency with this,
they uniformly taught that no man had a right
to hope for falvation, until renewed by the fpirit
of God, and that many will finally be fhut out
from the kingdom of heaven.

From page 170 to 178 of Dr. H's publication, he attempts to fhow " that it is evidential of the " truth of this doctrine of free fovereign grace " as illuftrated" by him " that there is no poffi- " ble danger in believing, and living according " to the genuine dictates of it." This will be denied. The reafons affigned for the fafety of believing and living according to the dictates of it, are the two following. Firft, that he believes like other orthodox people, in all points, except the number of the faved ; and fecondly, that concerning the number of the faved, there hath been great difference of opinion in the chriftian church. With refpect to the firft of thefe reafons, it hath been fhowed, that his fingularity of fentiment is not peculiar to the number of mankind who fhall be faved ; but alfo concerning the manner of falvation and man's title to it ; and that he hath departed from that fcheme of faith and holinefs under which he ranks himfelf.

As to what he fays of the difference of opinion, that hath been concerning the number which will be faved, and the duration of the millenium, it only amounts to this ; that becaufe other people, who believe on the exprefs teftimony of God, that part of men will be loft, cannot agree in opinion, when attempting both without right and evidence, to tell how great a part that will be ; that it is therefore as fafe for him to fay none will be loft, as it is for them to difagree concerning the proportion.

My reafons for fuppofing, there is the higheft danger in believing and living according to Dr. H's fcheme, are thefe.

1ft. To make out a regeneration, repentance and faith, which will reach all mankind, he hath left holinefs out of their nature ; alfo, his law and gofpel are placed at fuch variance, they cannot be reconciled.

2d. It is alfo believed, that the eternal punifh-ment of fome finners is exprefsly declared in the word of God. There is every reafon to fuppofe danger in difbelieving what God hath revealed, and in living according to that difbelief; even though we are wholly unable to fee how the dan-ger arifes.

3d. Considering what human nature is, the tendency of this doctrine will be to promote vice, and make men carelefs concerning their own fal-vation. I do not think any obedience which flows from fear to be holy. It is effentially de-fective, and is no evidence men are in a fafe ftate. The obedience of chriftians flows from love; ftill it is true, that chriftians are in a ftate of great imperfection, and in their deep backflidings often need the fame kind of addrefs, as is proper for finners who never had a holy love of God. Though a fear of punifhment is not in its nature holy; it ftill ferves an excellent purpofe in Christ's mediatorial government of men, in fuch a ftate as we now are. The Apoftle faith the law is a fchoolmafter to bring men to Christ. It is by the law, the penalties of the law, and the real danger of fuffering thefe penalties; that fin-ners know their need of a Saviour. Thus they are made confiderate, convinced and tremble. We allow all this is not holinefs, yet it is neceffary to bring the minds of men into fuch a ftate, as experience teaches God will ufually have them to be, before he beftows holinefs by his renewing power. This is alfo neceffary to prepare them to improve holinefs after God is pleafed to give it. Take away all fear of mifery from men, and you bring them into a perfect fecurity, and it hath not

R r

been God's usual way to make such persons the partakers of his spirit by a holy regeneration. God did not reveal the future punishment of ungodly men to gratify our curiosity. It was to answer an important purpose in the work of salvation, and therefore it is not safe to live in the disbelief of it.

Sec. 16. From page 164 to 170, and in many other parts of his book, Dr. H. says, that all have endured eternal and everlasting sufferings in Christ, as their vicar, substitute or head. To prove this we find the following argument in page 165. " The obeying, and suffering human " nature, was as much united to all the attributes " of Deity, as to any one of them; to Deity in " all his infinite perfections; to the eternity of " Deity as much as to his omniscience, almigh- " tiness, or any other attribute. And the suffer- " ings of Christ are eternal sufferings, just in " the same way that they are infinite."——Now what is truth in this case? The truth is that the sufferings of Christ were neither infinite, nor eternal; almighty nor omniscient. It was only the finite, human nature of Christ that suffered. A finite nature cannot endure an infinite quantity of suffering in the short time of his passion. His sufferings were extreme. So great as infinite wisdom saw to be best, and sufficient to answer the whole purpose for which they were intended; but they were not infinite; neither were they eternal. Eternal, means duration without end. Christ's sufferings have long since had an end, and therefore they are not eternal sufferings. The efficacy of Christ's sufferings did not depend on their being either infinite or eternal; but on their having an infinite value in them to promote the end for which they were intended. Herein was the manifold wisdom of God, that he could find suf-

terings of infinite value which were neither infinite in quantity nor eternal in duration. The
use of the sinner's suffering, if he had suffered eternally; also the value or use of Christ's sufferings, I have already explained. The mediator's
sufferings were in his human nature, which was
capable of suffering; the value of them was derived from his divine and infinite nature. So
that there is no sense in which it is proper to call
the sufferings of Christ either infinite or eternal.
If the sufferings of Christ be in no sense eternal,
then the denunciation of God, these shall go a-
way into everlasting punishment, remains yet to
be fulfilled, on those unhappy persons who remain
in unbelief. If Christ never suffered eternal
punishment, it is certain they never suffered it in
him, and must endure it in their own persons, or
the word of God will fail.

Dr. H. makes two attempts to explain into a
consistency with his scheme, Christ's description
of the solemn process in the day of judgment, recorded in Mat. xxv. One is in pages 167, 168.
" God will show infinite approbation to the char-
" acter of his own Son, the Son of Man, as fed-
" eral head in union with his redeemed crea-
" tures; placing it at his right hand; a phrase
" denoting approbation and honor,—and he will
" manifest infinite wrath, indignation and ven-
" geance against the evil character of man, pla-
" cing it at his left hand. The place of his Son
" will on that day be at his right hand, as it al-
" ways was and always will be."——Had our
author forgot, when he wrote the above, that the
Son of God is to be the judge, and that his idea
involves not only the absurdity of judging characters without persons; but also that of the judge
placing himself at his own right hand.

His other attempt to explain away CHRIST's account of the laſt judgment is from page 66 to 68. And here he ſeems to labour heavily under his own argument, in order to bring it to a concluſion agreeable to his belief. After having told us that all mankind will appear in two characters before the bar of GOD; in their own which is infinitely guilty, and in the character of CHRIST which is infinitely worthy.—That in their own character all ſhall ſtand on the left hand, and in the character of Chriſt all on the right. After having deſcribed all as ſentenced both to eternal happineſs and eternal miſery, he raiſes the queſtion which ſentence ſhall take place. His own words are, " They are deſignated both ways, and op-" poſite ways—they can go but one, and they " are all to go together—Which ſhall get the " victory ?—Which voice or ſentence ſhall tri-" umph ? Which ſhall reign ?" To this queſtion he anſwers, *But where ſin abounded grace did much more abound, that as ſin hath reigned unto death, even ſo might grace reign through righteouſneſs to eternal life, by Jeſus Chriſt our Lord.* Rom. v. 20. This is Dr. H's anſwer. I have another anſwer to give, which is alſo the voice of the inſpired man. *They ſhall be tormented with fire and brim-ſtone, in the preſence of the holy angels, and in the preſence of the Lamb : and the ſmoke of their tor-ment aſcendeth up forever and ever.* Rev. xiv. 10, 11. Both theſe anſwers are from the word of GOD, and the queſtion ſtill returns which ſhall get the victory ? But I think the reader muſt by this time be ſenſible, that Dr. H's paraphraſe hath not changed the old aſpect of CHRIST's deſ-cription of the day of judgment.

FROM page 178 to 182, Dr. H. attempts to raiſe an odium on thoſe who think different from him by repreſenting that they think the greateſt part of mankind, will be a thousand times more miserable, than if there had been no gospel, and only a few individuals will be exalted, at the expence of a much greater number who are eternally wretched.

SUCH representations as he makes, are very apt to take hold of mens prejudices against the sovereignty of the divine government. Respecting the number of the saved we give no opinion. Of the proportion between the saved and the lost we are utterly ignorant, and are willing to rest the matter in the determination of a GOD, who is the infinite friend of happiness, and knows how to produce the greatest degree of it in his universe. We esteem the answer of our Saviour to the curious inquirer, whether only a few would be saved, a sufficient check to our own curiosity on the same subject; but we learn from it that some will not be saved.

NOTWITHSTANDING the dark aspect in the present age and generation, through the prevalence of infidelity and its natural offspring, the denial of vital piety and experimental religion; we hope that the saved will be vastly more numerous than the lost; and firmly believe there will be more happiness in the creation of GOD, than if sin and misery had never entered. Respecting those who are lost, we believe they will be treated as they deserve—That they will appear to be very wicked beings, deeply in love with their own sin, and of a most odious character; and not as Dr. H. represents, a number of honest, worthy and laborious people made miserable for the sake of aggrandizeing a few unworthy favourites.

HE tells us page 182, " A sermon is not made " up of contradictory parts, if it be wholly a gos- " pel sermon. Now, the doctrine I plead for, is " the only plan that ever was exhibited, as con-

" fistent with itself." On this I remark, must not a sermon be made up wholly of contradictions on Dr. H's plan; for he tells us both law and gospel must be preached in every sermon, and that these are directly contrary and opposed to each other.

In order to prove the contradictoriness of the best preachers since the reformation, he describes their doctrines in the following words. Page 184. " God hath elected to eternal life a part of man-
" kind, and Christ made an atonement for that
" part only; which part are elected to the end,
" and to all the necessary means and qualifica-
" tions; which God will bestow upon them in
" his own way and time. All the rest of man-
" kind shall as certainly perish, and that justly,
" the fault being all their own. Now we invite
" and command every one to believe in Christ
" to salvation, every one alike: for in him there
" is a fulness for all.

Any man will see, that the above representation is contradictory. The reader must remember it is in the Doctor's own words, and formed by him-self to answer his own purpose. How some have preached, and what inconsistencies they have held up, I pretend not to say. Good and learned men may fall into inconsistencies, of which every gen-eration furnishes new evidence.

Wrong apprehensions of the atonement have been the source of innumerable other errors, and none have been more fruitful in error, than Dr. H's own apprehension; which supposes there was an actual transfer of the transgressor's sin and guilt, so that they became the sin and guilt of Jesus Christ, and that in this sense he suffered for them. I have already attempted to show that such a transfer is both morally wrong and nat-urally impossible. The contradiction arises from the following paſſages in Dr. H's ſtating, " God " hath elected to eternal life a part of mankind, " and Christ hath made an atonement for that " part only"—" Now we invite and command " every one to believe in Christ to ſalvation, " every one alike, for in him there is a fulneſs " for all." The error of this ſtating, is in ſaying that Christ made an atonement ſufficient only for a part; and the contradiction is in directing all to come, when there is proviſion made only for a part.

But it hath been ſhown this idea of the atonement is erroneous, it being in its nature as ſufficient for all as it is for one, and that the want of coming is the only cauſe of deſtruction. Directing men to come to Christ, is the ſame as directing them to be holy, and however ſufficient the goſpel atonement is, if they will not be holy, they cannot be ſaved. Thoſe, who have preached that there is an atonement ſufficient only for a part of mankind, if there be any ſuch, ought to make very ſerious inquiry whether they have not preached wrong.

Having removed the charge of contradiction, which aroſe from a miſrepreſentation of the atonement; I will now propoſe, and attempt to anſwer a queſtion, which though it be not directly mentioned by Dr. H. may occur to ſome minds.

Queſtion. How is it reaſonable to direct them to come to Christ, who are not elected to eternal life, and to whom God will never grant his renewing and ſanctifying grace.

I shall not evade this queſtion, by ſaying the preacher doth not know whom God will ſanctify and whom he will leave in ſin, and may therefore intreat all to believe. It is doubtleſs the duty of thoſe whom God will never ſanctify, to love him and embrace the goſpel; and all men may be exhorted to the whole of their duty. The two following remarks, it is fuppofed, will give a juft anfwer to the queftion.

1ft. God might have left all mankind to perifh in fin, without any injuftice to them. If he might juftly have left all to perifh, he certainly may with the fame juftice leave a part, if he fees it to be the beft manner of governing the univerfe thus to do. His felecting choice, was made from motives of public good. He choofes and he paffes by from the fame motives ; to advance the gene-ral interefts of the intelligent fyftem ; and thofe, who are paffed by, have no more and no other reafon to complain of their treatment, than all mankind would have had, if a Saviour had not been provided for any. The removal of all dif-ficulty from the way of impenitent finners, except their own will; lays God under no obligation to remove that alfo.

2d. The obligation to come to Chrift doth not arife from the affiftance, which God gives by his fpirit in coming. God gives his fpirit to affift the finner in complying with a previous obliga-tion, and not to create the obligation. This will appear plain, if we attend, to what is meant by coming to Chrift. Coming to Chrift is loving his character—delighting in his moral qualities and perfections, which are in their nature excel-lent—obeying and choofing him as our Lord, and his law as our rule. All this is as much the finner's duty before he comes, as it is afterwards ; and if the affiftance of the fpirit be never granted, his duty is not hereby changed or leffened. Ob-ligation arifes from the moral fitnefs of the thing commanded ; and it is fit Chrift fhould be loved. Whether finners hearts be right or wrong, duty is the fame.

It is reafonable a finful being fhould be told to love God, becaufe the moral excellence of the divine character is the ground of obligation ; and the obligation is as much on thofe who oppofe, as it is on thofe who delight in him. The bufi-nefs of the preacher is to tell men to do their duty, to love God, and come to Jefus Chrift, whether the fpirit be granted, or whether he be denied. There is every reafon to fuppofe, that after the day of judgment, when it will become certain the fpirit will be granted no more to the impenitent, finners own confciences will preach to them the duty of loving God, in more decifive language than man ever uttered ; and a conflict between their hearts and confciences will be no fmall in-gredient of mifery.

Sec. 17. There is, faith Dr. H. page 187, a fentiment or impreffion on the hearts of all men concerning the dead, favouring his argument, and that on the death of the vileft finner, it would wound our feelings to hear it faid, he is certainly gone to an eternal hell.

It is readily allowed, fuch a conclufion con-cerning any one is unwarranted. The ftate of individuals is no where revealed, neither is there any fufficient evidence for a certain judgment of their condition. God may fanctify and forgive the moft vicious, in their laft moments ; taking them as brands out of the burning, and it would be very rafh in us, to fet any other bounds to his fovereign acting, than he hath fet to himfelf, *that many fhall feek to enter and not be able.* The beft confolation, on the lofs of friends whofe conduct hath been unhopeful, is this ; they are in the hands of a God who can and will do right and beft. Dr. H. makes mention of the tender affection of parents ; but this is merely an addrefs to the

S f

selfish paffions; and by thefe the world will not be judged. In page 189, he reprefents it exceeding ftrange, if there be a ftate of punifhment after death, that the fcriptures have not given us information of particular perfons who were configned to it.

Men often think it ftrange that the fecrets of divine government are not revealed to them. But what could be the benefit to mankind, of fuch information as he mentions? Would it make them better to have fuch a warning? Our Saviour hath decided this, for if *they hear not Mofes and the prophets, neither will they be perfuaded though one rofe from the dead.* The evils from fuch a revelation would be many. To mention no other, the afflicion of friends would often be extreme. Society cannot be maintained in fuch a ftate as this, without natural affection; and there is no reafon to make this principle an inlet of forrow, when the alternate rifing of hope and fear will more powerfully affift the furvivors in their own preparation, than a certain knowledge either of the glory or mifery of their departed friends.

Dr. H. hath taken much pains in pages 189, 190, 280, 281, to fhow that Judas hath come to a good end. I think there is much in fcripture againft his opinion, and fee but little ftrength in his remarks to fupport it, at the fame time, if it could be proved that Judas were now in bleffednefs, it would very little effect the evidence for eternal punifhment. But as fome appear to think this circumftance an important one, I will remark upon it. In page 281, Dr. H. tells us the text in Mark xiv. 21, which is tranflated " *good were it for that man if he had never been born,* ought to have been thus, *good were it for him, if he had not been born that man,*" and then he appeals to the learned that he is right. I think the learned need not be troubled, for every fchool boy in Greek, knows whence the variation arifes, and that it doth not alter the fentiment. The words of a fentence in different languages ftand in different order of location. No two languages agree in this ; and the different placing of words in a fentence is one thing which makes the peculiar idiom of particular languages ; ftill this doth not alter the meaning of the fentence, to thofe who have a knowledge of both languages. In the prefent inftance, the tranflators of the Bible, have placed the words according to the Englifh manner of placing words in a fentence. In Dr. H's tranfla-tion, he hath placed the words according to the Greek manner of placing words in a fentence ; but the meaning is the fame.

To be born, means coming into exiftence. According to the tranflators it is, * " *It were good for that man if he had never come into exiftence.*" According to Dr. H. following the Greek pla-cing of words, it is, *Good were it for him if not come into exiftence that man.* I afk what is the difference of fentiment, in thefe cafes ? I think none. In both forms, exiftence is reprefented to be an evil to the poffeffor, but exiftence cannot be an evil to the poffeffor, on any condition but that of endlefs mifery. An eternity of happinefs following after any limited duration of mifery, will overbalance it and make exiftence a bleffing.

IN page 191, 1 Cor. viii. 11, is mentioned as an argument, the words are, " *And through thy knowledge fhall the weak brother perifh for whom* CHRIST *died.*" He fays, the word *perifh* means eternal mifery as much as damnation doth, and that it cannot mean eternal mifery in this place.

AND what is the confequence ? Not furely that it never means eternal mifery. Words are often limited by the fubject and connected fentiments.

I do not think that the word perifh means eternal mifery in this place; at the fame time, I can fee no abfolute proof that it doth not; for there is a fenfe in which Chrift died for thofe who perifh eternally.

What Dr. H. fays of infants in pages 192, 193, doth not feem to contain any argument, and certainly was an infertion in his book ufelefs to his fubject, unlefs it was meant to infinuate that thofe who differ from him condemn all infants to a future punifhment.

Concerning the ftate of infants I have little to fay. They are in the hand of a good and wife God, and the Redeemer is their judge. The moft rigid in fentiment, with whom I ever converfed, go no further than Dr. H. doth; that God might juftly make all the human race miferable, and infants are part of the human race. There are thoufands of dying adults, whofe departure would be lefs gloomy than it is, if there were half the reafon to hope well for them, as there is to hope for dying infants.

Sec. 18. Beginning at page 208 to 217, Dr. H. endeavours to fhow, that unlefs all men are faved, Satan will obtain a victory over Jefus Chrift; and that the eternal mifery of fome, reprefents the Son of God and Satan as mainly united in defign.

The principles he affumes to prove this, may be feen in the two following quotations. Page 212. " On the part of the adverfary, the matter " contended for, is the entire, complete, eternal, " univerfal mifery of all mankind: the Son of " God does fully, and flatly oppofe Satan, in this " very thing; otherwife there is no war between " them, i. e. if the Devil is driving at one thing, " and the Saviour oppofing another. But the " oppofition is direct and full." Page 213.

" Satan never fo much as hoped; or in the leaft
" aimed to obftruct the happinefs or glory of
" God; for he always knew it was utterly im-
" poffible for him to do it, in the leaft degree.
" The compleat, eternal mifery of all mankind
" was the fole point he aimed at." On Dr. H's
defcription of this matter I remark;

Firft. It is fo worded as to reprefent the Son
of God engaged with one of his apoftate creatures in a mere matter of will, fuch as often takes
place between guilty men.

Secondly. He tells us that Satan had no defign
to obftruct the glory of God, and the reafon affigned to fhow he had not, is this; that he knew
he could not injure it.

What Satan's knowledge in this matter was,
no man can tell, but fuppofe he had fuch knowledge. Did not our author know, that an unholy
mind wifhes and attempts things againft knowledge; and that herein confifts the folly of fin.
Doth not the murmurer know that he cannot alter
the ways of providence? Doth not every finner,
who tranfgreffes againft the divine government,
know that he cannot overcome omnipotence? It
is not a rational profpect of overcoming and placing himfelf on the throne of the univerfe, which
makes a wicked being to fin; but it is becaufe he
loves fin and felf. Creatures actions will flow out
in conformity to their hearts, whether they fucceed or fucceed not. If all wicked angels and
men knew, that by a divine overruling, their efforts would increafe the glory of God, they
would ftill endeavour to difhonour him, and gratify themfelves.

If a knowledge that he could not fucceed, hath
prevented Satan from aiming againft the glory of
God; why hath not a knowledge of Dr. H's
fcheme of univerfal falvation, long fince prevented

him carrying on this war with the mediator? It is natural to suppose that a despair of success, would be equally efficacious in both cases to remove his depravity and resistance.

MAN was the creature of GOD, made by him and for his own glory. Satan had no cause of quarrel with man, but what arose from a previous enmity against his maker, his kingdom, and his glory. To counteract the counsels, will, government, kingdom and glory of GOD, and to gratify his pride were his motives in seducing. What knowledge this apostate had of the improbability of success, in the beginning of his rebellion, is not for us to say. Doubtless before this, he hath a full conviction that he shall be confounded, and under this belief he trembles; still this conviction hath no tendency either to reclaim or restrain him. The heart will pursue measures dictated by its own enmity and self-love; and sinful beings will act as much against reason, as those do who are in the deepest distraction or idiotism. It is on this account, that fools and folly are names used in the scriptures to describe sinners and their sin.

2. JESUS CHRIST will have a compleat victory over Satan, though part of mankind are lost; and his triumph may be greater than if all were saved. That which makes GOD most glorious and blessed, and produces the greatest happiness and holiness in his kingdom, will make the Saviour's triumph the most compleat and perfect that it can be. Satan's design against man, was accessary to his more impious design against GOD and his kingdom. CHRIST's design was to make GOD and his kingdom most glorious and blessed. In this consisted his compleat opposition to the designs of Satan, and not in saving every individual of the human race; for GOD hath wisdom enough to confound Satan more compleatly by the loss of some, than he would be by the salvation of all men.

Satan will fee God more glorious in the eyes of his holy creatures ; more fervently loved ; and more faithfully ferved by them ; than if an apoftacy had not taken place.—All the divine perfections will be brought into the view of creatures by thefe means, and happinefs be thus greatly advanced.—Though fome are loft, there will be more holinefs and happinefs among the children of Adam than if none of them had fallen.—Satan will fee human nature greatly exalted above him, and the Son of Man will be his judge.— He will fee fo many of mankind as fovereign mercy is pleafed to fave, compleatly taken out of his hands, and made more glorious and bleffed than if he had never tempted them.—He will know that God could have faved all men in the fame manner, if infinite wifdom had not referved them for the confufion of his defign.—He will fee himfelf and thofe who are with him, left as a conftant experiment and difplay of the bafenefs and unreafonablenefs of a finful temper.—His reafon and natural confcience will condemn what his heart loves.—While he hates the kingdom of God, he will know that the manifeftation of his own wicked temper, is the very means of inftructing the fubjects of that kingdom, in the excellency of holinefs ; the unreafonablenefs of fin ; the fitnefs of the divine law ; the glory of God in giving fuch a law ; and he will be fenfible that his continued hatred of God's kingdom, only makes it more glorious ; fo that he muft be the involuntary means of ftrengthening, through eternity, the caufe that he wifhes to deftroy. He will find loft men, who fell through his means, now become his tormentors (for there is as much reafon to fuppofe that wicked men will torment him, as there is that he will torment them.) He will find himfelf a more miferable being than if he had never seduced the human race. His confusion will be in proportion to the display that is made of the nature of sin. The final impenitence of some men, in the face of gospel mercy, will give the highest manifestation of the total baseness of sin, that can be made. So that the sinners whom he hath seduced, will serve as a glass, to reflect back the baseness of his own principles in his own sight, and in the sight of the holy universe, more brightly than it could appear by looking on him alone. Thus the loss of some men will add to Satan's confusion, and to the disappointment of all who continue united with him in design. In this way, CHRIST's victory over Satan will be a more compleat one, than if all men were saved.—This is meant by CHRIST's destroying the works of the Devil, and his being the plague and destruction of death. There will be more holiness and happiness in the universe, than if sin and misery had never entered; and all the designs of GOD's enemies will be turned on their own heads; partly by the exercise of sovereign mercy, and partly by the execution of justice. GOD will show that he can conquer, both by forgiving and by punishing, and make his enemies the footstool, by which he ascends a glorious throne of love. Even when he punishes, he can exercise more love, than if he had never punished. In the just punishment of those who choose sin, there will be as full evidence that GOD is love, as there is in the praises of Heaven.

IN page 217 Dr. H. says, " That though sin is " an infinite evil, we cannot in the least hurt GOD " by it, or infringe on his infinite and uninter- " rupted happiness." And he seems to think this an argument against eternal punishment. Here he mistakes in two points. For first, it is conceived that no argument arises from this consideration.

Secondly if there were any argument, it would be againſt the evil of ſin, which he has juſt ſaid to be infinite, and not an argument againſt the puniſhment of it. If there be an infinite evil in ſin, as is conceded, it is juſt it ſhould be eternally puniſhed, whether GOD be hurt or not. Page 220 he adds on the ſame ſubjeᶜt. That ſin belongs to the pure, wiſe, holy and good government of GOD ; and therefore becauſe it belongs to his government, GOD need not puniſh poor ſinners to retrieve any harm done to him.

I ALLOW with Dr. H. that ſin belongs to the infinitely wiſe plan of the divine government. I allow that it will never harm GOD ; but the reaſon it will never harm him, is becauſe eternal puniſhment is alſo part of the ſame plan. If eternal puniſhment was not part of the ſame plan, ſin would do harm both to GOD and his kingdom. Whatever hides the divine charaᶜter, will eſſentially harm the univerſe of creatures; for their happineſs depends on a true knowledge of the GOD who governs them. For the ſupreme governor not to puniſh ſin would hide his charaᶜter, and thus leſſen the general happineſs of the univerſe. And whatever diminiſhes the general happineſs of the univerſe of creatures, would directly militate againſt his own happineſs, which conſiſts in making the greateſt poſſible bleſſedneſs around him. The only reaſon that ſin can do no harm to GOD, is becauſe that puniſhment is part of the ſame infinitely wiſe plan.

PAGE 221. Dr. H. ſpeaking of the divine decrees ſaith, " What our hearts revolt at, is the at-
" tributing ſuch decrees to GOD, as are contrary
" to his nature. *God is love.* Attribute no de-
" crees to GOD but thoſe of infinite love, in har-
" mony with all the perfeᶜtions of Deity, and

" they will fet eafy on our minds."——I wifh to
attribute no decrees to GOD, but fuch as are confiftent with the character of love, infinite and un-
caufed. If the production of the greateft happinefs in the intelligent fyftem be a work of infinite
love, the doctrine now vindicated is fuppofed to
be confiftent with it. The greateft happinefs of
the whole, and not the greateft happinefs of every
individual, is the object of infinite love, and the
only one that can be worthy of it. To fay, that
the higheft happinefs of the whole and alfo of every individual can be united, is faying more than
man knows. This is a point which can be determined, only by that wifdom which inhabits
the praifes of eternity.

PAGE 222. Dr. H. makes the following fuppofition, " that if JEHOVAH was in all things elfe as
" he now is; but only had a difpofition to infi-
" nite malevolence, as he now hath to infinite
" love and benevolence, poor fuffering creatures
" could not even then impeach his juftice fimply
" confidered: for their whole beings and all the
" pain and all the comfort that could ever affect
" them, would be GOD's own abfolute property,
" to difpofe of, as he pleafed."——In remarking
on this paffage, I cannot refrain calling the reader's attention to our author's idea of juftice.
He doth not feem to conceive that it is a part of
benevolence, or that its excellency arifes from its
being an exercife of benevolence; for he here exprefsly fays, that an exercife of infinite malevolence might be juft. Is not this making power
the rule of right ? On thefe principles may not a
kingdom of infinite malevolence be, as juft as a
kingdom of benevolence ? Juftice is always lovely, and on thefe principles may not a kingdom of
infinite malevolence be infinitely lovely ? On
thefe principles would not Satan be as juft a being

as Jehovah is, if he had power without any honefty on his fide, to give him the victory? Or how
are the cruelties of this world to be called unjuft,
for there hath been power on the fide of thofe
who committed them. This is fetting all principles of juftice afloat, and is very congenial with
the paffions of the age. My author having paf-
fionately exclaimed to his readers, on the character of a God punifhing fin " Is this your God.".
Suffer me to reply, is this your God, who would
be as juft by the torments of infinite malevolence,
as he now is by a government which benevolently
feeks the greateft happinefs of the whole.

Page 222 of Dr. H. " We are taught, in the
" word of God, that all our backwardnefs in be-
" lieving to the falvation of our fouls, lies in the
" enmity of our hearts: at leaft, if this was all
" removed, we fhould, under gofpel light, read-
" ily believe." In the next page he informs us,
in what this enmity ccnfifts. " When we hear
" the pure doctrines of free grace, our hearts
" fay " this is too good news to be true". man-
" kind in a ftate of nature, find no fuch difpofi-
" tion in themfelves; and they do, and will im-
" agine, that God is in this regard " altogether
" fuch as themfelves."——I recite this paffage
to fhow the Doctor's notion of that fin in the
human heart, which keeps them from gofpel obedience. That it confifts in thinking fuch news
as the gofpel hath brought us " is too good to
be true." The event will determine whether his
apprehenfions are juft. If thofe who receive his
doctrine, from this time forward, fhow themfelves
the moft holy, pure, humble men in the world;
if they are devoted to God and religion, deny all
evil lufts and appetites, and appear to begin a
heaven of holinefs while they are here on earth;
it will be fome evidence in the Doctor's favor.

But if they are not more eminent in gofpel obedience than other men, it will be evidence that
there is fome caufe of difobedience, befide thinking the gofpel news " too good to be true."

Sec. 19. In page 225, Dr. H. begins an argument, which with his illuftration of it, is continued to page 245. His words are thefe " This
" doctrine of infinite, fovereign, and univerfal
" grace, flowing wholly out of the nature and
" difpofition of God to mankind, is wholly con-
" fiftent with his rewarding every man according
" to his works ; and is the only doctrine of fal-
" vation that is fo." Further on, fpeaking of
thofe who differ from him, he fays. " They
" have always underftood this doctrine as rela-
" ting, not only to the different degrees of hap-
" pinefs among the faved, and the different de-
" grees of mifery among the damned ; but alfo
" principally to the great difference in the eter-
" nal world, between all who are faved and all
" who are damned : Each defcription being com-
" pared with the other, or the faved compared
" with the damned." In the fame page by way
of proof he adds. That no one " will pefume to
" fay, that believers in this world, are as much
" better than other finners, as Heaven is better
" than Hell ; or that there is, or ever was, fo
" great difference in moral character, between
" any two men on earth, as there is between
" Heaven and Hell." In the above paffage Dr.
H. totally miftakes the opinion of thofe who are
oppofed to him. They believe that men will be
rewarded according to their deeds in the following fenfe. That the degree of punifhment in
miferable individuals, will be in exact proportion
to the quantity and degree, which the fin of one,
bears to the fin of another ; alfo that the happinefs of the faved, in comparifon with each other,

will be in proportion to their refpective graces : But they do not believe that the rewards of falvation and of damnation, bear the fame proportion to each other, as the moral character of faints and finners do to each other in this world. Dr. H's reprefentation of what hath been the common opinion in this matter, is as novel in the Chriftian church, as his whole fcheme is ; and what he afferts, cannot be gathered from a fingle author of any refpectability. I will firft, defcribe what is meant by finners being rewarded according to their deeds. Secondly, what is meant by the faints being rewarded according to their deeds. Determining thefe points juftly will give the anfwer that is needed.

1. THE word of GOD defcribes finners as being deftitute of all holinefs. Thofe things in them, which may be for the benefit of fociety in this world, arife from their felfifhnefs and pride, and are not holy or morally good in the fight of an omnifcient fearcher of hearts. The character and actions of finners are wholly unholy, though not equally fo. The comparative degree of punifhment inflicted on different finners, by a rule of the moft ftrict juftice, will be proportioned to their different degrees of fin ; and juftice without any mercy will make the apportionment.

2dly. THE word of GOD reprefents thofe to be faints, who are renewed, and in whofe hearts a work of fanctification is begun, by the fpirit of CHRIST. Still the fanctification of real chriftians in this life is far fhort of perfection. There is much pofitive fin remaining in them. Their moft gracious affections are deficient in degree, and in ftrength of exercife. If they were to be rewarded by fuch a rule of juftice, as is ufed in meeting out the punifhment of finners, they alfo muft be miferable. But the reward of faints is of free grace or mercy, granted through the merits of CHRIST. In the comparative appointment of happiness, it hath generally been supposed, infinite wisdom will have a regard to the degree of sanctification in this life, and that the scriptures intimate this will be the case. A GOD of sovereign wisdom may, if he pleaseth, make a rule to himself in the apportionment of unmerited favours. There may be a propriety in having such a rule, and the rule mentioned may be the most fit; still if the same persons were to be rewarded, on the same principles that unbelieving sinners are, and by the same rule of apportionment, it would forever exclude them from happiness. Thus it appears that Dr. H's argument, from mens being rewarded according to the comparative quality of their deeds; is so far from proving universal salvation; that if there be any force in it, it proves none will be saved.

WHEN he asks "Whether there is, or ever "was so great a difference, in moral character "between any two men on earth, as there is be-"tween heaven and hell?" I readily answer, there never was or will be, and the saved, if they were to be rewarded in justice according to their moral character in this world, would doubtless fail of salvation.

I WILL further observe on this subject, that a very critical limitation of the divine conduct, in the apportionment of rewards is not wise. The design of GOD in his word, seems to be to give us some idea of the rule that will be observed in the day of judgment, and in the commencement of mens happiness or misery. As justice requires that commencing misery should be proportionate to the degree of sin; so sovereign grace is pleased to encourage, that the happiness and glory of the saints, shall be in proportion to the degree of their holinefs in this life. At the fame time, it is not conceived to be inconfiftent with any reprefentations of God's word, to fuppofe, that fome, both of the holy and unholy, may in that world make more rapid advances in holinefs and fin than will be made by others. We fee it to be thus in this world, and nothing that we know, forbids it fhould be thus in the world to come ; and in fuch a cafe, it is reafonable to fuppofe, the exifting reward will bear a proportion to the holinefs or unholinefs of character.

The reafon, why Dr. H. depended fo much upon this argument, comes plainly into view by his attempts to enforce it. Though he fpeaks much in the courfe of his book, of regeneration, faith, repentance, of chriftians and good men, as diftinguifhed from the bad ; it is ftill apparent that all he meant by thefe words, is, that fome are lefs wicked than others ; and though he fpeaks of a fpecific difference or difference in kind, between fin and grace in the heart, his meaning is, that different degrees of wickednefs are not the fame thing.—As wealth and the five fenfes, are fpecifically different.

He therefore tells us, page 234, " When we " fpeak of the good heart of believers, and of " their good and holy lives, and when we find " thofe epithets in fcripture, they are never to be " underftood in ftrictnefs of fpeech ; but only in " a comparative fenfe, i. e. lefs wicked in the ex- " ercifes of their hearts, as to the matter of thofe " exercifes, than unbelievers are, or than they " themfelves were in a ftate of unregeneracy."— " But it is certain that in ftrict propriety of " fpeech, no pofitive goodnefs belongs to any " character on earth."——If Dr. H. had told us there is no perfection in this life, it would have been readily granted. Perfection is not neceffary to entitle a believer to the promise of salvation. Positive goodness is entirely different from perfection; denying any positive goodness, is denying the reality of sanctification in the people of CHRIST and removing all distinction between sin and holiness. May there not be positive sweetness to the natural taste, without perfect sweetness? May there not be positive love, without its being perfect, or so great as it ought to be? And with respect to all holy exercises in the heart, may they not be realities, while the strength of exercise is deficient. It is in the sense of deficiency that the most holy exercises of believers are supposed to be sinful, and not from a total want of positive goodness.

ON Dr. H's idea, the following question with innumerable others, will become very difficult to answer. What are that regeneration, love, faith, and repentance, which have no positive goodness in them?

THE long comparison between Paul and Pharaoh, was doubtless introduced to disprove the real holiness of christians. Though I find myself, very unable to determine the comparative quantity of sin and guilt in different persons; I am ready to grant, if it be required, there was more sin and guilt in Paul than in Pharaoh. The question, as it respects final salvation, is not who hath most sin, for GOD can forgive the greatest sinners. But the question is who hath any holiness? If Pharaoh had no holiness, he was certainly lost. If Paul had some holiness, for which we have the express testimony of GOD's word, he was certainly saved. To gratify and give the fullest scope to Dr. H's argument, I will even allow, that the smallest vice in Paul's heart after his conversion, contained more sin and guilt than the whole wickedness of Pharaohs life. Still nothing is proved by this. Paul, with his fin, had fome holinefs in his heart, and his fin and holinefs were entirely diftinct and different in their moral nature, hence he compared his inward life to a warfare ; but Pharaoh with his fin, had no holinefs— he was all fin. As Dr. H. fays *" The atonement ftands by itfelf alone and unmixed"* as the meritorious ground of falvation ; ftill our perfonal renovation by the fpirit of God, is neceffary to make men partakers of its benefits, and this renovation doth not appear to take place in all men.

SEC. 20. IN page 245, Dr. Huntington fays, " The doctrine I plead for, has a great tendency " to afford believers adoring and fubmiffive exer- " cifes of mind, in view of all the fin and calam- " ity they find in the world."——That all men ought to adore and fubmit to the divine government even in its moft afflicting difpenfations, is unqueftionably true. If ignorant men cannot fee, how the fin, mifery and judgments that have been in the world are neceffary for the beft and moft wife government; this is no evidence they are not fo, or any reafon againft fubmiffion. The wifdom of God is higher than the wifdom of man. It doth not appear by what Dr. H. hath faid, that he helps this point in the leaft degree.——GoD is love, and he will invariably purfue that difpenfation in the government of creatures, which will produce the greateft happinefs and glory. This is all the reafon for rejoicing and fubmiffion which a good mind needs. The Dr. in all that thinking upon this fubject which he defcribes to us, doth not appear to have attained to the following truths. That the greateft happinefs is the object of benevolence, and that the juft mifery of fome may be a means neceffary for this end. If his fcheme affords any peculiar argument for contentment and fubmiffion, it is the felfifh one, I will be contented and fubmit to GOD, becaufe he will make me a very great and bleffed being. He particularly mentions believers, though he need not have confined it to them ; for this argument will alfo make finners fubmit, fo far as it goes in their favor ; and if a little addition could be made to it, that every one of them in particular fhall be greateft in the kingdom of the univerfe, and their proud and felfifh wills be gratified in all refpects, it would give them perfect fubmiffion.

FROM 251, to 254, of Dr. H's book, he hath an eulogium upon the charitablenefs of his own fcheme.——If charity confifts in bringing fin and holinefs to a common nature, without allowing between them any diftinction of pofitive qualties ; then doubtlefs his fcheme tends greatly to charity. So true is he in his confequence, that if his ideas of the chriftian and the finful character are univerfally received, all terms implying moral diftinction will foon be dropped from the language of mankind ; and the world will be charitably united, in thinking that the poffeffion or the want of perfonal holinefs is a matter of no confequence for another world.

THE argument which is drawn, page 254, to 258, from the inftitution and ufe of chriftian ordinances, it is fuppofed totally mifreprefents their nature and defign ; and that in this view of them, inftead of being called, means of increafing grace, as they have often been denominated, they ought to be called means of finking mankind into a deep fecurity, under a folemn profeffion of holy obedience, when no fuch thing is intended. On Dr. H's opinion of divine grace in the heart— that there is no pofitive goodnefs in the beft faints —that a fanctified temper is in no fenfe neceffary for a title to heaven—that all the difference is

some are positively more wicked than others—
that the ordinances are only seals of universal salvation and not of any personal holiness in those
who use them; we might consistently baptize
those who never heard of a Saviour, for they will
as certainly be saved as those who have had the
information.   Also we might commune with the
inebriated Corinthian church, which Paul anath-
ematizes, thinking these men are only a little
more wicked than others, for there is no positive
goodness in any.

IN page 258, Dr. H. says, " *That no man*" on
the principles of those who oppose him, " *can do*
" *his duty; even if his whole heart and disposition*
" *were perfectly right.*" The method he takes
to prove his assertion is this, " *It is our duty to*
" *acquiesce in* GOD's *will in every event; but an*
" *holy heart cannot do this in such an event as his*
" *own eternal damnation, or that of any of his fel-*
" *low men.*" If any man feels himself perplexed
by the above, I will endeavor in a few lines to
help him out of the difficulty.——It is our duty
to acquiesce in GOD's will in every event. It is
GOD's will that holy beings be happy, and sinful
beings miserable, and this is a most righteous and
benevolent will, which the good of the universe
requires should be carried into execution. All
good and benevolent creatures will acquiesce in
this purpose of GOD. Take such an one as Dr. H's
supposition mentions, whose whole heart and disposition is perfectly right. It is the will of GOD
that such be happy, so long as they remain holy,
and in this they can certainly acquiesce. Suppose
this holy being should be informed of his own
future apostacy, when his whole heart and disposition will be perfectly wrong. He would still
say, it is GOD's will that when I am become perfectly wrong I shall be miserable, and as his will

is right and for the general good, I acquiefce in it ;
—he will continue to fay thus while he is holy ;
but the firft moment he is perfectly wrong, he
will become a difputer againft the punifhment of
fin. A creature who is perfectly right or holy,
is willing that all beings fhould be treated according to their moral character, and doth not wifh
to make his own cafe an exception to the rule.

IN page 262, Dr. H. tells us that if all the human race were to pafs in fucceffion before a good
man, he would fay, and pray with all his heart
let every individual be faved.——If GOD had
given no intimation to the contrary he doubtlefs
would ; but when the contrary is exprefsly revealed, his defire and prayer for every individual
would be with this limitation ; if it be confiftent
with the infinitely wife and good will of GOD,
who beft knows how to govern the univerfe. We
have no right either to defire or pray for an event
that is known to be againft the divine will.

THE prayer of our Saviour on the crofs " Father forgive them for they know not what they
do" is fundry times mentioned by Dr. H. as fa-
voring his fcheme ; but it is not feen that in this
prayer there is even a diftant intimation of his
doctrine. In the 17th of John he tells us exprefsly there are fome for whom he doth not
pray ; and if the prayer on the crofs had been
expreffed in the moft general terms, which is not
the cafe, ftill the prayer in John would ferve to
limit our underftanding of it. CHRIST's prayer
on the crofs was defigned for two things. Firft,
to fhow that his heart was free from enmity and
hatred againft his unjuft murderers, thus difplaying for our imitation the chriftian temper. It
was an expreffion of the nature of benevolence,
and to fhow us that a good being can fuffer without revenge ; and not any expreffion of the num-

ber that were to be faved by his fufferings. Secondly, fome of his crucifiers were afterwards
brought to repentance ; and if that prayer is to
be confidered as ftrictly interceffory, it doubtlefs
meant thofe perfons whom he knew would be re-
claimed by the fanctifying grace of God. Though
Dr. H. feems to think that CHRIST's crucifiers
were fo much more wicked than other men, that
if any of them were faved, all the reft of mankind
certainly muft be ; there is no evidence they were
more finful than men of the prefent day, who a-
gainft greater light, crucify CHRIST afrefh and
put him to open fhame, by their immoral lives or
by denying thofe truths which he laborioufly in-
culcated.

WHEN Dr. H. afferts page 263, " that all the
" divine attributes will be more glorified in the
" falvation, than in the perfonal damnation of
" any finner" and that therefore all will be faved,
he takes that as granted which is denied. Alfo
when he fays " that we derogate from the glory
" of the plan of redemption, in the fame propor-
" tion as we hold, that any number be they more
" or lefs, are perfonally loft ;" he afferts that of
which he hath produced no proof. There is not
a fingle intimation in the fcriptures, that the
glory either of God or of the gofpel plan confifts
in faving every individual. The glory of God
and the bleffednefs of his kingdom, will be moft
promoted, by bringing the divine character and
all his perfections, into the fulleft poffible view of
creatures ; and nothing appears but that the eternal punifhment of fome is as neceffary for this,
as the eternal falvation of others.

AN argument of Dr. H. page 264, is in the
following words. " That doctrine which repre-
" fents all fin, all moral evil, in the moft odious
" and abominable afpect, has thence one evi-

" dence of being a true doctrine."——To this propofition I agree. And there is no event in the univerfe will give fo odious and abominable an afpect to fin, through all eternity, as the impenitence of fome finners in the face of gofpel commands. To fee them continuing in fin, when all difficulty befide their choice is removed from the way of falvation, above all other things will fhow the implacable malignity of unholinefs. The contraft, between the offers of redeeming love and the refufal of impenitence, will be the higheft conceivable difplay of the exceeding finfulnefs of fin. This view of the nature of fin, will illuftrate the excellence of holinefs, and the lovelinefs of a holy government, thus increafing the happinefs of God's holy kingdom. There is much room to fuppofe, this is one reafon why God fuffers fome to be loft.

SEC. 21. PAGE 267, " No man on earth can " ever obtain affurance of his fafe eftate, or any " good hope towards God, on any other foun- " dation than the real and univerfal grace of " God." This is allowed to be true on Dr. H's notion of the chriftian character.——After he had removed all holinefs from the hearts of good people, he might well fay there is no poffible ground for affurance, except in the doctrine of univerfal falvation. The hope of affurance in thofe who attain it, arifes from a knowledge of thofe gracious affections in their own hearts, to which the promife of God is made. A rational hope is in exact proportion to the evidences of perfonal holinefs. Neither is there any reafon mens hope of heaven fhould be greater, than their confcioufnefs of a beginning preparation for it. The contrary would be attended with the moft mifchievous effects, rendering them fecure in evil. Let all finners have Dr. H's affurance of falvation, and the unbridled exercife of their lufts, would foon convince mankind, that whether this doctrine be true or falfe for another world, it is very unfafe for the prefent peace of fociety.

Dr. H. apprehends page 268, his fcheme would foon remove from the world, vifible deifm and oppofition to the books of divine revelation.———— I am of the fame opinion. But how would oppofition to the fcriptures be removed? Not by making men better. It would be removed by lowering down the requirements of fcripture, and denying the exiftence of that holinefs, which. hath been fuppofed neceffary while we are here, as a preparation for compleat falvation to come. Let men be brought to believe, that the gofpel, promifes eternal felicity to all however vicious their lives are—that this gofpel is only news of happinefs and hath no law of holinefs in it—that there is no pofitive goodnefs or holinefs in the beft, and all the difference to which we are exhorted in fcripture is being lefs wicked than we have been; and they will readily receive the fcriptures, and even confider them as a warrant for the fafe practice of vice. How readily would men fly from natural confcience to fuch fcriptures as thefe, and love Christ abundantly becaufe he had made it abundantly fafe for them to fin. Deifm, is an oppofition to the revealed truth of God, and is natural to the unholy heart. Many who do not profefs, feel and live under its influence. Deifm doth not arife from mens different underftanding of fcripture; but their different underftanding of fcripture, in a great meafure arifes from a natural deifm of the heart, or oppofition to the holy truths of divine revelation. In this cafe, Dr. H. hath miftaken the effect for the caufe. When men find the fpirituality of God's word difagreeable, they endeavour either to put fome new conftruction upon it, or to reject it, and while their hearts are agreed in a diflike of holinefs, they take different methods of avoiding it.   From hence arifes a diverfity of opinions founded in the natural corruption, felfifhnefs, and pride of the human heart.

Dr. H. was doubtlefs acquainted, that one argument which has been urged againft his fcheme, is its tendency to deftroy the ufe of all means, and make men negligent in the performance of prefent duty.   He therefore attempts to turn this argument in his own favour, page 271.   " There " is no other doctrine of grace, that will fo en- " courage the ufe of all the means of grace and " falvation, and fo enforce upon our minds, the " fitnefs and propriety of all the inftitutions of " the gofpel."——Let us inquire on which fide of the queftion this argument hath weight.   He affigns a reafon for his opinion in the following words.   " The greater our hope is in the ufe of " means to obtain any important end, the greater " will be our exertions in every cafe, without " exception.   Full affurance of fuccefs will ex- " cite the greateft exertions of all, provided we " know that fure fuccefs is only in this way."—— Looking over this argument, the error appears to be in the following claufe.   " Provided we know " that fure fuccefs is only in this way."   In the prefent cafe, fuccefs means the obtaining of final falvation ; and according to Dr. H, this fuccefs doth not depend on the ufe of any means while we live.   The man who ufes no means, and lives the moft abandoned and impious life, he fuppofes will be regenerated and have repentance and faith given him by death.   Every creature may fee in this cafe, that fuccefs doth not abfolutely depend on any means we ufe while living.   Unholy men will fay, thefe means of religion are difagreeable to me, and I can omit them if I choose. Death is also disagreeable, but that I cannot escape; therefore let death do the whole—let it come in the place of all this prayer—reading of the scriptures—meditating upon a GOD, a law, and an eternity that are disagreeable to me. This will certainly be the determination of all those, who do not delight in the services of religion for their own sake. The fallacy of Dr. H's reasoning lies in the clause I mentioned " provided we " know that sure success is only in this way" for according to him, sure success may not only be in this way, but also by the way of death, a way from which no man can escape. Let the unholy once think, that salvation is as sure as death, and they will remain very quiet in vice.

Dr. H. often speaks of the powerful inducements to religion, afforded by his universal grace. But what are they? The principal one which he mentions, is this; the more religious men are in this life, the greater their reward, their comparative dignity and glory will be in another world. This is wholly a selfish motive. It is destitute of holiness, and amounts to nothing more than this; I have determined to compound with GOD, and restrain some of my most audacious lusts. He hath promised that in the same proportion, as I live religiously in this world, he will make me a very great and glorious creature in the world to come. It is a good bargain, I will therefore make it. Very little doth the Doctor tell us, of a delight in GOD, a pleasure in his glory, or happiness in complying with moral obligation. So long as a person's prevailing motive to perform religious duty, and to abstain from vice, is his own personal exaltment in the future society of heaven, it proves that he hath not even the beginning of a heavenly

W w

temper. The faints, in that world, will doubtlefs be free from this felf-exalting difpofition. To exalt God will be their defire, and it will give them as much pleafure to fee him exalted by the fervice and dignity of others, as by their own. A love of the general good will fill their hearts, and if they fee that moft promoted by their taking the loweft place in heaven; then the loweft place will be their choice. If a higher place is given to them, their pleafure in it will not be, becaufe it is given to them, but becaufe God and his kingdom are moft benefited thereby. The pleafure they will take in rifing above fome and falling below others, will be the fame in kind and degree, and from the fame motive, and without any thing, in either cafe, that is felfifh.

In page 274, is the following. " It is another " token of true gofpel faith, and truly evangelical " principles, that, in the exercife of them good " people find themfelves happy in their own " lot."——Let us firft determine whom Dr. H. calls good people. Doubtlefs he will allow that regenerated people are good people; and who regenerated people are we find from a claufe in the next page. " I am very fenfible that no man " will, or ever can fully and cordially believe in " fuch a charaƈter of God, and fuch a falvation, " without the fpecial energy of divine power and " grace, which is fitly called regeneration." Regeneration is therefore believing in his fcheme of falvation, that is, in univerfal falvation, and thofe who thus believe, he doubtlefs did allow to be good people. And wherein confifts the fingular virtue of a man, in being happy and contented with his own lot, as it refpeƈts another world, when he fuppofes that blifs eternal is in his path, and there is no poffibility of miffing it. But let us try this contented univerfal believer, who hath no pofitive holinefs in his charaĉter, with pain, ignominy and fuch extreme diftreffes as men often meet—try him with fuch croffes as CHRIST tells his people muft be their portion in this life ; and it would not be ftrange to fee his contentment vanifh. To make a holy contentment, it is believed there muft be fome pofitive good in the heart, and fome love of GOD for what he is in himfelf ; and that it cannot be produced merely by being a little lefs wicked, or believing in an after falvation.

INTERSPERSED between page 277 and 282, Dr. H. hath many obfervations on the impoffibility of mens rejoicing in the divine fovereignty, unlefs on the plan of univerfal falvation.——The argument, if there be any, is fo diffufely expreffed, that it is difficult to be colleĉted ; but by the current of his difcourfe, I fuppofe it to be as follows. *The law of nature is as much the law of* GOD, *as his word is. By the law of nature all men defire happinefs, and* GOD *will not in his government do any thing to counteraĉt or crofs his own law in us, which is a defire to be happy.*——If this be not the argument intended, I fee none ; if this be the argument, the following reply is fuppofed to be fufficient. When GOD gave the law of nature defiring happinefs, he alfo gave a moral law direĉting the only way in which happinefs can be obtained. Both by reafon and revelation he hath enab!ed the creature to underftand this moral law. He alfo informed the creature, that a departure from the moral law, would difappoint the law or defire of happinefs. If now the creature as a free agent, and with full underftanding on the fubjeĉt, difappoints the law or defire of nature for happinefs, by his chofen tranfgreffion ; this doth not imply any oppofition between the laws of GOD ; but only proves that the creature by departing from one law of God, hath loſt the benefit of another law of God. Sin will never make a creature happy, and when he finds himſelf unhappy by tranſgreſſion ; inſtead of thinking the laws of God in nature and in his word are contradictory, he ought to think that he is himſelf counteracting both. If God did not make the ſinner miſerable by puniſhment, the natural law of happineſs and moral law of duty, would indeed be contradictory ; but now they are harmonious. So that the deſire of happineſs in all creatures, which Dr. H. calls a law of God, proves that the threatenings of the moral law will be carried into eternal execution on the impenitent.

In a number of remarks beginning at page 284, Dr. H. intimates his expectation, that all the fallen angels will alſo come to a ſtate of happineſs, though he knows not the manner how.——It is not ſtrange, that thoſe who can read the ſalvation of all men in the word of God, ſhould alſo believe the ſalvation of fallen angels ; but as their fate is wholly diſconnected with the fate of men, and as there is not a ſingle intimation, in the word of God, that any of them will ever be ſaved, further obſervations will be uſeleſs.

Still more to confirm his doctrine, Dr. H. hath introduced an argument in page 292, of the following import, that his ſcheme " exhibits God " to our view, as conducting the affairs of our " ſalvation analogous to all his other conduct." A little further on, ſpeaking of the temporal enjoyments we receive from God, it is ſaid, " Yet " he gives us all things, in a way ſuitable to our " natures, as rational creatures and free moral a- " gents, by the exerciſe of our minds and bodies, " that we may have at all times proper exerciſe ; " for this is wholly neceſſary to our felicity."—— But how do the Doctor's ſentiments correſpond with each other ? Firſt, that there is an analogy, in God's manner of beſtowing, temporal bleſſings and eternal bleſſings. Secondly, that all temporal bleſſings are given in the exerciſe of our bodies and minds. But thirdly, that eternal and the richeſt of all bleſſings, will be given by death, to thoſe who never through their whole lives have exerciſed a ſingle faculty, either of body or mind, in religion. Such he ſuppoſes to be as certain of heaven, as thoſe who have exerciſed all their faculties in religion, through their whole lives. The Doctor's argument appears to confound itſelf.

Dr. H. ſeems to ſuppoſe page 295, that his plan helps us to the beſt ſolution of the queſtion, which ſo often ariſes among men " Why did God " ever bring moral evil into his eternal plan, or " ſuffer it to exiſt ?" —It doth not appear that he hath caſt any new light on this ſubject. He ſuppoſes that it was done, to increaſe happineſs on the whole ; and we who oppoſe him think the ſame. We alſo ſuppoſe, for this reaſon, there will be the ſame need of the eternal continuance of natural and moral evil in the univerſe, as there was for their firſt exiſtence ; and we have confidence in God's eternal wiſdom and goodneſs, that he will admit no more of either than are neceſſary for the greateſt good. And even Dr. H. ſays, page 317, that if this be the caſe, " we " ought to" acquieſce in ſuch a fearful event, " yea even to wiſh for it."

Sec. 22. From page 296, to 301, Dr. H. attempts to ſhow, that univerſal ſalvation " is ſup-" ported, by the doctrine of God's unlimited " wiſdom and power" and that the contrary belief is ſuch a limiting of the divine perfections, as is inconſiſtent with the nature of an infinite being.

The following extracts, I think will place his argument in a point of view more forceable, than

it now ftands with his interfperfion of words.
" All will allow, that if all the good ends could
" have been anfwered and accomplifhed, without
" the eternal mifery of a multitude of mankind,
" that then it had been better, and that GOD
" would have chofen it."——" To fuppofe that
" GOD could not have anfwered all thefe glori-
" ous ends, without this eternal mifery of fo
" many creatures, is to fuppofe that he was lim-
" ited by the very nature of things."——" But
" pray what is the nature of things? And whence
" doth the nature of things originate? Certainly
" from GOD and his attributes only. For in that
" period of duration when there was nothing ex-
" iftent but GOD, where was the nature of things,
" or the neceffity of nature, but in GOD only."
——" This lays a limitation on the moft high,
" arifing from the nature of his attributes."——
The Dr. then goes on to fay that thofe who differ
from him " Suppofe GOD hath formed a fyftem
" as full of happinefs as was poffible, and a glo-
" rious fyftem on the whole. That he would
" have kept out of this fyftem, the eternal mifery
" of any creature, if he had been able, but was
" not able through the neceffity of his own at-
" tributes fo to do, therefore formed the beft
" fyftem he could."

Dr. H. was fenfible his argument as much difproves the exiftence of temporary evil, which being matter of fact cannot be denied, as it doth the
exiftence of eternal evil, and therefore he adds,
" It is in vain to fay here, that this argument would
" equally exclude out of the fyftem, all the moral
" and penal evil, that ever did exift, or ever will.
" Becaufe, on the gofpel plan, according to my
" fenfe of it, all the evil of every kind that hath
" exifted, or fhall exift, is real good in the whole
" connection; not only to the fyftem in general,

" but to every individual in it, capable of happi-
" nefs."

In remarking on this argument I will endeavor
Firſt, To ſhow, that this argument, as the Dr.
foreſaw would be objected; does exclude out of
the ſyſtem, all the moral and penal evil, that ever
did or will exiſt; as much as it doth eternal evil.
We know evil hath exiſted and therefore the argument is a falſe one. And the Dr. hath aſſigned
no ſufficient reaſon why it is vain to object this
againſt his argument. Secondly, I will make
ſome remarks upon " the limitation of the moſt
" high ariſing from his own attributes."

Firſt. We may by the ſame argument prove,
that moral and penal evil have never been ſeen
and felt by mankind, and we will take the ſame
argument. *All will allow, that if the ſame good both
to the whole and to individuals, could have been effected, without the paſt ſix thouſand years of pain
and ſin, it would have been better, and God would
have choſe it. To ſuppoſe, that this could not have
been the caſe, is to ſuppoſe that God is limited by the
nature of things. But this nature of things origna-
ted from God and his attributes.* This lays a limitation on God from the nature of his attributes;
ſo that he could not make the whole, and every
individual in the whole the moſt happy, without
the paſt ſix thouſand years of pain and ſin. But
ſuch a limitation cannot be on God from the nature of his attributes; therefore there hath not
been any pain or ſin. We ſee that Dr. H's reaſon
againſt turning the argument in this manner is no
reaſon at all. And the argument will as readily
prove, there hath been no ſin and miſery, as that
there will not be both eternally.

I ſhould not have paid ſo much attention to
this argument, if I had not often heard it urged,
with much more logical preciſion and force than

it is ſtated by Dr. H. and with laviſh praiſe as though it were invincible.

2dly. I WILL make ſome remarks, upon the limitation of the moſt high, ariſing from his own attributes; which I hope will lay this cloud of duſt. The fallacy of Dr. H's argument lies in ſuppoſing that it implies imperfection in GOD, to ſay, that he is limited in the exerciſe of his government, by the attributes of his nature. A limitation on GOD by the attributes of his own nature, is ſo far from implying imperfection; that it is abſolutely neceſſary for infinite perfection. Unchangeableneſs, is reckoned among GOD's attributes; and what is this but a limitation againſt change, ariſing from the very nature of his infinite and holy exiſtence?—By the plenitude of his holineſs, GOD is limited againſt ſin.—By his truth, he is limited againſt breaking his promiſe.—By his benevolence, he is limited againſt making a univerſe leſs happy, than the greateſt poſſible quantity of happineſs. If there was not from the very nature of his attributes, a limitation on his agency, in the exerciſe of government, we could have no firm expectation of the eternal happineſs, either of all or a part of mankind.

IT is therefore evident, that a freedom from all limitation implies imperfection. This may be illuſtrated in natural as well as in moral ſubjects. As an inſtance; GOD is limited and cannot make a thing to be, and not to be, at the ſame time. If this were poſſible, it would be no perfection in him, and would only imply a power of making exiſtence and happineſs, and deſtroying them by the ſame volition. Limitation, in creatures ſometimes implies imperfection; but in GOD as it ariſes from the attributes of his own nature, it implies the infinite and eternal plenitude of his perfection. A good man is by his truth limited againſt ſpeaking falſe, and while he remains true, he cannot be falſe. A benevolent man, by his love, is limited againſt doing leſs good than it is in his power to do; and this limitation, is the excellence of his character. In the ſame manner, GOD by his infinite benevolence, is limited againſt making every individual happy; for it would, on the whole, be doing leſs good than he can do in another way.

AFTER all, I am ſenſible that what I have ſaid will not ſatisfy the unholy and repining heart. Such a heart will ſay, I wiſh a GOD who would make all individuals happy.—Such a GOD would appear to me much more excellent and perfect. This is not doubted. While ſin appears excellent to any mind, neither the GOD who exiſts, nor his government will appear excellent. The riſing of mens hearts againſt the doctrines of revelation is no evidence they are not true, or that GOD will not govern according to what is written.

SEC. 23. IN page 301 Dr. H. endeavours to ſhow, that he alone is on that ſcheme of free grace, which Paul preached, and that on the opinion ſupported by others, " Men are ſaved by their " own merit, ſo far as we can have any notion " of merit in a creature." Further on he ſays; " All the idea we can poſſibly have of merit in " creatures, is the following : that there is ſome- " thing good in the creature, which GOD con- " ſiders as a condition of his ſalvation; and " which in the order of nature, precedes his ſe- " curity of eternal life."——In reply to this, it is only neceſſary to deſcribe what Paul meant by grace or free grace, and I conceive it to be this. That the ſinner is wholly undeſerving of every favor, and the ſovereign, ſelf-moved mercy of GOD is the ſource of all his bleſſings. In ſelf-

X x

moved grace GOD chofe his people to eternal life—In the fame grace he effectually calls or renews them—In the fame grace he juftifies, compleats their fanctification and glorifies them. The gift and actual poffeffion of effectual renovation, which is the firft bleffing received in the heart, gives them no right of worthinefs to claim the fecond; or the fecond to claim the third. The continuation of bleffings flows as much from GOD's felf-moved grace, as the firft bleffing did. After the firft bleffing is granted, acting on the principles of juftice to the finner, GOD hath the fame right to deny a fecond, as he had to omit granting the firft.

WHEN the unfanctified finner becomes a chriftian by the renewing of his heart; he hath no right to fay, my character is now become fuch, that I have right to expect further bleffings on the ground of my own worthinefs; for on this ground, he hath no more right to expect a continuation of GOD's bleffings, than he had to claim a renovation by the holy fpirit, when he was in a ftate of total fin. Self-moved grace in GOD, exercifed through the merits of CHRIST is the fource and caufe of all the bleffings, that will be granted to the faved through eternity. The chriftian's expectation of falvation, is not from any worthinefs which his graces gave him to claim a reward; but from the fovereign promife of GOD. GOD hath been pleafed to exprefs his own purpofes in the form of a promife. The promife is made to faith and repentance, not becaufe thofe graces give a right of worthinefs to the perfon poffeffing them, but for other wife reafons.

THIS I conceive to be Paul's apprehenfion of free grace in election, effectual calling or fanctification, and in the final glorification of the faints. Still the confequence doth not follow, according to Dr. H's idea, that thefe graces are not necef-

fary in the order of nature to give the chriftian
fecurity of eternal life. Thefe are neceffary, both
in the order of a divine appointment, and in the
order of nature, as the whole Bible declares. In
the order of a divine appointment, as the promifes fhow ; becaufe GOD who grants in fovereign
and free grace had a right to prefcribe his own
manner of granting. In the order of nature alfo,
becaufe a holy Heaven cannot be enjoyed by an
unholy foul, as all fouls are without the renewing
of the fpirit of GOD ; fo that without perfonal
fanctification free grace cannot fave a fingle finner.

By the law of Mofes there were a number of
ritual uncleanneffes, for which the purification was
wafhing and remaining unclean until even. Dr.
H. page 205 tells us evening time means death,
and that becoming clean at that time, teaches us
all men will be cleanfed and made fit for heaven
by death. I will endeavor to explain this matter.
Thofe ritual uncleanneffes, were doubtlefs typical
of mens moral uncleannefs by fin. The purga-
tion of wafhing was typical of fanctification
by the fpirit of GOD ; and being unclean
until even, or the time of the offering of the
daily evening facrifice, reprefented cleanfing
by the blood of CHRIST. The daily evening
facrifice was typical of CHRIST's facrifice ;
fo that the whole meaning of the tranfaction was
this ; that the moral pollution of man is removed
by fanctification and believing in JESUS CHRIST;
and it had no more relation to the day of death,
than it had to the day of mens birth.

HE alfo infers the fanctifying power of death
and corruption, from *fowing feeds*, mentioned in
the law of Mofes, being clean in certain cafes,
which if deftined to another ufe would have been
unclean. His reafon for this is, that Paul fpeaks
of the bodies of faints as fown in corruption and

raifed in incorruption. But here the type according to his own application is directly againft him. For he tells us that the "Body goes into "the grave an awfully polluted thing: but does "not arife fo." In the cafe of thefe fowing feeds they are clean fown, and if there be any argument, it is that there muft be a cleannefs by fanctification before the day of death, in order to be raifed in incorruption.

Dr. H. mentions, page 329, the following paffage in Rev. v. as another reafon of his belief. *And I beheld, and heard the voice of many angels round about the throne, &c.—And every creature which is in heaven, and on the earth, and under the earth, and fuch as are in the fea, and all that are in them heard I, faying, bleffing and honour and glory and power, be unto him that fitteth upon the throne, and unto the Lamb, forever and ever.* I fuppofe, the argument, from thefe words, is, that all creatures are reprefented bleffing God, and therefore are in a happy ftate. But we muft obferve, that this vifion of St. John, defcribes the very beginning, and not the conclufion of the great fcheme that was reprefented to him, in a fucceffion of vifions. The caufe of their joy was that the Lamb, had prevailed to open the feals. And as the feals were opened, the moft awful fin and rebellion againft God were difclofed; and the difclofure ends, with an account of the final judgment, by which many were fentenced to eternal death. So that by every creature in heaven, earth and fea, in this paffage, cannot be meant all creatures who exift, and the generality of the expreffion, every creature, only intends the great number of holy beings who rejoiced, and the harmony of their feelings in the caufe of God.

Dr. H. in many places, brings the charge of prejudice againft thofe who differ from him. As in the following, page 261. "If it were poffible

" for people to diveſt themſelves of the long,
" deep, and rooted prejudices ariſing from the
" limitarion ſcheme."——He hath many ſimilar
obſervations.   I do not mention this to retort the
charge.   To cry out prejudice, in thoſe who
think different from us, hath no good tendency,
and can neither enlighten the underſtanding, nor
ſweeten the heart.   All men, of all parties, are
liable to prejudice ; and thoſe who think themſelves exempted are very ſelf-ignorant.   In the
caſe of differing opinions, on any queſtion, we
ought not to ſay, *you are prejudiced, becauſe you
think different from me ;* but candidly to examine,
on which ſide of the queſtion, the danger of prejudice lies.

THERE are two ſenſes, in which the word prejudice is modernly uſed.   The firſt, which is the
moſt natural and original meaning of the word, is
judging without an examination into the evidence.   The ſecond, is judging contrary to evidence, through ſome ſelfiſh inducement.

Is there reaſon to think thoſe who believe endleſs miſery, are peculiarly expoſed to prejudice, in
either of theſe ſenſes ? Who can ſay they do not
examine ? Is not the evidence before them ? Have
they not the ſame inducements to examine ? And
in maintaining their opinion, do they not appeal
to evidence for its ſupport ; frankly owning, that
their own bold aſſertions are of no weight in the
point, unleſs ſupported by the word of God.

OR if we take the word prejudice, in the ſecond ſenſe mentioned, *judging contrary to evidence,
through ſome ſelfiſh inducement,* on which ſide of
the queſtion doth the danger of prejudice lie ?
Men of both opinions are creatures liable to prejudice, and where is the ſtrongeſt temptation ?
Where the greateſt temptation is ; there is the
probability of finding the moſt prejudiced men.

I will state the point, and leave every reader to judge for himself, on which side of the question, the danger of prejudice through a selfish inducement arises. The point is this; if all men are saved I am certainly safe; but if part of men are forever miserable, I may be one of the number. Which opinion will selfishness incline a man to take?

But it may be said, have not men a proneness to continue in the customs, practices and opinions of their fathers; and is not this a prejudice, in the present instance, against the doctrine of universal salvation?

I answer, men through a respect for the opinions of their fathers, may be prevented from examining; but it is conceived there is no such respect for their fathers, as will make them believe both against their interest and against evidence, when it is set before them. In the present point, we do not retreat from examination—we seek evidence—we call for it—show that the word of God intends this, and we will believe it. I do not know a single universalist, whom I do not think candid enough to own the following. That by far the greatest part of mankind, in the present day, would wish to believe universal salvation, if they could find evidence for it in the holy scriptures. What then doth it signify, to tell of bigotry, prejudice and superstition. Let all parties remember, that all men are liable to prejudice, and instead of fixing the charge on those who differ, examine whether they are not themselves the prejudiced persons; and seriously attend to the subject, that they may find on which side of the question, the danger of prejudice lies.

Sec. 24. I have now taken notice of the principal things mentioned by Dr. H. as arguments for universal salvation. The attentive reader will obſerve, that his arguments are few in number, but very frequently repeated and placed in many points of view ; which may to ſome give them the appearance of a multitude of arguments.—— This hath made it neceſſary for me, in a number of places, alſo to fall into repetition. Much of his book is an addreſs to the paſſions, interſperſed with certain paſſages of holy writ, which appear to be his favorite proofs. The following I conceive to be a ſummary of his ſcheme. That the goſpel is news, mere news, all news, and hath no law in it.—That law and goſpel are diametrically oppoſite.—That theſe two diſpenſations of God, oppoſe each other from beginning to end.— That a God all vengeance and delighting in torment, would have as juſt a claim to our obedience, founded on the right of property, as a God of rational benevolence. That property according to men's ideas of it in the things of this world, is the ground of moral obligation. That righteouſneſs, ſin and guilt, may by the will of God be negotiated, and transfered from one being to another, in the ſame manner, that the alienable and material properties of this world are between man and man.—That Christ became a ſinful and guilty being.—That the righteouſneſs of Christ actually becomes the righteouſneſs of men.—That Christ actually aſſumed not only human nature, but alſo the ſin and abominable wickedneſs of human nature.—That Christ was eternally puniſhed.—That as all fell in Adam, ſo in Christ, long before they had an exiſtence, a work of ſanctification hath been actually going on, in ſome kind of myſterious, ſeminal ſenſe, in every individual from the time of the firſt promiſe. That regeneration, faith, love and repentance do not imply poſitive goodneſs ; but only a leſs degree of wickedneſs.—That the ſpecific difference between sin and holiness, in the regenerate and unregenerate, is only such a kind of difference; as there is between, holiness, wealth and the five senses; that is, not the same thing.—That faith is not necessary to give a title to salvation; but only to make men know they shall be saved.— Hence it follows, that a saving faith consists in believing all men shall be saved; and that the only office of what have been called the christian graces, is to give men peace of mind under the threatnings of the law.—That there is no such thing as fitness for death by a sanctification of the spirit, and that those peculiar distinctions which have been called personal holiness in men, naturally tend to produce pride.—Together with many other sentiments and maxims, which it is conceived subvert holiness, and reduce it to a common moral nature with the corruption of the human heart.

THESE appear to be leading sentiments in Dr. H's scheme, and from many passages both in his introduction, and in the body of his work, he seems to suppose that a period of new light is breaking on the world, and that all men will soon become of his opinion. The following passages show that he wrote with such an apprehension. Page 16. " I am well aware, that such an open " advancing step, to pour light into the minds of " men; though it is no other, in the nature of " it, than what has been many times done, may " as in former times, in all probability, be an oc- " casion of great alarm, in the minds of many " pious, good people."—" When HE who ruleth " the spirits of all men, is determined to make it " appear to the world, he always makes the truth " press so hard on the human mind as to find " vent. Witness the case of Elihu, Jeremiah, " Paul and many others. The most of those,

" whom God has made inftruments, to give ad-
" ditional light and guidance to his church and
" to the world, have felt much reluctance on the
" part of human nature, and worldly confidera-
" tions, from Mofes to the prefent day. But al-
" mighty God always finds an effectual way to
" draw out of their fouls, whatever he is pleafed
" to pour in with fpecial defign for the benefit of
" mankind." Page 40. " There have been re-
" markable æras, in which fomething like a flood
" of light has poured into the world." Sundry
other paffages fimilar to the above may be found ;
and I make no doubt but the Doctor fuppofed
himfelf the defigned inftrument of great enlightening to the church on this fubject. Imaginations
of this kind are not uncommon. Every age hath
produced inftances of thofe, who fuppofed that uncommon light was poured into their minds, with
a fpecial defign for the benefit of mankind. While
we pafs their zeal without crimination ; we ftill
fuppofe their fentiments, muft be judged like the
fentiments of other men, by fuch rules as are furnifhed in nature and revelation. When thofe
preffures of mind to enlighten mankind, which
Dr. H. mentions, as in the cafe of Paul and others, have come from God ; he hath generally
enabled them to work miracles, or given fome extraordinary fign in providence, as a witnefs that
the preffure was from the fpirit of truth and holinefs.

Sec. 25. It appears to me, by carefully attending to Dr. H's book, that his notion of the atonement, and a deficient idea of the nature of holinefs, were the two principal things which led him
into his fcheme. His lateft idea of the atonement,
implying an actual transfer of all the fin and guilt
of men to Christ ; fo as to make them his own,

.Y y

as much as though he had committed the sin perfonally, I have endeavored to disprove. But it appears from what he says, that previous to this he had an apprehesion, which is believed to be erroneous; and seeing the defect of that led him into his last opinion. His first idea of the atonement, we learn from several places, but particularly from the introduction, where he states the difficulties in his own mind, which finally led him to embrace the sentiment of universal salvation, page 11, speaking of his own preaching, and the number of the saved. "I can very willingly let "alone the number and the names; that sits "easy on my mind. But what shall I do with "the principles I have advanced, as things re- "vealed and belonging to every sinner in the "world? How can I on these principles, these "revealed doctrines, invite and command every "sinner to believe to salvation, and in the name "of CHRIT too, tell every one, without excep- "tion, that CHRIST has laid a foundation for "this universal faith and salvation; when I be- "lieve he did, in his death, lay a foundation only "for a part; that only a part are given to him, "and that other foundation can no man lay than "that which is laid, which is JESUS CHRIST." It appears, the Doctor's previous conception was this. That a part of men were given to CHRIST. That he came and made an atonement for these only. How then is it sincere to invite those for whom he never made an atonement? Whereas, his conception ought to have been this. A part of men were given to CHRIST.—The atonement he made was as sufficient in its nature for all men, as for these.—It opened such a door for the return of all men, that nothing but their own unholiness can prevent them entering.—The atonement did not remove unholiness either from the saved or the loft. The obligation to return by repentance doth not arife from the atonement; but from GOD's nature, the nature of fin, of men, and their relation to GOD; fo that it is as much a duty of the finally impenitent to turn to GOD, as it is of thofe who do really return. There is as much propriety in telling the difobedient, as there is in telling the obedient to do their duty.—The atonement, at this moment, bears the fame relation to the man who will repent and believe a year hence, as it doth to the man who will never believe and repent.—It hath done as much for one as for the other; and in fight of this atonement, there is the fame duty incumbent on both, the immediate duty of repenting and believing; and of courfe they are both to be invited and entreated in the fame manner. To what then relates the truth, that a particular number are given by the Father to CHRIST, or is it not a truth? It is a truth, but hath no particular connection with the doctrine of atonement, in the confideration of this fubject. All whom the Father hath given to CHRIST he will effectually fanctify; and the reafon he doth not effectually fanctify the remainder of finners, is not becaufe there is a deficiency in the atonement; but becaufe the general good requires them to be left, and it is alfo juftice to them to be thus paffed by.

If the Dr. had entertained thefe ideas of the atonement, he would not have met that difficulty, which he mentions, as a principal caufe of turning from his ancient fentiments; but would have found himfelf at liberty without any deceit, and even in contemplation that fome of them would be loft, ftill to tell them. *Here is a door open for falvation, if the ftate of your hearts will permit you to enter. The atonement of CHRIST is as fufficient for all men, as it is for a part.* GOD is ufing means, *which have a rational tendency to reconciliation. No objection now remains but that which you find in your own temper. It is reasonable you should love this God, Saviour, law and gospel. Their excellent character and nature, and the relation you bear to them, are the origin of this reasonableness. As I ought to exhort you to all reasonable duties, I may exhort you to receive God, Christ and his gospel with love ; and receiving them in this manner is that faith, which will entitle you to salvation. But if you do not receive, you must be lost through the unholiness and unbelief of your own hearts.* This is all that a gospel minister hath a right to preach, and this may be said, without that difficulty, which the Dr. reprefents in his own way.

If any suppose that Christ made an atonement sufficient only for a part of men ; I do not see the propriety, of their exhorting all men to repent through him ; and Dr. H. was right in feeling the difficulty, that arose from his first apprehension of this subject. But there was no need of his going from this, to another extreme ; an actual and applicatory atonement to all men, by means of a transfer of his righteousness to human nature generally. This idea of a transfer, is so contrary to nature, right, and reason, that if it were admitted, it would make more infidels than universalists. A few persons would become universalists ; but is probable that a greater number would be ready to say, this transfering of merit, demerit, righteousness, sin and guilt, is so unnatural and impossible in the present system of being, that on this account, I must reject the whole revelation in which it appears to be a main pillar.

Another thing which appears to have led the Doctor into his belief, was a defective idea of the nature of holiness. When mens apprehensions of the nature of holiness once become right, it harmonizes their conceptions of the law and gospel, in all their precepts and doctrines, and the use God makes of them in the government of mankind. The Dr. uses Calvinistic words and phrases, and in sundry of the definitions with which he began, appeared fair to carry himself through a Calvinist; but before his whole system is divulged, it is evident he uses these words, in a sense totally different from what they have been understood by Calvinistic writers. He might with much more truth, have titled his Book, Calvinism overturned, than Calvinism improved. Indeed, I conceive, his opinion of final salvation, to be less dangerous, than some other things he hath advanced. He begins with allowing the total depravity of human nature, and that this depravity confists in enmity against God ; but afterwards says, that the cause of sinners enmity against God, is because they think he is their enemy, or in a state of enmity against them. Also, that this depravity began immediately on the promise being made to Adam, to be seminally or federally removed ; that no man since, hath been half so unholy as total depravity is. It is only therefore, in a relational connection with Adam, that human nature and all men are totally depraved. The depravity began to be removed long before they had an existence. It is not seen how, on this representation, any man since Adam can be charged with such a depravity.

FURTHER, He also speaks of regeneration, and of God's grace communicated to the heart. But what is this? There is no positive goodness, and of course no holiness in it, for all moral goodness is holiness.

FROM these considerations, it appears, that his notions of holiness and unholiness in men, were such as Calvinists must call very deficient.

To confirm this it may be obſerved; that he ſays very little of the agency of the divine ſpirit, in the great work of mens ſalvation; and when he mentions the holy ſpirit, appears to conceive his influences to be rather reſtraining than ſanctifying. A work on the underſtanding and conſcience, rather than a work on the heart giving a new moral taſte and reliſh, and producing a real conformity to the moral perfections of God. So that I conceive, in order to eſtabliſh univerſal ſalvation, Dr. H. has exploded the eſſentials of the Calviniſtic underſtanding of the holy Bible, and only retained names and phraſes with his own meaning to them. The venerable Calvin, Owen, Hooker, Edwards and others, on whom he frequently calls, as vouchers for the truth of his ſentiments, were as different from him in their ideas of depravity, holineſs, and the way of a title to ſalvation; as they were on the queſtion, whether all men will be ſaved.

There are periods, in which particular doctrines are much the ſubject of popular inquiry; and whether all men will be ſaved, is the inquiry of the preſent. But many, who are not in the opinion of univerſal ſalvation, embrace ſentiments, which are as dangerous to themſelves perſonally, as this would be, allowing it to be falſe. Such are all thoſe, who do not think, there is any depravity in men directly oppoſite in its nature, to . the holineſs of God, of his law, and of heaven. Who think there is no higher principle than ſelflove or ſelfiſhneſs, by which rational minds can be influenced. Who think that regeneration is nothing more, than ſome ſuch reformation, as men may make from a regard to their own ſafety; and not a change in the moral taſte of the heart. Who deny the ſpecial work of the divine ſpirit, in awakening and ſanctifying men. Theſe ſentiments are more prevalent than univerfalifm, and very near akin to that, in the effects, they will have upon mens opinion of their own perfonal ftate and danger. Thofe who embrace thefe fentiments, are by them, fortified againft the theatenings of the law.—They will not fearch their own hearts.—They are not the fick ones who feel the need of a phyfician.—When confcience accufes they quiet it by fome little reformation.— Though they believe that fome men will be miferable, not feeing their own hearts, nor knowing their own need of a change of heart; they cannot think that they are themfelves the perfons. Thus they live as quietly, as unguardedly, as much without felf-examination, prayer and thinking of another world; and as much without any preparation for it, as they would do, if they fuppofed all men going directly to heaven.   As I before expreffed, Dr. H's reprefentation of unholinefs and holinefs, are as dangerous by nurturing thefe notions, as they be by inculcating, the univerfal, fanctifying power of death. It is principally for this reafon, that I followed him in his remarks on regeneration, faith, repentance, and the nature of grace in the foul; and not becaufe I fuppofed that what he fays on thefe topicks, would be confidered as availing arguments, in his principal fubject.

Jehovah is a holy God, and heaven is a holy place. If the gates of heaven were thrown open to all the univerfe of creatures, and an invitation made to enter; none could abide the holy prefence, or wifh to remain in it, but thofe whofe hearts delight in holinefs. Holinefs in creatures is like to the holinefs of Deity. It is a benevolence, which is oppofed to felfifhnefs, and makes the general good and glory its object of fupreme delight. Neither will the nature of heavenly happinefs alter, for it is unchangeable, as the nature of the GOD who forms it. Why then fhall we try to form thefe unavailing hopes of heaven, which are not founded, in the thorough fanctification of our own hearts? Why fhall we think lightly of a holy fpirit, and his divine work on the heart? Or amufe ourfelves with grace from GOD, when we do not find its prefent effects, affimilating our difpofition to the temper which appeared to be in CHRIST, and to the fcriptural reprefentations of praife and worfhip, with which heaven is perpetually filled.

I HAVE now finifhed my propofed remarks on Dr. H's publication, and have endeavoured not to mifreprefent him. I fuppofed, that juftice to the truth, required of me to remark as freely on his fentiments, as though he had not been my particular friend in life.

LET him who reads, remember that GOD is the fupreme judge of men and of truth; and endeavour to obtain a very real fenfe of that eternity, into which all the living will very foon be removed.

PART IV.

A serious Address to the reader on the subject of future punishment.

THE subject on which I address you is of infinite importance. To lose eternal happiness and suffer eternal misery, is an evil which surpasses all description.——If there be those who are forever miserable, their existence will be an eternal evil to themselves; and the misery will doubtless exceed in degree any thing that is now conceived. The progressive improvement of the mind in knowledge, is a sufficient proof that the degree to which that misery shall arise, will exceed present apprehension; as eternity does time. Such is the nature of the human mind, that it admits a constant increase of happiness or misery, and to what a great degree of each, will an eternal increase arrive! This is one consideration, that will swell above all account, the happiness or misery of creatures who have an eternal duration of existence. It must be a growing happiness or a growing misery. We can follow it in imagination, until we are astonished by the quantity; but are no nearer to the true amount than when we began the estimate.

THROUGH this eternity we are all to exist, and the question is, whether it will be a happy or a miserable one? If it be happy the happiness will be our own; or if it be miserable the misery will be our own, and when it overtakes us cannot be escaped by any possible means. Certainly we

Z z

ought to dwell on this idea until our minds are deeply affected with it. He must be partially delirious who places such an interest as this, at the smallest risk. If there be but one chance in a million of our falling into a miserable eternity, and there be any means by which that chance may be lessened, he is an infatuated man who doth not attend to them. What is the longest life, ever enjoyed by a mortal, compared with the endless duration that is to follow? If a whole life of the most extreme misery, were the means by which we might avoid one chance in a million of being eternally miserable, wisdom would choose the present, to avoid the future; but that good GOD in whose hands we are, does not require present distress, to avoid future misery. Wisdom's ways are pleasantness and her paths are peace, as much for this life, as they be for the life to come. True religion which secures a blessed eternity, secures also the greatest happiness in this world; but it is to be obtained only by believing the truth, and performing the duties enjoined in GOD's word. To have the pleasures of religion in either world, we must be religious. It is the greatest absurdity, to think that a life spent in sin, will end in the happiness of a holy and religious life. Expecting any thing of this kind; is expecting against the course of nature, as much as it is against what we conceive to be the predictions of God's word.

SEC. 2. THE following questions are proposed with candid feelings, and ought to be considered with candour and seriousness by every reader; for every reader is as much interested in them as the writer is.

DOTH not the present desire to believe, if possible, the final salvation of all men, arise in a great measure from a fear of punishment? Is not the eager attempt to seek evidence against the doctrine of future mifery, made with a defign to quiet confcience, and to render the pleafures of the prefent world reconcileable with future fafety? Can thofe who believe, or try to believe in univerfal falvation, folemnly place themfelves before God, and fay, my motive for feeking evidence of this doctrine is more to promote thy glory, than it is to make my own confcience eafy in a ftate which I know to be dangerous, unlefs all men are faved. Or would they, if they knew their own ftate to be perfectly fafe, be fo eager to give much praife to God for faving all men; before the event has proved that he requires any fuch praife to himfelf? I charge no man with being moved by fuch motives as are here intimated; and am fenfible that all have a perfect right to form an opinion for themfelves; but ftill in a queftion circumftanced as the prefent is, we ought all to fearch our own hearts, and find whether our paffions, our fears, and that love of fin which is natural to all men, do not prejudice us and make that appear to be evidence which is no evidence; and that appear to be rational, and promotive of divine glory, which would tarnifh the holinefs of his government.

Sec. 3. Before any man decides pofitivly againft a doctrine, which hath been the general opinion of the church, and of innumerable good men who have had the fcriptures in their hands and have fearched them diligently; he ought to make deep inquiry into the ftate of his own heart—into his motives for differing from the vaft numbers who have judged before him—into the nature of his fears—into his love or diflike of that fcheme of doctrine, which is moft intimately connected with the doctrine of eternal mifery.

The man, who fuddenly and pofitively judges, different from the opinion of thoufands who have gone before him, perfons, who in many refpects, have had better advantages for judging than he has himfelf, difcovers the rafhnefs of prejudice.

I AM fenfible there is a progrefs in the opening of truth—that new truths are difcovered—and errors both of fentiment and practice detected ; but it muft alfo be allowed, there are new errors, and old errors often come forward in a new drefs ; and no wife man will fuddenly and without very weighty evidence difcard what has been long thought to be truth, and important to be known, for human happinefs. Though we are not to call any man mafter in refpect of opinions, or build our faith upon the judgment of others ; there is ftill a defference due to what hath been the general opinion of the deliberate, ftudious and pious, for thoufands of years.

AN infallible church on the one hand ; and on the other, a total difrefpect to the opinions of great and good men ; are two extremes equally dangerous, and equally forbidden by common fenfe. It is a well known fact, that the general opinion of the chriftian world, with an open Bible before them, for nearly two thoufand years, has affirmed the doctrine of eternal mifery. There have been only fome folitary inftances, in comparifon with the whole of men, who have doubted it. Thefe, feemed to be permitted by providence, as a means of ftirring up inquiry ; and inquiry hath always ended in giving more clear conviction to mankind in general, that there will be future and eternal mifery. I do not mention thefe facts as a proof of the doctrine, but only to fhow that it is unwife to reject without great deliberation, what hath been fo long, and fo generally received as truth.

SEC. 4. I KNOW it is faid by fome, that the clergy and many others are interefted in eftablifh-ing this truth, and that by keeping alive the fears of mankind, their craft is fupported.

THIS is the fame outcry that hath been in the mouth of infidelity from the beginning. It is an eafy cry to make, and ferves an admirable purpofe for thofe who have much voice, and little argument. The writer with refpect to himfelf, can hear this with the utmoft indifference ; and no one is fit to minifter in CHRIST's fervice, who cannot hear it without any emotion except it be that of pity. The only reply that he wifhes to make to fuch an infinuation, is this. That it fhows in thofe who make it, a very great ignorance of human nature, and of the means by which a priefthood, may promote their own temporal intereft and pleafure in the world.

So long as natural confcience is in the human mind, there will be an order of men, devoted to the ftudy and inftruction of that, which is called religion. We find it in all places, in all nations, in all fchemes of religion, even the univerfalifts themfelves purfue the fame track.——This fhows, that the chriftian inftitution of public teachers is confonant to the nature of fociety, and a thing which the common fenfe of mankind deems to be for public benefit. It is not the preaching of eternal mifery, but common feeling and natural confcience which preferves a priefthood, and enforces this law of CHRIST in the chriftian world. Were all of the facred profeffion to be at once put into their graves, men would inftantly make a race of fucceffors ; and it will continue to be fo, while there is a natural confcience in the human mind. Thofe who think there will be a time, when the priefthood will be abolifhed ; with all the wifdom and philofophy which they boaft of poffeffing, fhow a moft extreme ignorance of human nature. Let irreligion prevail, ten times more than ever it yet hath, the consequence would not be the abolition of a priesthood; but the introduction of one so corrupt as to be worse than none. It is this which the church fears, and not the abolition of public teachers. So far as the priesthood wish to promote their own temporal interest and pleasure, their temptation is to hide the awful and sin reproving doctrines of God's word, and not to overteach them. All who have been conversant in the business of a minister's life, know that the worldly temptation, is to teach things too smooth, and too complying with the notions of a sinful world; and not the things that are too terrifying. If the priesthood consulted their own temporal interest or pleasure, they would cover all those sin restraining truths, and soothe human vice; and this would be the direct way to answer purposes that are merely worldly. Through the power of natural conscience, few men dare or ever will dare, to live without something which they esteem the visibility of religion—they choose a clergyman to commend their last hours to God, —to commit their dust to the earth, and as a kind of refuge, to whom they may fly when the terrifying providences of God awake up their consciences. The man who will do these things, and at the same time flatter them in an easy and prayerless life, has a much fairer opportunity to serve his own worldly ends and interests; than others have, who pursue the opposite course. So great is the temptation of the priesthood to prophesy smooth things, and suffer mens consciences to lie at ease; that considering the corrupt nature which they possess in common with their brethren, it is strange they are so faithful as they be; and it proves the mighty power of God; who, though he has sinful men to serve him as instruments, will cause his truth to be spoken. It really shows a great ignorance of human nature, to pretend that it is prieftcraft which keeps alive the doctrine of eternal mifery ; and thofe who are thoroughly acquainted with the nature and feelings of men, whether they be of the priefthood or not, will never pay any regard to fuch an infinuation.

SEC. 5. WHEN men fearch the fcriptures to obtain evidence of the final falvation of all, it implies that the fcriptures are fufficient to determine the point ; and that the truth of this fubject is there contained, if we can but difcover it. I therefore afk ; Is it not incredible to fuppofe, that almoft the whole chriftian world, with the bible in their hands, fhould have been miftaken in their underftanding of this point, and that the truth was referved for the difcovery of men at this late day ? The great defign of the fcriptures is to teach falvation, with the way and means of giving it to finners ; and when this is the great object for which the holy fcriptures were written, can it be fuppofed, they are fo written as never to give a general apprehenfion that all men will be faved, but quite the contrary ? GOD is certainly able to exprefs the truth, fo that it would be generally underftood ; it has been generally underftood ; but in a manner totally different from the univerfalift faith.

How comes this to happen ? Has God exprefsfed his word with ambiguity ? How has the great truth, which he meant to exprefs, that all men will be faved, been almoft univerfally overlooked, until this favored period ? Has there been any new guide to an underftanding of the fcripture ? Did God mean that the world fhould be in the dark until now ? Are the men who have made the difcovery people of more piety, more prayerful, of more holinefs in their lives, greater partakers of the directing influences of the fpirit ? more close and painful and learned examiners of the bible, than fifty generations of our fathers have been ? No such thing appears with respect to the present character of men of any party; nor is it credible that a book coming from God, on purpose to teach salvation, should be so expressed, as that only one in a hundred thousand understand it aright, and all others understand it directly the reverse.

Much has been, and much may justly be said concerning a progressive increase of knowledge in the world and in the church ; but what is said on this subject, ought to be said wisely. By an increase of knowledge ; the consistency, the harmony and the glory of the gospel, and of the divine government will doubtless be rescued from misconception ; long received truths will be better explained and reconciled ; and the agreement between nature, providence, reason, and divine revelation will be discovered ; but we have no reason to suppose, that any essential truth of the gospel, or of the divine government of rational beings has been generally hid. None but novices in sacred science can think this is the case. The very general agreement of mankind, that a great number of men will be eternally lost, is an evidence that the thing is plainly revealed in scripture.

It is common for persons, who think they have made a discovery from the scriptures, contrary to general opinion ; to suppose a period of new and great light is commencing, and that they and their coadjutors in sentiment are destined to illuminate the globe, and set mankind free from the shackles of error and fear.—A thousand such expectations have failed.—The enthusiasm of infidelity has burnt down to the snuff and expired, as often as the enthusiasm of fanatical believers.

ᴌ—And it will appear after all, that great and effential truths have been long known, and that
men have ever had evidence for fuppofing, there
will be eternal mifery in the univerfe. The confidence of a few who think contrary, may be
much fooner fufpected, than either the perfpicuity
of the fcriptures, or the common fenfe of millions
of men, who have examined into this fubject with
much prayer, and great apparent honefty and
goodnefs of heart.

SEC. 6. SUFFER me, in the next place, to affure
thofe who are making themfelves eafy in the
doctrine of the falvation of all men ; that this
doctrine will not give them peace in death or enable them to face it with boldnefs. Many have
an idea, that if they can find evidence of this
doctrine, it will enable them to meet any event
with calmnefs; even death itfelf; but this is a
great miftake. And if thofe in this belief die in
peace, their peace is owing to fome other caufe
befide their fingular belief in this matter. It is
not in the power of any fpeculative opinion to
make men die happily. The chriftian is not made
happy in death, folely by the doctrines which he
fpeculatively believes ; or by a doctrinal hope of
being in a fafe ftate. That which enables a chriftian to be happy in death, is an approving confcience, and his prefent enjoyment of a holy GOD
and of the truth. Speculative opinions may make
men eafy in fcenes of worldly quietnefs, and when
there are no worldly evils near them ; but mere
opinion is a miferable fupporter under trials, or
when danger looks us in the face. Suppofe a
perfon on his death bed, and expecting eternity to
open on him every moment. Suppofe, in this
fituation he has a lively view of the holinefs of the
divine nature, the infinite rectitude of JEHOVAH,

A a a

of his government, of his law, and the moral purity of that heaven to which good people go. In this ſtate let his conſcience be awakened to ſee himſelf—to compare himſelf with a holy GOD—a holy commandment—and the ſpotleſs holineſs of thoſe pure creatures who ſurround the throne of GOD. When he fears death, tell him all men will be ſaved, or ſuppoſe he is a perſon who has been in that opinion ; it will not remove his fear. Tell him GOD has promiſed it, and read to him the ſuppoſed promiſe. Neither will this make him happy. Conſcience within tells him that he is baſe—that his temper is bad—he feels that he ought to be condemned and to be puniſhed. This inward conviction will be higher evidence there is danger, than he ever can have that there is any promiſe from GOD all men ſhall be ſaved. When his own conſcience ſo pointedly condemns him, he cannot ſuppoſe that a GOD of infinite reaſon and holineſs will approve. Or even go ſo far as to ſuppoſe, that contrary to the conviction of his own conſcience, GOD ſhould approve him while he condemns himſelf. Still this will not make a heaven. There can be no heaven without an approving conſcience. All other ingredients, without this, will not make one. His condemning conſcience within him, is a gnawing worm, that will gnaw eternally unleſs removed by ſuch righteouſneſs and holineſs of heart as purifies the conſcience. Conſcience is not the opinion, which we have of the judgment that GOD will make concerning us ; but is our own judgment concerning ourſelves. One who has never been told that GOD makes any judgment, may ſtill have an accuſing conſcience ariſing from a knowledge of the evil nature of his temper and actions. The ſpeculative doctrine of the ſalvation of all men, can never therefore of itſelf give firmneſs in death; becaufe it cannot give a good confcience. It is on this account, that fo many who live fecurely with fome kind of reliance on this opinion, die in fear.

Sec. 7. But it may be enquired, is it not the promife of God's grace through Jesus Christ, on which the chriftian dies triumphantly, and can he thus die without a promife? It is allowed the promife is one thing neceffary for a happy death; but it is far from being the only thing. A purified confcience or confcioufnefs of fanctification begun is as neceffary as the promife. If the dying chriftian hath not fome knowledge of his own fanctification; if his own confcience doth not bear a witnefs of fome holy difpofitions and graces in him, he cannot have evidence of forgivenefs. His fanctification is his only evidence of a right to the promifes. When he feels in himfelf a beginning holinefs, wrought by the power of God's fpirit, it enables him to rely on divine grace for the forgivenefs of paft fins, and the removal of prefent imperfection; but if he feels no prefent efficacious help from the gofpel, it muft be difficult for him firmly to rely on future deliverance.

Sec. 8. From what has been faid, it appears that it is not in the nature or power of a fimple promife, and a fpeculative knowledge of it, to give happinefs. The foundation of happinefs and mifery are laid in the mind itfelf. It is not the threatnings of the law without fin which make the finner miferable; but his own temper. Neither is it the gofpel promifes without holinefs, which make a chriftian happy. Suppofe all threatnings of the law to be repealed, and the denunciation of an eternal hell to be taken away; this would not make the finners of this world happy beings. The fin that is in them makes them wretched—envy frets them—enmity bites them—; an empty heart folicits them—unfulfilled expectations difappoint them—and a condemning confcience burns up all peace, and leaves only the bitter afhes of remorfe.—This condemning confcience does not arife from the threatnings of the law, but from their own knowledge of the nature and fitnefs of things, and the relations of fociety. Some feem to have a very miftaken idea, that if they can fly away from all legal threatnings, and take refuge in a gofpel promifing falvation to all men, they have gained the point they wifh; but this is wholly miftake. A threatning law cannot be a fource of mifery to any creature, unlefs he hath fin. Neither can a promifing gofpel, make the creature happy without holinefs.

We hence fee it was not poffible, that falvation fhould be brought forward by the wifdom and goodnefs of God, upon any other fcheme than that of a heart renewed and fanctified by his fpirit. The original nature of things, of minds and of rational fociety, have connected holinefs and happinefs—fin and mifery. This nature of things is to continue through eternity, and God did not mean to change it by a gofpel of grace. He did not mean to alter and accommodate the nature of things to the reign of fin; but through grace by Jesus to forgive the guilt of all paft fins, to thofe who fhould be renewed and made holy by the fame grace. There is no poffible way of removing the mifery of a finful being, but by removing his fin, or annihilating his exiftence.

Sec. 9. On this ground ftands the gofpel of Jesus Christ. The law condemns finners; but it is their own fin and not the law which makes them miferable. The gofpel begins their deliverance from mifery in a renewal by the holy fpirit. The firft efficacious thing, which the gofpel does for finners is to fanctify them. I fay the firft efficacious thing; for all the doctrinal knowledge—all the means ufed with men under the gofpel difpenfation—and all that God has been doing from eternity, in this great defign of grace, is not efficacious to give peace and remove guilt; or in other words to make a heaven in the foul; until a renovation of the heart takes place. This quenches that hell, which already burns in the finful mind, and will continue to burn without a reftored conformity to God and his law. If the finner's mifery confifted only in an apprehenfion of eternal punifhment, God might remove it by faying he would never inflict the penalty; but fuch an apprehenfion, even if we make the moft of it, is but a circumftance of mifery, and not the effential part of it. The effential part of it, is the unchangeable effects of fin arifing in the mind, the firft moment it begins to be unholy, and which will continue fo long as it remains unholy. What additional punifhment God may ufe, beyond that arifing from the nature of fin with which we are now acquainted; it is not for us to fay. The fcripture plainly intimates there will be fome additional judgments; but if there be none fuch, the fources of mifery now open, are fufficient to make a ftate of mifery beyond what we are able at prefent to comprehend, fo that it will forever appear fin punifhes itfelf.——On the other hand, Christ faid to his people, the kingdom of heaven is within you, and this is the kingdom of happinefs. The fources of heavenly happinefs are opened in the foul, the firft moment of its renovation to holinefs. An increafe of holinefs will make a more bleffed heaven, than any faint on earth did ever yet imagine.

Sec. 10. On thefe ideas, what doth the believer of the falvation of all men gain for himfelf by his new efpoufed doctrine ? Has he removed himfelf one ftep away from mifery, and towards bleffednefs ? Though his belief may have fwept away, in his opinion, the threatening penalties of the law, which ufed to arife and frighten him in the hour of fin; has it fwept away the corruption of his heart, which was his real mifery ? Has it made him refemble a holy GOD, and love a holy law, which are the fources of heavenly happinefs ? Has it altered his nature in any refpect; and is he not as finful, as miferable as ever he was? Has he not yet to go through the fame procefs, the fame means, the fame departure from fin, the fame abhorence and loathing of fin; that he muft experience if he ftill fuppofed fome finners would be eternally miferable ? Is falvation made an eafier bufinefs than it was before ? Does he find it more eafy to refift temptation ? Are his appetites better governed? Have his finful paffions ceafed ? Does he find himfelf, walking more like the example of CHRIST, meek, holy, heavenly, undefiled by the world and feparate from finners? No ! In none of thefe things is he changed by his new faith; but is the fame man, the fame finful man, and confequently the fame miferable man. In fhort his doctrinal belief is a thing which has no operation in his own fanctification, and does not make it more eafy to refift any fin, or perform any duty. It does not make fin any more reafonable, nor reconcile the judge of the univerfe to it. It does not break the eternal, the unchangeable connection between fin and mifery. The only alteration in his own cafe, by his new doctrine, is this. He would formerly fay, I am now miferable and do not know but I fhall be fo eternally. But he would now fay; though mifery is yet upon me; I expect hereafter to be freed from it.

Sec. 11. Here an important queftion arifes. Does this certain expectation of being hereafter freed from mifery, give men any advantage in efcaping it ; and does not the opinion, as human nature is conftituted, rather tend. to fix them in that fin which is the real caufe of their mifery ?

In determining this queftion, it muft be kept in view, that all mifery is the effect of fin and made by it, and that we are miferable fo far and fo long as we are finful.—Therefore the fame things, and only thofe things that affift us in efcaping fin, will affift us in efcaping mifery ; and then the queftion comes to this.—Does the certain expectation of being hereafter freed from mifery, give us any affiftance in efcaping fin.—— I think we need not paufe a moment to anfwer this queftion. There is no truth or fact better known than this, that a fear of punifhment is fo far from promoting crimes, it is one of the beft means of preventing them. It would be a hard thing to convince the civil government of any ftate in the world, or the common fenfe of mankind, that to remove the fear of punifhment would prevent thofe fins which the laws of men forbid. A fear of punifhment is one of the moft certain reftraints on a finful temper. I am fully fenfible, a holy obedience muft arife from higher motives than a fear of punifhment. But it is true that a fear of punifhment reftrains the excefs of fin, makes men ferious and confiderate, and puts them upon the ufe of fuch means, as God is often pleafed to accompany with his fanctifying grace. Remove a fear of punifhment, and fin becomes exceffive—depravity matures rapidly—the paffions and appetites of corrupt nature flame out without a check—men forget God through amufement and temptation, and forgeting him, they cannot ferve him. Forgeting him they abound

in vice, and it is more difficult to escape those
sins, from which misery necessarily springs. Human nature is such in this world, and daily experience evinces it, that the certain expectation of
there being no punishment for sinners in the
world to come, promotes corruption instead of
giving any assistance in escaping it. So that the
certain expectation of all men being happy hereafter, is so far from giving any assistance in leaving sin, that considering human nature as it is, it
increases the difficulty. The very persons who
rejoice in this new dicovery, must own one of
these two things ; either they expect to be made
happy and saved in their sins ; or the salvation
they expect, and of which they profess to be certain, is made more difficult by their knowledge,
than it would have been by their ignorance ; and
for this plain reason, their belief of the salvation of
all men, has removed one of those means, by
which sin the inseparable cause and companion of
misery is prevented.

Sec. 12. Suppose it should be answered ; we
have no expectation of being saved in our sins,
and those who expect the salvation of all men,
believe as much as any others do, the need of
sanctification in order for salvation. To this I
reply. If this be the case, what still have you
gained by this new belief, and how is salvation
placed more within your reach than it was before ?
If you suppose a renewal of your hearts, a sanctification of your whole mind, and a departure
from all sin, to be the necessary means of salvation ; this is all which those who differ from you
require. To these conditions we fully agree salvation is promised. On our ideas of the gospel,
when you have atttained this, you are safe from
eternal misery ; and on your own ideas you are
miserable until this is attained. So that your

new faith has not made the way of falvation any eafier than before ; fin is as contrary to your happinefs as ever it was—there is no alteration in duty, and you have only attained to a dry fpeculation which gives you no affiftance in practice, and leaves the work of falvation as hard and difficult for finners as it was before. On every view of this fcheme of belief, nothing is gained by it in removing men from mifery and bringing them to happinefs.

SEC. 13. By tracing the fubject we have come to the following conclufions.—That a mere fpeculative belief of the falvation of all men will never enable any one to die in peace.—That it cannot purify the confcience, without which no creature can be happy.—That fanctification muft go with the promife to produce happinefs ; and a knowledge of the nature and effects of his own initial fanctification, is what comforts the chriftian, and affures him the gofpel hath any fafety for finners. —That the happinefs of falvation grows out of the holinefs of falvation, and can be made in no other way.—That the continuation of fin is the continuation of mifery, and muft always be fo.—That the belief of univerfal falvation can give no affiftance in efcaping fin.—And confequently, that if it were true it would give no affiftance to any man in making his calling and election fure.—Alfo, if a fear of punifhment tends to reftrain crimes, the difcovery, if it were true, would be a dangerous one. It then becomes us to make the following inquiry ; whether a love of fin and fear of its confequences be not a principal thing, which makes the doctrine fo pleafing ? I do not mean in this inquiry to caft any reflection on thofe who profefs a belief of fuch an event, for it would undoubtedly be as pleafing to millions of others as it is to them. While all men hate mifery they naturally love that fin which is the caufe of mifery. A fear of mifery is a principal reftraint on thofe who are not gracious. The threatenings of the law harafs them, and when their hands are ftretched out to pluck the forbidden fruit, confcience whifpers fee thou touch it not, left thou be forever miferable. This inward controverfy between a love of fin and a fear of mifery is one caufe of unhappinefs. And when men hear a propofition for the falvation of all, it delufively feems to them as though they have now found a way to reconcile that fin which they love, with the fafety which they wifh. Their feelings will naturally be thefe. " I am now relieved from my " fear of punifhment. The fweetnefs of a world " ly life, was conftantly mared by my appre " henfions of fome future ill. I was called upon " to live for eternity ; but fince I find that my " eternity is fafe, I may now live wholly for " time. I was afraid my unholy heart would " prove dangerous, by cutting me off from hap " pinefs in another life ; but fince I find future " happinefs to be fecure, this unholinefs appears " dangerous to me no longer."——If there be in the human heart a natural love of fin and dread of mifery, thefe muft be the feelings of men in confequence of difbelieving future mifery.—It is natural it fhould be fo, and nature will take its courfe.— All errors are not equally dangerous in their practical effects. Thofe who oppofe the doctrine of univerfal falvation, fuppofe it to be one of the moft dangerous which was ever broached, both to the happinefs of fociety in this world, and to the final falvation of finners.—That it removes a principal reftraint from a finful world— opens the flood gates of vice—and leads unpardoned finners to neglect the ufe of thofe means, which God hath inftituted to inftruct us, and which he is pleafed to accompany with the renewing and fanctifying influences of his fpirit.

Sec. 14. To bring the matter to a trial by our own confciences, whether a love of fin and fear of its confequences, be not a principal thing which makes this doctrine fo pleafing, I will defcribe two methods of preaching it, with their probable effects on the minds of men.

The firft method is this. The time fhould be fpent in defcribing " the amazing love of God " in giving his fon to redeem finners.—The love " of Christ in dying for all men —That every " fon of Adam, in confequence of his death, is " delivered from the penalties of the law.—That " glory, and nothing but glory awaits every " creature.—That we fhall all come to higher " glory, at death, than if we had never finned.— " That as fin abounds, fo grace will much more " abound.—That nothing is to be feared after " death, and God will take care when we leave " this world, we be bleffed enough." Yea, fuppofe the preacher in a moment of enthufiaftic univerfalifm fhould break upon his auditory, with the pleafing news, " they had no fins—that " Christ had taken them all upon himfelf—a- " toned for them all—and that if fin is to be " confidered as belonging to any one, it is to the " Son of God."——What would the probable effects of fuch preaching as this be upon a finful world, for it is to a finful world, preachers of every denomination have to fpeak.—If men could bring their own confciences to believe the doctrine ; if they could, in the face of plain declarations in the holy bible, think the preacher was right, and a fafe guide ; we might expect a crouded, an applauding auditory ; and every man would leave his feat delighted, becaufe he had heard good things concerning himfelf. Should thefe hearers, go from their religious fervice into a fcene of temptation, the victory over them would be eafy. After the enemy of fouls had thrown out his bait, he would need only repeat the fermon to make men fwallow it.

Or fuppofe, the following method of preaching this doctrine fhould be adopted. " Though
" you are all to go to heaven in the end, remem-
" ber there is a mighty and a moft holy God.—
" Though he has fuffered you to rebel againft
" him, he will through his powerful grace in Je-
" sus Christ, make you mourn bitterly for the
" rebellion in which you now are engaged. But
" while I tell you, that you are all to go to heav-
" en ; be affured the temper which is now in you
" is entirely contrary to heaven.—You are fin-
" ners by nature. You have joined with fatan
" the great enemy of God. Thofe finful prac-
" tices in which you live, your love of the world,
" the flefh and its lufts, your want of love to
" God, and the pure, fpiritual duties of a holy
" life, are highly difpleafing to the Lord. And
" though he intends by his power and grace to
" fave you in the end, and thereby bring great
" glory to himfelf, it is certain he is now oppof-
" ed to your whole temper. He abhors your
" fins, and is angry with you every day. There
" is no excufe for your prefent temper and vices.
" —That tafte, by which you relifh them now,
" is moft unreafonable, and all good beings in
" the univerfe, though they wifh you well, abhor
" your difpofitions. It is juft you fhould be pun-
" ifhed, now and forever. Though we hope
" better things of you in fome period of eternity
" to come, nothing can be faid as yet, but that
" you are of your father the devil, and you de-
" light to be like him. According to your ca-
" pacities, you are as odious and wicked as he
" is. It is your duty to become of another char-
" acter, and wholly leave the fins you now love.
" Though we expect in future, through the pow-
" er of God to call you brethren in Christ Je-

" sus, we cannot call you fo now.—Turn from
" all your fins which are very many, and very
" great.—Mourn, mourn bitterly for them.—
" Confefs you have acted a vile and ungrateful
" part, againft the God who made you, and the
" Saviour who has died to bring you to heaven.
" Love God, think of him, and meditate upon
" his law.—Take much pains in fearching out
" the corruption of your own hearts.—Spend
" much time in reading God's word and medita-
" ting upon the holy life of Jesus.—Learn to
" view the world, its fins, its interefts, its lufts
" and its amufements, as you will view them
" when you come to judgment and to heaven ;
" and hate fin from this moment forward, as much
" as the Son of God hated it when he died on
" the crofs to banifh it from the univerfe. Be-
" take yourfelves to your clofets, fpend much
" time in prayer, and live in all refpects in that
" felf-denying manner Christ did, when he
" came to be your example.

THIS is a fpecimen of the fecond method of
preaching univerfalifm. And I now appeal to
the confcience of fome of thofe, who have received the doctrine, and to an innumerable number of others who wifh to receive it but dare not ;
whether this laft method would be agreeable to
them.———I prefume that many have franknefs e-
nough to own, this laft method would be as difagreeable as the common manner of thofe who
are oppofers of the doctrine. The reafon is plain
enough.—The firft fpecimen which I offered,
leaves mens finful and guilty character out of
fight.———It does not open to them the plague of
their own hearts, alarm their confciences, call
them to behold a fin hating God, or to forfake
their fins. It calls them to look on glory and
bleffednefs, tells them thefe belong to all of you,
and overlooks that holinefs and repentance which

are the only means by which men can come to
blessedness; and thus soothes them in a sinful and
easy life.   A man may be a hearer of the first
specimen his whole life, and never feel reproved;
or led to look on the odiousness of his sinful character and the repentance and reformation which
prepare for heaven.   But by the second specimen
of universalism, a bad heart is charged on men;
God's holiness and the holiness of heaven is af-
serted; the baseness of human nature, and our
need of a total change are asserted.   The necessity
of an immediate forsaking of every sin, and performing all religious duty is declared.   The hearer's conscience is brought to condemn himself,
and to feel the necessity of parting with the sin
which he loves; and if he be an unsanctified
hearer, tho' eternal salvation be promised, he does
not want the promise on such conditions.   Here
the truth of this business comes out.   The human heart is very deceitful.   We often think we
are honest inquirers, when an unobserved desire
to unite ultimate safety with the sin which we
love, or to delay religion, are at the bottom of
our opinions.   In all such cases, a love of sin and
dread of its consequences are the cause of mens endeavors to make this doctrine a true one; and
while they think benevolence to men, and a desire of glorifying God is their sole motive, a selfish love of their own sin is the real cause.

PERHAPS some, who suppose holiness is necessary for salvation, may be biased by a present love
or sin, through the desire of delaying a religious
life.   When they know that they must be holy
to enjoy heaven, they wish not yet to commence
a life of strict religion.   But if some men are not
saved, one day's delay may be infinitely dangerous
to them.   Here there is a strong temptation to receive the doctrine, if possible, that they may quietly neglect that life of strict religion, which their

own confciences know to be proper, and the real preparation for glory to come. Confidering the bias men have to fin; their unwillingnefs to part with it; and the trouble an apprehenfion of future mifery gives them; it is really ftrange, that after all the pains which are taken to diffeminate this doctrine, and all the pains men take to convince themfelves of its truth, there are not more converts to it than we find; and this circumftance proves there is glaring teftimony to the contrary, in the holy fcriptures.

THAT method of preaching the gofpel, will be difagreeable to many, which opens the fountain of iniquity in the heart, and declares the Lord a juft and glorious GOD in punifhing it, and the neceffity and wifdom of immediately leaving all fin and becoming holy as GOD is holy. This is the thing, with which corrupt human nature contends, and even the doctrine of univerfal falvation, might be fo preached, that a vaft proportion of mankind would not wifh to hear it. When the preacher gives fuch a faithful defcription of the nature of fin and the need of leaving it, that the hearer through the accufations of confcience, feels more unhappy by contemplating his own guilty felf, than he is pleafed with thinking he fhall be a very great and happy being, in fome diftant period of futurity; then he will condemn the preacher as being too rigid in his opinions, and whether he declare the falvation of all men, or the contrary, his miniftration will become difagreeable. Of whatever denomination among chriftians a man be, he is not worthy to be a preacher of the gofpel of GOD; unlefs he can patiently take on himfelf, that odium which he knows to come from fuch a caufe, and calmly abide all the confequences, as a wife GOD may fuffer them to take place.

SEC. 15. PERHAPS fome will fay, though we are now unholy we really take delight in medita-

ting on a holy salvation to come.——But suffer
me to inquire, whether such a state of the heart,
be not impossible ; and I think there is no difficulty
in making it appear to be so. Doubtless those, who
say, they are pleased with the thought of escaping
misery and being forever happy are sincere ; for
they may be pleased with this from the principles of sin ; but they are not pleased with a holy
salvation. A holy salvation consists in loving
God for all that he is in himself.—In loving his
law—in loving our neighbour as ourselves—and
in loathing ourselves for all the evil things we
have ever done.

CAN any man, when he looks upon his neighbour and hates him, honestly say, I now hate this
man most sincerely and am determined to do him
all the hurt in my power ; but I rejoice in the
doctrine of universal salvation, because it assures
me, that a short time hence, I shall love him as I
do myself, and do him all possible good.

I NOW love this vice, and am determined to continue in it for the sake of my love to it ; but I rejoice in the doctrine of universal salvation, because
it assures me, in a very short time I shall hate and
detest it with my whole heart.

I NOW love this sin and cannot bear to be part-
ed from it ; but I triumph in the doctrine of universal salvation, for it assures me, I shall in a short
time, look back with detestation upon what I am
doing, and loathe myself that I have done it.

I CANNOT now bear to behold God, because
his pure nature is contrary to my heart ; at the
same time, I delight in the doctrine of universal
salvation, because it assures me I shall soon hate
every thing that is now in my heart, look upon a
holy God with delight, and devote myself both
in body and spirit to his service.

ARE not these things contradictions ? Can they
be found in the heart together ? We therefore

conclude, that when unholy perfons rejoice fo much in the idea of the falvation of all men, it is not becaufe they are delighted with the thought of univerfal holinefs; but they conceive the doctrine as making fin more fafe, and its confequences lefs dreadful than have been fuppofed.

I may further add in this place, that no unholy perfon wifhes for fuch a heaven as the fcriptures promife. The heaven which God has promifed, is the completion of a holy temper and holy enjoyments; and I think it is very inconfiftent to fuppofe, when men cannot bear the little beginning of heaven, there is in a holy life in this world, that they fhould at the fame time wifh the infinite fulnefs of it. When thofe who are now unholy, think they really intend to be holy in fome future time, it is one of the delufions of a corrupt heart. That they intend and wifh fomething we know; but to be holy is not the thing which they intend. They intend to avoid mifery—they may intend to make fome vifible alterations in their conduct— they intend, when they come to heaven, to conform as well as they can, on their own principles, to the nature of the place; but they do not intend to love that which they now diflike. The notion of an unholy heaven of perfect happinefs, is fo inconfiftent with nature as well as with revelation, that few will own they have any fuch apprehenfion, left it fhould make them ridiculous; ftill their hearts would choofe fuch a heaven, if they could be freed from the fear of punifhment.

One very good way of trying our own hearts on this fubject, is to examine what our ideas of heaven are. What do you mean by heaven? Do you mean any thing more by heaven and falvation than freedom from mifery and the poffeffion of happinefs? Which is the moft pleafing to us, in contemplation of univerfal falvation; either this, that there will be no more fin and all will be holy, or that there will be no more mifery? The fcriptural heaven is defcribed as a place, ftate, and condition of moft perfect holinefs.   Every object and event will bring a holy God into view.   To fee him continually, and in every thing, will be the bleffednefs of the place ; and to praife, worfhip, and adore him will be the employment.   Is it in contemplation of this ftate—all devotednefs to God—all obedience to a moft holy law—all felf-abafement and humility—all confecration to divine glory and the public good, that the doctrine of univerfal falvation appears fo pleafing? The fcriptures give no reprefentation of heaven different from this, and if we cannot meditate with delight on fuch a ftate, and feel as though the bleffednefs of heaven confifted in its holinefs ; it is evidence that a love of fin, is the ground of joy in the doctrine.

Sec. 16. I have no doubt that a part of thofe who think all men will be faved, believe the holy fcripture ; ftill fome who call themfelves univerfalifts, often exprefs themfelves in the following manner : " If I believed the fcripteres taught the " doctrine of eternal punifhment, I never could " receive them as the word of God.   I once " difbelieved the fcriptures, but fince I find the " falvation of all men promifed, I can freely re- " ceive them as the word of God."   Is it not alfo common to find many, who allow the fcriptures to be in part the word of God, and in other parts incredible.   What is this, but to fet up reafon as a more fure guide than revelation? Can revelation be any guide of faith and practice, if all the men of this world, may fet afide its divine authority, when not conformable to their tafte, and to their notions of the beft way to govern a univerfe? Is it fuppofeable after God had given a revelation, that he would fuffer it to be fpurioufly intermixed with the opinions of men ? In fuch a cafe, the intermixture would wholly defeat the whole end of revelation, as we could not tell which is from God, and which from human corruption. Or do thofe perfons, who fuppofe that part of the holy fcriptures is true, and part fpurious, conceive they are capable of deciding for mankind ? What evidence can they give us that they are able for the tafk ? There is an evident likenefs between thofe who call themfelves univerfalifts of this kind, and infidels. One clafs are difbelievers, depending on reafon alone ; and the other are difbelievers in a new drefs, with a mixed dependence on reafon and revelation; but allowing to reafon the fovereign prerogative of determining what it is fit God fhould reveal and do. The leading feature of likenefs between infidelity and this kind of univerfalifm, is highly worthy of notice, and is really fuch an attack on divine revelation, as when carried to its whole length will banifh chriftianity out of the world. Doubtlefs many who believe the fcriptures, have been amufed, hoping to find this fentiment in them ; but they ought to be warned on what dangerous ground they are walking ; and how eafy it will be to flide into the moft grofs infidelity. Thoufands have travelled the road, who began only in doubting the plainly revealed doctrine, of eternal mifery for the impenitent ; and ended in difbelieving the whole fcripture of God. There is no medium between believing the whole fcripture and rejecting the whole. God has all power and can direct events as he pleafes. Is it fuppofeable, he would give us a revelation attefted by the moft remarkable figns from heaven, and command us to believe and obey it ; and at the fame time, fuffer a fpurious intermixture to be incorporated with his own word, and handed down to future generations ? Either this, which is incredible, muft be

the cafe; or we are under obligation to receive
the whole Bible as an authoritative revelation.
When men begin to judge between the parts of
revelation, and fay, let this be fet down as truth,
becaufe I can fee its fitnefs—it is according to my
reafon and agreeable to my relifh; but let this be
rejected, and I will not own him for my God,
who would fay and govern in this manner; they
have affumed the place of infinite wifdom, and
are not far from the moft grofs Deifm and perhaps Atheifm. I enlarge on this, becaufe it is
become fo common to hear people own this thing,
which is only with a little more appearance of
modefty hanging out the colours of infidelity;
and the people who do it are either infidioufly
artful, or ftrangely beguiled by the pride of human reafon. When they have had confcience a
little longer in the fchool of an unholy heart, they
will probably deny the whole fcripture. They
have already placed the books of revelation on a
footing with all other books; containing fome
truth and fome things that are incredible; and
on this ground, it is not feen why they fhould be
reverenced more than any other writings.

Sec. 17. Through the weaknefs of human
reafon, and mens corruption of heart, the beft
things are liable to abufe. Freedom of inquiry
is to be indulged, and will forever end in a more
full eftablifhment of truth. But freedom of inquiry gives no right for licentioufnefs of fentiment. Mens right to inquire and think for
themfelves, gives them no right to think wrong.
That liberty of opinion which is the boaft of the
day; is by fome miftaken, for a liberty of thinking any thing that is agreeable to their own tafte
and wifhes, and of judging moft pofitively, what
God can, may and will do in the eternal government of a univerfe of creatures. In things that
relate to the character and government of an infi-

nite GOD, free inquiry ought to be conducted in a moft ferious and reverent manner; and with a humble fenfe, how unable we are to fearch out the deep counfels of the LORD, and judge of his wifdom and righteoufnefs. There muft forever be the greateft conceivable diftance between infinite and finite. Though we may inquire, we are not to fit as judges with GOD; what is beft to be done, or how far he may go in punifhing fin; but our inquiry is permitted, folely for our own advantage, that we may know our duty, our danger, and the glorious object of our moft humble adoration. There hath been a day in the world, when freedom of inquiry was prevented by civil tyranny, and inquifitorial torture. Thanks be to GOD! Thofe impediments to knowledge have been in a great meafure removed. The folly of men is apt to go from one extreme to another; from adoring a wooden crucifix, to a denial of GOD's infinite right to govern the univerfe as he fees to be beft. The bigotry of ignorance, and licentioufnefs of opinion, are in the fame degree unfriendly, to piety and the happinefs of men. New thinkers, are apt to fuppofe they can think right on every thing, and by the decifion of their own reafon will determine pofitively on the events of an eternity to come, and place themfelves on a level with eternal wifdom. JEHOVAH governs a univerfe—the immenfity of this univerfe is inconceivable—the nature and character of the governor is incomprehenfible—the prefent is the beginning of an eternal duration—GOD looks on the whole—he knows what is beft for the whole —and who befide him can tell? Is it not prefumption in the finful children of men, to fay what is beft and what is right in the eternal government of GOD? Frail child of duft! Who art but of yefterday, and haft feen but a point in the vaft kingdom of that GOD who made thee! Thou knowest not the heart of a single creature that is around thee, and but very little of thine own heart! How often art thou incapable of judging rightly in the little concerns of this world! Thou knowest not what is for thine own good for an hour to come! And dost thou sit in judgment on the great JEHOVAH and his ways? Dost thou take on thee to say what is for the highest good of the universe? Art thou able to appoint the penalties of a law, that is designed for the eternal direction of all beings? Canst thou say, how far and how long misery may be used? What need there is of it, and what good may come out of it? Dost thou know the infinite chain of connections, dependences, and influences that take place between being and being; and which arise from a sight of the various characters and rewards that are appointed to them? Can it be for thee, to reject any part of the scriptures because they are not according to thy prejudiced taste? Feeble creature! When GOD shall bring the to the bar of universal judgment; with myriads of intelligences superior to thee in intellect—When all around thee shall swarm with rational life, of which thou hadst no conception, how wilt thou be surprised at the vastness of the LORD's dominion! And if there were no other sin lying on thy conscience, this rashness, in limiting the righteousness of GOD, would by thy self-conviction sentence thee to the misery which thou now deniest to be just.

SEC. 18. I MAY also address universalists and those who are endeavoring to make themselves so; on the ground of prudence. If your opinions are right, we who oppose you are certainly safe.— On your principles, we shall be saved; and the mistake under which we labor, will not impede our happiness in another world; but if our opinion be right, you are in a most endangered state; for the sentiments you embrace, will naturally keep you from ufing the means of deliverance. Unlefs you have arrived to infallible certainty, in this matter, you muft allow thofe who differ from you to be the moft-fafe and prudent. If you are right they run no rifk. If there be only one chance in many millions, that they are right, there is the fame proportion of rifk, that you will loofe eternal happinefs and fall into eternal mifery.—— And O how awful ought the thought to be, that fuch a thing is poffible. Can you pretend to infallibility in this point? If not, and it is fuppofed none will pretend to it; you cannot act a prudent part, unlefs you do in all refpects conduct like thofe who think different from you, and endeavor to make your falvation fure, on the fame grounds they expect to be faved. Of what avail to you then are your peculiar fentiments, if you muft give them up in practice to be prudent men. If you act prudently, they do not fhorten your way to heaven, or make it any more eafy to get there.

Sec. 19. The principal things, intended in the beginning of this addrefs, have been fet before you. The writer believes many of them to be worthy of moft ferious confideration, before any one comes to a final conclufion, that the doctrine of eternal punifhment, is the fiction of interefted ecclefiaftics and gloomy minds. Whatever the truth may be, he is confcious of none but honeft motives, in endeavoring to defend what he believes to be the doctrine of the holy fcriptures; and hopes that in the end it will appear, he was moved by a love of God's glory and the good of men. He concludes, with mentioning the danger of being given up to judicial blindnefs, by a long refiftance, of what God hath determined to be fufficient evidence of the truth. What if God fhould take the doubting, at their own word, and fay concerning them. I will grant no

more light. I have warned them in my word—
in my fanctuary—by my providence and by the
courfe of nature. I have warned them by their
own confciences, and the fecret admonitions of
my fpirit. They had rather enjoy a few days of
earthly eafe, believing I have prepared no punifhment for my impenitent enemies; than to feek
me in the way of holinefs.—Therefore let them
have their way. ' Let them fee and perceive not
—let confcience fleep and become feared—let
death continue to fweep the earth, their turn will
foon come, and in that war there is no difcharge
—let nature go on in her courfe and all her laws
be facred—let holinefs and fin meet the end prepared for them—let the holy, be holy ftill; and
the filthy, filthy ftill—let time roll, until all its
years are fwallowed up in eternity! That eternity, where every creature will come before his
judge—let this be the cafe, and though they are
loft, God is glorified—though they are miferable,
God hath a holy and glorious kingdom in which
he will be praifed forever and ever.